*People and the Land through Time*

EMILY W. B. RUSSELL

# People and the Land through Time

## LINKING ECOLOGY AND HISTORY

*Yale University Press*
*New Haven &*
*London*

Printed in the United States of America.

Library of Congress Cataloging-in-Publication Data

Russell, Emily Wyndham Barnett, 1945–
    People and the land through time : linking ecology and history / Emily
W. B. Russell.
        p.   cm.
    Includes bibliographical references and index.
    ISBN 0-300-06830-1 (cloth: alk. paper)
           0-300-07730-0 (pbk.: alk. paper)
      1. Human ecology. 2. Human beings—Influence on environment.
    I. Title.
    GF41.R87   1997
    304.2'8—dc21   96-37098
                        CIP

A catalogue record for this book is available from the British Library.

The paper in this book meets the guidelines for permanence and durability of the Committee on Production Guidelines for Book Longevity of the Council on Library Resources.

10 9 8 7 6 5 4 3

In memory of my father, Samuel Treutlen Barnett, Jr.
A true southern gentleman whose inquiring mind was a
never-ending source of inspiration

# Contents

# Figures

# Tables

# Preface

When I started studying ecology, I hoped to be able to explain the composition of plant communities by understanding the interactions of species' physiology and population dynamics with microenvironments. Reading and research, however, have convinced me that while these interactions are important for determining what species *can* grow somewhere, the history of a site and region plays a major role in determining what species actually *do* grow there. This idea is not new, even within the discipline of ecology, but until recently ecologists have downplayed it in their efforts to discover general laws that govern species distributions, ecosystem properties, and other ecological processes, regardless of time or space. On the other hand, historians are realizing that the environment in which people live has influenced human history, so that they too must be sensitive to changing environmental conditions.

Concern about a deteriorating environment caused by human activities pervades our current view of the world. Many people are of the opinion that, unless we mend our ways, we risk disaster. Many also see scientific research, especially ecological research, as the potential source of solutions to environmental problems. In dealing with scientific research related to the environment as altered by people, however, scientists are faced with an overlay of causation that has varied over time and space with changing human culture.

I have written this book to help point to different aspects of current environments that bear the imprint of various past human activities, which must be considered in order to understand the current processes. The emphasis is on remnant effects on current communities, ecosystems, and landscapes and on how factoring these effects into ecological studies can help elucidate processes. Along the way, it should become clear how differently people have viewed, understood, and used the nonhuman environment and how these differences contribute to impacts as well as, in complex webs of feedback, to changing activities and attitudes.

In conducting historical ecological research, I have been convinced of the importance of distinguishing between time as a measurable dimension of duration, such as one day or one year, and historical time as a specific duration, such as 6 June 1952 or 1735. The partitioning of the processes that we observe between those that are based on the nonspecific unit of time and those that are historically constrained will help us tremendously in relating theoretical studies to actual responses of real ecosystems.

I have two main goals in this book, one related to research and the other to environmental management. I hope to stimulate further research on the role that history, specifically human history, has played in shaping communities, ecosystems, and landscapes and conversely, the role that changing environments have played in human history. I have tried to do this by pointing to the ubiquity of residual as well as current human impacts on the environment and by demonstrating that these impacts have changed over time, up to and continuing in the present. Second, those who plan and manage natural areas should learn that their systems are never static and that the present conditions are merely stages in a continually changing mosaic. They cannot be frozen in time.

My examples are drawn from all over the world, from a wide variety of biomes, though emphasis is placed on temperate systems, especially in the eastern United States and in western Europe, as these are the ones with which I am most familiar. They are discussed as illustrations; references are given for readers who would like more definitive discussions of the individual examples. The concepts apply, however, anywhere.

I expect this approach to be useful both as an introduction to historical ecology for professional ecologists, environmental historians, historical geographers, and historical anthropologists and as an advanced undergraduate and graduate textbook for such courses as historical ecology and environmental issues. I start with an exposition of the importance of considering the past of ecosystems and then introduce techniques that can be used for reconstructing this past. I then discuss a variety of ways in which people have affected the environment over time, from using fire to laying out property boundaries. I conclude by discussing how a historical ecological approach contributes to an understanding of some issues of current concern: changes to lakes, biodiversity, and sustainability.

I hope that readers will carry away an excitement for including human history in ecological studies and ecology in historical studies. This integration of the disciplines has great potential for both and presents challenges that must be met if we are to deal responsibly with our role in the biosphere.

# Acknowledgments

My interest in historical ecology probably began when I was a child digging up old horseshoes in our garden and finding old stone walls in the woods where I played. I owe a great debt of gratitude to my parents, who were always enthusiastic supporters of my interest in science. Many people have contributed to the development of my ideas on historical ecology in addition to those who have more recently commented on various versions of this book and have contributed technical expertise. My teachers at The Baldwin School and at Denison University required me to write and to study the humanities as well as the sciences, preventing too narrow a focus. A year's study at the University of Paris introduced me to the residual impacts of people on the forests of France and to the idea that all forests have experienced some human impact. Further studies at Duke and Rutgers universities continued this emphasis on the interplay between people and their environments. This book grew directly from a joint biology and history graduate seminar I taught at Duke University in 1990, while I was supported by a National Science Foundation Visiting Professorship for Women. The lively discussions among students with different intellectual backgrounds inspired me to begin the long process of writing a text that would build on and disseminate this enthusiasm for interdisciplinary interactions.

Over the years, discussions with many individuals have contributed to the development of the ideas expressed here. I would like especially to acknowledge W. Dwight Billings, Michael Binford, Grace S. Brush, Norman L. Christensen, Harold L. Cousminer, William Cronon, Ronald B. Davis, Richard T. T. Forman, David R. Foster, Steven P. Hamburg, Sally P. Horn, Daniel A. Livingstone, Peter L. Marks, Mark J. McDonnell, Steward T. A. Pickett, Robert L. Sanford, Jr., John C. F. Tedrow, George Theokritoff, Peter L. Tobiessen, Charles Watkins, David Wigston, and the attendees at the fourth Cary Conference, "Humans as Components of Ecosystems." Faculty and students participating in seminars in Rutgers University's Quaternary Studies Graduate Program reinforced the importance and exciting potential of interdisciplinary research. Thompson Webb III read and provided invaluable commentary on the entire manuscript, which was also improved by the comments of three anonymous reviewers. My editor, Jean E. Thomson Black, has been a wonderful source of support, encouragement, and gentle pressure to keep moving on this work.

For assistance with the illustrations I thank Susan Hochgraf, F. Mason Barnett, and James Gasprich. I greatly appreciate the generosity of all of those who have allowed me to use their data, photographs, or illustrations from their publications; these are individually acknowledged in the respective figure captions. For financial support during various phases of this project I thank Yale University Press, the National Park Service, the National Science Foundation, and the Mellon Foundation.

Last but definitely not least, I thank my husband, Frederick H. Russell, for widening my perspectives, challenging my ideas, and patiently putting up with and supporting me when I was distracted and frustrated by this project. His belief in the value of what I was doing and in my ability to do it gave me the push I needed to complete it.

# PART I

# Questions and Clues

Reconstructing the past to evaluate its effects on present ecosystems is like a puzzle, where the researcher knows the outcome but not the rules. It requires the integration of a wealth of diverse information. Written records document past human activities as observations of the natural world by literate people. Some past human activities have left traces on the landscape that persist to the present. And organisms themselves have left a record by their remains in sedimentary deposits. Each kind of record provides a unique type of information, each with its own spatial and temporal scale. By integrating these sources, a historical ecologist can piece together a picture of past activities and communities in order to formulate and test hypotheses about causes of past changes and the contributions of past processes to present ecosystems and landscapes. This process of integration requires careful attention to the compatibility of the different kinds of information, in terms of scale and biases, and an awareness of the appropriate kinds of critical analysis used for interpreting the various categories of data.

In the next four chapters, I introduce the three major categories of sources that inform historical ecological studies: written records, traces left on the landscape, and sedimentary records. I suggest ways in which each makes unique contributions to these studies as well as offer caveats relative to biases and limitations. These chapters do not provide detailed instructions on how to use the different sources; such detailed how-to information may be found in the various texts I mention, and these should be supplemented by courses and consultation with practitioners in the various fields of study. But first I will raise some of the kinds of questions that historical ecologists ask.

# History Hidden in the Landscape

## Introduction

Human impact on the land is ubiquitous, although it differs in kind and intensity from one place to another, from one time to another. The causes of some impacts, such as cutting forests or draining marshes, are obvious, but other causes, such as polluting the air or introducing pathogens, are more subtle. Reminders of past human activities persist even in such apparently pristine environments as the tropical forests of Africa[1] and many areas designated as wilderness in North America. Historical ecology seeks to explain many enigmatic features of present ecosystems and landscapes by deciphering the legacies of past human activities.[2]

I shall use the simple definition of an ecosystem as an assemblage of organisms and their environment that acts as a unit.[3] A landscape is an assemblage of ecosystems—for example, forest, lakes, and streams—which also interact, though less directly than the components of ecosystems. Ecologists try to understand the organization and functioning of these complex systems by asking questions like why there are more species in one ecosystem than another and how this affects the ability of the system to resist disruption. Discovery of general laws that explain such relations would allow us to predict and anticipate responses of ecosystems to future change. The scientific research that may uncover such general laws depends on the repeatability of observations and experiments.

Past as well as present human influences on these systems complicate matters. Technology, the ways people view the environment, and other aspects of human cultural development change in unpredictable ways. People's past interactions with their environments are repeatable only in their barest essentials. Rebuilding a stone wall to reproduce the effect of a wall on adjacent fields, for example, can possibly duplicate the physical effect of the wall on the climate of the fields, but it cannot reproduce such critical features as the seeds that were redistributed by the removal of rocks from the fields hundreds of years ago. Such imperfect duplication has several consequences for ecological studies. First, if those past interactions have left a residual impact, study of current conditions alone cannot detect its cause. For example, selective logging in the past for a preferred firewood species such as hickory may affect the composition of a forest stand for many years after logging ceases, but the reason for the scarcity of hickory can only be inferred from knowing the logging history.

Second, past human influences are cumulative and superimposed on each other and on changes in climate.[4] A typical suite of activities in a forested area of eastern North America in the nineteenth century was logging, followed by fires, followed by grazing of sheep, and finally recovery of the forest. Logging favors species like chestnut that can sprout prolifically from the cut stumps or those like birches that can reproduce by seed in open sites. Fires eliminate fire-sensitive species like hemlock and red maple. Grazing by sheep discourages species that sheep find especially palatable. No one of these activities taken alone can explain characteristics of the resulting forest, nor can several of them taken out of order.

Third, the ubiquity of human impact means that it is very difficult, if not impossible, to find systems that are devoid of human influence. Two stands selected to compare the effects of different species composition on some feature of nutrient cycling will differ in past land use as well as in species composition, so a simple comparative study cannot yield results that are attributable simply to differing species composition.

All is not lost, however. In fact, these consequences of human activities open up an exciting arena of integrative research. Many anomalies in current ecosystems may be explained by past human impacts. By interpreting the historical record, in all its guises, we can infer past human activities, including their spatial and temporal patterns, and by comparative studies establish how they have worked to shape the present land. Rather than serving as an impediment, the study of past human impact is an entry point into

Figure 1.1. Desert of Nevada (Carson Valley, five miles north of Miden in Douglas County). Note the sharp contrast between rectangular irrigated fields between two large, straight irrigation ditches and irregular patterns of vegetation and physiography outside them. (F. J. Marschner, *Land Use and Its Patterns in the United States*, Agriculture Handbook #153 [USDA, Washington, D.C., 1959], plate 87)

the great diversity of possible interactions of species with their environments and will assist us in making predictions that are more appropriate to a world fraught with human influences.

## What We See Today

Changes in the intensity of human activities over space confront us everywhere, on many scales. On a regional scale, extensive forests alternate with towns and cultivated fields in the Appalachian Mountains of eastern North America, an apparent contrast between untrammeled wilderness and domesticated nature. Similarly, the deserts of the American southwest contrast sharply with irrigated agricultural fields, visible even from the air as regular fields superimposed on the irregular matrix of the surrounding desert (fig. 1.1). In Hawai'i, verdant rain forests differ markedly from orderly, low-diversity pineapple plantations (fig. 1.2). The natural, pristine appearances of the Appalachian forests, southwestern deserts, and Hawai'ian forests are,

Figure 1.2. Island of Maui, Hawai'i. Contrast the lush vegetation in a valley along the northeast coast of Maui (*top*) with pineapple plantations in the interior (*bottom*). Non-native species, however, are common in the unmanaged as well as the planted sites. (Photos by the author, 1992)

however, to a large extent mirages; all have a distinctive imprint of past
human activities. Logging and agriculture have leveled almost all the forests
of the Appalachian Mountains sometime during the past two hundred
years.[5] In the southwest, overgrazing and the pumping of water for irrigation and other uses have reduced many dry grasslands to desert shrublands,
thereby altering nutrient cycling and causing erosion.[6] Non-native species
have decimated native populations of plants and animals even deep in the
forests of Hawai'i.[7]

These past human activities have left both obvious and subtle imprints on
many aspects of these systems, for example, on the species that are present
and characteristics of the soils. Which species did logging favor, and which
did it eliminate or diminish? Can one separate the direct effects of grazing,
such as a decrease in the populations of palatable species, from the effects of
changed water tables caused by irrigation? What have been the processes of
extinction and introductions in the past, and how have they affected current
community composition? How have these processes changed over time in the
past, and which characteristics of the present communities and landscapes
reflect them?

Some major categories of ecosystems—extensive swamps, say—appear to
the casual observer to be undisturbed by humans. Here, apparently natural
patterns often serve to conceal past, more active, human management. Most
marshes in the northeastern United States, from the pocosins of North Carolina to tidal marshes along the Chesapeake Bay to remnants of glacial lakes
in New Jersey, have been ditched and drained. Although most ditches are
generally no longer maintained and active uses have ceased, these past uses
have left lasting impacts on the ecology of the extant ecosystems, in a
changed water table, past fires in the dry organic soils, and changed species
composition from mowing and grazing. On the other hand, over the past two
centuries, human activities have also indirectly created new marshes on the
piedmont of Georgia in North America, by upland erosion and subsequent
sedimentation along streams.[8] These human-made marshes offer potential
sites for the study of critical factors responsible for developing and maintaining these systems.

Traces of abandoned human settlements both reveal and conceal past uses
of the land. "Lost villages" abound in Europe and North America, revealed
by place-names on old maps, by obscured physical remains, and by pictures
(fig. 1.3). They are now, however, often hidden by pastures, plowed fields, or
regenerated forests.[9] To historians these villages are of interest for what they
reveal about human behavior in the past. Why did they come into existence

Figure 1.3. Site of Quartz Mill, near Virginia City, Nevada. The top picture was taken in 1868, the bottom one at the same place in 1979. Only a few stones remain to mark the site of the structure a hundred years later. (Top: Timothy O'Sullivan, 1868: quartz Mill near Virginia City [U.S. Geological Survey]. Bottom: Copyright 1979. Mark Klett for the Rephotographic Survey Project. "Site of Quartz Mill, Virginia City, NV")

and why did they disappear? More geographically oriented questions consider the relation of village locations to spatial features of the landscape. Deserted villages raise ecological questions as well. A village represents a concentration of people who used natural resources for fuel and food, disturbed the soil by plowing or just trampling, and produced wastes. The influence of these on the regenerated vegetation may persist in patterns that are quite obscure when compared with the current physical environment.

## Recreational Landscapes Shaped by Past Land Use

Shenandoah National Park in the Appalachian Mountains of the southeastern United States and the Adirondack Park in New York State consist of thousands of hectares of forested, mountainous terrain, much of it designated as wilderness. Neither includes wilderness extensive enough to fit Aldo Leopold's definition of a wilderness area as "a continuous stretch of country preserved in its natural state, open to lawful hunting and fishing, big enough to absorb a two weeks' pack trip, and kept devoid of roads, artificial trails, cottages, and other works of man";[10] but they contain thousands of hectares with little obvious evidence of human impact except old logging trails and rough dams.

Past agriculture, logging, and mining have devastated the natural vegetation, fauna, and physical landscape of both parks, however. Grazing has eliminated palatable herbs and shrubs as well as tree seedlings in many areas of the Appalachians. Cultivation of demanding row crops like corn and tobacco depleted soil nutrients and encouraged erosion on steep hillsides. Logging encouraged tree species that sprout quickly after cutting, such as American chestnut, producing the "sprout hardwoods" forest type of the late nineteenth and early twentieth centuries.[11] Then, in the first half of the twentieth century, the introduced chestnut blight killed all of the mature chestnut trees.[12]

In 1880, an observer described the northern part of "the Adirondack wilderness" as "scarred all over with . . . fires. In some places miles in length and breadth of valuable timber and smiling landscape are desolated."[13] The extent, frequency, and, probably, severity of these fires, generally attributed to human carelessness, were most likely much greater than they had been in the past, slowing recovery from logging. But by 1900 most farmers had abandoned the steep lands of the Appalachian Mountains, and the logging industry had moved its attention westward.[14] Forests began to regenerate on these abandoned lands, which were no longer economically viable. The beauty of the forests and mountains began to attract the attention of vacationers.

Wealthy individuals acquired some of the most spectacular land for vacation estates, while federal and state governments took possession of much of the rest, which had little economic potential. Development of vacation estates usually required extensive tree cutting for scenic vistas,[15] while development of a park included abandonment of most remaining farms and the building of roads, campgrounds, and other "improvements" deemed necessary to human enjoyment of the area. To say, then, that the landscape of these parks consists of forests regenerated by some natural process of secondary succession on land that was abandoned after logging or farming ignores major factors that affect such succession, including the diversity of prior land use and the time and reason for abandonment. Such components help explain some of the patterns of vegetation today.

Another kind of wild and rugged landscape valued for recreation is the open heathlands of Great Britain, from Exmoor and Dartmoor in the south to the Lake District in the north. Although the presence of sheep and stone walls in these areas attests to continued human impacts, the very origin of these treeless heaths centuries or even millennia ago is associated with past human activities. Land clearance that started with early agriculture and continued to Roman times, in conjunction with climate changes, poor soils, and overgrazing by sheep, has resulted in permanent deforestation.[16] Similar human factors appear to be responsible for extensive heaths in parts of western Europe as well.[17] In addition, land management continues to affect them in complex ways.[18] Because of economic incentives in some places there is less grazing, allowing nonheath shrubs to invade, while in others the incentives have encouraged farmers to plow the heath and plant grass for more intensive grazing.[19] The very existence of the heaths is tightly linked to past and present human intervention as well as to climate in ways that have not yet been adequately elucidated.

## Two Ecological Problems with Historical Explanations

Two studies highlight the importance of historical ecology in deciphering current community and ecosystem dynamics. The populations of many migratory birds in North America are apparently declining. The search for a cause focuses on habitat change over the past century.[20] Forest cover in this region was at its lowest point at the end of the nineteenth century. The forests that have recovered since then are dispersed, creating landscapes with many edges, quite distinct from the prelogging, prefarming forest. This landscape pattern encourages various predators and parasitic birds, such as brown-headed cowbirds, which were probably not common several centuries

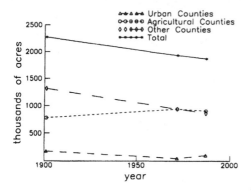

Figure 1.4. Changing forest cover in New Jersey, 1899–1987, by land use region. (Data from Vermeule, The forests of New Jersey, and Ferguson and Mayer, *The Timber Resources of New Jersey*)

ago when the land was more heavily forested. Although the area of forest in some parts of this region continues to increase late in the twentieth century, the populations of some neotropical migrants continue to dwindle, possibly owing to human disturbance of their wintering range in the tropics.[21]

More detailed consideration of the historical trends may shed additional light on this dilemma of dwindling populations. Forests were most fragmented in the late nineteenth and early twentieth centuries, when not only was cleared farmland at a maximum in most of the northeastern United States, but also destructive forestry practices led to a patchwork of cut and burned-over forest stands. Brown-headed cowbirds and barn cats would have proliferated in the agricultural regions. Over the past century, on a regional scale, many forests have become larger and less actively disturbed as the demand for wood products has shifted west and south and farms have been abandoned.[22] On a more local scale, however, the changes have not been so straightforward. For example, forest cover increased between 1900 and 1972 in previously agricultural sections of the state of New Jersey, almost doubling in many areas (fig. 1.4). At the same time, in heavily wooded sections, forest cover declined by up to a third, mainly because of development as people moved out of the cities to the country.[23] Many urban counties lost almost all of their former forest land, maintaining only small areas in parks. Overall, the proportion of land in forest declined in the state over the first three-quarters of the twentieth century, but this broad pattern obscures more local changes that occurred on the scale of bird habitat.[24] From 1972 to 1987 much forest area in formerly agricultural counties was developed, and newly abandoned farms were more apt to become housing developments than forest.[25] In addition, even where forest has survived and expanded in the twentieth century, there has been a proliferation of trees characteristic of disturbances, such as birch (*Betula* spp.), and loss of others, such as eastern hemlock (*Tsuga canadensis*).[26] More investigation into the responses of the neotropical migrants to past changes in their environment at a variety of temporal and spatial scales may suggest why they did not become extinct when the regional forest cover was at its most fragmented in the mid–nineteenth century and why they are currently dwindling when the forest cover is not declining as rapidly as it did in the eighteenth and early nineteenth centuries.

Although a strong case has been made that changing human impact has caused the decline of these bird species, the introduction of non-native species presents other questions. Over the past century a non-native species, cheatgrass (*Bromus tectorum*), has spread widely in the shrub steppes of the North American intermountain west, causing major changes in the ecosystems there. Scattered and sketchy records as well as the few relict stands suggest that the native vegetation consisted of shrubs and perennial bunch grasses, but cheatgrass now dominates large areas.[27]

The increase of cheatgrass in the 1920s and 1930s appears to be part of a self-reinforcing pattern: overgrazing allows the cheatgrass to invade the plant community, then in late spring the grass forms a very dry fuel which carries fires, destroying fire-sensitive shrubs like *Artemisia* and bunch grasses. By killing the shrubs and bunch grasses, the fires create additional excellent habitat for continued expansion of the cheatgrass, whose seeds are spread by livestock and railroads. Overgrazing and railroads, however, were present before the maximum spread of the grass, which probably arrived as a contaminant in wheat seed before 1900. Why then did it wait until the 1920s to become so invasive? Is it possible that the cool, moist climate of the late teens and early twenties[28] that led to expansion of agriculture into areas previously too dry for it hastened the dispersal of this weedy species? Or did it just take this long for the population to become well established? The combination of historical with biological and environmental inquiry opens new areas in the search for answers, which may lead to action to prevent other such invasions.

The changing pace of technology, human population growth, and attitudes toward the natural world permeate all of these changes, from modifying the physical environment to make possible the production of crops to preserving so-called wilderness. It has also affected the records that people have kept and the basis on which we can judge the magnitude of changes. This cultural, human context lies in the realm of historians, geographers, and archaeologists.

## Interdisciplinary Considerations

"The causes of the earth's big environmental problems—deforestation, loss of biodiversity, pollution, climate change, and so forth—are all rooted in human behavior."[29] This sentence may appear banal at first glance but is startling in context. It introduced a news brief in the journal *Science* referring to a National Research Council report that called for interdisciplinary research on the "human dimensions of global change."[30] I would add that the recognition of these specific issues as problems and the division of research into current disciplines are themselves the result of human behavior. They must be placed in a historic context because the relevant "human behavior" is not a static, isolated characteristic of the species but rather a historically conditioned and highly variable one.

Environmental historians and historical geographers consider the conceptual, political, and economic frameworks within which people have acted and how these frameworks have influenced their interactions with the natural environment. Historians concentrate on explaining human nature and contemporary human affairs,[31] at the same time revealing to ecologists the underlying human causes for the patterns of successional stands on the landscape. Conversely, ecologists can point to environmental consequences of certain activities, which in turn affect human responses to the environment. For example, in Illinois, soil quality and topography are often not suited for the use to which land has been put.[32] Such cultural forces as land surveys, overriding more resource-oriented concerns, influenced the distribution of these land uses.

There is a wide gulf between stating the need for interdisciplinary work and engaging in it; different disciplines ask different questions, look for answers in different kinds of data and sources, and use different criteria to judge the quality of the answer. To cooperate fruitfully, researchers must recognize their differences and respect alternate points of view. Answering an ecologist's, a historian's, and a geographer's questions as they relate to one subject may be of interest, but for us to gain the full value of interdisciplinary research the answers must amplify each other. Cooperation may even lead to questions that themselves are interdisciplinary and would not have been posed in any of the separate disciplines.

A minor example may suffice to make this point. In the second half of the nineteenth century in the northeastern United States, the tanning industry cut many thousands of hemlock trees for their bark, an ingredient in the tanning process.[33] Ecologists are interested in this phenomenon because of its effect on species' distributions and on the ecosystem dominated by hemlock.[34] Environmental historians are interested in why the industry grew when it did: What factors of industrialization, capitalism, and international trade determined the demand for tanbark at that time, rather than earlier?[35] Historical geographers might question the distribution of tanbark sources with relation to transportation and energy sources as well as demand.

Answers to all of these hypothetical questions fit together to create a story that no one could tell alone. Until the mid–nineteenth century, extract of oak bark was used for tanning hides in small tanneries powered usually by water.[36] By the 1850s, however, farmland had replaced much oak forest, in part because good soil and climate for many oak species corresponded with good agricultural land. Large stands of hemlocks persisted in steep, remote areas like north-central Pennsylvania and south-central New York.[37] The cattle industry by that time was producing large numbers of hides from cattle slaughtered in central stockyards, near railroad and steamboat transportation. Industrialists, using steam power and capital intensification, were able to build tanneries to process these hides only where there were large stands of bark-bearing trees, and these were the hemlock stands.[38] So the hemlocks were ruthlessly destroyed, not because their bark was favored or because they grew in especially convenient locations but from a combination of ecological and cultural factors that came together at a certain time in history. The same would not happen today. Attitudes toward the resource were as important in determining its destruction as was its inherent usefulness.

The attitudes of historians toward research that includes the natural environment have changed considerably over the past few decades, allowing more fruitful collaborations between historians and ecologists. In 1967, W. A. Walsh, a historian writing on the philosophy of history, asserted that "the historian is not concerned, at any point of his work, with nature for its own sake; only with nature as a background to human activities."[39] By 1985, however, some historians no longer saw the environment as merely a backdrop for history, but rather as a legitimate focus for research.[40] In that year, the historian K. E. Bailes described the newly emerging field of environmental history as "the study of what impact economics, politics, social structure, technologies, and value systems have had on the natural environment and the use of natural resources."[41] In the words of A. W. Crosby, "Environmental historians have discovered that the physical and life sciences can provide quantities of information and theory useful, even vital to historical investigations," and they have used this approach to interpret many aspects of human history.[42]

Historical geographers, on the other hand, have a long tradition of studying the interactions between past human activities and natural environments. In introducing the major themes of historical geography in 1941, Carl Sauer regarded humans as agents of physical geography, including plant and animal ecology, while in 1966, S. R. Eyre and R. J. Jones observed that "in a sense, all Geography is historical geography, in that nothing in the present can be explained without reference to the past."[43] In addition, they considered all geography to be human ecology, concerned with the "interaction between the natural and the psychological, between the blind forces of nature and the self-conscious activities of men."[44] The *Journal of Historical Geography,* which appeared in 1975, focused on patterns of human settlement, agriculture, and natural resource management. An incoming editor in 1990 emphasized the breadth of the field: "Research in historical geography is required neither to adhere to a specified set of methodological conventions, nor to demonstrate an immediate utility."[45] The emphasis, however, as with environmental history, remains on the human element.

Historical ecology shifts the emphasis to the natural environment itself. Turning Walsh's statement inside out, human activity is of interest to ecologists only as it affects nature.

## Humans as Geographic Agents

In 1864 George Perkins Marsh published *Man and Nature; or, Physical Geography as Modified by Human Action,* the first comprehensive exposé of the ability of people to modify nature in significant ways.[46] On the title page of the first edition was a quotation (undated), "Not all the winds, and storms, and earthquakes, and seas, and seasons of the world, have done so much to revolutionize the earth as Man, the power of an endless life, has done since the day he came forth upon it, and received dominion over it."[47] Mary Somerville, in *Physical Geography,* published in 1863, also made the observation that humans had exerted a major geographical influence on the earth.[48] Until this time, the assumption had generally been that although people had certainly cut down trees and thus depleted local supplies of timber and even contributed to soil erosion and siltation, these were really not major modifications of the potential of the land, but rather minor, temporary side effects. The loss of agricultural potential or of fisheries in large areas of the world was attributed to natural causes, such as climatic change.[49]

Marsh demonstrated that the activities of people—their cutting of forests, overgrazing, and other practices—had led to loss of soil, silting of harbors, and other major geographic problems. It was possible even that the actions of people, especially in cutting forests and mining, had changed the very climate of some regions. Although others had made such observations locally, it was only in the mid–nineteenth century that attention was focused on the general nature of the impacts. In many U.S. states around the mid 1800s, concern about such problems led to the establishment of state geological surveys, whose task it was to catalogue the natural resources of the states and make recommendations about how they could be preserved. The official recognition of the problems indicates that they were taken seriously.

At the same time, the development of ecology in North America, Great Britain, and continental Europe exhibited an ambivalence toward human impact, in part conditioned by local conditions. Early-twentieth-century ecologists in North America predicated a stable natural type of vegetation for a region, determined above all by the climate, called the climax vegetation.[50] Deviations caused by local topography or bedrock were classified according to their relations to putative climax vegetation. Hypothetically, all vegetation in a climatic region would converge on the climax condition, albeit slowly where erosion and soil modification had to modify such limiting physical conditions as topography. This appealing simplification of the bewildering variety of current vegetation won wide acceptance in North America, and even today persists as a major organizing concept in the explanation of plant ecology to students and laypersons. Maps of the vegetation of the United States, for example, generally indicate the "potential natural vegetation", that is, the climax, rather than the actual plant cover.[51] A major goal of ecology was, then, to understand the determinants of the climax vegetation of a region, and by comparing these factors over space to arrive at general organizing principles to explain the characteristics and dynamics of different plant communities. Ecologists in North America have thus sought "natural" stands to study or test their theories. There has also been the implicit assumption that once freed of active human management, vegetation would develop along lines dictated by natural forces; the past human element could essentially be ignored. In other words, there is a teleological tendency in nature that is unaltered and unalterable by human actions.

On the other hand, in western Europe and other regions with a longer, more obviously pervasive human impact on the landscape, the idea of climax vegetation did not take hold, at least in part because there were no so-called virgin stands left. Maps of the vegetation of France, for example, made according to the Zurich-Montpellier school of phytosociology, describe and classify existing, not potential, land cover. The human element there cannot be ignored.

In England, the oldest woodlands date at least from the Middle Ages, having been actively managed for various timber products over hundreds of years.[52] Some of the most interesting ecological studies there focus on species spread and distribution under different kinds of human management on different substrates. The British ecologist Arthur Tansley exemplified the ambivalence toward the role of human impact when he stated, "It is true that ecological problems are complicated by man's activity. . . . But the plants themselves are working in the same way, tending towards the same effects, whether man is at work or not."[53]

This idea is captured by the dual concepts of the fundamental and realized niches of species.[54] Most simply, the fundamental niche refers to the interaction between the physiology of a species and the limiting environmental variables that allow the species potentially to survive indefinitely. This corresponds to Tansley's idea of the plants' "working in the same way, tending towards the same effects." The realized niche is the subset of conditions in which the species is actually found. This includes Tansley's complications arising from man's activity as well as competitive interactions with other species. However, lest we be tempted to define human interactions in the same terms as competition with other species, we should be continuously aware of the importance of human culture, people's "ability to comprehend their relationship with the world around them and to manipulate that relationship to conscious purpose."[55]

Anthropological evidence suggests that humans, including those in hunting and gathering cultures, have long exerted an influence on the land. Even before the advent of intensive agriculture about four or five thousand years ago, it is unlikely that "the earth retained its pristine form, and any modifications of its physiography, fauna or flora [were] ascribable to natural causes."[56] No ecosystems could be understood apart from past as well as present human impacts. Intensive agriculture and industrialization have had even more lasting and extensive impacts.

In 1956, W. L. Thomas Jr.'s interdisciplinary *Man's Role in Changing the Face of the Earth* brought together the thoughts of outstanding scholars on these impacts, but it had little direct or immediate influence on academic disciplines, especially ecology. By the 1970s, however, the topic was attracting more attention from ecologists, especially paleoecologists, leading G. E. Likens and M. B. Davis to conclude that "[it] is clear that the magnitude of changes caused by man in decades are equivalent to those occurring over thousands of years without him".[57] Although many ecologists today still ignore human impact in attempting to explain the natural world according to scientific principles, especially if it is not immediately obvious,[58] an ever-increasing number are realizing that "their concentration on natural ecosystems is, in many cases, rather naive or even misleading."[59] Acknowledging the acceleration of change in recent centuries, B. L. Turner et al.'s *The Earth as Transformed by Human Action*, published in 1990, focused on only the past three hundred years.[60]

N. L. Christensen attributed ecologists' current resurgence of interest in history to four factors: (1) predictive models structured only on the natural world often account for very little of the total variation observed in ecosystems; (2) historical impacts have a much longer lifespan than ecologists had previously thought; (3) landscape-scale processes critically shape their component parts and are nearly always influenced by past human activities; and (4) one can expect the influence of human impacts to increase in the future, so prediction will necessarily have to include human factors. In addition, the whole system is dynamic, varying on several scales, so that the effect of an action at one time may differ from that same action taken at another time. For example, the abandoning of an agricultural field during a period of dry years may have very different effects on future forest regeneration than the abandoning of the same kind of field in the same area during a period of wet years. Historical uniqueness, for example, the specific conditions at a given time, may modify the impact of the more easily observed variable of time.[61]

In addition, recent paleoecological research suggests that ecosystems, even those with minimal human impact, constantly change at a variety of scales from decadal stand-level responses to such local disturbances as windstorms to centennial regional responses to changing climates. The search for a typical "climax" type of vegetation for a region is bound to fail because of the constant reshuffling of species under the influence of changing climates, species migrations, and microevolution.[62] The human element serves to magnify the impacts of these influences.

To be rigorous, historical ecology must establish clearly stated hypotheses to explain the impacts of past human activities and their explicit consequences. In a way, the experiments have already been done, but, as contrasted with controlled experiments in the field or laboratory, we know the consequences but not the experimental treatment or controls.[63] Possible "treatments," such as climate change and specific human activities, are posited with the likely consequences of each. The full panoply of historical techniques can then be applied to either refute or support the hypothetical causes.

In the rest of this book, I shall introduce the major sources of information used by those who study historical ecology, emphasizing the underlying principles that justify their use and what each kind of source can and cannot contribute. These will not be detailed, how-to discussions but rather attempts to acquaint practitioners in one field with some of the basic assumptions behind data use in other fields. I shall then show how ecologists, historians, and geographers have used these techniques to elucidate various aspects of human impact on the environment. I conclude with a discussion of how the historical perspective can help elucidate current ecological problems.

# The Written Record

The abundance and diversity of written accounts of the natural world attest to people's abiding interest in the earth that sustains them. Travelers write diaries and letters describing the new lands they visit. Farmers and others keep track of their daily activities in diaries. Governments collect statistics about the land they govern. All of these and more constitute evidence for reconstructing the past environment and the human actions and attitudes that affected it. In any historical study of a literate period these sources present unique information on human activities as well as provide the basic temporal framework for analyzing other kinds of data. Like any observations, however, each represents only a small portion of reality, seen through necessarily biased eyes. They cannot, therefore, be used as direct statements of reality in the past but must be interpreted with awareness of potential bias. For historical ecology in particular, inadvertent revelations about the natural world often provide the most revealing insights into the structure and function of past landscapes.

My discussion will focus mainly on documents available for the United States, the country with which I am most familiar. The general precepts apply to any historical documentation, however, and can be applied much more widely.

## Unique Values

Most important, written documents offer a temporal context for studying the history of human impact on the landscape. They are a rich source of
information on people's lives but are usually less explicit about the landscape, except where its elements are useful for economic activities like farming and transportation. By reading between the lines, however, we can deduce
a wealth of information on the natural environment and on how people have
affected it. Such sources as the date of the wine harvest in France, for example, have been used to infer changing climate in the past.[1] Economic and
social systems often determine structures of landscapes and their components, and only by using historical documents can we discover how these systems interacted with the natural environment. The historical ecologist can
then frame hypotheses to interpret the environment in the context of past
human actions. Historical documents as well as other kinds of evidence can
be used to test these hypotheses, not by experimentation, but rather by the
corroborating or refuting of the hypotheses.

The broader technological and political contexts of documents must be
grasped before ecological changes are interpreted and their importance eval-
uated. For example, the proliferation of railroads in the mid– to late nineteenth century led not only to deforestation as trees were cut and used to
produce railroad ties and fuel but also to greatly increased ignition of fires,
affecting vegetation all along the railroad lines. The timing and locations of
the lines and the politics of allocating public land to the railroad companies
for supplies of wood affected their impact on the natural vegetation in ways
that can be learned only through the study of written records.[2]

Historical documentation alone can elucidate such political activities as
wars, which have had major impacts on the environment. The effects of
wars, for example, are often not just the obvious ones of direct damage by
troop movements and battles, but also include unique exploitation of natural resources. In England during the Second World War, peregrine falcons
and other birds of prey were destroyed along the east coast to prevent them
from killing passenger pigeons, causing a precipitate drop in their populations.[3] Although this population decrease was rapidly reversed after the war,
it must have had at least a temporary effect not only on the populations of
the target species, but also on their prey. Comparisons of bird populations
between 1950 and the present could thus be influenced by processes of recovery from this human action as well as by other activities that are more
current.

Although various kinds of isotopic dating techniques can give a fairly precise date to some object from the past, historical documents are necessary to

establish what was happening in the human world that might account for the changes that are interpreted from the fossil record. Historical accounts may even help date physical records when isotopic dates are unavailable but fairly distinct changes in the record can be correlated with likely human impact. This technique has been widely used in North America to date sediment that was formed about the time of European colonization. European settlers rapidly cleared the land for agriculture, thereby causing a rapid increase in the amount of pollen produced by weeds of open fields, such as ragweed (*Ambrosia*), which was preserved in lake sediments. If one can find written records that date the beginning of Euroamerican clearing near a lake, then one can use the historical sources to date the sediment. In the absence of the historical documentation, it would not be possible to find a probable cause for this shift in vegetation or to date it as precisely.

Historical documents often do not specify a precise location, but some are sufficiently definite to contribute to our understanding of local ecological relations. In one study, recent human-caused fires in Maine seem to have favored the habitat of several rare species, increasing their frequency over what it probably had been in the natural vegetation.[4] This conclusion could not have been reached without the use of historical documents, carefully analyzed for a specific site.

## Methodology

A convenient, useful first classification of historical documents is whether they are primary or secondary. A primary document is one written more or less contemporaneously by the person who made the observation or collected the data.[5] Secondary sources are those that use primary sources to interpret a past event or condition of which the author has no firsthand experience. This distinction is not hard and fast, however. For example, some documents may be primary sources for one purpose and secondary sources for another. A nineteenth-century description of an American Revolutionary War battlefield site that noted where the various units were deployed is a secondary source for establishing these locations because the author relied on local oral history to determine the sites. But when the author mentioned that he walked up a hill and past a pasture where the forest had just been cut, he provided primary evidence for forest clearing at the time he visited. The text is also a primary source for analyzing attitudes in the nineteenth century, why he visited the site, what he thought was worth writing about it, and why he wrote his descriptions in the first place, that is, that there was a market for such memoirs.[6]

It may also be difficult to know whether an author was really describing firsthand experiences or was just reporting what had been related to him or her or even generalizing from other experience. For example, an often-cited description of the forest composition in the New Netherlands (New Jersey and eastern New York) by Adriaen Vander Donck in the eighteenth century is repeated by him almost verbatim in several places as descriptions of local vegetation, in sites many hundreds of kilometers apart and obviously different. The description of each site is given, however, as if it were local; it was, rather, a set piece put in wherever he needed a forest description.[7] There is no doubt that Vander Donck, who lived in New York for several years, had firsthand experience of the vegetation, but his descriptions are not useful for determining local forest composition. Often the rarity of such descriptions makes it tempting to regard them as valid, without adequate analysis. It is perhaps better in these cases to have nothing.

The distinction between primary and secondary sources can also apply to scientific writing. Articles reporting results of research may be considered to be primary sources presenting original observations filtered through the pen of the author. On the other hand, review articles, which summarize and synthesize the work of others, might be considered secondary. These are very useful, just as other kinds of secondary sources are, and usually contain original insights into the research problem, but if the actual experiments are to be discussed, the primary source, or article in which the research was reported, is a more reliable one.

In order for past scientific publications to be adduced as evidence of ecological conditions in the past they must be treated in the same way as other, more literary primary sources. In comparing published data on past vegetation in several parks in New York City with current vegetation, Robert Loeb showed where there must have been errors in the earlier reports because they were grossly inconsistent with the current locations of trees and species composition.[8] Although it is not usually possible to make such detailed comparisons as this, his results raise a cautionary flag when it comes to using past published (or unpublished) data as completely reliable and unbiased. Approaching them as historical sources rather than as straightforward data sets is helpful in using them to best effect. One must ask why they were done, which affects coverage and specificity of the data collected and reported, and what biases may have influenced the results.

Primary sources appear on the surface to be accurate, usually objective original records of contemporary conditions, and within limits many are. The key to using them effectively is determining these limits and deciding what questions to put to them.[9] At one extreme, one can be very critical of the sources, treating them in effect as a lawyer treats hostile witnesses.[10] The other extreme is to treat them as completely reliable, accurate accounts of the truth. If the criteria being used for evaluating them are made clear, a reader has a better chance to evaluate the interpretation.

A historical ecologist who relies on written, historical sources is searching for different information than is a political historian using the same sources, and sees them from a different set of paradigms. Ecologists are usually interested in what the document reveals about the external world, what kinds of plants and animals there were, the weather, and other physical descriptions. For example, on 1 May 1732 sworn testimony of a certain John Hayward in New Jersey stated that "he was approached in the forks of the N. Branches of the Raritan R. to become part of a band rounding up the many horses roaming loose in the woods at that time of year to put on weight for plowing to sell them in Maryland or elsewhere."[11] The economic historian may find evidence here of illegal trade in horses among the colonies. There is evidence of the lawlessness of this early frontier between plowed land and uncut forest. And for the ecologist, there is evidence both of the progress of clearing and of early grazing within the uncleared forest. What we cannot tell is whether this was an isolated incident and why John Hayward was "approached" or decided to give testimony, facts that might help establish the value of the evidence. All evidence needs to be corroborated before it can be more than a tantalizing suggestion of conditions in the past.[12]

A series of observations such as that made by a census survey may reveal changes in the environment over time, from which we can infer causes. Changes in definitions, techniques, and even census-takers can, however, make comparability difficult. In the United States Federal Census Agricultural records, for example, the definition of a farm has changed over time, as have the categories of land use within each farm. Even the reported area of political jurisdictions can change. In reports on forest area of the state of New Jersey, for example, the area of the state was reported as 2,578,700 acres in 1899 and 2,553,100 acres in 1972, a 4 percent difference.[13] Such adjustments can make it problematic to assess changes from one census period to the next. Even a census survey taken at different times of year may affect comparability, for example, of farm population in summer and winter.[14]

Another example of complications in a series of records is the apparent decline in silica measured in water taken from Lake Michigan into the water treatment plant in Chicago from 1926 to 1962. The decline appears when the data are analyzed over the entire period, but when they are partitioned into two sets, based on a change in analytical technique between 1948 and 1949, the major difference appears to be between the two sets, with no significant decline from 1949 to 1962.[15] In another series of statistics, data for wheat yield in part of England from 1823 to 1857 suggest that yield increased from thirty to fifty bushels/acre. Survey techniques apparently inflated the yields, making them difficult to compare with modern estimates. In addition, it appears that most of the change occurred between 1838 and 1842, which corresponded with a change of estimator, so this may account for the apparent increase in yield (fig. 2.1).[16]

Outright fraud is possible. For example, in 1755, the governor of North Carolina bemoaned the fact that some surveyors made up corner trees (trees found and marked at the corners of surveyed lots) without actually doing the surveying, taking advantage of the design by which all lines were surveyed along cardinal directions.[17] Using the trees noted in these surveys as a sample of contemporary vegetation would obviously not result in a reliable picture.

Assuming that human activities have had a major impact on most landscapes, at the beginning of a study of landscape history, or historical ecology, one must find out what these activities have been and how they have changed. This is rarely a straightforward project. The relevant historical record is almost always sketchy in time as well as imprecise and incomplete. These complications do not invalidate the record but do require attention to the methods of collecting and recording the observations. At least some disagreements among historians may be traced to differences in the interpretation of the documents. Making these explicit can contribute to reaching an accord on the range of possible inferences.

It is a tautology to say that written records are the products of the mental processes of the writer and are thus not simple, direct records of a past situation, but it bears emphasizing, especially for nonhistorians. The attitudes and perceptions that prevailed when a document was composed necessarily color what was written. For example, ecologists and environmentalists know George Perkins Marsh primarily for his cogent exposition of the major depredations enacted by humans on their environment over the centuries. They may be surprised to learn that in 1882 he wrote, "I am more than ever impressed with the superiority of the artificial [managed] forest, both in quantity and quality, as compared with that of the natural and spontaneous growth,"[18] a statement consistent, however, with observations he made earlier in *Man and Nature,* including, "The sooner a natural wood is brought into the state of an artificially regulated one, the better it is for all the multiplied interests which depend on the wise administration of this branch of public economy."[19] As much as Marsh was an innovative and perceptive interpreter of human impact on the environment, he was also a man of his

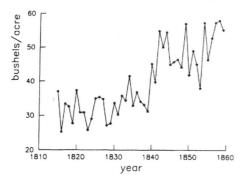

Figure 2.1. Yield of Wheat, 1823–57, Liverpool Merchants' Results. Note steep increase between 1837 and 1843, which may be attributed to change in estimator rather than a steady increase in yield over the thirty-four years of the records. There is no known other change at that time to account for the steep increase. (Data from Healy and Jones, Wheat yields)

age, one who saw the natural world as a wealth of resources for the wise use of humankind. Similarly, we are of our age, and our attitudes are deeply imbued with current values and perceptions.

A few examples of the current diversity of perceptions, depending on professional or cultural biases, emphasize the role that attitudes play not only in our reactions to our environment, but even in what we see when we look at it and record our impressions. A few years ago, I attended a workshop on fire management of barrier islands. On the workshop field trip to Canaveral National Seashore, much of the vegetation that we saw consisted of impenetrable palmetto scrub (fig. 2.2). If I had visited this location on my own, I would have regarded the thick scrub as a hindrance to walking off the trails and would have wondered why people who built houses in it had not cleared more area around their houses to let in light and breezes. After I had attended a day and a half of lectures and discussions with specialists in fire ecology and fire management, however, this vegetation became "fuel load," poised to carry highly destructive fires that would threaten the human habitations. The crucial transformation was that I not only grasped the significance intellectually, but actually perceived the vegetation as fuel, a culturally conditioned response.

A cultural bias may be illustrated by the observations that an English medievalist and his wife made about a preserved forest in Princeton, New Jersey. Being accustomed to the carefully managed woods in England, my friends were quite distressed by how messy the woods were; they needed "tidying up" (fig. 2.3). They were referring not to human litter, which was not in evidence, but to natural litter, dead branches and fallen trees. To an American the site looks the way a preserved forest should look, with forest plant litter in varying states of decay forming a patchy cover on the forest floor. The combination of lack of neatness and waste of wood carries quite

Figure 2.2. Palmetto scrub at Canaveral National Seashore, Florida. (Photo by the author, February 1984)

different connotations to others. Neither attitude is inherently right or wrong; they are merely culturally conditioned points of view, although the different methods of managing the forest would have varying impacts on nutrient cycling from woody debris. Throughout history, however, attitudes have had consequences for how people treat the environment, what they deem worthy of study, and how they express their observations.

Both general and local contexts color what is written and how it is expressed, especially in public documents. Census and other land records, for example, catalogue areas in different crops but generally cite no details of forest composition because the records were made not to serve as ecological descriptions but to evaluate the agricultural productivity of the land. Probably the most complete inventory of land resources a millennium ago is the Domesday Book, an inventory the Norman conquerors made in Great Britain in A.D. 1086. Assessors based most estimates of the area of land in woodlots on supply of woodland for swine grazing, length and breadth of woodlots, and area in acres, though it is unclear how much an acre was in 1086 (fig. 2.4).[20] This enumeration of property offers a tantalizing glimpse into land use then but includes only major categories of land—fields, ponds, and woods—because its purpose was to regularize the land tenure system, not to describe the land cover.[21] The most detailed environmental information from the past

Figure 2.3. Contrast the tangle of dead fallen branches at the Institute Woods, Princeton, N.J. (*top*) with the neat, clear understory of a beech woods in Juniperhill Woods, England (*bottom*). (Photos by the author, spring 1985 [Juniperhill] and spring 1995 [Institute Woods])

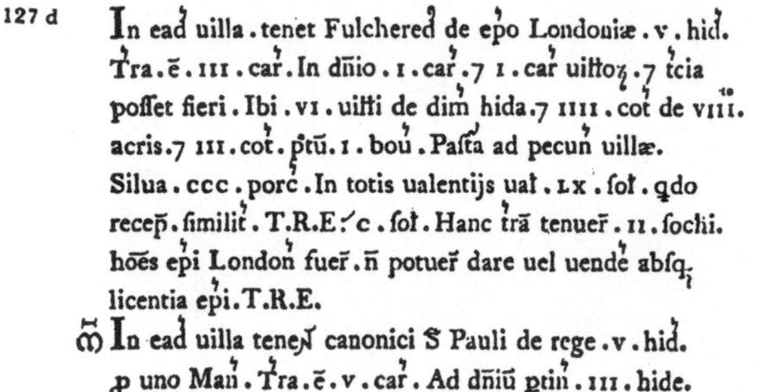

127 d

In ead uilla.tenet Fulchered de epo Londoniæ.v.hid.
Tra.ē.iii.car.In dñio.i.car.7 i.car uitto៵.7 tcia
poffet fieri.Ibi.vi.uitti de dim hida.7 iiii.cot de viii.
acris.7 iii.cot.ptū.i.bou.Pafta ad pecun uillæ.
Silua.ccc.porc.In totis ualentijs ual.lx.fot.qdo
recep.fimilit.T.R.E.ʻc.fot.Hanc trã tenuer.ii.fochi.
hōēs epi London fuer.n̄ potuer dare uel uende abfq,
licentia epi.T.R.E.

M̃ In ead uilla teneɲ canonici S Pauli de rege.v.hid.
p uno Man.Tra.ē.v.car.Ad dñiū ptin.iii.hide.
7 ibi funt.ii.car.Vitti.ii.car.7 tcia pot fieri.Ibi.viii.
uitti.qfq, de.i.uirg.7 vii.uitti.qfq, de dim uirg.
7 vii.bord.qfq, de.v.acs.7 xvi.cot.7 ii.ferui.ptū
v.car.Pafta ad pecun uille.Silua.c.l.porc.Int totū
ual.viii.lib.qdo recep fimilit.T.R.E: x.lib.Hoc M̃
tenuer idē canonici S Pauli in dñio.T.R.E.7 ē de uictu eo៵.

*In Osvlvestane hvnd.*

In *Tyeverde* tenet Durand canonic S Pauli de rege
ii.h̃ træ.Tra.ē.i.car 7 dim.Ibi funt.iii.uitti de dim
hida.7 dim uirg.Pafta ad pecun uille.Silua.c.porc.
H̃ tra ualet.xxx.fot.qdo recep fimilit.T.R.E:ʻxx.fot.
In ead uilla tenet Gueri canonic S Pauli.ii.h̃ træ.
Tra.ē.i.car 7 dim.In dñio.ē car.7 dim poteft fieri.
Ibi.ii.uitt de.i.uirg.7 i.bord de.vi.acs.7 iii.cot.
Silua.l.porc.H̃ tra ualet xxx.fot.qdo recep.
fimilit.T.R.E:ʻxx.fot.Hoc M̃ jacuit 7 jacet in æccta
S Pauli.in dñio canonico៵.

Figure 2.4. Page from Domesday Book, trans-
cription on left with translation on right. Note
that forest is described generally by how many
pigs it will feed. (From *Domesday Book*. Vol. 11.
*Middlesex*. J. Morris, ed. [Phillimore, Shopwyke
Manor Barn, Chichester, West Sussex PO20
6BG, 1975], 127d)

describes economically or politically valuable aspects of the environment but
only indirectly includes the kind of detail that ecologists seek.

Details of other aspects are often found in local and informal descriptions
or travel accounts. The value of these depends on the knowledge of the person making the statement but often supplies unique documentation of land
cover or other environmental features for specific times and places. Interpretation then requires consideration of the reasons for the record and the
context in which it was written as well as the actual content.

13   In the same village Fulcred holds 5 hides from the Bishop of         127
London. Land for 3 ploughs. In lordship 1 plough. 1 villagers'
plough; a third possible.
  6 villagers with ½ hide; 4 cottagers with 8 acres; 3 cottagers.
  Meadow for 1 ox; pasture for the village livestock; woodland,
  300 pigs.
Total value 60s; when acquired the same; before 1066, 100s.
  Two Freemen held this land before 1066; they were the Bishop
of London's men; they could not grant or sell without the
Bishop's permission.

14 M. In the same village the Canons of St. Paul's hold 5 hides from
the King as one manor. Land for 5 ploughs. 3 hides belong to
the lordship; 2 ploughs there. The villagers, 2 ploughs; a third
possible.
  8 villagers with 1 virgate each; 7 villagers with ½ virgate
  each; 7 smallholders with 5 acres each; 16 cottagers; 2 slaves.
  Meadow for 5 ploughs; pasture for the village livestock;
  woodland, 150 pigs.
In total, value £8; when acquired the same; before 1066, £10.
  Before 1066 the Canons of St. Paul's held this manor in
lordship; it is for their supplies.

  [also] in OSSULSTONE Hundred*
15   In TWYFORD Durand, a Canon of St. Paul's, holds 2 hides of land
from the King. Land for 1½ ploughs.
  3 villagers with ½ hide and ½ virgate.
  Pasture for the village livestock; woodland, 100 pigs.
Value of this land 30s; when acquired the same; before 1066, 20s.

16   In the same village Gyrth, a Canon of St. Paul's, holds 2 hides of
land. Land for 1½ ploughs. In lordship 1 plough; ½ possible.
  2 villagers with 1 virgate; 1 smallholder with 6 acres; 3 cottagers.
  Woodland, 50 pigs.
Value of this land 30s; when acquired the same; before 1066, 20s.
  This manor lay and lies in (the lands of) St. Paul's Church, in
the lordship of the Canons.

These written records afford only scattered glimpses into the past. Because the questions that historical ecologists ask today are rarely those asked by people in the past, there is no one compendium of sources, and further, these records have not been maintained systematically, as have birth and death records and legal documents. Historians are always faced with fragmentary evidence and must assess the representativeness of what has been preserved. Some records have been deemed important enough for some purpose to be edited and printed, so are easily available. These usually give an overview, but because the reason for their assembly was usually not the reason we want to use them, they almost always have to be supplemented by unpublished sources, whether to establish the history of a local site or even to trace overall trends. Unpublished records survive in a variety of collections: libraries, historical societies, clerk's offices and other depositories of public documents, business archives, and sometimes in attics and old trunks. Librarians are often unaware that their manuscript collections contain environmentally interesting information; I have often been told that some diary would contain nothing of interest, only to find that inadvertent or indirect comments were quite valuable. For example, an eighteenth-century diary from Morris County, New Jersey, commented on the presence of smoke in the air from "many meadows afire underground."[22] Combined with other evidence, this suggested that draining of the meadows had allowed them to dry out so much that the highly organic soil was able to burn; furthermore, it is a clue as to why the vegetation that grew back after the drainage ditches were no longer maintained is apparently different from what was there before draining. It may be that the change in soil composition from highly organic to more mineral after the organic matter burned provided the appropriate habitat for different species. By relating an understanding of ecological and physical processes to historical evidence one can often posit novel explanations for current systems.

### Kinds of Primary Documents of Use in Historical Ecology
PUBLIC RECORDS AND STATISTICS

Governments collect a wide range of descriptive statistics about land and people under their control.[23] Most of these have to do with the kinds and amounts of natural and agricultural resources available for exploitation and the numbers of people, often divided into such categories as gender, age, and status. Land surveys often include natural features and corner witness trees. Wills and especially estate inventories describe properties as well. Tax rolls contain valuation of property and crops. All of these kinds of documents provide what a scientist using historical documentation is most comfortable with: numbers and precisely delimited categories. For reconstructing land use at specific times and changes over time and space they are invaluable. The information was usually compiled more or less systematically and is often quite detailed. The data record, albeit indirectly, locations and rates of forest clearance and use of other natural resources as well as field abandonment. For example, an estate inventory in New York made on 21 February 1823 included "15 Sheep with 2 lambs," indicating that lambing had just started by 21 February, "$25 worth of "Grain in the Ground," probably winter wheat or rye, "$4 worth of "Cyder and Casks," evidence of an orchard, and "1 Lumber Sleigh" and "1 lumber Chain and ax," indicating the existence of uncleared woods probably on the property.[24]

The major quantitative evidence of forest composition is trees recorded in surveys. Testing for bias in choice of species in systematic surveys suggests that it was not important enough to skew the results seriously, even though trees were chosen in part because of their size, age, smoothness of bark, and other practical criteria rather than to represent the forest composition.[25] When these data are summarized they can be used to generate maps of forest distribution and composition at various spatial scales at specific times. Yet even surveys in which sampling was not systematic and the sampling interval was very long provide a first approximation of the distribution of different kinds of vegetation. Qualitative descriptions along with enumeration often reveal even more about the land cover. For example, a late-eighteenth-century survey of land in New York State included trees marked in a grid with corners spaced about one mile apart. In one such survey half of the eighteen trees in one block were beeches (*Fagus grandifolia*) and none hemlocks, while the qualitative description was of "hemlock-beech" vegetation on the uplands. Beech is more convenient to blaze than hemlock so may have been overrepresented in the survey.[26] In another area few trees were blazed, but the survey included a graphic description of the early phases of natural secondary succession: "Entered low land covered with thorns and briars. Large pine trees blown up by the roots. A great thicket."[27] In other words, in many cases, qualitative descriptions contain information critically important for corroborating or modifying the impression gained from quantitative documentation.

MAPS AND PHOTOGRAPHS

Maps and photographs furnish the most graphic evidence of past land cover and use. Maps incorporate an interpretation of certain features of the landscape, often including bodies of water and topographic features as well as human constructions like roads, towns, and political boundaries. Some of the historic maps that are most useful for reconstructing past landscapes have been those drawn for military purposes. The planning of troop movements and battles requires intimate knowledge of the terrain, including some details of forest cover, so armies have included well-trained surveyors. Natural features on these maps, such as streams and hills, often correspond closely with what is there today, so the details are spatially comparable over time. Once the contemporary map-making conventions for an era are clear,[28] many details can be interpreted, among them overall vegetation type (for example, deciduous or coniferous forest) and steepness of slopes. Even maps that are several centuries old can be highly accurate, depending on how well known the area was to the mapmaker. A map made in 1777 by the British surveyor of the Saratoga battlefield in New York is remarkably accurate near the British headquarters but decreasingly so as the distance from the headquarters increases, that is, as danger of colonial snipers increased (fig. 2.5).[29]

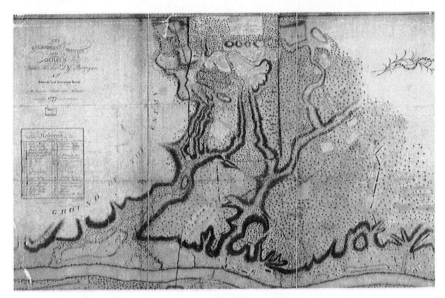

Figure 2.5. Military map of 1777, Saratoga Battlefield, Saratoga County, New York. Note ravines and hills delimited by hatchmarks to show steep slopes, cleared fields, and forest cover. Part of W. C. Wilkinson, The encampment & position of the Army under His Excy. Lt. Gl. Burgoyne at Swords and Freeman's Farms on Hudsons River near Stillwater, 1777. (Photo courtesy of Saratoga National Historical Park)

Sixteenth- and seventeenth-century maps of North America are most accurate near the coast but often quite vague inland. Mountains described by native Americans may be placed rather haphazardly, and mythical lakes and rivers abound. Illustrations on maps are notoriously useless for reconstructing the local scene. In the late nineteenth century, however, some carefully surveyed maps include forest cover which corresponds remarkably well with current vegetation. Maps like these can be used to interpret recent patterns of forest regeneration.[30] As with other documents, however, it is essential to pay attention to definitions of terms: for example, the term *forest* may mean noncultivated brushlands in the United States but serves as a legal rather than vegetational description in Great Britain. As long as one bears in mind that maps include details relevant to their purpose and that accuracy is often not uniform, they can be used to very good effect to reconstruct a past landscape.

It is most rewarding to be able to work from photographs, a more or less direct record of what was present. Fascinating comparisons have been made between photographs taken at one location at two or more points in time.

Where distinctive landmarks are present for relocating of sites, these photographs often record dramatic changes in plant cover in great detail.[31] When the Mexican and American governments constructed monuments along their common border in the late nineteenth century, for example, the surveyors took an archive photograph of each monument. Photographs of these same markers taken almost a century later document vegetational change in their vicinity as well as differences across the border caused by different land use.[32] In drawing conclusions about changes in the intervening century, one cannot, however, ignore the impacts of human activities before the first photographs were taken or the impact of disturbance caused by constructing the monument. A comparison of other photographs of the American west taken in the nineteenth century with the same places in the late twentieth sheds light not only on land use and vegetational changes, but also on the intentions of the earlier photographers. Many nineteenth-century photographic sites were carefully chosen for their dramatic landscapes or were photographed in ways that enhanced their dramatic effect in order to let people of the eastern United States see what the west was like.[33] Thus comparisons of photographs over time can indicate changes in vegetation, but they, like other historical documents, must be interpreted in context, not just as objective data.

Photographs of actual human activities such as tree planting hint at possible impacts of these past activities. For example, photographs and written records document that in the 1930s the Civilian Conservation Corps in the United States cleared the understory and planted small trees among scattered larger ash (*Fraxinus americana*) and red cedar trees in young second growth stands in a park in New Jersey (fig. 2.6). The photograph shows that plantations may be much more complex than straight rows of one species in one size and that they could take place within an existing young forest.

Aerial photography, particularly vertical aerial photography, lends itself even more readily to interpretation of landscape change. Such photographs, which date at the earliest from the 1920s or 1930s, use technology developed during the First World War. The United States Department of Agriculture has repeated stereo coverage of much of the land area since the 1940s or 1950s. Since the late 1960s, satellite imagery, in a variety of wavelengths, has also been available, so changes in land cover can be charted in some detail.[34] These images still present problems of interpretation in terms of ground cover classification and scale but supply ample data to interpret changes over time. The categories are gross and may refer primarily to plant canopy classes, but this is nevertheless an excellent frame of reference for analyzing short-term changes in landscape patterns at a variety of scales.

Figure 2.6. Civilian Conservation Corps plantation at Morristown National Historical Park. The young stand of red cedars and what appear to be ash trees was cleared of undergrowth and then underplanted with small trees. (Photo courtesy of National Park Service, United States Department of the Interior, taken in 1934)

### OTHER KINDS OF DOCUMENTS

A plethora of other kinds of documents adds context and detail to interpretations. Correspondence and diaries record individual perceptions of landscape features which often explain more cryptic information available from formal documents. Whereas an agricultural census return may record the number of cords of wood cut on a farm, a farm diary may include details of how the farmer used the wood and when and how he cut it. For example, cutting small trees for "hoop-poles"[35] (small, straight stems used for making barrels) had a different effect on forest vegetation than cutting larger trees for fencing. A preference for twigs as winter fodder similarly implies different impact and management than would leaf collecting.[36] Some descriptions were written for blatantly commercial reasons. Advertisements of property for sale or other descriptions designed to attract people are an obvious example, although some sound quite convincing. Landscape paintings and other artwork also contain clues to past landscapes, though these must be especially carefully interpreted in context.

Laws relate both to the actual state of affairs and to attitudes about a politically ideal state, based on contemporary ideas of how to get to and maintain this state. They regulate activities both to protect resources and to protect property rights, so it is important to be aware of why a law was written. Laws sometimes state the opposite of the truth, that is, how it ought to be. Thus, regulations on cutting white pine or other timber in various American colonies in the seventeenth and early eighteenth centuries reflected not a scarcity of timber in the colonies but rather the desire on the part of the British government to prevent individuals from poaching timber.[37] Closed hunting seasons for some species in twelve of the thirteen American colonies by 1776,[38] however, reflected both a diminished herd and a perception that deer hunting should be protected. Closed seasons did not indicate opposition on the part of the governments to hunting, but quite to the contrary, a commitment to revive the resource for further hunting. In addition, just because an activity was not regulated does not mean that it was permitted; it may mean that not doing it was taken for granted.[39] Does the imposition of a "closed" season for hunting deer in the eighteenth century, for example, suggest that previously hunters had paid no attention to the period when fawns were being born? or does it mean that deer populations were becoming so limited that hunters were tempted to kill even does with fawns, ignoring former unwritten taboos? One cannot always rely on laws to state the obvious. In other words, the meaning of laws in terms of natural resources must be interpreted in the broader context.

Historical documents are a valuable source of information for historical ecological studies. They exhibit a wide variety of detail, reliability, and availability. The information gleaned from them must be placed in the context of a larger question in order to be anything more than a chronicle, but in such a context they provide explanations for some changes in the landscape, changing use over time, and a chronological framework in which to put other research findings.[40] With a little imagination one can usually mine more information from them than at first appears possible.

# 3

## Field Studies: Bringing Documentary Evidence Down to Earth

The evidence gleaned from written sources comes to life for ecologists when they apply it to specific landscapes and their component ecosystems. They can then evaluate the importance of historical factors in affecting the structure and functioning of these systems. Physical and biological remnants like cultivated plants and old ditches also reveal many details about what people did in the past and where they did it, and this amplifies archeological, historical, and geographical understanding. Because written records are often not spatially precise or detailed, making the connection between documents and landscapes often involves painstaking fieldwork to decipher the physical remains of past land use in terms of historically documented activities, logging or farming, to name just two. The physical traces left on the land are clues that confirm and frequently amplify the documentary record. By establishing patterns of past landscapes we can see the variety of uses that have shaped the present and the interactions over time between changing uses and changing cultures.[1]

Even if the major focus of a study is historical and not ecological, one should first compile the natural abiotic features of the research area—climate, microclimate, bedrock and surficial geology, and soils—at an appropriate scale. These factors determine the possible ecosystems, including species composition and structure. In addition, they affect human activities.

For example, there are most likely no remaining examples of undisturbed, virgin vegetation on excellent agricultural soils. Farms have taken the place of forest and prairies in most places, and even woodlots have served for cordwood, lumber, poles, and casual grazing.[2] On the other hand, ecosystems in remote mountainous parts of the world may be relatively untouched by people, especially if they have no valuable mineral deposits or are hard to reach. Abiotic features and location strongly influence both potential natural vegetation and human activities; the two are inextricably linked.

### Relating Documentary to Field Evidence

Although some patterns of vegetation, such as medieval coppice woodlands (stands of multiple-stemmed trees that have originated by sprouting after repeated cutting), obviously relate to past human activities, more subtle patterns may also owe their existence to past human activity. For example, in 1987, one roughly rectangular patch of oak–yellow poplar forest in eastern Pennsylvania, about thirteen hectares, had more yellow poplar and black birch (*Betula lenta*) than the surrounding forest. In addition, there were many dead red cedars (*Juniperus virginiana*) in this area. Because red cedar rarely grows under a forest canopy in this region, it is a strong indicator of forest regeneration after field abandonment.[3]

Written records describe an active iron furnace at this site from 1771 to 1883. In an aerial photograph from 1937, most of the current yellow poplar forests were open fields. None of the current oak forests was an open field in 1937, but remains of old logging roads and the leveled circles of old charcoal hearths seemed to indicate that these forests had been heavily cut to make charcoal to fuel the furnace. This suggested that the stand had originated as an abandoned field well before 1937, while the nearby forest was still being cut for charcoal. An abandoned road and foundation supported this inference.[4] Any study of the effect of cutting for charcoal on subsequent forest development must therefore exclude this stand. Documentary evidence thus supplied a composite picture of the history of the forest in general, but a field survey considering historic land use was necessary to differentiate this stand with a different history.

Historic surveys commonly contain sufficient information to enable an investigator to infer probable vegetation and even quantitative species composition of sites sometime in the past. Comparison of these with the present, coupled with indications of intervening activities, suggests the consequences of the past land use on current plant and animal communities as well as on soils, nutrient-cycling, and other ecosystem properties. Field studies search for evidence of such past features and for their resultant effects through a variety of techniques.

## Field Techniques for Historic Reconstruction

Many anthropogenic features like old stone walls, banks and ditches, abandoned roads or clearings, and rows of old hedgerow trees embedded in younger forest are obvious as one walks through a field or forest.[5] By superimposing these on historic maps or aerial photographs one can generate a detailed reconstruction of the past patterns of fields, woodlots, roads, and buildings at different times.[6]

These patterns show up in aerial photographs and in other remotely sensed images at a wide range of scales, revealing past activities ranging from large-scale irrigation projects to individual farm sites and woodlots. Because some patterns are easier to discern at a distance, remote sensing often bridges the gap between written documents and actual field reconnaissance. It may be difficult to locate a specific site on the ground, but if it has left a distinctive mark visible in aerial photography or other remote imaging the location can be pinpointed.

Patterns visible in remotely sensed images are often enigmatic, however, and require ground-level study, which may still not reveal the function of the patterns. In aerial photographs of an area of New York taken in 1948 and in 1992, a square field about twenty meters on a side had a striped appearance, the stripes being about three meters wide. Although not immediately noticeable on the ground, once the stripes were identified in the aerial photographs, the pattern, consisting of wide, shallow, parallel undulations in this one field only, was obvious (fig. 3.1). The pattern most closely resembles medieval "ridge and furrow" microtopography, but here found in New York, not Europe (fig. 3.2). It has a distinct effect on vegetation; because of poor subsurface drainage the troughs are wetter than the ridges. When and why they were constructed remains a mystery, though clearly they are a past human construction that continues to have a significant effect on the vegetation.

Soils too reflect past activities.[7] In some soils, cutting of forest cover precipitates severe erosion, which may leave quite obvious steep-sided gullies which persist long after agriculture or logging has ceased.[8] Sheet erosion removes surface soil, sometimes washing off all the soil and leaving exposed bedrock but more often removing all or part of the surface soil horizon.[9] Fires, possibly human set, often leave distinct layers of charcoal in the soil, in tropical rain forests as well as in temperate forests.[10] Plowing homogenizes the surface horizons of the soil, so that upper level zonation is destroyed or

Figure 3 1  Field at Saratoga National Historical Park with unidentified parallel ridges. These ridges also appear in the 1927 aerial photograph of the park. Aerial photograph taken in 1992 for Saratoga National Historical Park.

obscured.[11] Most obviously, especially in the tropics, where most nutrients are sequestered in the vegetation, agriculture leaves soils depauperate in available nutrients, to the long-term detriment of regenerating vegetation. Agriculture also often raises the pH of soil by bringing base-rich minerals from lower horizons as well as by the addition of lime, while regenerating forests cause detectable decreases in pH.[12] Conversely, deforestation in the uplands of England millennia ago probably contributed to acidification of soil as heaths replaced the forests.[13] These processes may then have indirect

Figure 3.2. Medieval ridge and furrow landscape that has been preserved by pasturing, Leicestershire, England. The reverse S-curve of some of the pattern is characteristic of much ridge and furrow in the Midlands of England. (Cambridge University Collection of Air Photographs, copyright reserved)

effects in lowering the pH or raising the trophic status of streams and lakes or both.[14] The existence of any of these, and many other, conditions indicates past land use and directly affects current ecosystems as well.

Archeological studies focus on physical remains of specifically human activities. They can show where and how people lived at some time in the past, and to some extent how they used natural resources. By extrapolation, they can indicate population densities. For example, assemblages of house sites in the Maya region of Guatemala allow archeologists to make estimates of changing populations there, which increased slowly from as long ago as 3000 B.C. to a peak of perhaps two hundred persons per square kilometer around A.D 800. They then declined precipitously in the ninth century A.D. and did not exceed their former density until recent times.[15] Remains of food and cooking implements provide insight into the kinds of resources that were being exploited.[16] These population changes can be related to changing conditions of a local lake.

Historic as well as prehistoric archeology permits reconstruction of past environments and uses. For example, in northern Australia extensive stock-yards are common in an area of few trees. Measurement and counting of the logs in these structures as well as research in historical documents furnish evidence that the region was much more heavily forested in the past. Once cut, the trees have been unable to recover, but their remains as well as some historical records testify to their former existence.[17]

The actual plants growing on a site also hint at its history. An even-aged stand of trees generally originated after some major disturbance, whether natural or anthropogenic. Other indicators may suggest the nature of the disturbance, for example, natural disturbances usually do not have rectilinear outlines, whereas artificial ones like agricultural fields often do. Changes in age and composition across a straight line thus suggest a human element. Some plantations are obvious, but others that have utilized native species can be less so. Field data may indicate past harvesting when a species is lacking on sites where it is expected and the sites are near locations of past human activities.[18]

Another clue to past use lies in the structure of individual plants, for example, in coppices. These usually consist of one species, with more or less regularly spaced clumps of stems (fig. 3.3). Scattered among the coppice stems are often larger individuals grown as "standards" to produce larger wood. The basic structure of the stand may persist long after the coppice management has ceased.

Even in North America, where coppicing was usually practiced in a rather casual way, there are stands with many multiple-stemmed trees: that is, they may have been cut in the past and have regenerated as sprouts rather than as seedlings. Such an origin for the trees in a forest imposes a distinct pattern of age and size classes and species composition, known as sprout hardwoods, characterized by extensive stands of prolifically sprouting taxa such as American chestnut and oaks.

Ground-layer flora also reflects past land use. In eastern Pennsylvania, for example, forty-year-old yellow poplar stands that regenerated on an abandoned agricultural field had an herbaceous layer rich in such non-native weeds as field garlic (*Allium vineale*) and Japanese honeysuckle (*Lonicera japonica*), whereas these species were not present in the herbaceous flora of yellow poplar patches of approximately similar age and size in sites that were in all probability never used as fields.[19] In England, old field edges can often be located by the presence or absence of woodland species that spread only very slowly into nearby regenerated woods. Others, such as sanicle (*Sanicula europea*), indicate old fields.[20]

Figure 3.3. Hazel coppice, Wallis Wood, Surrey, England. Note the regular spacing of the sprouting stools, which were cut in the previous year. (Photo by the author, spring 1985)

In a study of the relation of understory flora to origin and type of woods in New England, G. G. Whitney and D. R. Foster found that the origin of a stand as old-growth or old-field succession influenced the distribution of more species than did the relative numbers of conifers and broadleaved trees present in the stand (table 3.1).[21] The interpretation of such differences depends on thorough knowledge of the local flora and site histories.

These and many other indicators of land use that are fairly easy to discern in the field present the historical ecologist with a static picture, a sort of snapshot of the present consequences of a past inferred activity. The connection between the past and present is inferred. There are several ways to tease out a more dynamic, moving picture of change over time. These involve finding traces on the landscape of a succession of past events and studying some kind of time series in the field.

As woody plants die, their remains are often buried by additional litter before they decompose completely, especially in cool moist climates and acid soils. Trees that are toppled by storms produce distinctive mound and pit

Table 3.1. Comparison of common understory species in different woodland types.

| Species/habitat | Primary woodlands | | Secondary woodlands | |
|---|---|---|---|---|
| | Conifer | Broadleaf | Conifer | Broadleaf |
| **Species with generally >10% occurrence in primary woodlands, <5% in secondary** | | | | |
| Acer pensylvanicum | 32 | 73 | 0 | 0 |
| Aralia nudicaulis | 36 | 30 | 0 | 2 |
| Chimaphila umbellata | 20 | 12 | 0 | 0 |
| Epigaea repens | 12 | 3 | 2 | 0 |
| Medeola virginiana | 12 | 12 | 0 | 0 |
| Polypodium virginianum | 32 | 3 | 0 | 0 |
| Viburnum acerifolium | 10 | 52 | 4 | 2 |
| Viburnum alnifolium | 76 | 48 | 2 | 0 |
| **Species with generally >10% occurrence in secondary woodlands, <5% in primary** | | | | |
| Dennstaedtia punctilobula* | 0 | 0 | 0 | 42 |
| Lycopodium clavatum* | 0 | 0 | 22 | 27 |
| Lycopodium obscurum | 2 | 0 | 9 | 13 |
| Maianthemum canadense | 2 | 0 | 41 | 12 |
| Polytrichum commune | 0 | 0 | 17 | 8 |
| Pteridium aquilinum | 2 | 3 | 17 | 19 |
| Pyrola spp., esp. elliptica and rotundifolia | 0 | 0 | 35 | 17 |
| Rubus spp., esp. flagillaris* | 0 | 0 | 36 | 38 |
| **Species with major occurrence in broadleaf woodlands, ≤5% in conifers (No difference between secondary and primary)** | | | | |
| Aster acuminatus | 5 | 36 | 0 | 36 |
| **Species with little or no preference** | | | | |
| Dryopteris carthusiana | 25 | 18 | ?? | 17 |
| Gaultheria procumbens | 92 | 48 | 26 | 29 |
| Mitchella repens | 56 | 30 | 37 | 19 |
| Vaccinium angustifolium | 39 | 24 | 39 | 23 |
| Total number of sites | 59 | 33 | 46 | 52 |

*Described in Gleason and Cronquist, Manual of Vascular Plants, as preferring open or disturbed sites.

Source: Whitney and Gordon, Overstorey composition.

Figure 3.4. Uprooted beech, Forêt de Lyons,
France. Note the large amount of soil pulled up
by the roots. (Photo by the author, spring 1995)

patterns in which the root mass was pulled from the soil (fig. 3.4). Erosion and decay slowly smooth these mounds over time, but their traces may remain for centuries, especially if other trees fall on them. Farming smooths these remains, so that an old agricultural field that has reverted to forest leaves a fairly level surface, unscarred by a maze of mounds, pits, and ridges formed of decayed logs, root masses, and root hollows. Study of the consequences of this kind of microtopography for regeneration of plants and distribution of animals can indicate ways in which a younger forest may be distinct from an older one even after many decades of growth.

Even where stems have broken off rather than pulling up their roots, the tangle of superimposed stems can be dissected to trace the history of tree deaths. This very painstaking procedure yields a detailed picture of changing species composition and disturbance events, which may then be related to patterns of natural and human disturbance.[22] Although studies such as this can be done only on small areas and their results are site-specific, they afford unique, detailed glimpses into temporal patterns of change and the importance of disturbances to the structure of the forest vegetation.

In many climates, trees write their own long-term records, both in growth form and in details of their annual growth rings. The obvious distinction

Figure 3.5. Row of trees that previously formed
the edge of a field. The field was on the right
and old forest stand to the left. Note the large
branches to the right and leaning trunks. (Photo
by the author, spring 1995)

between tall, straight trees and spreading, thick-trunked ones is a sure clue
to their origin in a thick growth of other trees or in the open, respectively, a
phenomenon governed by the remarkable flexibility in growth habit of many
species, including beech (*Fagus* spp.), oaks, and maples (*Acer* spp.). A
straight, clear trunk on one side balanced by low branches on the opposite
or a trunk that curves to one side is evidence of the edge of a large gap, clearing, or field when the tree was young. It is not a remnant of an old forest left
when the clearing was made (fig. 3.5).

A cross-section of a tree trunk reveals age, episodes of suppression and release, nutrient status, climate, fires and other disturbances such as defoliation, and other information (fig. 3.6).[23] Tree ring studies used as proxies for reconstructing past climates require large numbers of sections from a region and complex correlation with the effects of climate on tree growth. The study of trees in individual stands may also give insight into the development of individual stands. For example, many species of trees respond to thinning of a stand by accelerated radial growth, so that growth rings record the date of these episodes.[24]

Additional long-term data come from general observations and censuses. Herbarium specimens, especially those for which the collector recorded detailed locations and made repeated collections, reveal past population distributions. Annual bird censuses document the presence and absence of species in specific areas and sometimes include information on abundances. The United States Breeding Bird Survey, for example, has compiled at least semiquantitative data on breeding bird abundances in the United States since 1965.[25] Banding records can give more easily quantified records. Records of the take in hunting, "bag records," may give signs of changes in population densities, albeit modified by technological and licensing changes.

In studies often referred to as "space-for-time,"[26] stands of different ages at a given time are assumed to represent a temporal sequence, in which older stands resembled the younger ones in their earlier years. Such studies have been widely used in the eastern United States, where natural regeneration has colonized many agricultural fields abandoned over the past century.[27] They serve as a basis for detecting general trends of change over time, although they assume that the conditions obtaining when the fields were abandoned are not important. They are further complicated by subsequent, usually unrecorded management, for example, clearing of undesirable species and selective harvesting, and other disturbance like grazing.

## Long-term Studies

A quite different approach to determining changing patterns over time depends on repeated observations of one site—a permanently marked plot, for example, or at least easily distinguished stands—over a long time period. Repeated observations in small forested areas in Wisconsin, for example, showed that the numbers of native forest herbs decreased between 1954 and 1975, probably in response to human disturbance.[28] In a virgin hardwood forest in Pennsylvania, a rephotographic study showed that the amount of

Figure 3.6. Cross section, Sequoia. Note convoluted structure of the trunk, which includes fire scars. (Photo courtesy of Anthony C. Caprio)

*Table 3.2. Change in understory cover in rephotographed plots over twenty years.*

| Photo date | Trend since 1942 | Number of plots | Percent of plots |
|---|---|---|---|
| 1947 | − | 9 | 43 |
| | o | 11 | 52 |
| | + | 1 | 5 |
| 1952 | − | 12 | 57 |
| | o | 7 | 33 |
| | + | 2 | 10 |
| 1957 | − | 12 | 57 |
| | o | 5 | 24 |
| | + | 4 | 19 |
| 1962 | − | 13 | 62 |
| | o | 4 | 19 |
| | + | 4 | 19 |

− decrease
o no change
+ increase

*Source:* Hough, A twenty year record.

understory decreased in thirteen of twenty-one plots between 1942 and 1962, probably because of deer browsing (table 3.2).[29] These studies document changes over time but we can only speculate on the causes.

Some long-term studies include experimental manipulations of sites to mimic human or natural disturbances. Probably the oldest of these is at Rothamsted in England, initiated in the mid–nineteenth century in response to the invention of "artificial manure," that is, chemical fertilizers. Its aim was to test ideas about long-term use of nutrients by agricultural crops and the source of nitrogen in plants.[30] Owing to its length, this experiment has yielded an invaluable set of data on the long-term consequences of the experimental treatment; at the same time, however, it precludes the quantifying of such changes as increases in weeds and growth of soil fungi.[31]

Data gathered in an annual initiation of succession on paired plots in agricultural fields in New Jersey, started in 1958, focus on changes in species composition. Prior use of the fields was not, however, uniform; some had been actively cultivated and others merely mowed. Other features—among them seed sources from plots that had already been abandoned and weather—changed with time, so even in this carefully designed experiment the plots did not differ only in age. Overall patterns that emerged have suggested general characteristics of succession, although extrapolation to regional patterns, where conditions of abandonment and prior treatments differ, was more difficult.[32]

The effects of watershed-scale disturbances, for example, clear-cutting, on nutrient cycling is the primary focus of another long-term study, one being carried out at the Hubbard Brook Experimental Forest in New Hampshire.[33] In this project, long-term records have afforded new insights into such ecosystem-scale processes as productivity, biomass accumulation, and nutrient cycling, and these discoveries have been incorporated into predictive models.[34]

All three of these studies have yielded valuable insight into change over time and how human impact leaves residual effects, though none has been focused particularly on the residual effects of previous land uses. The long-term nature of the studies prevents us from drawing erroneous, short-term conclusions about long-term processes and allows us to test hypotheses derived from space-for-time studies. On the other hand, these studies themselves are tied to time and place, and even if experimental are not repeatable in a strict sense.[35]

Long-term observations, whether studies of experimental plots or just monitoring of populations, are a critical part of predicting the effects of land use on plant and animal communities, ecosystems, and landscapes. It may be easy to see that a species has declined or increased in abundance recently, but long-term observations are necessary to place this observation in perspective, that is, was the species more or less abundant just prior to the recent decline than it had been, say, a few decades before? Such studies allow us to form a hypothesis to explain changes, and to see if the consequences of these hypotheses are consistent with the evidence, in the search for understanding of process and causation.

## Statistical Analysis of Historical Data

Historical studies yield quantitative data: species counts, acres in different land uses, population densities. Even when specific counts are not available, categorical data, such as logged or farmed, coppiced or not, can be treated statistically. An index of the intensity of previous human disturbance may help one evaluate the relative importance of these factors in altering the composition of woodlots.[36] Simple comparisons between data collected some time in the past and similar measurements made later show trends over time, which can be compared through a variety of multivariate analyses.

Changing landscape patterns can be analyzed by quantifying past land uses shown in historical photographs.[37]

Historical data are not, however, quite as easily used in statistical analyses as are data collected according to a well-designed sampling scheme. If plots with measured data in the past were neither permanently marked nor randomly located, there are no statistically robust ways to compare the data with that collected later. Unpredictable biases in location of the plots make comparisons suspect, except perhaps when there are major changes, like the absence of a formerly very common species. The competence of the observers is also critical. For example, the abilities of various observers involved in the United States Breeding Bird Survey are not uniform.[38] These potential problems do not negate the value of these data for quantitative comparisons but suggest that just because historic data are quantitative does not necessarily mean that they can easily yield statistically valid comparisons with current surveys.

Data from historical studies can also be used to build mathematical models of ecosystem change, to test hypotheses about the causes of the changes, and to predict future change. These models generally have focused on climate and natural disturbances but may appropriately be modified to include human disturbance as more quantitative data become available.[39]

Reconstructing the past of a stand or a landscape is somewhat like solving a mystery. The current condition can be described in detail; the characters are all there; clues to the past, both to past conditions and past processes, are present as well. But assembling them all to form a coherent explanation of how one got to the present is a formidable challenge. Some aspects will never be explained, some clues are misleading, and some turn up only because of insightful questioning of the witnesses. Seeing critical connections requires previous experience and often serendipitous inspiration. Familiarity with all likely explanations is essential. In addition, each case presents unique factors or has a unique solution. This does not mean, however, that general patterns and processes cannot be discerned; in fact, generalizations allow insights and can be tested in other unique situations.

The role of the historical ecologist, or the successful investigator, is to distinguish the general principles from the specific deviations. This, of course, requires a subjective abstraction of certain characteristics for study, such as nutrient fluxes, energetics, or community indices. The validity of these is then tested by studying longer-term records or by making predictions. Because ecosystems are dynamic, hypotheses must be tested over time. It is not possible to extrapolate backward from a single current study because a single

end point can arise from several possible beginnings. One must use historical analysis to elucidate the processes that led to the current "end" point.
Similarly, because of potentially divergent paths in the future or future unanticipated changes in conditions, it can be difficult or impossible to predict.
The record that maps the route taken to the current situation is the best indicator of future alternatives, and it reveals the variety and changing nature of
change, especially as humans have manipulated the environment in an array
of ingenious ways.

# The Sedimentary Record

Many organisms write their own records in sediments, deposits that accumulate over time. A constant rain of particles—pollen grains, fine mineral dust, microscopic charcoal—falls on any surface. In lakes, these settle to the bottom with the remains of dead organisms like algae and protozoa (microscopic animals). On land, they mix with accumulating dead plant litter which is preserved under very acid or dry conditions. As new, younger layers bury the older, they build a sedimentary record. By looking at the sequence of organic remains and other materials in a deposit and understanding the processes by which they got there and were preserved, we can analyze changes in the environments from which they came. These carry the record of the past much farther back than do written documents or current field study and introduce different spatial as well as temporal scales, thereby providing critical evidence of past human impact on vegetation.[1]

Human bias is much less important in formation of this kind of record than in written documents; the bias in the sedimentary record is more constant, being dependent on the characteristics of the organisms, how they got to the sediment, and the conditions of preservation. As with any other kind of record, human bias is introduced in the choice and interpretation of the record.

## Kinds of Evidence Found in Sediment

A large variety of organic and inorganic components make up sediment and soil. Some, like algae and aquatic plants growing in a lake or plants growing on a soil surface, originate in situ, while others, like pollen blown into a lake from surrounding vegetation or silt washed in by erosion, come from elsewhere. After deposition, chemical and physical processes alter both the physical and biological fractions of the sediment, so that the record requires translation before it can be read as a record of the environment that produced it. I shall discuss only a few widely used techniques for making this translation.[2]

Pollen grains (and some spores) produced by plants furnish some of the best evidence of past plant communities. They are made in large quantities, they resist decay in anaerobic, acidic, and/or very dry conditions, and their ornamentation and structure allow identification of some even to species (fig. 4.1). By using theory based on the production and dispersal of pollen and empirical studies that compare current pollen input with current species distributions, we can infer past species distributions from the record of pollen in sediments.[3] Some species, such as pines (*Pinus* spp.), which rely on the wind for pollination, produce copious buoyant grains, while others, such as maples, which are insect-pollinated, produce little pollen, which is not dispersed far from the plant. Pollen released near the ground in a wooded landscape rarely is lofted far, while some of that released by canopy plants may travel long distances.[4] Grasses and many agricultural weeds are well represented in the pollen record, but some important crops, like potatoes and beans, leave little record because they produce little or no windblown pollen. Many important tree taxa in the tropics are insect- or bat-pollinated, so they, too, are poorly represented in the pollen rain.[5]

Because of the tendency of most pollen to fall out of the air fairly near its source, forest soils contain pollen that represents the vegetation within only a few meters of the depositional site and thus record the past on the scale of single agricultural fields or of small gaps in the forest cover.[6] In a small pond, one less than one hectare in area, most of the pollen comes from plants within about twenty meters.[7] A larger lake collects relatively more pollen that has traveled farther, up to a few hundred meters. In even larger lakes, a major proportion of the pollen comes from the larger region. Thus, depending on the size of the sedimentary basin, the pollen may record plants from micro sites up to regional landscapes.

Patterns of species distribution measured in the field compare well with patterns of distribution of the pollen of these species in surface sediments.

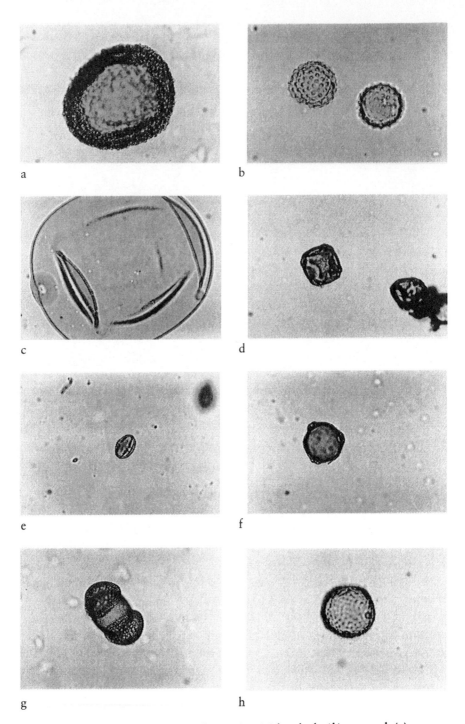

Figure 4.1. Some representative pollen grains: (a) hemlock, (b) ragweed, (c) corn, (d) alder, (e) chestnut, (f) birch, (g) pine, and (h) elm. (Photos by the author)

For example, the proportions of spruce (*Picea*), hemlock, and oak pollen in the surface sediment of a suite of lakes from Maine to New Jersey correspond with the changes in vegetation from spruce-dominated with little or no oak in the north to less spruce but more hemlock in the central region to almost no spruce but much more oak in the south. At a finer scale, the proportions of different taxa in surface samples correspond with their relative proportions in the local vegetation, corrected for factors related to production, dispersal, and site characteristics.[8]

Large fossils like leaves, fruits, and parts of insects usually record only local communities, though more directly and specifically than pollen.[9] For example, species of birch are recognizable from fruits but not from pollen. The discovery of such fossils in a deposit usually confirms that the plant was growing on the site.[10] Because of large differences in seed production by different species, however, the results are seriously biased toward those that yield more and better-preserved seeds,[11] and the record is generally restricted to plants that grew very close to the basin.

Most pollen, seeds and leaves, and insect parts are allochthonous materials, those brought to the site by wind, water, or people. Along with these remains of living organisms are inorganic materials, among them clay and silt, that imply erosion in a watershed.[12] In addition, increased mineral input from erosion changes the productivity of a lake and the chemistry of the sediments, which provide clues to human activities where these caused the erosion. Sedimentary data thus shed light on the impacts of human activities on the physical as well as the biological environment.

Autochthonous materials in lake sediments, those produced within the lake rather than transported to it from elsewhere, consist largely of the remains of algae, especially diatoms (algae which produce microscopic shells with distinctive ornamentation) (fig. 4.2), and other plankton, precipitates from the water column, and compounds made by processes within the sediments.[13] Study of these remains in sediments reveals details of changes in water quality. For example, since the time of European colonization in the upper Chesapeake Bay, diatom populations have shifted from species that are primarily benthic (living on the bottom) to those that are primarily planktonic (living in the water column). This shift, along with other indicators of changed sedimentary input, implies increased turbidity and sediment accumulation.[14]

In other studies, comparison of suites of diatom species from lakes with known pH with those found in sediments allows reconstruction of pH of lake water in the past.[15] In all phases of sedimentary analysis, many lines of

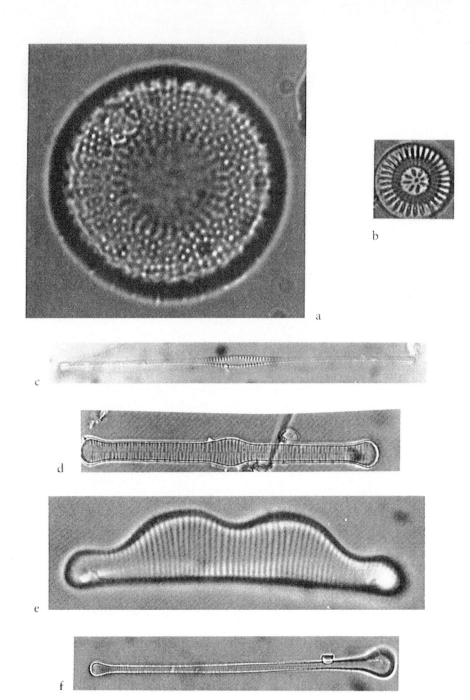

Figure 4.2. Some diatoms associated with cultural eutrophication and acidification: (*a*) *Stephanodiscus hantschii*, (*b*) *Cyclotella stelligera*, (*c*) *Fragilaria crotonensis*, (*d*) *Tabellaria quadriseptata*, (*e*) *Eunotia bidentula*, and (*f*) *Asterionella formosa*. (Photos courtesy of Ronald B. Davis and Dennis Anderson)

evidence coupled with good ecology are needed to reconstruct the historical conditions that produced the assemblages.

Even autochthonous sediments do not directly reflect conditions in the water column, however. Fish and other animals may differentially eat some species, some communities such as littoral ones may be underrepresented, and changing lake conditions may accelerate or slow the dissolution of remains before they can be incorporated into sediment.[16]

More esoteric sources of fossils also offer evidence of changing landscapes: for example, pack rat middens in which the collections of the rats are fossilized in urine. Coprolites are fossilized feces that contain plant remains which not only reveal the diets of the animals that produced them but also represent a sample of the surrounding vegetation.

## Collecting and Processing the Sediment

Sediment is usually sampled by extracting a vertical core from it or by taking a vertical suite of samples from the wall of a soil pit. It is assumed that deeper sediments in the core or pit are older, which is true in most lake sediments and peats. Using a variety of techniques, one then concentrates or isolates different components from subsamples of the sediment core. Identification and enumeration of plant and animal fossils document changing communities, while physical and chemical analyses of the bulk sediment reflect sedimentary processes. Charcoal analysis gives evidence of local fires.

Precise, accurate dating of sediments is critical for correlating them with documented human activities as well as for comparing data from different sediment cores. Radiometric methods supply numerical estimates of the ages of samples. The most commonly used for Quaternary sediments are carbon 14, which provides ages of organic materials up to about 45,000 years ago, and lead 210, which is useful for sediments less than 150 years old. The precision and accuracy of radiometric dates rely on the investigator's understanding of the principles of production and incorporation of the radioisotopes into the sediment, calibration with other dating techniques, and other factors.[17]

Nonradiometric techniques are especially useful for dating cultural horizons in sediment cores because the relation between carbon 14 and tree ring dates for about the past 500 years are nonlinear.[18] The sediment of some lakes has annual deposits called varves, which can be counted to obtain precise, accurate ages. Evidence of human activities may itself constitute a precise and accurate dating horizon, for example, the appearance of pollen of plants native to Europe and the increase in species of open fields near the surface of eastern North American sediments.[19] This increase corresponds with land clearance by European colonists, which can be absolutely dated through historical documents.

Once several dates have been obtained for a core, dates for intervening samples are interpolated. Vertical mixing of sediment, both within the lake and in the processing of the sediment, homogenizes the record for a number of years, so that questions asked and sampling intervals must allow for this running average. Dates from widely spaced intervals often do not allow close correlation with actual years because sediment accumulation per year may have varied within the intervals.

## Analyzing the Data

The results of a sedimentary analysis are usually presented in a two-dimensional graph in which the y-axis is inverted, with zero (the surface) at the top and increasing depth in the sediment down the axis. Lower is older. Distance along the x-axis represents the contributions of the different taxa or other components of the sediment, such as charcoal or minerals. Changes in the proportions of pollen of different taxa over depth in the sediment imply changes in the amounts of the different taxa near a lake over time (fig. 4.3).

The numbers in the data set may be expressed in various ways to emphasize different features of the data. The most often used calculation for pollen is percent of pollen grains counted, which corresponds well with spatial patterns of species distributions and allows data to be compared over large regions. Pollen influx, a measure of the amount of pollen that settles on the sediment per unit time, is an estimate of pollen production, allowing differentiation between sparsely vegetated landscapes, like tundra, and forest.[20] Influx varies, however, from lake to lake and even within a single lake and thus is not as generally useful for regional comparisons.[21] For diatoms, percentage data are comparable for lakes with similar chemical composition and can be used for comparing lake chemistry.

A variety of statistical analyses enable one to recognize patterns in the data.[22] Principal components analysis extracts patterns of covariance, which can reveal the important trends in a data set, especially when compared with data on current ecosystems. For example, through principal components analysis it could be seen that the patterns in the overall pollen assemblage in surface samples of sediment from a large number of lakes tracked those found in the vegetation in Michigan.[23] The statistical analysis confirmed that

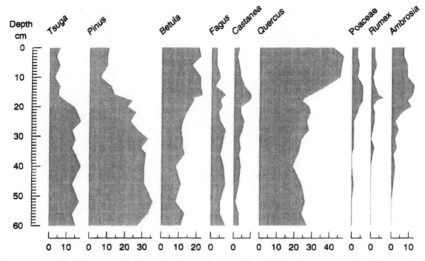

Figure 4.3. Pollen percentage diagram from Giles Lake, Pennsylvania. (Plotted using Psimpoll, courtesy of Keith Bennett)

the pollen reflects the overall vegetational trends and thus serves as a good proxy for reconstructing vegetational patterns at this scale. Maps of the values from principal components analysis emphasize the magnitude and directions of changes in overall vegetation caused by recent human impact (fig. 4.4).[24]

In other kinds of studies, pollen data are corrected by factors that relate the percentage of the pollen grains in the sediment to the percentage of trees in the local vegetation.[25] Dissimilarity coefficients calculated to compare fossil and modern pollen samples are potentially an objective way to find analogues of past spectra in current vegetation.[26]

To detect significant changes within the pollen diagram, both agglomerative and divisive classification techniques have been used to reveal sample clusters, which may correspond with changing climate or human activities.[27] Time series analysis is another technique used to detect low frequency cycles indicated by the data.[28]

One can also map pollen data from a number of sites to provide a spatial representation of changes over time. "Isopoll" maps are analogous to topographic contour maps, on which for a given time, say, 5000 B.P., points (sites) with the same percent of a given taxon are connected, producing a contour map of the taxon's abundance at that time (fig. 4.5).[29] Similarly, "isochron"

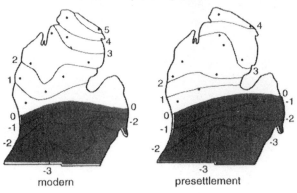

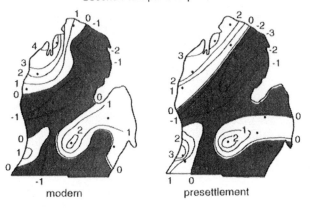

Figure 4.4. Comparison of principal components of modern and presettlement pollen data in lower Michigan. (Modified from Webb, A comparison of modern and presettlement pollen, figs. 9, 10, with permission of Elsevier Science—NL, Sara Burgerhartstraat 25, 1055 KV Amsterdam, The Netherlands)

maps have contours that connect similar dates for certain changes in the pollen diagrams, for example, the first major increase in proportion of a taxon.[30] The proportions of certain taxa at individual sites or dates of arrival can also be indicated by symbols of different sizes or colors to emphasize the patterns of change.[31]

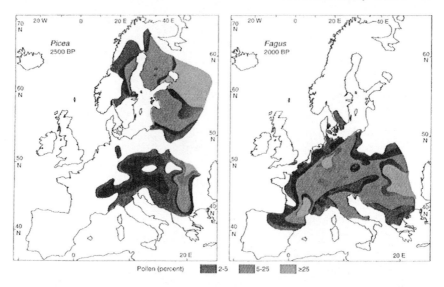

Figure 4.5. Isopoll maps of *Picea* and *Fagus* in western Europe at 2500 and 2000 B.P., respectively. Note spread of *Picea* from north, while *Fagus* has more concentrated populations toward the south and west. (Modified from Huntley and Birks, *Atlas*, fig. 5.108, 5.180. Reprinted with permission of Cambridge University Press)

## Interpreting Human Impact

Early in the twentieth century, Scandinavian researchers observed that the pollen of tree taxa changed over the length of sediment cores, from trees characteristic of cold climates, such as spruces, to indicators of more temperate climate. They used this evidence to infer a progression of postglacial climates. In the 1930s and 1940s F. Firbas and Johs Iversen attributed some changes in the pollen record to human activities. Firbas interpreted the spread of hazel (*Corylus*) in some western European sediments as the result of human activities rather than climate.[32] Iversen related a sequence of changes in tree and herbaceous pollen to a cycle of land clearing and abandonment, a "landnam" episode. Other features of the cycle were a preceding charcoal layer and a decrease in the absolute amount of pollen.[33] In spite of some debate about various other factors that have influenced these changes,[34] pollen evidence has been used in many parts of the world to support the contention that early agricultural human cultures had major effects on vegetation, though the effect became much greater when agriculture became widespread and permanent.

The pollen record of human impact at Giles Lake, a small lake in northeastern Pennsylvania, is a typical record of agricultural clearing in northeastern North America (see fig. 4.3).[35] Major increases in the amounts of ragweed, dock (*Rumex*), and grass pollen above thirty-eight centimeters were accompanied by decreases first in hemlock, then in pine and beech, and increases in birch and oak. The amount of chestnut increased temporarily, then returned to low amounts. For several hundred years before that, there is no evidence of changes in the predominantly hemlock-, oak-, and pine-dominated vegetation.

Were the transformations caused by changed climate, human disturbance, insect infestations, disease, or some combination of these? To answer this question, we must first infer a date for the beginning of the increase in herbs at thirty-eight centimeters. *Ambrosia* is a native genus, and both *Rumex* and grass include many widespread native species. However, not one of them is common in the pollen record of northeastern North America until the very upper levels of the cores, strongly suggesting a relation with European-style agriculture.[36] This relation is supported by lead 210 dating, which can be extrapolated down the core to assign a date of about A.D. 1800 to thirty-eight centimeters, approximately the date of local European colonization as established from historical documents. The occurrence of so much open ground indicated by the high percentages of herbaceous pollen seems an unlikely result of any reasonable climatic change. We know that clearing introduces and encourages weeds such as these, so we accept the explanation that their increase was caused by postrevolutionary clearing for agriculture.

There is less historical documentation for specific changes in forest composition related to human activities. There are records of logging pine, especially white pine, and of cutting hemlock for tanbark. Oak and birch recolonize open areas, and chestnut sprouted vigorously after it was cut, before the chestnut blight decimated it in the early twentieth century. Beech, hemlock, and white pine are especially susceptible to damage by fire, which generally seems to have increased after European settlement of the area. All lines of evidence thus converge on the conclusion that human activities caused the loss of hemlock, beech, and pine and the large increases in the amounts of birch and oak in this vicinity. Climate and other physical factors do not adequately explain these changes, although it is possible that the cool climate of the so-called Little Ice Age from about 1450 to 1850 contributed to the patterns of change.[37]

Human impact can also be studied through pollen taken directly from archeological sites. This requires different assumptions about sedimentation

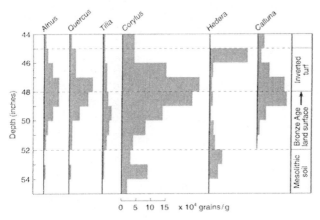

Figure 4.6. Pollen concentration diagram from a
Bronze Age barrow, Sussex, England. (Modified
from Dimbleby, *The Palynology of Archaeological Sites,* fig. 24)

processes, however.[38] A typical habitation site includes old pits, fill, refuse
deposits, and other reworked materials. Buried soils are often of great interest on such sites. Not only are the fossils reworked and possibly neither con-
temporaneous with the site nor local, but the matrix frequently is poor for
preservation and so contains only a very low concentration of somewhat
degraded specimens. Thus problems of contamination and differential destruction loom large in analysis of these sites. A pollen profile through a Bronze
Age barrow illustrates the complexities involved (fig. 4.6). This diagram from
soil expresses the pollen as grains/gram of soil because there is not a regular
accumulation of pollen incorporated in sediment over the years, but rather
a series of temporarily stable soils. The oldest "Mesolithic Soil" is generally
low in pollen but has relatively large amounts of ivy (*Hedera*) pollen near
the top. The soil was perhaps fairly well mixed, possibly by earthworms, but
not enough to move such a large amount of ivy pollen downward. Ivy was
used as fodder for domesticated livestock in early agricultural cultures and
perhaps was brought to this site even in the preagricultural Mesolithic period
to attract red deer.[39] Whatever the reason for the importing of ivy, this much
ivy pollen is unlikely to occur under undisturbed conditions, so people probably brought it to the site. The Bronze Age soil overlying this is well stratified. The large amount of heather (*Calluna*) pollen suggests moist, acid
conditions, not conducive to earthworm activity, and the large amount of
hazel (*Corylus*) hints at open vegetation. The "inverted turf" at the top is in

many ways the mirror image of the soil beneath it, so came from turf cut into the Mesolithic soil and inverted on the Bronze Age soil surface. Each layer suggests some impact of people in the area.

These few examples illustrate the wide variety of sedimentary sources that give clues to past human influences on ecosystems. The interpretation of any of these kinds of evidence depends on knowing the ecology of the organisms and their interactions and dynamics at local, ecosystem, and landscape scales. If beech and maple forests undergo reciprocal replacement, for example, noting a shift in importance between them may merely be noting this community dynamic, not some change in human use of one or the other.

Although these methods have their own biases and limitations, empirical studies comparing modern pollen rain to some measure of modern forest vegetation substantiate claims that the methods are robust.[40] The gross similarities of many studies in a region further increase confidence in the methods. Conclusions can be drawn with assurance for a number of theoretical reasons as well. Given a few years' averaging to account for differences in weather as it affects pollen production, it is reasonable to assume that individuals of each species produce pollen at more or less constant rates,—or at least that a forest composed of a certain proportion of each species will produce pollen at a constant rate—and that it will be carried approximately constant distances, given more or less constant climate. Thus an unbiased sample of this production should give an equally unbiased sample of the vegetation that produced it.

Fossils and other components of the stratigraphic record thus allow us to take the records back in time and to consider changes that have not been recorded in the written record or cannot easily be deduced from field studies or from the relatively short existence of long-term field studies. Many changes that have occurred in the past will most likely not be reflected in long-term studies, which cannot duplicate conditions and processes that no longer obtain. For example, studies have identified modern analogues of fossil pollen spectra over the past ten thousand years, but no modern analogues for much earlier samples.[41]

Many taxa are never (or almost never) represented in the fossil record, so inferences about them can be made only with reference to their association with those taxa that are present. Similarly, some taxa cannot be differentiated, for example, the species of oaks. Some places are less well represented than others. A clearing in the forest far from a body of water will in all likelihood not appear in the record. A preponderance of palynological, or pollen, studies has been done in glaciated terrain because the bogs and lakes that best preserve pollen and spores are there. Thus the spatial coverage of the data and detail of the inferences are quite variable. However, as more sites are found, the results generally serve to amplify rather than to radically alter conclusions drawn from earlier studies.

Stratigraphic studies tell a story that no other method can. Debates about the relative importance of migrational strategies, habitat preferences, and climate in determining rates of spread and decline of species have focused on interpreting postglacial plant migrations.[42] Analysis of dense networks of pollen sites has allowed investigators to differentiate the roles of climate and substrate characteristics in controlling distribution of tree species in the central Upper Great Lakes Region of North America.[43] By considering variation on several scales, research has revealed that the factors controlling the patterns over time change as climate has changed. Such analyses indicate the detail that can be gleaned from palynological evidence that is analyzed closely at different scales. In conjunction with other sources of information, these same techniques provide clues in the search for answers to questions about the factors that determine current ecosystems and human impacts on them.

# PART II

# The Diversity of Human Impacts on the Natural World

Human interactions with ecosystems act as disturbances, as actions that disrupt the ecosystem's equilibrium or more or less regular trajectory of change. Nonhuman events like fires, immigration of new species, and wind-, ice-, and snowstorms also constitute disturbances. The first two human interactions that I shall discuss, fire and human-mediated species introductions, mimic natural disturbances. Human use of forest resources resembles uses made by other omnivores and perhaps storm damage, but with increasing technology has expanded well beyond those levels of activities. Agriculture, in which people disturb the soil itself to win produce from it, has brought with it even more intense and diverse impacts on the natural world. Finally, farthest removed from nonhuman disturbances are those brought about by the most distinctively human activities, those associated with political systems, urbanization, wars, and industrialization. None of these categories of activity occurs in isolation from the rest; acting together, they have altered the ecosystems and landscapes that would have existed in the absence of humans.

In these chapters, I shall discuss some major aspects of these activities in order to indicate how people have altered "natural" processes and structures, both directly and indirectly. Examples from a wide variety of systems suggest the diversity of impacts that have contributed to the systems that we study today.

# Fire: Mimicking Nature

Fire-prone ecosystems dominate many parts of the world, including the savannas of Africa, the grasslands of North America, and the shrublands of the Mediterranean. Among fire-prone forests are the oak savannas of Minnesota, pine forests of North America, and gum tree (*Eucalyptus* spp.) forests of Australia (fig. 5.1). To what extent do these ecosystems owe their existence to human-ignited fires? How have past fire regimes, determined by changing culture and technology, affected the current structure and function of these and perhaps other, less obviously fire-dependent ecosystems? Finally, what are the implications of this history for current management of these systems?

The essence of human nature includes manipulating fire. Long before people learned to light fires, they were able to keep embers alive and transport them for starting hearth or cooking fires. Fire must even then have been approached with ambivalence; under control it provided heat, light, and a source of fascination, while uncontrolled it could be an awesome and terrifying threat to life and shelter. This ambivalent attitude pertains also to the effects of wildland fires, whether they appear as beneficial or destructive.

The role of fire in the development of ecosystems is inextricably linked with human activities as well as with climate. The interactions of humans and fire have altered over time, with major consequences for current trajectories of vegetational change. I shall first review briefly the characteristics of

Figure 5.1. Pictures of fire-dominated ecosystems: (*top*) An oak savanna at Agassiz Dunes Nature Preserve (Nature Conservancy), Minnesota. The trees are all bur oak (*Q. macrocarpa*), and the ground cover is a mix of grasses, forbs (broadleaved herbaceous plants), and some small shrubs such as *Artemisia*. This area is burned about every six years and grazed by deer and moose. (Photo by the author, 1983). (*bottom*) Long-leaf pine stand (*P. palustris*), Weymouth Woods, Southern Pines, North Carolina. This is burned every few years. The understory is turkey oak (*Q. laevis*) with a highly diverse array of grasses and forbs. (Photo by the author, 1990)

fire-adapted communities and their antithesis, then turn to some ways in which people have taken advantage of these. Wildland fires, those that burn nonbuilt areas, continue to excite interest in the news media and research; an international bibliography of wildland fire published in 1992 claimed to include thirty-five thousand citations.[1]

## Naturally Ignited Fires and Fire Adaptation

Lightning and volcanos ignite most fires that are not started by people. Both have been present since long before the evolution of land biota, so at least some land organisms and processes evolved in the presence of fire. The likelihood that lightning will start a fire depends, however, on a complex interaction of climate and vegetation, not just on an ignition source. If plant cover is patchy because of the predominant life-forms and low rainfall or soil nutrients, a fire, once started, cannot spread. Climate also influences the frequency and season of lightning strikes. In a humid, cool climate both the frequency of lightning strikes and the susceptibility of vegetation to fire are low, while in a seasonally dry climate a similar frequency of lightning strikes may cause frequent fires. These two interconnected factors, plant cover and lightning storms, establish local natural fire regimes, which vary greatly. In the continental United States alone, the average annual number of lightning fires per million acres of forest varies from fewer than 1 in the mid–Atlantic region and 21–40 in southern Florida to more than 60 in Arizona.[2] Estimates of the percentage of wildland fires ignited by lighting vary from close to 100 percent in some years on the montane savanna of Belize and about 80 percent in Arizona and New Mexico, down to 2 percent in the northeastern United States.[3] Even at this low proportion, the U.S. Department of Agriculture reported 2,726 lightning-caused fires in the northeast between 1961 and 1970, enough potentially to have major effects on ecosystems in the area.

Many species of plants have evolved under these conditions, developing properties that not only protect them from being killed by fire but even help them carry it. The inflammable properties of many species, for example, blueberries (*Vaccinium* spp.) and pine, may perpetuate fire-dependent communities. The leaf litter of gum tree is highly inflammable, carrying fire very effectively. Once species such as these are established it is very difficult for fire-sensitive taxa to invade because of the frequency and intensity of fires they support.[4] Even many of these pyrophytes, however, cannot withstand very frequent fires. Fires that burn the leaves of gum tree, for example, do not affect subsequent leafing out of adult trees, but they kill seedlings.[5] Although fire stimulates sexual reproduction in some species, too frequent fires may eliminate them.[6]

Consider a very hot fire in a prairie. It sweeps across the grassland, apparently destroying all life in its path. Dense smoke carries off charred particles of organic material while the heat volatilizes much of the nitrogen in the vegetation. But soon after the fire is over, animals emerge from holes, patches of unburned prairie, and peripheral habitats where they escaped the inferno. In only a few days, buds at or below the ground surface that were protected from the heat begin to produce new green sprouts. Nutrients that had been tied up in the organic matter have been released and spur growth of the new sprouts. Some tree and shrub seedlings that had no protection from the heat are killed outright, but plants that survived flourish and provide abundant forage for herbivores that return quickly to the regreening grassland.

In a dense pitch pine (*Pinus rigida*) forest, a fire may start on the forest floor and then climb to the canopy by way of lower dead limbs or dense understory, finally reaching the green needles and "crowning out." It will then rush quickly through the treetops as well as over the ground, sometimes leaping over living trees, leaving most trees and shrubs as well as herbaceous vegetation and young pine seedlings apparently killed in a mosaic of burned and unburned patches (fig. 5.2). But the trees are more resilient than they appear at first. Their thick bark protects meristematic tissue (tissue made of cells that can divide to produce new cells), which quickly reorganizes to send out sprouts from the trunks and woody underground stems (fig. 5.3). Blueberries and oak trees also have protected buds that quickly sprout, and the blueberries fruit copiously the year following the fire.

Following a fire in the New Jersey Pine Barrens, an inconspicuous sedge (*Scirpus longii*) which appeared to be almost sterile for many years before the fire produces many flowers and fruits after it. Its newly generated seeds also germinate especially well in the burned seedbed.[7] Large flocks of towhees converge on the newly burned forest, feasting on the pine seeds released from the serotinous cones, which open and release seeds only when they are heated above a certain temperature. The mineral soil provides ideal conditions for seeds to germinate. Fire rejuvenates this fire-adapted community and eliminates invading species like red cedar.

A surface fire in a lodgepole or longleaf pine forest singes the bark without harming the living stem cells, so that the trees survive. Long clusters of needles protect the terminal buds of the young seedlings of longleaf pine (*Pinus palustris*), which allows them to recover quickly after a fire (fig. 5.4). Fire kills susceptible plants and diseases and prepares the seedbed for many native plants by changing the nutrient status as well as removing thick litter.

The complexity and diversity of evolutionary adaptations to fire and the ubiquity of naturally ignited fires lead inexorably to the conclusion that the

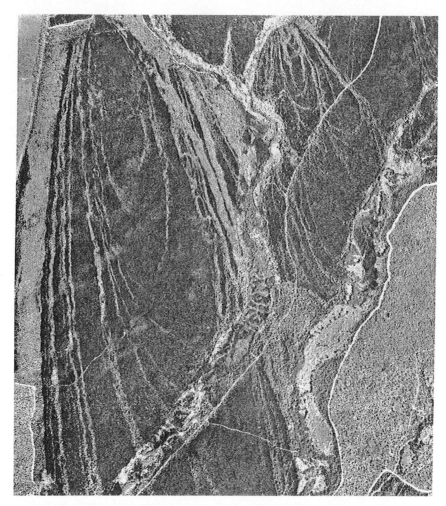

Figure 5.2. Vertical aerial photograph of a portion of the New Jersey Pine Barrens, a few weeks after a major fire. Black is burned, light-colored not burned. Note the elliptical pattern of spread of these fires from the ignition points at the top of the photograph. These crown fires burned through the pitch pine and cedar swamps, being stopped by a larger stream. Note the strips of unburned forest, where the fires "rolled over." (Black and white copy of color-infrared vertical air photo, USDA, photo courtesy of Richard Lathrop)

Figure 5.3. Pitch pine (*Pinus rigida*) in the New Jersey Pine Barrens sprouting from underground lignotubers. (Photo by the author, 1991)

basic patterns of pyrophytic communities and biomes developed in the absence of humans. The stratigraphic evidence in many regions supports this conclusion. Fossil soils and grasses from East Africa indicate "grassy woodland and wooded grassland" about 14 million years ago, well before the evolutionary divergence between apes and hominids 5–10 million years ago.[8] Such plant communities are most likely to have been at least in part maintained by fire or at least resilient in the face of fire. In Australia, pollen analysis suggests that the shift from *Casuarina*-dominated forests to those dominated by gum tree occurred about 130,000 years ago and was associated with a large increase in fires. In all probability a change in climate caused this associated shift in vegetation and fire frequency, not human colonization, which is dated by archeological remains to about 40,000 years ago.[9] (Some, however, use the evidence of changed fire frequencies as evidence ipso facto of human intervention, so would date the arrival of humans in Australia to 90,000 years before there is any archeological evidence of it.)[10] In Madagascar, where evidence of human colonization does not predate about 1500 years B.P., there is ample charcoal in sediments back as far as 36,000 B.P., indicating widespread fires.[11] Even in more densely forested areas such as the spruce-northern hardwoods of northern North America and the deciduous

Figure 5.4. Grass stage of longleaf pine. The
cluster of needles protects the apical meristem of
the seedling. (Photo by the author, 1990)

forests of the southeastern United States, fires are invoked as a disturbance
factor necessary for maintenance of the communities,[12] and since similar
communities, and certainly the species that make them up, presumably
existed before people immigrated to North America they must have been
adapted to naturally ignited fires.

### Prehistoric Human Uses of Fire of Limited Extent

The search for a causal connection between human activities and fire
incidence usually starts with an independent dating of the evidence of a
change in vegetation and fires and of related human settlements. In very
recent sediments, for example, in a sediment core from a lake in northeastern Pennsylvania, there is a major increase in charcoal at the same depth as
an increase in pollen of ragweed and a decrease in hemlock (fig. 5.5). It
appears that the spread of agriculture, occurring here after about 1800 A.D.,
was associated with an increase in fires in the surrounding forests. We may
then hypothesize that people set the fires, either on purpose or by accident,
and that these fires contributed to the decrease in hemlock in the forests. Similar connections between local changes in vegetation, increased fire incidence, and local human settlement have also been made elsewhere, for
example, in Ontario and the northern Great Lakes.[13]

Another fruitful approach to relating human activities to past fire frequencies is to compare past patterns of fires recorded by sedimentary charcoal with patterns of human settlement. For example, the most dense human

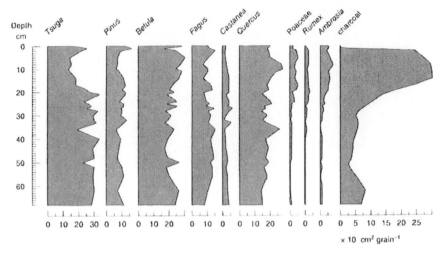

Figure 5.5. Pollen percentage diagram of Lake Lacawac (Nature Conservancy), Pennsylvania. Charcoal was estimated microscopically from the same sediment as the pollen. (Plotted using Psimpoll, courtesy of Keith Bennett)

populations in New England for the past several millennia were in coastal and riverine areas, where concentrations of charcoal in lake sediment are greatest; thus, people may have been responsible for the higher fire frequencies.[14]

Although there is controversy about the earliest use of fire by humans, burnt bones excavated in a cave in Swartkrans, South Africa, are evidence that hominids were using fire before 1.0–1.5 million years B.P.[15] Once humans were building fires, they would have become a new and possibly important source of ignitions.

Fires have many uses, some carefully controlled in size and temperature and others more widespread. The hot temperature of fire melts pitch, hardens pottery, changes wood to charcoal, and smelts metal ores, in addition to making raw foodstuffs more palatable and digestible.[16] The use of fires for such purposes as well as for heat and light has indirect effects on the local vegetation, as wood is gathered to feed the fires. These fires may also unintentionally initiate less controlled wildland fires. There is little evidence that hunter-gatherers carefully extinguish fires.[17] Such fires, then, may have had local impacts, from fuel collection to chance ignitions of larger conflagrations.

Fires purposely set for specific purposes in natural vegetation had even greater potential effects on the landscape at a larger scale. Such fires served many purposes: they cleared land for agriculture, attracted game to the new growth, stimulated fruiting of many species, and favored hunting.[18] For these purposes, fire was taken to the fuel, and it could escape from the bounds that were intended. For example, during dry periods in the late nineteenth century, fires used to clear fields or improve forage for livestock as well as campfires used by hunters caused large wildfires, altering the vegetation in the western United States and Siberia.[19]

Fire was also used to drive game into a stockade or narrow valley or over a steep cliff.[20] On the edges of prairies, fire may have been used to drive game into the oak openings (areas with scattered oak trees and shorter grass), where it was more easily killed.[21] Such fires had major local effects, yet it is also possible that they escaped from control. To attract rather than to chase game, hunter-gatherers burned small prairie and meadow areas very early in spring to provide early forage, for example, for moose and other herbivores in northern Alberta, Canada. Trees killed around the edges of these fires furnished excellent, immediately usable firewood.[22] Fire also served in warfare as a kind of "scorched-earth" tactic, and this kind of fire, too, could escape control.[23]

All of the uses of fire described so far were planned to be of limited extent. They burned large expanses of land only by mistake, when the fire escaped the bounds set for it. Their impact on regional vegetational patterns would have been to shift the vegetation slightly toward more fire-prone systems.

The question of purposeful burning of large areas presents much livelier debates. In North America, for example, it is difficult to reconcile such contrasting statements as "it is at least a fair assumption that no habitual or systematic burning was carried out by the Indians [in North America]" and "the record for Indian burning of all woodlands of the eastern United States is so complete" as not to be worthy of comment.[24] In Australia too there is no consensus on the uses or importance of fire set by aborigines. On the one hand, M. Williams noted that in south Australia "[aboriginal man]'s one effect on the landscape was the burning of the natural vegetation, possibly to drive game to slaughter, and, of course, accidentally," while on the other hand, T. Lewis concluded that purposely set fires, mostly to improve forage for herbivores, had a major impact on the flora and fauna of Australia.[25]

Purposely set fires could have altered the overall patterns and structure of the landscape in major ways. S. Pyne has written that "humans . . . overwhelm, redirect, and regularize [the] fire regime" of a natural savanna.[26] This is arguably true of other kinds of vegetation as well. People intensify natural fire regimes so that their role in modifying vegetation by fire has varied according to the burnability of the local vegetation, the local climate, and the population density and cultural activities and development of the people.

In southern Africa, which has a very long history of human habitation and dry climate, humans apparently have been using fire extensively in such open vegetation types as savannas for more than 150,000 years, so that such human-set fires have been an integral part of the development of the vegetation under changing climate, especially in the past 10,000 years.[27] When B. H. Walker attributed savanna vegetation to the four factors water, nutrients, herbivory, and fire, he noted that although naturally ignited fires were common in southern Africa, humans had been setting fires for at least 50,000 and probably as much as 100,000 years, so that the human role had to be taken into account in interpreting the causes of the savanna vegetation.[28]

The balance between human-set fires and climate as causes of open, non-forested vegetation in other parts of the world is more problematic. A complex of climatically and topographically influenced fire regimes maintain the prairies of North America, but the sources of ignition have included people for many millennia. Forests survived in the nineteenth century along the prairie/forest border where they were protected by firebreaks,[29] but was this protection from natural or human-caused fires? A Jesuit father traveling in the mid–nineteenth century noted that Indians in different parts of the prairies had different attitudes toward fires; those of the east burned the prairies, but farther west they were afraid that fire would scare the game and reduce their own cover.[30] In 1819, a traveler in North America, William Blane, commented on the annual firing of the prairies but did not think that these were the cause of the prairies because he noticed that prairies increased in magnitude to the west, which was not consistent with fire as the primary cause but rather with climatic control.[31] The ecologist Henry Gleason was of the opinion that Indian-set fires were essential to maintaining the prairies because there were not enough naturally caused fires.[32] Geological evidence, however, points to widespread prairie vegetation (indicated by fossil grassland soils) in the Tertiary period, long before humans evolved.

Similar debates concern smaller patches of prairie like the barrens of Kentucky.[33] As early as 1802, A. F. Michaux thought that fire was responsible for the unusual vegetation there, attributing the fires to aborigines and later white settlers, who burned to attract game and for cattle pasture. B. B. McInteer, however, thought that fire, dry soil, and climatic conditions interacted to cause the Kentucky prairies, that is, that they would not have existed there through fire alone. Or, inversely, one could not create such "prairies" just anywhere in deciduous forest by burning it. Humans may not be the primary cause of open grassland vegetation, but they may well serve to expand its extent by increasing the incidence of fires.

The impact of human-set fires on deciduous forests is even more elusive because most deciduous forests are not obviously fire-dependent and the documentary evidence for widespread fires is inconclusive.[34] Those of northeastern North America, for example, contain such fire-sensitive species as

American beech and eastern hemlock along with the more fire-resistant oaks and varying amounts of pines. Oaks and pines probably dominated vegetation in many areas in earlier, interglacial periods, before humans occupied the continent, so their existence is not tied to human-set fires.[35] Fire-sensitive species like beech and hemlock were much more common in the pollen record before the arrival of European colonists than they were after, and the input of charcoal to sediments increased greatly in most areas with the arrival of the Europeans.[36] In other words, the incidence of fires in the forests most likely increased after European colonization, so that whatever the use of fire had been by the native Americans, it was less severe than that of the colonists. Finally, too frequent fires would result in forests dominated by pine or would even eliminate forest vegetation completely, while the pollen and documentary evidence is of mesic (that is, requiring moderate moisture) deciduous forests for most of the Holocene through most of the region.

At several sites in the Netherlands and northern Germany, sedimentary charcoal layers and human artifacts accompany the replacement of pine and birch by herbaceous species about 12,000 B.P., implying the possible role of humans setting fire to the forests and at least locally eliminating the pine and birch.[37] Some recent interpretations of these vegetational changes attribute them, however, solely to climatic deterioration, including increased drought.[38] A pollen study in southern Germany found an abrupt decrease in beech pollen at the same time as an increase in hazel, dated at about 5500 B.P. A concomitant increase in the input of charcoal to the sediment has suggested that people caused the change by setting fires, although there is little pollen of cultivated plants or weeds in the sediment.[39]

These studies indicate that it is very difficult to factor out the relative roles of natural and human ignitions in vegetation. Even in such diverse vegetation as the highlands of Costa Rica and the Amazonian rain forest, it is problematical to distinguish human set from naturally ignited prehistoric fires.[40] Changes in climate that affect vegetation may cause an increase in fires, but the possibility of a human factor must be included in any attempt to explain the change in vegetation.

The role of human-ignited fires is thus set against a complex of evolutionary adaptations, climate, plant migrations, and human population and culture. Plant and probably also animal species evolved adaptations to fire before the evolution of humans, or even hominids. These plants and animals conceivably formed communities that were maintained by fire as controlled by climate, topography, and fuel production before humans entered the story. Once humans began to use fire, however, their fires interacted with these factors to modify the vegetation.[41] This role of human-set fires has since varied with time, as both cultures and climates have changed. We cannot clearly detach humans from the environment, that is, decide what "natural" fire regime might maintain a vegetation type in the state that existed before human impact on it, because the farther back we go in historical reconstructions the more difficult it becomes to separate humans from other causes of ignitions. It is unlikely that humans at the hunter-gatherer stage modified vegetation from fire-resistant to fire-prone without a concomitant change to a climate more favorable to pyrophytic vegetation. On the other hand, humans must have hastened and expanded changes that were stimulated by climatic change.[42]

### Intensifying Human Impact

The development of agriculture and later of industrialization greatly increased the potential of humans to alter ecosystems. Although the extensive use of fire for "slash-and-burn" agriculture in the tropics is often discussed, fire has been a common tool of farmers in temperate and boreal zones as well. In Finland, charcoal content of finely laminated sediments indicates a fire-return interval of 95 years between A.D. 470 and 1100. After A.D. 1100, pollen indicators of agriculture like hemp (*Cannabis*) and cereals became common as the amount of charcoal in the sediment increased. Between A.D. 1600 and 1900, when the fire-return interval had decreased to 30 years and agriculture was well established, pollen of juniper replaced that of birch, pine, and probably spruce. Apparently the spread of fires and probably of grazing as well altered even the forests that were not converted to agricultural fields.[43] The Finns had long been known for their practice of burning forest to clear land, a practice they carried with them into Sweden, to the dismay of the Swedes, and into North America.[44]

Others carried on the practice of using fire in agricultural fields and often in surrounding forests as well, though with an attempt to keep the fires under control. In the village of Newark in the North American colony of New Jersey, for example, a seventeenth-century ordinance required that six citizens be chosen "to appoint a fit season to burn the woods, and it is agreed, that every male from Sixty years to sixteen, should go out one Day to burn Woods. . . . Item., if any man shall set fire on the meadow before the tenth of March . . . he shall be fined Ten shillings."[45] Laws to control fires attested to a persistent problem of escaped fires that lasted well into the twentieth century throughout North America.[46] In addition to large, even-aged stands of such species as lodgepole pine in western North America and pitch pine in the East that attest to past fires, there are complex patterns such as those caused by irregular burning (see fig. 5.2) that most likely persist for centuries.

Much of the land that was not suitable for agriculture was cut over repeatedly in the eighteenth and nineteenth centuries in North America to make charcoal to fuel furnaces for the smelting of iron, which was needed in the manufacture of tools critical in agriculture and industry and weapons. The making of charcoal to fuel furnaces required setting fire to mounds of wood in the midst of the forest. Slash left in the cut over forest was excellent fuel for a fire and during the charcoal-making process escaped sparks sometimes set it on fire. Itinerant graziers, too, burned the cutover land to improve pastures. In addition, by the late nineteenth century, railroads penetrated many remote forested areas, bringing locomotives spewing ashes and sparks that ignited numerous fires.[47] Even stills, used illegally to distill alcoholic beverages, were a source of ignition in some forests of the eastern United States.[48] Logging in the nineteenth and twentieth centuries left slash that often burned after a human-set fire.

Even with an increase in ignitions in some parts of the landscape, however, the changed landscape configuration most likely led to fewer fires in isolated woodlots. For example, an old white oak in an isolated twenty-four-hectare woodlot in New Jersey had five scars from fires that burned during the first seventy-five years of its life, before agricultural clearing in its vicinity, but only one from the succeeding two and a half centuries.[49] As fire frequency increased in extensive tracts of forest, it probably decreased in remnant forest patches. By the early twentieth century in New Jersey, foresters noted that "it is often due to fire that the hardier and less valuable oaks take the place of [white] pine, also that black oak takes the place of the more valuable white oak and hickory" in extensive forested areas.[50] At the same time, white oaks persisted in woodlots, enhancing the differences between the two kinds of forest. Landscape patterns as well as specific kinds of past uses thus exert unique influences on plant and animal community composition.

## Changing Attitudes Toward Wildfire in Postcolonial North America

The culturally induced changes in fire regime that were superimposed on those driven by climate and evolution have led to the conditions that exist today. Ecologists studying the role of fire in vegetation in the late twentieth century face a very different fire environment than did those who commented

on it earlier in the century. Increased population density has increased ignitions, both accidental and intentional, in many parts of the world, but better fire-fighting ability has at the same time limited the sizes of fires in many
areas. These recent changes affect both the questions that ecologists ask
about the role of fire in ecosystems and their attitudes toward fire, whether
fire is seen as friend or foe. The role of fire in increasing the productivity of
such resources as wood and pasture is distinct from its role in maintaining
or reconstructing hypothetical "natural" ecosystems to preserve biodiversity.

The rapidity of change in North America from hunting, gathering, and dispersed agriculture to widespread agriculture to industrial nation makes it an
ideal place to consider the importance of changing practices and perceptions
to understanding the ecological role of fire. When European colonists first
arrived in North America, they came generally from countries in which,
because of a scarcity of wood, wildfires were not tolerated. Fire may have
been an accepted tool for clearing, but uncontrolled fire in forests at large
was anathema. Fires in the forests of eastern North America, possibly ignited
by aborigines, presented them with awesome spectacles of destruction.
Colonists did not generally condemn Indians for setting fires in the forests,
however. Some of them attributed the open understory of many woodlands
to Indian-set fires, although they did not discuss how such fires might have
changed the species composition of these forests or even threatened their
continued existence if the fires were continued for many years.[51]

By the end of the nineteenth century, however, the propensity of the Indians to burn the forests and the destruction wrought by such a practice were
widely censured. For example, in Kentucky, the geologist Nathaniel Shaler
thought that "when the whites came to this country this savage custom
[annual firing of the forest undergrowth as well as grasslands] had deforested
an area of at least five thousand square miles. In another two hundred years
the Indians would probably have reduced the larger part of the surface of
Kentucky to the condition of prairies."[52] In an article entitled "The Use and
Abuse of Forests by the Virginia Indians," Hu Maxwell of the United States
Forest Service stated that "at the time of the first explorations the Indians
had succeeded in deforesting thirty or forty acres for every individual in their
tribes, and were proceeding with the work of destruction from the sea to the
mountains and beyond"[53]. Although these interpretations do not explain
why the forest destruction had not proceeded farther by the time of European colonization, they do favor a perception that the Indians' impact on the
extent of the forest was enormous. To explain why they saw the effect as so
great, one must look to the forest environment and attitudes at the end of
the nineteenth century.

By 1900, cutting for lumber, charcoal, and other products had led to badly damaged forest stands, which recovered only slowly from the successive logging and burning. Those concerned with natural resource protection saw the terrible damage wrought by the fires and condemned them.[54] A "Memorial of the American Association for the Advancement of Science [AAAS], in relation to the need of attention to our future forest supplies," adopted by the AAAS at its meeting in 1880, encouraged state legislatures to protect the forests by, among other things, "laws tending to prevent Forest-fires, by imposing penalties against the willful or careless setting of such fires" and by attempting to control them. "The waste from this cause, in some years, greatly exceeds the amount of timber used, and there is no question connected with forest supplies that demands more serious attention."[55] The Department of Agriculture carried out a mail survey of the incidence of fires nationally in 1880. A vanishingly small number had been ignited by lightning and a very few by native Americans (table 5.1).[56] Of the vast majority ignited by "white man," almost a third were intentionally set, and even most of those that were accidental resulted from intentionally set fires that escaped from their intended limits, such as an agricultural field or campfire.

In 1900, Gifford Pinchot described the damage that wildfires did to the forest of New Jersey, including the destruction of standing timber, young trees, and the humus of the forest floor. He observed that "there is no doubt that forest fires encourage a spirit of lawlessness and a disregard of property rights."[57] While noting that light fires in pine forests were not particularly damaging, he did not advocate their use. Fire was bad. In the face of this attitude toward the deleterious effects of fires, and even their moral perils, some people easily extrapolated the conditions they saw in the early twentieth century to the prehistoric forests and Indian-ignited fires. If contemporary fires were bad, then fires set by Indians must also have been bad.

In the early twentieth century, fire also seemed to be a factor that interrupted the natural directional changes unfolding in forest or other vegetation. The only role of fire in succession was to set the process back.[58] Ecologists sought general principles to explain patterns of vegetation, based on natural, or nonhuman, factors. Fires were clearly caused mainly by humans, so they were unnatural and not part of nature's grand scheme.

Attitudes toward fire began to change in the mid–twentieth century. Fire control had been greatly enhanced. For example, in the 550,000-hectare New Jersey Pine Barrens, about 22,000 hectares burned annually from 1906 to 1939, while only 8,000 hectares burned annually in the succeeding four decades.[59] In the United States national forests, 5 million acres burned in 1910 and 2½ million in 1919, but fewer than 300,000 acres per year between

*Table 5.1. Fires in the United States in 1880 as reported to the United States Department of Agriculture.*

| Cause | Number | % of total |
|---|---|---|
| Natural causes—lightning | 3 | 0.6 |
| Indians (hostility) | 21 | 4.5 |
| White man | 443 | 94.9 |
| Of those 443: | | |
| Intentional | | |
|   Improvements of pasture | 85 | 19 |
|   Incendiary | 37 | 8 |
|   "Tramps" (carelessness?) | 6 | 1 |
|   Escaped backfires | 3 | 1 |
|   Clearing ground for finding chestnuts | 5 | 1 |
|   Clearing ground for finding mica | 1 | + |
|   Subtotal | 137 | 31 |
| Accidental | | |
|   Fires escaped from clearing | 93 | 21 |
|   Hunting (usually neglect of campfires) | 75 | 17 |
|   Carelessness by travelers, etc. | 69 | 16 |
|   Locomotive sparks | 55 | 12 |
|   Charcoal burning | 11 | 2 |
|   Steam mills | 2 | + |
|   Burning oil well | 1 | + |
|   Subtotal | 306 | 69 |
| Total | 443 | |

*Source:* Hough, *Report upon Forestry*, 206–07.

1935 and 1949. The sizes of fires had decreased over this period as well, from an average of more than 100 acres/fire before 1930 down to 40 acres from 1931 to 1940 and 31 acres in the decade after 1940.[60] At the same time, many forests that had been heavily logged and burned in the second half of the nineteenth century were recovering.

Although the U.S. Department of Agriculture Yearbook of Agriculture, "Trees," published in 1949, still regarded fire primarily as a threat to forests, it admitted that some kinds of fires could be beneficial to some forests. One chapter detailed the use of controlled burns to improve southern longleaf pine timber, especially for preparing the seedbed and controlling brown spot disease in young trees.[61] On the other hand, wildfires were thought of as detrimental: "Wildfires are bad, a scourge to man and beast."[62] Ecologists and foresters alike viewed fire as a retrogressive force, one that set natural plant succession toward climax vegetation back to an earlier stage. Any fire would fulfill this retrograde role, but fires caused by people were especially deleterious. The use of fire in pine stands served to keep them in an arrested stage of succession, in which maximum productivity of timber and game was achieved without considering other ecological characteristics of the stand.

After the middle of the twentieth century, as ecologists recognized the complexity of successional pathways and the ubiquity of disturbances, they began to evaluate the possible roles of fires in nonpine forests. The issue of changed fire frequencies since aboriginal times became central. It was taken as fact that aboriginal fires had been widely prevalent and frequent (anywhere from annual to decennial). Current fire suppression resulted in much lower frequency of fires at a site. Perhaps this change was responsible for apparent shifts in vegetation and for the dearth of oak reproduction in many areas that had been described as oak-dominated when European colonists first arrived.[63] Two kinds of studies were initiated to test this hypothesis. One compared accidentally burned stands with unburned ones on otherwise fairly similar sites. The other experimentally burned sites on a regular schedule.

A typical early study of the effect of wildfire on forest vegetation compared tree species present on burned and unburned stands on similar soils in Rhode Island.[64] Although white, scarlet, and black oaks (*Quercus alba, Q. coccinea,* and *Q. velutina*) dominated both burned and unburned stands in terms of number and sizes of trees, red maples (*Acer rubrum*), red oaks (*Q. rubra*), and eastern hemlocks were relatively more dense and larger in the unburned stands. Differences were greater in the smaller size classes, with many more red maples, white pines (*P. strobus*), eastern hemlocks, hickories (*Carya* spp.), American beeches, and black birches, all fire-sensitive taxa, in the unburned stands. There were few woody plants less than one foot high in any stands, although the unburned sites had more small white oaks and red maples than did the burned sites. Statistical analyses rejected the hypothesis that the proportion of oaks was the same in burned as in unburned plots. The main conclusion of this study was that "the prevalence of oak both in burned [and] unburned stands is apparently the result of a long history of disturbance and burning." In other words, the long-term history of the stands, not just the current conditions, played a major role in determining their current composition.

The pasts of the burned and unburned plots were different, however. Only one of the twenty-one burned plots had regenerated on an abandoned agricultural field, whereas six of the nine unburned plots had a history of previous plowing. Even the unburned plots on virgin, or unplowed, soil were only

50, 60, and 108 years old, so none represented forest stands as they existed before Europeans colonized the area. This makes it difficult to extrapolate to the possible roles of Indian-set or even naturally ignited fires in the precolonial forests. The results pertain more to methods that could be used to perpetuate oak-dominated forests in previously disturbed sites.

Fire can be isolated as a factor in experimentally burned plots to test directly the effects of fires in similar sites. Prescribed burns on paired test plots show directly the effects of such fires on cover, species composition, mortality, biogeochemical cycles, and microclimate, data that are useful for managing these kinds of forests.[65] It is not clear, however, just how experimental fires relate to historic fires, which probably burned at different seasons and intensities and in forests of varying ages.

Such studies have confirmed many predictions of the different susceptibility of species to fire damage, and they have modified others. Many fire-sensitive species can withstand light fires when they are more than four inches or so in diameter at breast height.[66] Not only frequency but amount of area burned, timing, and other factors change the effect of fires on the landscape pattern as well as on species composition.[67] A landscape may include a mosaic of communities that were very recently burned and that were burned at various times in the past. At different stages of development communities have different susceptibility to fire. Periods of frequent, less intense fires that burned patches of small size may have alternated with periods of less frequent, but more intense fires that have left homogeneous patches of similarly aged stands (fig. 5.6).[68] Human fire suppression may have created conditions for more intense fires than might ordinarily occur, while frequent, light, prescribed fires would produce a much larger homogeneous area of lightly burned sites than would exist under natural conditions.

## Relationship of Human History to Current Fire Management

Fire influences ecosystems both by its presence and by its absence. Communities adapted to fire may disappear if fire is suppressed, while those that are not so adapted may disappear if fire is introduced. Humans have both introduced and suppressed fires and thus altered natural fire regimes. They have also altered fire regimes by changing the fuel supply, for example, by logging and leaving slash or by suppressing fires. The ecosystems resulting from these changes influence both perceptions of appropriate goals and the potential for fire management. For timber production, for example, the goal is usually to maximize one or a very few economically valuable species. Managers may prefer to ignore history, clear and plant the site, and then use fire

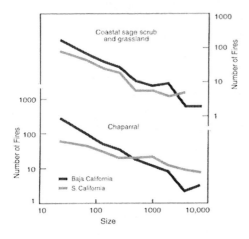

Figure 5.6. Number of fires compared with their sizes in two kinds of fire-dependent vegetation in California. (Modified with permission from Minnich, Fire mosaics, fig. 3. Copyright 1983 by the American Association for the Advancement of Science)

at appropriate intervals, timing, and intensities to favor maximum yield. This is a system almost as thoroughly dominated by people as an agricultural field.

At the other extreme is the goal of maintaining or creating conditions as they would exist without people, a "natural" landscape. This is, for example, frequently a goal of national parks in the United States.[69] This is not as easy as it might appear, however. We cannot just remove people and expect that their past influences will disappear. Past fire suppression may increase the likelihood of very intense fires that would lead to soil erosion on steep slopes. Past high fire frequencies or other disturbances may have eliminated fire-sensitive species and replaced them with those that perpetuate fire-dominated ecosystems. For example, in Hawai'i, the elimination of many native shrub and herbaceous species by grazing and their replacement with grasses have produced large areas of fire-prone vegetation that prevents native species from regenerating.[70] In North America, the question may be whether fires set by native Americans should be viewed as part of the "natural" ecosystem, to be replicated, or as an intrusive, human disturbance, to be avoided.

Any balance between fire suppression and prescribed fires is predicated on some subjectively determined desired outcome. Because we do not really know what the vegetation of any area was before human influence on the fire regime, it is not possible to set this fantasy as a well-defined goal. Another common goal is to maintain a system as it is or was sometime in the recent past. Preserving habitats for rare or special species is another goal for much conservation land. To achieve any of these goals by fire management, one must analyze the patterns and importance of past fires, whether naturally ignited or set or suppressed by humans, in the context of processes that maintain whole ecosystems.[71]

Perhaps fire management is coming full circle. Prehistoric people used fire for well-circumscribed purposes: game drives, keeping certain grazing areas open, clearing agricultural fields. At least some of these activities, such as clearing fields, continued into historic times. These people all lived close to the land, depending on its sustained bounty for their livelihood. During the nineteenth century in North America, however, exploiting such natural resources as timber was detached from sustainable use. After harvesting a forest, timber companies moved to new sources.[72] Itinerant graziers moved in and set fires with little regard for the future of the stand. Locomotives emitted sparks that set massive fires. Fires set to clear fields escaped into the forests. Fires were casually ignited with no plan, thereby making fire a scourge because it was no longer consciously used as a management tool. Reaction against these highly destructive fires led to the perception that all fires were bad, prompting suppression policies, epitomized by the highly visible Forest Service's Smoky the Bear campaign. It then became increasingly apparent that eliminating fire in many systems led to changes that were perceived as bad: a decrease in grouse populations in pine savannas, establishment of heavy fuel loads leading to highly destructive fires, crowding of saplings in conifer forests, in general a change in the vegetation in directions that were often not those desired by the owners of the property. So fires were reintroduced as management tools. Preindustrial peoples had observed the effects of naturally ignited fires and then, necessarily by a long period of trial and error, established methods of fire management that fit their needs. The methods used undoubtedly did not always work the way they were intended. Similarly, we are only in the early stages of discovering what fire regimes meet our often conflicting goals. Preindustrial peoples at least started with a fairly clean slate; we must begin after centuries of human-moderated changes, so historically modified landscapes dictate both our goals and our techniques.

# 6

## Extending Species Ranges

Over the millennia, people have wittingly and unwittingly transported many species from one region of the world to another, just as they have ignited fires. Neither role requires a high degree of cultural specialization. Most of the transported species have not survived for long in their new habitats, at least not without human attention, but some have found congenial homes where they have flourished. For example, about 10 percent of the higher plant species in Poland and California were introduced by people, as were close to 50 percent or more in the island realms of New Zealand and Hawai'i (table 6.1). Note that we usually consider a species to be non-native if it was introduced to a new area by human agency, although many human introductions, such as the rabbit in England, are so well entrenched that they have become integral parts of their new environments, rendering the distinction between native and non-native almost moot.

The migration of species into new habitats has been a characteristic of dispersal and evolution for as long as organisms have existed; it is not just a function of human activities. Changing climates and land bridges have provided the major stimuli for species to migrate in the past, often leading to the evolution of new species in new habitats. That species' ranges are dynamic was a central tenet in Darwin's exposition of the theory of evolution, although he admitted that he did not understand many details of migration.

*Table 6.1. Proportions of non-native species in a variety of floras.*

| Region | % non-native species |
|---|---|
| Poland* | 10 |
| California** | 11 |
| Western Germany* | 16 |
| British Isles* | 18 |
| Finland* | 18 |
| New Zealand† | 48 |
| Hawaii‡ | 65 |

*J. Kornas, Man's impact upon the flora and vegetation of Central Europe. In *Man's Impact on Vegetation,* W. Holzner, M. J. A. Werger and I. Ikusima, eds. (Dr W. Junk Publishers, The Hague, 1983), 277–86.
**H. A. Mooney, S. P. Hamburg, and J. A. Drake, The invasion of plants and animals into California. In Mooney and Drake, *Ecology of Biological Invasions,* 250–72.
†Mark and McSweeney, Patterns of impoverishment.
‡M. P. Moulton and S. L. Pimm, Species introductions to Hawai'i. In Mooney and Drake, *Ecology of Biological Invasions,* 231–49.

"I do not pretend to indicate," he wrote, "the exact lines and means of migration, or the reason why certain species and not others have migrated; why certain species have been modified and have given rise to new groups of forms, and others have remained unaltered. We cannot hope to explain such facts, until we can say why one species and not another becomes naturalized by man's agency in a foreign land; why one ranges twice or thrice as far, and is twice or thrice as common, as another species within their own homes."[1]

As Darwin emphasized, humans have played a unique role in the dissemination of species. They not only carry other species around by chance, caught in their hair or carried in their bodies as seeds or pathogens, like other animals, but also have purposely distributed species that they particularly value, for example, domesticated animals and crop plants. Their use of non-somatic energy has also allowed humans to far exceed their native potential for distance and speed of dispersal, rendering them the most effective dispersal agents on earth. By bringing new species to distant places, humans have effected great changes in native floras and faunas throughout the world much more quickly and in greater numbers than migration would have in their absence. In addition, of course, the human species itself is probably the most successful migrant of all, having colonized all habitable parts of the world and even some that are not really quite habitable, such as Antarctica.

Interest in the general problems caused by species introductions by people was sparked by publication in 1958 of Charles Elton's "The Ecology of Invasions by Animals and Plants," which compiled and analyzed an impressive array of species that people had introduced into new environments.[2] Ecologists adopted the term *invasion* to describe these introductions in such books as *Ecology of Biological Invasions,*[3] *Biological Invasions,*[4] and *Ecology of Biological Invasions of North America and Hawai'i.*[5] It appears that whereas people immigrate or colonize new territory, the species they bring with them invade it. Webster's unabridged dictionary defines *invade* as "to enter, as an army, with hostile intentions; to enter, as an enemy, with a view to conquest or plunder; to attack."[6] The term implies an attitude of conquest or hostility, which is applicable more to people than to plants, microbes, and other animals. It has gained popularity, however, probably because it implies damage by the newly arrived species and implicates people. Until recently, studies of such "invasions" have focused on damage to economically valuable crops and structures, defined in monetary terms, but many current ecological studies emphasize modifications of communities composed of native species. By displacing and preying on native species, causing diseases, and other means, these immigrants may rapidly alter the species composition of native communities.

History has played a crucial role in the study of these species' invasions; as Elton noted, "If we are to understand what is likely to happen to ecological balance in the world, we need to examine the past as well as the future."[7] Invasion is a time-transgressive process, so we need a temporal perspective to understand it. The past offers not only examples of past introductions, successful and failed, but also a backdrop for studying patterns of recent species establishment. We can study not only which introduced species succeeded where and when, but what conditions prevailed that facilitated or prevented the spread of the species. Failure or success has depended on a complex interaction of the physiology, growth habits, and population dynamics of the species, the evolutionary history of the local biota, and human alterations of the ecosystems that may have primed them for successful establishment of non-native species. History serves here as a prelude to the present as well as a series of comparative studies.

I shall first discuss here some species migrations in the absence of human vectors, then turn to the specifically human role in disseminating species and to some ways in which historical studies may contribute to an understanding of the ever-changing roles of these species in their new habitats.

## Migration in the Absence of Humans

By a combination of paleontological and ecological inferences, biologists have reconstructed several major patterns of migration of species without human intervention. Individuals of a species, given enough time, most likely will inhabit all parts of their environment that satisfy their requirements for survival, including limitations due to interactions with other species. They often cannot, however, cross such barriers as high mountain ranges and large bodies of water, which may separate two regions of appropriate habitat. If a species can tolerate a large variety of environments, it may in time range over large areas. For example, the red fox (*Vulpes fulva*) and fireweed (*Epilobium angustifolium*) live in northern regions all around the globe. Species with restricted habitat requirements, however, may have very restricted ranges, for example, globeflower (*Trollius laxus*), which grows only in wet, limestone seeps in the northeastern United States.

Changes in a species' range are caused either by an evolutionary change in the species' tolerances or a change in the environment, including other species. Species and their environments interact and vary constantly, at different rates, mostly imperceptible to us. We are most familiar with the changed ranges of species as reconstructed for the last glacial period. Ample stratigraphical data in North America and western Europe record species' migrations under a climate that was changing too fast for most of them to evolve adaptations. Even so recently in the past, however, it is difficult to decipher the factors that controlled rates of migration. As the climate moderated during the waning of the most recent continental glaciations, species migrated at different rates along different pathways. In eastern North America, for example, some, such as the oaks and hickories, migrated north along a broad front, while others, such as hemlock and beech, migrated north and west along a more restricted corridor.[8] Beech and hemlock, which both reached the Great Lakes region from the east, migrated at different and variable rates, suggesting that factors in addition to climate may have affected their movement.[9] For example, differential dispersal of seeds and soil conditions are two factors that may mitigate the response to climate change for some species.

These examples refer to species' migrations along a continuous continental surface, with no species added that were not present on the continent before the climate changed. Competitive interactions would have been established over the millennia of evolution of this flora and fauna within a framework of continuous climatic change. Changed migration routes, however, introduce new species to an assemblage that has evolved in their absence. The reemergence of the Panamanian land bridge between North and South

America about three million years ago, for example, allowed species to move between the two continents. After the land bridge appeared, the number of species of land mammals and probably other taxa as well increased in both North and South America, as species expanded their ranges in response to the new habitat available to them. In North America the number of families (each with one or more species) of land mammals increased from twenty-seven to thirty-four, while in South America it increased from twenty-three to thirty-six. The numbers of families subsequently decreased, leaving North America with four fewer and South America with seven more than before formation of the land bridge.[10]

Many invading species are only temporarily successful. They may succeed initially because habitat is available, but competition with other species and perhaps changing climatic or other environmental conditions play a primary role later. In isolated habitats such as islands with few species, immigrations have also led to evolution of new species. Examples include the impressive diversification of finches on the Galápagos Islands and of honeycreepers on the Hawai'ian Islands.

These brief historical examples hint at overall patterns in the adaptations of species to new habitats. Most new introductions fail, but some succeed at least for a while by a process of interactions with preexisting biota and physical habitats and of evolutionary changes, and the new species may replace those that were local. Immigration usually increases diversity at first by simple addition of new species. Successful new immigrants may experience explosive population increase at first, then fall back to more moderate densities. Some initially successful species later become extinct. In an isolated or fairly new (on a geological timescale) habitat such as an island, with many unoccupied niches, species diversity may continue to increase as the new immigrants diversify over a long period of time (at least thousands of years). These processes have been going on for as long as there have been organisms on earth, at the slow pace of climatic change, plate tectonics, and evolution. Humans have accelerated the pace of migrations and creation of new habitats many times over the natural system but cannot alter the basic processes governing success or failure.

## Preagricultural Humans as Immigrants and Dispersers

Many regions have seen waves of human immigrations, each bringing with it its own baggage of new species from distant places. Climatic change initiated some of these migrations, for example, the great trek northward following the retreating glaciers in Europe and Asia and the Late Glacial peopling of North America. Other animals and plants surely migrated along similar paths as the people.

The rate of early human migrations was limited to the speed of walking or wind- and muscle-driven boat travel until the past thousand years or so. By these methods people successfully colonized most parts of the world, in large part because of their ability to build shelters, to use fire to keep warm, and to learn to hunt and gather new species. Their impacts thus included the killing of other animals and collecting of plants for food and wood for fuel and building shelters.

People also carried organisms with them, even before the invention of agriculture. Preagricultural people of North America, for example, traded the fruits of Kentucky coffee tree (*Gymnocladus dioicus*), American chestnut (*Castanea dentata*), and butternut (*Juglans cinerea*), and probably even propagated them near their settlements.[11] Kentucky coffee trees, for example, which are not common in Wisconsin in undisturbed habitats, characterize some Indian village sites there.[12] In addition to bringing new species with them, these people also changed habitats by establishing villages and altering fire regimes. These altered habitats provided sites in which new species could thrive.

## Cultivators as Dispersers

The development of agriculture increased the rate, distance, and number of dispersed species as well as providing ideal disturbed habitats for them. Most plant species bred for agriculture could not survive without constant human attention and did not generally become naturalized parts of the flora,[13] so the first indicators of agriculture were generally plants of open or disturbed habitats, mostly local species (fig. 6.1). These "weedy" plant species were probably restricted to such disturbed habitats as agricultural fields, pathways, and roadsides.

Many domesticated animals, on the other hand, flourished without human attention. In the Near East, domesticated goats, sheep, pigs, and cattle date back at least seven thousand years.[14] Although it is unlikely that they directly transformed forests into shrub communities, they may have prevented the regeneration of trees once areas cleared for agriculture had been abandoned. The ecology of these regions reflects not only climate and soils, but also the impact of millennia of grazing and browsing by introduced domestic species, especially goats.[15]

Other intentional introductions characterized western Europe well before the age of the great explorations. For example, Romans took walnut (*Juglans*

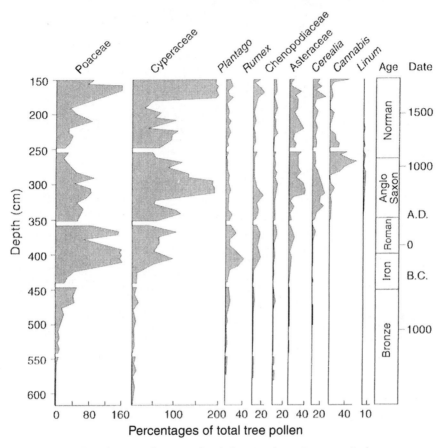

Figure 6.1. Pollen diagram from England showing large increases in hemp
(*Cannabis*) and flax (*Linum*) pollen in the Anglo-Saxon period along with that
of cereal grains. (Modified from J. Turner, Post-Neolithic disturbance of British
vegetation)

*regia*) and sweet chestnut (*Castanea sativa*) with them as they conquered ter-
ritories north and west as far as the British Isles, greatly expanding the ranges
of these species.[16] Chestnut subsequently became a common woodland tree
in England. In the twelfth century, the Normans introduced rabbits to the
British Isles from France or Spain, perhaps as a food source. As early as the
beginning of the fourteenth century these animals had become pests on
arable lands, though estates continued to protect them as late as the nineteenth century.[17] Most complaints about rabbit damage referred to cultivated
crops, but it is probable that they were responsible at least in part for the
failure of reproduction of many trees as well.[18]

Some species have more restricted habitats in their adopted homes. White dead nettle (*Lamium album*), a widespread herb of woodlands in its original home in the Caucasus, and goutweed (*Aegopodium podigraria*), a common European woodland herb, have not moved from disturbed sites into woodlands in England, even though they have in all likelihood been there for hundreds of years.[19]

Explorations and especially colonization after about A.D. 1400 accelerated the spread of plants and animals to new habitats much farther afield. Colonists took with them seeds and livestock, not relying on the bounty of the lands where they settled for food and clothing. Colonists also introduced flowers and shrubs as well as such birds as house sparrows and starlings. Unintentional hitchhikers included rats, agricultural weeds, and pests and disease organisms. All of these species apparently flourished in the disturbed habitats created by the new colonists.[20] Most did not, however, move into undisturbed habitats.

During this period, the introduction of feral animals onto islands that had no native mammals devastated native animals and vegetation. Sailors often introduced pigs and goats to islands in the hopes of stopping there for meat on later voyages, with no thought to anything except provisioning. At least as early as 1439 there were herds of feral sheep grazing on the Azores, introduced by Portuguese sailors before any grants of right to settle there.[21] Pigs introduced by sailors to the island of Bermuda about 1500 had become so numerous by 1630 that they were regarded as pests to be exterminated. By then it appears that they had decimated the indigenous seabirds.[22] Ship captains introduced goats and sheep onto the Hawai'ian islands in the eighteenth century,[23] with disastrous consequences for the native flora. Rabbits introduced to the island of Porto Santa in the Madeira Islands in 1718 did so much damage to the vegetation that the land was soon unfit for human occupation.[24] So even before there were permanent settlements on many islands, introduced domestic animals had severely depleted native fauna and flora, and where there were people, introduced animals competed with them for food. Even on the large continental island of Australia, introduced rabbits devastated the native vegetation.[25]

By the mid–eighteenth century, the English colonists in eastern North America had planted many meadows to "English grass" for pasture, including a mixture of perennial grasses like timothy (*Phleum pratense*) and orchard grass (*Dactylis glomerata*), and herbs like clovers (*Trifolium* spp.) and burnet (*Sanguisorba minor*).[26] The British Board of Trade recommended to Parliament placing a bounty on hemp (*Cannabis sativa*) raised in the North American colonies in 1761 to encourage its cultivation, and hemp pollen appeared in the pollen record about that time.[27] Many of these taxa were able to spread without human assistance and are common in abandoned and mowed fields today, along with such native species as ragweed, little bluestem (*Schizachyrium scoparium*), and asters.

The dispersal of species by European colonists in the eighteenth century was a two-way process. Horticultural enthusiasts in North America sent seeds, fruits, cuttings, eggs, and other propagules back to their home countries. The correspondence of the eighteenth-century Philadelphia naturalist John Bartram with his fellow horticulturist Peter Collinson in London illustrates the commitment to introducing new varieties of plants and animals to England. In December 1737, Collinson reported excitedly that a shipment of turtle eggs from Bartram had begun hatching the day they arrived. The novelty of this prompted many visitors to see them; "such a thing never happened, I dare say, in England before." Letters from Collinson to Bartram illustrate the enthusiasm for American plant taxa: "Renew thy collecting of acorns; and if thee can, send specimens to each which is a great curiosity. Get what sassafras berries thee can; and send as many Red Cedar berries, in a little box by themselves, as thee can afford for half a guinea. . . . Send some Sugar Maple seed and Rose Laurel cones; and send a specimen or two of the Upland Rose and the Marsh Rose. Try what thee canst do to send us some cones of the Long-cone White Pine."[28]

Bartram also avidly pursued the reverse trade; witness a letter to Collinson in 1760: "The seed thee sent last fall was choice good and most of them come up. The ranunculus and anemone root grows finely and several bore fine flowers. The flags—iris—grow well and two of the bulbous is ready to flower. Many aconites is come up and polianthus by hundreds. Balm of Gilead and a pretty annual linaria hath been long in flower, sowed last February. I hope the yellow digitalis and double-blossom celandine is come up."[29]

Linaria and celandine both later became common weeds in northeastern North America, but none of the plants listed as sent from North America to London is listed in the British flora.[30] No doubt, along with the seeds and cuttings were insects, many of which proliferated in their new habitats.

Other countries were also introducing New World species in the eighteenth century. The Hessian forester F. A. J. von Wangenheim, who traveled to North America as an officer in a Hessian field corps in 1777, published a book in 1781 describing North American trees and shrubs, as they might be useful in German forests. These forests were already heavily managed for timber and game; his recommendations were especially directed to providing feed for the game.[31] At about the same time, North American species like the white pine (*Pinus strobus*), black walnut (*Juglans nigra*), black locust (*Robinia pseudoacacia*), and Douglas fir (*Pseudotsuga menziesii*) were being planted in Bohemia as well, for the same purposes.[32]

Not all introductions were intentional, however. Long-distance trade and conquest, especially in Asia, Europe, and northern Africa, furnished many opportunities for the early inadvertent dispersal of organisms that hitchhiked on people, livestock, boats, and wagons. The growth of the long-distance wool trade in the Middle Ages in western Europe exemplifies the processes by which species were inadvertently dispersed in the preindustrial world. Sheeps' wool accumulates a tremendous variety of seeds and other plant parts, until washing and carding release them. In the thirteenth century, many monasteries used wool to pay papal dues, distributing seeds with it, for example, from England and France to Rome.[33] Estates shipped bulk wool as well, for example, from England to Perugia (in north central Italy) in the fourteenth century.[34] In the late fifteenth century bulk wool from England went to Calais (France), Italy, Holland, and Zeeland (present-day eastern Denmark).[35] Centuries of shipments such as these contributed to the homogenization of the weed flora of the region.

Agricultural weeds transported across the Atlantic Ocean with crop seeds flourished in the New World. Pollen evidence suggests that plantains (*Plantago major* and *P. lanceolata*) accompanied the earliest European agriculture in North America.[36] Indian tribes even adopted *P. major* and other European weeds such as yarrow (*Achillea millefolium*) and dandelion (*Taraxacum officinale*) as part of their medical lore, giving them Indian names.[37] John Josselyn observed plantain, dandelion, and twenty other weeds during visits to New England in 1638 and 1663.[38] In central California, adobe bricks made before 1800 include pieces of many non-native grasses, for example, annual bluegrass (*Poa annua*) and common foxtail (*Hordeum murinum*).[39] Does the length of time such species have been present in a local assemblage affect their role in these communities? These natural experiments, in which a formerly fairly rare community of species of open habitats has expanded and incorporated a large number of non-native species, may shed light on the processes involved in such multispecies interactions.

Introduced species have also directly affected human populations. It is likely that the ancient Egyptians disseminated malaria and its vector, the Anopheles mosquito, just as Old World colonists spread smallpox, malaria, and other Old World diseases to the Americas.[40] Smallpox was, for example, probably responsible in large part for the decline of the native population of North America south of Virginia from about two hundred thousand in 1680 to fewer than sixty-eight thousand in 1730. At the same time, the European and African human populations of the area, protected from smallpox by early exposure and variolation, increased from about three thousand to seventy-two thousand.[41] The spread of this introduced disease, accelerated by the susceptibility of the native populations and also by their lack of treatment, contributed to a major shift in the genetic stock of the regional human populations as well as to changes in population density.

By 1800, therefore, and even earlier, people had caused major expansions in the ranges of many species, including plants, animals, and diseases. The number of species present in most continental areas had increased, as the rate of introductions exceeded the rate of extinctions. Island habitats did not fare so well; there species had no defenses against newly introduced predators, so extinction rates were high. The newly introduced plant species generally flourished in habitats disturbed by human activities like agriculture. Some mammals, including rats, stayed close to the newly created habitats, but others, such as goats and rabbits, ranged widely into native ecosystems. Any concern people expressed about these related, however, to their damage to economically valuable resources, not to the local species diversity.

## Dispersal in the Nineteenth and Twentieth Centuries

The human-mediated dispersal of species accelerated greatly during the succeeding two centuries. People intentionally introduced species to semi-natural environments for forestry, forage, sport, control of other pests, and other reasons. Inadvertent introductions also proliferated. Transportation became faster and easier, so trips between continents became more frequent and more rapid. A seed or insect that remains viable for only a short time under mild conditions, for example, can move from one continent to another as baggage on a jet flight, whereas it would have succumbed on a slow, cold ocean voyage. With more people traveling and more species carried, the chances that seeds and disease-causing organisms could spread increased. Most have failed to become established, but some have been moderately successful and others dramatically so. Increased frequency of introductions coupled with habitat modifications have improved the chances that a species might become established in a new environment.

Although people had introduced only about 110 tree species into Great Britain before 1800, they brought in more than 200 between 1800 and 1900 and 58 between 1900 and 1978.[42] On the islands of Hawai'i foresters used almost 1,000 non-native tree species in plantations between 1910 and 1960 to revegetate overgrazed rangeland.[43] The historical record, however, documents not only these large numbers of tree species introduced to new environments, but also the failure of most of them to reproduce successfully in native communities, even disturbed ones. Of the 211 species of trees introduced into England between 1800 and 1900, only one has become established on its own, and of 58 species introduced from 1900 to about 1978, none had established wild populations by 1978.[44]

About 20 of the 1,000 tree species introduced into Hawai'i have become naturalized. The concatenation of conditions, a young and isolated flora, very large numbers of introductions, and other major human modifications of the ecosystems allowed more species to become established (although still only about 2 percent of those that had been introduced). Strawberry guava (*Psidium cattleianum*), for example, introduced into Hawai'i from Brazil in 1825, has dispersed into uncut native forest stands, its spread in part facilitated by introduced pigs, which carry seeds and disturb the soil.[45] Spread also by pigs and non-native birds, firetree (*Myrica faya*) succeeds well in native forest stands, crowding out native species and changing the nutrient status of the soil by nitrogen fixation.[46] Both of these trees have succeeded in invading native ecosystems not only because of their innate characteristics, but also because of the conditions at the time they were introduced.

Planting for ornament and aesthetic appeal has contributed many introduced species as well. European floras list as "naturalized" many North American taxa that have escaped from cultivation. Pokeweed (*Phytolacca americana*), introduced into southern Europe for "ornament and for its berries which are used in dyeing," is often naturalized, or reproducing on its own.[47] The American tree boxelder (*Acer negundo*) was "widely planted" and now grows without cultivation as a "wayside shade tree" in southern Europe. In the nineteenth century, the pitcher plant (*Sarracenia purpurea*) was widely introduced into bogs in western Europe and England because of its interesting growth form, and it has become naturalized in many areas.[48] The floras do not describe these as "invader" or problem species, although they are all growing in more or less native, though disturbed, habitats. For millennia these regions have experienced intensive human impact on the vegetation, so that little habitat remains that would be described in less long-manipulated regions as natural. The process of integrating these species into the native vegetation is, however, still undergoing adjustment.

Hunting, fishing, and trapping have constituted another major impetus to the importing of species. Hunters imported European hares (*Lepus europaeus*), for example, into many parts of the world. In the 1990s, much of Ontario's and Quebec's agricultural regions support thriving populations of European hares, which apparently originated mainly from the release in 1912 of seven female and two male hares in Brantford, Ontario. These denizens

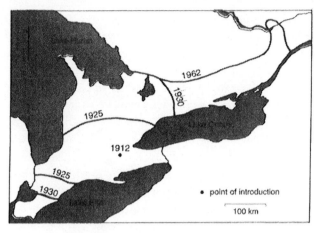

Figure 6.2. The spread of European hares
(*Lepus europaeus*) in southern Ontario from
introduction in 1912. (Modified from Dean and
de Vos, European hare)

of open fields, a habitat newly created in the region, had ranged up to one
hundred kilometers from the site of introduction by 1930 and three hundred
kilometers by 1962, possibly assisted by some supplemental introductions
(fig. 6.2). On the other hand, introductions of hundreds of hares in southern
New York State in 1893–1911 led to much more localized establishment until
about 1938, when populations began to dwindle rather than increase.[49] Populations in both areas have survived into the 1990s, but hares from Canada
appear to have had difficulty crossing the international boundary. Hares
have also been established in New Zealand, Australia, and South America.[50]
The nonspectacular success and spread of such introductions compared with,
for example, rabbits in Australia and red deer in New Zealand, may shed
light on the intrinsic properties of invasions.

Deer have been introduced into many habitats for hunting and aesthetic
appeal. In the nineteenth century, several introduced species established naturally reproducing populations: red deer (*Servus elaphus*) from England and
white-tailed deer (*Odocoileus virginianus*) from North America in New
Zealand and Sika deer (*S. nippon*) from Asia in the British Isles and New
Zealand.[51] The red deer have had dramatic effects in eliminating native vegetation and accelerating erosion, for example, in New Zealand.[52] In many
areas, native deer and elk populations that became very small by the nineteenth century because of overhunting and elimination of habitat, have
been rejuvenated by reintroductions and protection in the twentieth.[53] These

reintroductions of native species pose interesting questions about the roles of introduced species. In many areas in the absence of former predators and possibly other controlling factors, they are having negative effects on the regeneration of native plant species. If they were not native, we would automatically view them as harmful invaders, based on their impacts on native communities, but because they are native their role is more controversial.

Fish must hold the record for major impacts on native communities by species introduced for sport. They proliferate even in relatively undisturbed habitats. European brown trout (*Salmo trutta*) introduced from Tasmania to Auckland, New Zealand, between 1866 and 1880 quickly established naturally spawning populations widely on both islands. Rainbow trout (*S. gairdneri*) formed naturally reproducing populations in New Zealand after one introduction in 1883.[54] Non-native trout species are the only large freshwater fish in New Zealand and form the major sport fish there in the late twentieth century. In most western states of the United States, well over 25 percent of the fish are introduced species; they often dominate the fish fauna in biomass as well as diversity. Species are introduced not only on purpose, for their sport-fishing qualities, but also by escapes of "minnows" used as bait.[55]

The dynamics of fish and plankton populations in the Great Lakes of North America cannot be understood apart from the history of both inadvertent and intentional species introductions. The digging of the Welland Canal in 1829 to bypass Niagara Falls allowed the sea lamprey (*Petromyzon marinus*) to invade the Great Lakes above the falls.[56] The lamprey did not reach Lake Michigan until 1937, but when it did, it attacked the large native fish, virtually eliminating them.[57] A small fish, the bloater (*Coregonus hoyi*), apparently benefited from the loss of large fish, and its population increased. Competition for zooplankton with the non-native alewife (*Alosa pseudoharenga*), established in the lake in 1949, is blamed for the subsequent collapse of the bloater population. Later control of the lamprey at its spawning sites, the reintroduction of native trout, and the introduction of non-native salmon and European brown trout have again shifted species dynamics. Changes in the top predators have also affected both species distribution and morphology of plankton species as well as changing the bloater from an open water to a bottom feeder.[58] This abbreviated and simplified version of the Lake Michigan story only scratches the surface of the complex interactions of species tolerances and human activities, which can be understood only against a background of the history of introductions of species to the lake.

The idea of introducing organisms to control pests has a long history as well, and some of these control agents have ranged into native communities. Large land snails introduced to the Hawai'ian islands to control pests in pineapple plantations, for example, became dispersed, competing with a highly diverse native tree-snail fauna.[59] The mosquito fish (*Gambusia affinis*), introduced from southeastern North America around the world to control Anopheles mosquitoes and thus malaria, is now perhaps the most widespread freshwater fish in the world, where it has eliminated many native fish.[60]

In forests, on the other hand, inadvertently introduced diseases and insect pests have had the most impact. A fungus inadvertently introduced in the early twentieth century on imported nuts killed all of the mature American chestnut trees, for example. The gypsy moth, imported to produce silk, and the Dutch elm disease, spread by both native and non-native bark beetles, are two other inadvertently introduced pests that have had widespread effects on major native forest trees in North America. The Dutch elm disease has also killed elm trees in Great Britain.[61] The timing of their introduction—into forests that were recovering in the late nineteenth and early twentieth centuries from heavy logging—contributed to their spread and effects on forest species composition. In many northeastern forests, earlier successional species such as black birch and red maple responded to gaps occasioned by the death of chestnut trees, setting succession back to an earlier stage.[62] The current dynamics cannot be understood without reference to this major dislocation sixty to seventy years ago. Diseases of animals likewise have had major repercussions for population distributions and dynamics. To cite just one, the rinderpest panzootic introduced into Africa in the nineteenth century is blamed for major current anomalies in the distribution of wildlife there.[63]

Other major inadvertent introductions have been initiated at harbors, where ships offload large loads of ballast, which has included a wide range of organisms collected unwittingly at the outgoing port. For example, about 250 species of plants, mainly of European origin, were growing on ballast deposits in three harbor areas of New Jersey in 1881,[64] about 10 percent of which were naturalized in northeastern North America within a century.[65] Ballast water in the twentieth century became an even more important source of unintentionally introduced aquatic organisms, especially those adapted to oceanic or brackish conditions.

These examples illustrate the importance not only of the history of the introduction process itself for understanding present distributions, but also of the conditions at the time of introduction. Species usually gained a foothold in disturbed habitats, but once established there, many have to some extent been able to penetrate into more native habitat and affect succession to native species.

## Introduced Species: The Changing Emphasis

Predicting the spread of introduced species remains a risky job, as does predicting the effects of such a spread on native communities and ecosystems. Most introductions are not successful, but these unsuccessful, usually unintended experiments provide little information because they are poorly documented. Most information comes from the taxa that have deleterious effects on economically valuable crops or are regarded as beneficial and thus a positive success, as in the cases of introduced sport fish and biological controls. The early success of an alien species does not allow one easily to predict its eventual range.[66] Two species, charcoal hearth grass (*Eulalia viminea*), a grass most likely introduced inadvertently as seeds in grass wrappings of wine bottles, and Japanese bittersweet (*Celastrus orbiculatus*), were only "sparingly naturalized" in the northeastern United States in 1963, but by 1985 had become well-known pests in young forest stands. As late as 1991, a plant manual described Japanese barberry (*Berberis thunbergii*) as an escapee from cultivation into roadsides and thickets, even though by 1985 it had spread into well-established oak forests in New Jersey and elsewhere (fig. 6.3).[67] Basically, the change in distribution had happened too rapidly and too recently to be included in the manual, after the species spent a long period as a denizen of only disturbed sites.

The introduced species themselves often lead to changes in habitats that in turn facilitate their expansion at the expense of native species. Non-native grasses in Hawai'i like molasses grass (*Melinus minutiflora*) from Africa and broomsedge (*Andropogon virginicus*) from North America colonize disturbed microsites, forming almost complete cover. Both are fire-adapted, both carrying and surviving fires, but the native plants that they surround are killed by the fires. Thus they are creating the conditions that allow them to overwhelm the native species, including such trees as koa (*Acacia koa*) and *Metrosideros* (fig. 6.4).[68] Humans start most of the fires. Introduced species brought in to improve range for cattle pasture, disturbances caused by cattle and people, and fires generally ignited by human activity interact in ways that have led to the success of the introduced species at a specific time in history.

About 30 percent of the plant species in one- to two-year-old abandoned agricultural fields in a study in central New Jersey were non-native, but the proportion was only about 17 percent in stands ten to sixty years after abandonment. The proportion was a mere 5 percent in older forests in the same region.[69] The total number of species was highest in these old forests and lowest in ten-year-old fields (fig. 6.5). What role do these species play in these fields? Are the proportions related to the time of abandonment or to the age

Figure 6.3. Japanese barberry (*Berberis thunbergii*) growing in mature oak forest in northern New Jersey. (Photo by the author, spring 1995)

of the stands? Have some species been part of these successional sequences longer than others? Where did the species come from? The species assemblages that characterize these fields are new on an evolutionary timescale, and thus the interactions among them may be unstable. The consequences of such instability offer a challenging arena for research into the dynamics of communities and ecosystem processes.

People continue to plant exotics for erosion control, beautification, and other reasons. Consider the widely distributed packets of so-called wildflower seeds, which usually contain few or no wildflowers native to where they are to be planted, and the beautification of the roadsides in England by the planting of non-native narcissi that compete with the natives. Inadvertent introductions can also not be completely controlled, as species hitch rides on airplane wheels and the hulls of boats. Understanding the dynamics and potential of these aliens to alter native communities and species must start with understanding why, where, and how they are introduced.

Figure 6.4. Native ohia (*Metrosideros polymorpha*) forest in Hawai'i killed by fire. The native, nitrogen-fixing tree mamane (*Sophora chrysophylla*) is sprouting back, but there is no recovery of the ohia. The grasses are mostly non-native and carry fire effectively. (Photo by the author, 1990)

An extreme attitude toward non-native species is exemplified by the introduction to a National Park Service guide to the Hosmer Grove of non-native trees in Haleakalâ National Park in Hawai'i. Printed in 1990, the guide states in large letters, "You have entered a battlefield. Aggressive alien trees, planted as an experiment by a forester in 1910, are overcoming and supplanting native vegetation here."[70] The non-native trees are personified as truly evil.

A more balanced approach would entail study of the history of introductions, including the conditions of the community at the time of introduction and the pathways and rates of spread of the non-native species. Their integration into a native ecosystem may be more or less complete. Whether one regards introduced species as beneficial, as was most often the case in the nineteenth century, or as deleterious, how long they have been there and how they were introduced may help explain otherwise anomalous properties of the community. For example, black locust–dominated successional stands outside the native range of the species do not appear to be changing to more mature forests after seventy to ninety years. Studies that focus on such species may elucidate patterns that are otherwise obscure.

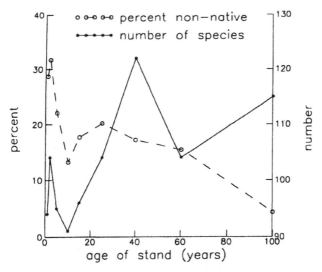

Figure 6.5. Comparison of species richness and proportion of non-native species in successional stands of different ages in central New Jersey. (Data from G. E. Bard, Secondary succession on the Piedmont of New Jersey, *Ecological Monographs* 22:195–215, 1952)

People have long viewed their role in intentionally transplanting species to new environments as positive. The new species improved diversity and economic value. The beautiful fall colors of sugar maple enhanced European gardens, while the addition of house sparrows (*Passer domesticus*) made American fields more homelike. Scots pine (*Pinus sylvestris*) and Norway spruce (*Picea abies*) yielded reliable crops of timber in North America, *Eucalyptus* spp. in Hawai'i, and white pine and Douglas fir in Europe. In evolutionary terms, they were seeing only the first phase of reaction to immigration, species enrichment. As species have adapted to their new environments and begun to enter those not as greatly disturbed, competitive interactions have become more apparent, including those with negative impacts for native species. The evolutionary process suggests that the dynamics will not be sorted out quickly; people can accelerate the process of transport, but the disruptions will take many years to resolve, and the outcomes will surely involve more extinctions among both invaders and native species.

# 7

## The Forest as a Resource

Forests and woodlands are a treasure trove of valued resources: nuts, roots, berries, and animals for food; wood for building, burning, and boating; and a vast assortment of other products such as pitch and tannins. In some ways human use of the forest has mimicked natural processes. Herbivores eat nuts and berries; carnivores kill and eat other animals; beavers and storms cut or knock down trees. But humans have intensified and extended these processes by removing products far from their source or burning them, thus changing the processes of nutrient recycling and soil retention, and by cutting forests over larger areas than a storm or beaver would flatten. The history of fire, as it modifies species composition and nutrient cycling, and of introduced species, as they become more important in forests, is also part of the history of forests; the web of interactions becomes ever more tangled as we consider more facets of human impacts on ecosystems.

In regions in which human populations have been scattered and demands mainly generated by subsistence, the use of these resources has had barely detectable effects. On the other hand, in much of the temperate zone, use has been intense and extensive, so that remaining forest structure and function can be understood only in the context of past and present patterns of use. Even where apparently unmanaged, stands often bear the imprints of a variety of past human activities, which affect current conditions, and the landscape-scale patterns of woodland distribution.[1]

To forest-dwelling hunter-gatherers, the forest was a source of many necessities of life: food, clothing, medicines, and building materials. It is hard to imagine that they regarded it as a hindrance, though they certainly feared some of its components, dangerous animals and spirits, to name just two. The advent of agriculture, however, heralded a new attitude. To plant crops, it was necessary to destroy trees. Forest products were still critical for heating, food, building material, and other necessities, yet the forest itself came to be viewed at least in part as a hindrance. As further population growth led to the clearing of more forest, remaining woodlands became more closely integrated into the agricultural economy, for example, for pasture and a source of materials such as firewood, fencing, and lumber.

Increased demand for construction and fuelwood led to increased exploitation of the forest, often with little regard for the future because there seemed to be inexhaustible expanses of exploitable timberland, though often at a distance.[2] Great Britain, for example, though largely deforested, did not perceive a serious lack of timber until after the First World War because it could import ample supplies from the United States and Canada.[3] Finally, as people recognized shortages or deleterious effects of deforestation, they began to develop silviculture that prolonged the productivity of timber resources as well as protected soil from erosion, attracted tourists, and, most recently, safeguarded the remaining biodiversity of the forests and possibly attenuated global climate change.

The history of forest use, then, can be viewed as comprising three stages: (1) hunting, gathering, and shifting cultivation, in which preponderantly local resources were used with little widespread active management (although recent research has found examples of very intense local management);[4] (2) primarily agricultural uses, with more intense disturbance at least in part because of increasing population with decreasing forest area for fuel and grazing; and (3) commercial, intensive use for industrial products and processes, with growing recognition of the value of the resource and the need to protect it.[5] In this last stage, conflicts arose between the aims of those who sought increased productivity and those who sought to preserve natural areas for their esthetic or biological roles, with major consequences for management of existing stands.

The structure and composition of forests reflect the variety of patterns and intensities of uses through time. Where human populations have been very dense and forested areas restricted, such as in much of western Europe, most woodlands have been molded by the interactions between natural site characteristics and human use.[6] Such intense use may result in distinctive landscapes, such as rows of pollarded trees whose branches have been repeatedly cut above browsing height (fig. 7.1). Other kinds of management produce

Figure 7.1. Row of pollarded trees in Brittany, France. (Photo by the author, spring 1985)

more natural-looking stands, even where the species composition and forest structure are intensively managed (fig. 7.2). In regions of less dense population and a shorter history of intense forest use—for instance, North and South America—the human interactions are even less obvious. Clear-cutting two hundred years ago, selective logging in the past century, loss of chestnut trees to introduced disease, and changed browsing and fire frequency have nevertheless left forests that superficially appear untouched by human disturbances.[7] Tracing the history of any of these stands by synthesizing historical documentation, stratigraphic study, and on-site analyses leads to a composite story that incorporates the influence of both natural site characteristics and human impact on the current forest composition and ecosystem functioning.

### The Impacts of Subsistence Hunting, Gathering, and Shifting Cultivation

The terms *hunting* and *gathering* imply an impact on forest ecosystems. Whatever was hunted or gathered suffered some consequences of human use. The evidence of this impact, however, is hard to find. There is ample evidence of what was hunted and gathered, at least of those organisms that left

Figure 7.2. Black Forest, Germany. Note the reproduction beneath these non-native Norway spruces. (Photo by the author, spring 1995)

preserved bones, seeds, or other parts. Even amounts can sometimes be inferred from the concentrations of remains at settlement sites and estimates of how long the sites were occupied. At many archeological sites, however, there are few or no remains of food, so that we do not know even what kinds of plants and animals people ate.[8]

It is even harder to estimate the resilience of species that are hunted or gathered. We would need to know what species were used, how their populations changed, and how the use caused the changes. Although it is assumed that hunter gatherers generally did not hunt (or gather) species to extinction, because that would have destroyed their food supply, such an argument assumes that these people could detect the potential for extinction before the population became too small to be saved by reduced hunting or gathering pressure. This may not have been true where species were under stress because of changed climate and vegetation at the end of the Ice Age and human populations were moving into habitat that had been unavailable earlier.

For most of the history of *Homo sapiens,* people have relied on hunting and gathering for subsistence. From the tropics to the arctic, from well-watered lands to near desert, they have used a wide diversity of foods and faced various challenges of survival during the hard times of year. Dependent primarily on natural cycles of productivity for their food, they seem to have lived in a world inhabited by spirits who could release or withhold the bounty of the earth.[9] A romantic view of these preagricultural peoples pictures them as living in small groups surrounded by an animated natural world from which they take only the small amount of game and plants that they need for survival, thereby exerting only a very minor impact on the environment. Recent research indicates, however, that this is an antiquated, culturally biased picture. Setting fires and eliminating species by overhunting are two well-known examples of how hunter-gatherers probably modified their environments in major ways.[10]

One of the most impressive illustrations of the ability of paleolithic hunters to kill enormous numbers of animals is the deposits of mammoth bones found in paleolithic sites in the Ukraine and Poland. At one site in the Ukraine, bones from ninety-five individual mammoths formed the support for one dwelling, and at another, in Poland, dated at 21,000 to 23,000 years B.P., during the full glacial period, three dwellings contained bones from sixty mammoths.[11] This did not, however, lead to local extinction of the mammoths, which survived in Siberia for at least ten more millennia.

Human and mammoth populations likely evolved on the steppes contemporaneously, given that both survived at least the last advance of the Pleistocene glaciers there. Similarly, in Africa, where human populations evolved, only 14 percent of the large (fifty kilograms and over), warm-blooded fauna have become extinct in the past one hundred thousand years.[12] Major waves of extinctions of large mammals, however, typified previously unpeopled continents such as North and South America and Australia after the arrival of humans, about ten thousand years ago in the Americas and forty thousand years ago in Australia (table 7.1). Of the fifty-eight species of large, warm-blooded animals present in South America in the past one hundred thousand years, only twelve are still alive, a mere 21 percent. In North America, only 14 percent have survived and in Australia 27 percent.

Humans and much of the extinct fauna did coexist on these continents, at least for a while. Butchering tools found with bones of these animals, along with marks on the bones that resemble those caused by the butchering of meat with stone tools, indicate that people did hunt and eat these animals.[13] Alternation of human and extinct ground sloth (*Mylodon*) remains at the southern end of South America in Patagonia means that at least this beast was able to survive long after humans had entered the region, though the two do not seem to have coexisted locally.[14] Coexistence of extinct species and humans in Australia lasted for many millennia, however. For these and many other reasons, hunting by *Homo sapiens* was likely not the sole cause of these

*Table 7.1. Extinctions of terrestrial megafauna species in the past one hundred thousand years on major continents.*

| Continent | Extinct in last 100,000 years | Still living there | Total | % extinct |
|---|---|---|---|---|
| Africa | 7 | 42 | 49 | 14 |
| North America | 33 | 12 | 45 | 73 |
| South America | 46 | 12 | 58 | 80 |
| Australia | 19 | 3 | 22 | 86 |

*Source:* Martin, Prehistoric overkill, 358.

extinctions.[15] The complexity of the niches of the fauna, changing climate and consequently habitat, and the advent of humans, whose culture also changed even during the Paleolithic, imply that the extinctions had multiple causes. Whatever the causes, humans probably played a role, and the loss of these large animals almost assuredly would have had major effects on the plants that were no longer eaten, trampled, and dispersed by these animals as well as on the populations of other animal species that survived.[16]

People have also affected forests (and other types of vegetation) by gathering plants. Many plants that supplied major portions of the food supply of communities, for example, wild rice (*Zizania aquatica*) in north-central North America or mongongo nuts (*Ricinodendron rautauenii*) in Botswana and Namibia, still flourish under continued harvesting,[17] although in Egypt, gathering has eliminated species like the carob-locust bean tree (*Ceratonia siliqua*) and papyrus (*Cyperus papyrus*) from their native habitats.[18] In North America, native Americans valued ginseng (*Panax quinquefolium*) for a variety of purposes, but it remained locally abundant when European settlers arrived. Collection for trade to China (through France) led to its becoming rare in the vicinity of Montreal as early as 1750[19] and eventually throughout northeastern North America. In some regions of North America, ecological experiments confirm ethnographic evidence that intensive management even increased productivity of some collected plants like redbud and rhizomes of bracken ferns used for making baskets and various tubers used for food.[20]

People have used a wide variety of plants for food, shelter, medicine, arts, and dyes; in the Upper Great Lakes region of North America, for example, 373 species of native plants provided local Indian populations with food, beverages, medicines, charms, smoking materials, and dyes.[21] A survey of fifty-eight modern hunter-gatherer societies found that twenty-nine depended mainly on gathering for their food supply, while only eleven depended on hunting. Plants contributed up to 80 percent of their food by weight, with fewer plants and more meat being consumed the farther north one went.[22] The use and dispersal of so much plant material would have altered some species' distributions in ways that would be difficult to discern. Although overuse of a rare species could have led to extinction, with little remaining evidence, it seems improbable that the native people would have used species that they could see were not common.

The cutting of trees for bark, boats, and fuel must have had local impacts, and as resources became scarce in one place, camps would have been moved to another. Migratory hunter-gatherer tribes move partly because they cannot obtain enough food or firewood in one place; this implies that they exert pressure on the resources. Changed vegetation associated with preagricultural people, for example, a consistent rise in alder (*Alnus*) pollen in sediment dated about 7500 B.P. through much of the British Isles, may be a response to forest disturbance by Mesolithic people.[23]

Documents from the seventeenth and eighteenth centuries that describe the forests of North America after they had been subject to millennia of hunting, gathering, and shifting agriculture do not allow modern readers to infer the impact of these activities on forest vegetation. The descriptions are vague, and they describe the vegetation at one time only and so lack the comparative data needed to assess impact. A seventeenth-century description of New Netherlands (eastern New York and New Jersey) described the timber that covered most of the land as "standing . . . without order as in other wildernesses."[24] The land produced "several kinds of timber, suitable for the construction of houses and ships . . . consisting of various sorts of oaks," "various sorts of Nut timber," very abundant hickory, chestnuts growing "wild without regularity," beeches (including *Carpinus caroliniana*), "axhandle wood (*Ostrya caroliniana*?), canoe wood (*Liriodendron tulipifera*— ed.)," and a long list of other trees, nuts, fruits, grapes, animals, birds, and fish. Juxtaposition in the list of "ash, birch, pine, lathwood [?], *Imberen* or wild cedar [?], linden, alder, willow, thorn, and elder" at the end of the list indicates the difficulty of reconstructing the structure of these forests. One might imagine the pine as growing on high, dry sites, with alder and willow in wet sites, but where were elm and hemlock or the maples? The only clear message is that oaks were the most abundant trees. Pollen analysis is consistent with this conclusion but has added little to analysis of the structure of the forest or the difference in impact of hunting and gathering as compared with early agriculture.[25] The lack of unequivocal cause and effect connection between humans and changes in forest flora and fauna before the advent of agriculture is not a sufficient reason, however, to discount the possibility of such an effect, although the impact was surely much smaller than the one that followed.

## *Agricultural and Domestic Uses of Forest Resources*
### EFFECTS ON PLANTS

The primary impact of farmers on forests is massive deforestation, but farmers also affect remaining forests by making much heavier use of the remaining forest resources than preagricultural peoples did. Overuse of forest resources has been blamed even for the downfall of many civilizations in the past,[26] though it was doubtless just one cause in a complex of interrelated problems that beset the civilizations.

Evidence of the effects of early agricultural societies on forest resources is hidden in many places. By identifying wood remaining in ancient buildings, for example, we can detect sources and uses of different tree species. The Anasazi in New Mexico used thousands of spruce and fir logs for construction timbers in the eleventh century A.D., carrying them from high mountains at least seventy-five kilometers away.[27] Farther east in North America, local use of bald cypress (*Taxodium distichum*) for buildings most likely depleted the populations of that species by A.D. 1400, restricting its northern distribution in the central part of its range.[28]

Literate sedentary societies have left evidence for past forest use in the form of inventories, maps, and tax records. The recorders of these documents were chiefly interested in the resource for economic reasons, so their observations are incomplete or difficult to interpret in terms of changes in forest composition and structure under varying kinds of use. They generally did not record most species present, for example. Using data from the Domesday Book (see fig. 2.4), Oliver Rackham has concluded that the region was largely deforested by A.D. 1086.[29] Others, however, using the same sources, doubt that any accurate enumeration can be gleaned from them but estimate that there was a lot of wood remaining at that time.[30] Such uncertainty in instances in which the records appear to be excellent suggests that analyses elsewhere will be even more difficult. Rackham's method of clearly stating his assumptions is a good start, one from which disagreements can be precisely defined and settled.

Use of forest resources had more obvious consequences in dryer regions. Overuse of forests may, for example, have led to the abandonment of villages in the Fertile Crescent of Jordan six thousand years ago. Buildings in the area had plaster floors made from lime produced by heating limestone. Plaster for one building required six oak trees, and four more were needed for beams. At that rate, the local population of twenty-eight hundred over a period of one thousand years would have depleted the local wood supply, especially as goats grazed in the cut-over forests, preventing regeneration.[31] Deforestation of nearby Lebanon also began as many as five thousand years ago. An inscription on a temple in Egypt announced the arrival there of forty ships laden with timber from Lebanon, probably before 2900 B.C. Two thousand years later, Lebanon was still supplying timber: eighty thousand loggers were supposedly employed to cut cedar and fir in Lebanon for the construction of a temple at Jerusalem about 1000 B.C.[32] This logging apparently destroyed almost the entire remaining forest covering about two thousand square miles (five thousand square kilometers). The forest was lost because of the demand for timber, not because of clearing for agriculture, leading to severe erosion and permanent deforestation. Past overuse of forest products in this seasonally dry climate played a major role in the evolution of the regional ecosystems as well as in the downfall of civilizations.

In tropical wet climates, the impacts were less distinct. The traditional uses of trees by the Bora tribe of eastern Peru offer a glimpse of the use of wood in a tropical, preindustrial region. The Boras planted trees in their clearings, including nitrogen-fixing trees, so that when they abandoned the clearings, there was natural regeneration that included useful species. They used the trees for construction materials, firewood, art, and food, including edible grubs.[33] The combining of analyses of archeological sites with stratigraphic information may detail some of the interactions of human populations and forest structure in the past and the consequences for present ecosystems.[34]

From the earliest introduction of domestic animals, people have valued forests as pasture. From about A.D. 250 to 700, Saxon immigrants in Holland brought large herds of cattle, which they pastured in the forests.[35] An Anglo-Saxon law in the late seventh century levied a fine of sixty shillings for cutting a lot of trees or sixty shillings for a single tree that could "shelter" thirty swine.[36] Sixth- to tenth-century Salic law details punishments for pig stealing, and documents refer to many scattered "denns" in the forest of England that were used for fattening swine. Forests of oak and beech were encouraged for the mast they yielded.[37] As population grew and woodland shrank, rights of grazing became more limited and controlled on common lands, although woodlots continued to serve as pastures. By the mid–fourteenth century, however, local shortages of timber led authorities to enclose some woods in England so that they could be managed for firewood.[38]

In northern areas of Europe, where long, cold, snowy winters precluded leaving stock outside to fend for themselves year round, farmers collected

Figure 7.3. Old woodland bank in Surrey, England. (Photo by the author, spring 1985)

leafy twigs for winter fodder, a practice that continued into the nineteenth century in parts of Norway.[39] Most systems of twig fodder collection relied on the sprouting abilities of certain species such as birches, ashes, and oaks. Wood could be cut at ground level, producing a coppice, or higher on the trunk (pollarding, shredding) so that young sprouts were out of reach of grazing and browsing animals.

These kinds of cutting provided wood for a variety of purposes in addition to fodder. Coppices, for example, yielded fuelwood, poles to train hop vines for flavoring beer, wood for charcoal, and stems for weaving into fences and hurdles. Ash (*Fraxinus excelsior*) was good for hop poles and hazel (*Corylus cornuta*) for fences (see fig. 3.3).

Individual coppiced woodlots in England can be identified by name back to medieval times, and the changes in boundaries noted on the ground even today by remnant banks and ditches built to keep stray livestock out of the woods and to delimit the boundaries (fig. 7.3).[40] The distinct assemblages of herbaceous species, invertebrates, and birds in these woodlots are closely related to their past management.[41]

Farmers in North America revived the practice of allowing domestic livestock to graze in forests. Because pigs, cattle, sheep, and even horses grazed at large, plowed fields had to be fenced for protection. In seventeenth-century New Jersey, for example, a farmer could be compensated for damages caused by wandering livestock only if the fences around his fields were at least four feet, three inches (1.3 meters) high. Cleared land was a rare commodity. By the mid–eighteenth century, however, as the ratio of cleared to uncleared land increased, laws in many areas required that livestock be fenced in rather than out of fields.[42] Advertisements for land for sale mirrored this change, as they began to emphasize the availability of timber or woodlots, commonly including wooded acreage on some agriculturally poor soil that was subdivided and sold separately from arable land.[43] Woodlots nearer to farms also were a source of timber in a wide variety of sizes for many necessary products, from construction wood to firewood, fenceposts, and barrel staves.[44] Farm use changed even forests that were never clear-cut; lack of direct use did not translate into lack of impact.

EFFECTS OF HUNTING

In the past millennium, humans have hunted few species to extinction except on islands. When combined with habitat change, however, hunting has eliminated some species, for example, the passenger pigeon in North America, and has reduced the ranges of many more. The drive to destroy predators like wolves has limited their ranges in such areas as western Europe and North America. Hunting for trade locally exterminated beavers in eastern North America in the seventeenth and eighteenth centuries. Although people may have substituted for predators in controlling prey populations, the roles of such species as passenger pigeons, especially in transporting seeds, and of beavers in damming creeks and cutting trees have been left unfilled. The dislocations caused by the loss of these animals most likely still affect forest structure. Where these changes in vegetation are subtle, however, local extinctions of large animals may go unnoticed, for example, in some neotropical forests in the twentieth century.[45]

On the other hand, management of land for hunting has had major impacts in many parts of the world for centuries. Aldo Leopold suggested even that game management might afford a means of developing a culture that showed how conservation and public benefit might coexist to their mutual advantage.[46] As early as the seventh and eighth centuries in the Auvergne in France, when the lowland area was so completely cleared of forest that people had to use straw for fuel, the surrounding mountains served as a preserve for huntsmen who supplied the aristocratic residences of the plains with game. Settled by Germanic immigrants, this area continued to include extensive forests as contrasted with the south of France, where settlers from the Mediterranean did not establish hunting preserves and defor-estation was more complete.[47]

The very term *forest* comes from the Latin *foris* and refers to "land out-side the common law and subject to special law that safeguarded the king's hunting";[48] that is, it had nothing to do with the existence of trees. Anglo-Saxon literature and the Domesday Book refer to deer parks and royal hunt-ing, so many hunting preserves probably dated from Anglo-Saxon times;[49] many of these and other large English "forests" are mainly nonforested heathlands. Much timber remaining by about A.D. 1600, however, was in the royal "forests," where clearing for agriculture had not been allowed.[50]

One of the first books dedicated directly to forest management, published in 1561, was entitled "Jagd-und Forstrecht" (Hunting- and forest law). For-esters employed by German principalities experimented with planting, includ-ing plants obtained from abroad, to improve the cover and feed for game. When peasants protested the extension of the seigneurial parks and the dam-age wrought by the game, the proprietors of the parks responded that if they did not protect the forests the increased numbers of peasants would destroy them entirely.[51] Management for hunting thus may have contributed to the maintenance of open and forested land in many areas.

Reintroductions of nearly extinct native species like the white-tailed deer (*Odocoileus virginianus*) in much of the northeastern United States have also had major impacts on the vegetation. Populations flourished on abandoned farmland that had reverted to a mosaic of brush and young forest, ideal habi-tat for the deer.[52] Long-term observations indicate that deer have damaged forest tree regeneration in many well-established forests. In Pennsylvania, for example, heavy deer browsing was blamed for destroying understory hem-lock and witch hobble (*Viburnum alnifolium*).[53] In Wisconsin, a comparison of seedling and sapling growth between browsed and unbrowsed stands showed that browsing limited hemlock regeneration.[54] If changed browsing by one herbivore can have such major effects on forest regeneration, and thus future forest structure, it is likely that changes in densities brought about by hunting in the past could likewise have had major impacts.

INDUSTRIAL USES AND TRADE

Industrial and other commercial uses of forest products have also played a part in forest structure for millennia, with intensification in the nine-teenth and twentieth centuries. Early iron, salt, and glass industries exerted large demands on wood for fuel, in the form of charcoal, which was made by burning wood slowly with insufficient oxygen for complete combustion, to yield a better fuel.[55] Iron furnaces used a lot of charcoal, often depleting the forests in their vicinity. As early as the beginning of the fourteenth century, the iron industry in England suffered in some places from a lack of wood for charcoal, and by the fifteenth century the shortage of wood for charcoal limited it more than did the shortage of ores.

In Domesday England, all salt was produced by boiling seawater or brine from a few inland brine springs; the Domesday tallies included more than a hundred salt pans.[56] Five centuries later, the salt producers at Lünebourg in western Germany used two hundred thousand cubic meters of wood a year, shipped from interior forests in Mecklenbourg for evaporating water from brine.[57] Coppices supplied much of the wood for these purposes,[58] and some specific changes in forest composition can be related to these uses of forest products, usually followed by grazing. Charcoal hearths and kilns found well above the current timber line in the French Pyrenees attest to forest destruction at high elevations for making fuel, probably followed by grazing, which prevented regeneration. A piece of charcoal from a hearth has been dated to A.D. 580–895. Charcoal from *Abies alba, Pinus sylvestris,* and *P. uncinata* has been identified from many hearths, but *P. sylvestris* no longer grows in the region.[59]

Coppices were characteristic of parts of Italy too. Although *Pinus pinaster* dominates the forests of the Cerbaie Hills in Tuscany in the twentieth century, until the late eighteenth century the forests apparently consisted principally of oaks and chestnuts. (Even the Michelin Green tourist guide to Italy describes the beautiful pine and cedar forests of Tuscany.) A map of woodlands of the region in 1682 showed oak, chestnut, and some elm managed as coppice with standards, primarily for fuelwood, poles, and shipbuilding. Grazing, fires, and the invasion of a fungus *(Phytophthora cambivora)* in chestnuts appears to have favored the spread of *Pinus pinaster,* which was planted along with *Quercus cerris* and *Robinia pseudoacacia* (from North America). At first shipbuilders objected to the pine lumber but eventually they accepted it, until in the mid- to late twentieth century it formed the main lumber cut in the forests. In the 1940s, as chestnut succumbed to a blight and elms to other pests, pine spread aggressively over most of the upland despite continued planting of broad-leaved species. Its success can be understood only by considering the effects of changed competition, disease, soil erosion and depletion, and other consequences of the long history of forest use as well as possible changed climate.[60]

Although well-defined coppices provided wood for many fuel uses in the densely settled parts of the temperate zone, more casual cutting regimes often followed by fires characterized much of northeastern North America, pro-

*Table 7.2. Proportions of different trees in historical records and in a recent survey in eastern Massachusetts.*

|  | Percentages of trees | | |
|---|---|---|---|
|  | 1676–1750 | 1849–1860 | 1981 |
| *Quercus alba* | 27.3 | 14.4 | 8.9 |
| *Q. rubra* | 7.2 | 1.4 | 19.2 |
| *Q. velutina* and *Q. coccinea* | 26.3 | 3.6 | 20.8 |
| *Quercus* unspecified | 0 | 20.9 | 0 |
| Other *Quercus* species | 0.9 | 2.8 | 0 |
| *Carya* spp. | 9.4 | 3.6 | 0.8 |
| *Castanea dentata* | 3.8 | 5 | 0 |
| *Acer rubrum* | 2.8 | 13 | 16 |
| Other hardwoods | 3.7 | 20.8 | 10.1 |
| *Pinus rigida* | 0 | 8.6 | 0.2 |
| *Pinus strobus* | 0.3 | 5 | 23.1 |
| *Pinus* unspecified | 18.2 | 0.7 | 0 |
| Total number of trees in sample | 319 | 139 | 569 |

*Source:* Whitney and Davis, From primitive woodland.

ducing the sprout forests.[61] Increases of disturbance taxa like birches and decreases in those most sensitive to fire, like beech and hemlock, are evident in the pollen record as well as in forest surveys. Oak and chestnut, which sprout readily, also benefited from the frequent cutting in the eighteenth and nineteenth centuries.[62]

Some more subtle changes may be related to specific uses of certain species as well as to lack of sprouting ability. White oak was and still is especially prized as a timber tree. In at least one area, Concord, Massachusetts, comparison of historical surveys with current forest composition shows a decrease since the late seventeenth to early eighteenth centuries in white oak and replacement by the less favored, vigorous sprouters black, scarlet, and red oaks and by the earlier successional red maple and white pine (table 7.2).[63] Variations in sprouting ability may be seen geographically as well as within species. For example, maple and beech sprout vigorously in the northern parts of their ranges in North America, but not in the southern, so frequent cutting in these two regions would have different effects on the resultant forest.[64]

Heavy use of trees for other kinds of products has affected certain species. The textile industry of nineteenth-century Europe, for example, used gum arabic from west African *Acacia senegal* for textile finishing. Trees close to the Sahara Desert produced large amounts of gum after being wounded by hot winds, so they were preferentially cut. Because the trees did not regenerate after cutting, partly because of overgrazing to feed workers, this practice eliminated trees at the northern edge of their range, progressively reducing the range of the species.[65]

The bark of certain trees, especially that of oak and hemlock, was used for tanning leather; estates that were in financial exigency often sold their good timber prematurely as tanbark to get cash.[66] Before the fifteenth century the Finns, consuming between seven hundred thousand and one million trees per year, exploited the tough fibers of basswood (*Tilia vulgaris*) bark to make boat rigging, baling materials, sails, and parchment. In the late nineteenth century, they used birch and basswood bark to make more than a million pairs of sandals and boots.[67] The Netherlands cut most of their timber to try to win land from the sea by building dams, sluices, locks, windmills, and dikes, which were often faced with wooden pilings that rotted and had to be replaced continually. Their large shipbuilding industry was constructing two thousand seagoing vessels a year by 1650. By then they were buying softwoods from the Baltic countries, especially Germany and Norway, and tropical hardwoods and dyewoods from Brazil.[68]

Even at the end of the nineteenth century in western Europe much wood was used directly for fuel. In France, for example, 80 percent of the beech used about 1880 was firewood. The next most important product was, however, a new one, railroad ties, which took 5.5 percent of the volume of wood. The third is perhaps surprising, 5 percent for wooden shoes.[69] In 1882, F. B. Hough estimated that three-quarters to seven-eighths of the total wood production of the Old and New Worlds (western Europe and North America) was used as fuel and predicted the total destruction of the forests of both continents if a substitute was not found.

Other late-nineteenth-century uses of wood included matches, oil extracted from nuts, resins, cork, and pine and fir distillate used as lighting oil. Paper birch in North America was a prime source of wood for spools, shoe lasts, and pegs. In the words of the nineteenth-century French commentator J. G. Lefèbvre, "Wood also serves for use in the preparation of an article that has become wonderfully developed in recent years—viz, in the form of pulp, designed for use in the manufacture of paper."[70] This use led in the twentieth century to major deforestation as well as to the establishment of plantations to grow renewable supplies of wood for pulp.

The lumber industry both removed the standing timber, often ruthlessly, and planted monospecific stands of frequently non-native species in its place.[71] Many years of coppicing, pollarding, shredding, logging, and other repetitious use of trees in woodlands of the temperate zone preserved some tree cover but changed the species composition of the forest trees as well as the associated herbaceous species and animals, changes that outlived the disturbance regime.

## Two Sides of the Same Coin: Forest Depletion and Forest Protection

In the twentieth century, the perception of the forests of the New World and the tropics as an inexhaustible resource has given way to concern about their depletion.[72] The response to this concern has been to protect still-existing forests and to replant cut-over lands, although much deforested land is merely abandoned in the expectation that forest will regenerate. In areas like the Black Forest of Germany, plantations are so extensive and long-standing that they form the major forest vegetation. Changing management goals and methods over time have altered the results of the original decisions about reforestation, so that each reforested stand is a consequence of a sequence of events, such as changing grazing regimes, selective harvesting, and modified fire regimes.

Even in the absence of humans, forests would undergo changes; soil development, erosion, and climatic change all continue unaided by people. Natural disturbances such as windstorms, fires, and disease and pest outbreaks create a mosaic of disturbed sites in which species thrive in bright sunlight.[73] This patchwork created by microclimate, topography, and natural disturbance constitutes the basis for natural regeneration. Wherever there was extensive clearing for farmland, however, remaining forests formed scattered patches in a sea of farms. These woodlots often were found in poorly drained land along rivers and streams, on steep slopes, or on otherwise poor agricultural soils. Their sizes, shapes, age, and composition were dictated by the local system of land allocation, the availability of good land, distance to the nearest alternative sources of wood, and a variety of other factors. Even if the lots were not intensively used by the farmers, this dissection changed both the physical environment, especially in terms of wind, and such biological features as seed supply and animal populations.[74] In addition to presenting different edge effects and distributions of seed sources, the varied sizes and shapes of the remaining patches of forest increased susceptibilities to further disturbance, for example, blowdowns and insect infestations.[75]

In the early stages of forest product use, however, when it was assumed that after a forest was cut it would return of its own accord to a condition similar to that which it had experienced before logging, most stands were cut and abandoned. Describing regeneration of forest of the Ivory Coast, A. Aubréville commented in 1938 that "there is no recognizable difference between forests which are incontestably virgin since remote times, and *ancient* forests which are found in regions which were worked over by man a long time ago. They have the same species and the same associations of species."[76] He was echoed by E. A. Bourdo forty-five years later in the observation that the forest "the settlers saw" in the north-central United States was probably not very different from older secondary stands today. The same processes of secondary succession were still at work.[77] Support for these statements is sketchy. Pollen evidence suggests the contrary, even in terms of genera.

Where harvesting focuses on only one or a few species, seed sources and regeneration niches may become rare, leading to a downward spiral in the species' population size. For example, in southern Brazil, the logging of araucaria (*Araucaria brasiliana*) forests in the twentieth century had reduced them from about 20–25 million hectares to about 445,000 by 1980 (fig. 7.4). Because araucaria does not grow well in plantations, it has been replaced by exotics like loblolly pine (*Pinus taeda*) and eucalyptus (*Eucalyptus* spp.). It is anticipated that because of the lack of seed sources and incentive to encourage this formerly dominant species this forest will disappear permanently from the landscape.[78] In China, shamu (*Cunninghamia lanceolata*) has been cultivated as a timber tree for at least a thousand years. Although it is common in plantations in hilly and mountainous regions of southern China in the twentieth century, it is rare in the wild and reproduces only when protected by nurse plants, so abandoning cultivation would probably not allow this native species to recover.[79]

In many parts of the world, from the temperate forests of North America to the tropical forests of Asia and South America, cutting of trees for forest products was intended as a prelude to agriculture. Such a decision, however, was commonly made in ignorance of the potential of the land as farmland. Such was the fate of much of the forest land of the Great Lakes area of North America. Farming was successful in the southern part of this region, so logging seemed an ideal way to make a profit on the land while clearing it for settlement.[80] Where climate or soils or both were inappropriate for agriculture, however, large areas were left to regenerate naturally. The extent of the logging reduced the seeds for the timber trees, white and red pines, while fires and abortive attempts at agriculture removed advance regeneration. Aspen (*Populus* spp.) replaced the white and red pine. Balsam fir, which frequently

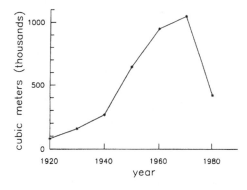

Figure 7.4. Exports of coniferous sawnwood from Brazil, 1920–80. (Data from McNeil, Deforestation, 21)

replaced aspen, was often killed by spruce budworm, leading to more fires, which favor aspen or jack pine.[81] Thus the consequences of logging in the past have been a major change in the composition of these forests, with little apparent potential for recovery of the prelogging state.

Selective logging may change forest composition, possibly for the long term. Sugar maple, a fairly common species in mixed deciduous-coniferous forests of the upper midwestern United States, increases after selective logging of the earlier successional northern white cedar (*Thuja occidentalis*) or white pine, hemlock, and yellow birch.[82] Selective disturbance thus accelerates the transition from shade-intolerant species to shade-tolerant ones, even in areas in which such progression has been aborted by frequent natural disturbances like fires and windstorms. Different cutting regimes in the Allegheny hardwood region of Pennsylvania have left a variety of stand types, varying both in structure and species composition (fig. 7.5). Even heavy sawlog cuts could produce multiaged stands, and only very complete clear-cuts of all stems greater than 1 inch (2.45 centimeters) in diameter resulted in truly even-aged stands. The effects of cutting have persisted for a century or more.[83]

Active attempts at reforestation or regeneration of forest resources also have a long history. It was the opinion of John Gifford in 1900 that "just as reckless deforestation leads to idleness, want and moral degeneration among those dependent upon the woods, so does afforestation have the opposite effect in the same if not greater proportion."[84] The ideal of a thoroughly managed landscape in which all the parts fit together into a harmonious, productive whole may be contrasted to both a wilderness, defined by a lack of order and a proliferation of useless and even potentially damaging plants and animals, and to the desolated landscape generated by overuse.

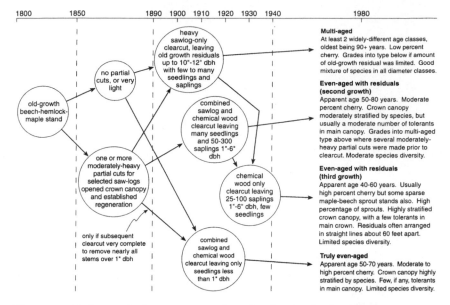

Figure 7.5. Pathways in forest regeneration after logging in the Allegheny hardwood region of Pennsylvania. (Modified from D. A. Marquis, History and origin of Allegheny hardwoods. In *Quantitative Silviculture for Hardwood Forests of the Alleghenies,* D. A. Marquis, ed. [General Technical Report NE-183, USDA Forest Service, Northeastern Forest Experiment Station, Radnor, Penn., 1994], 5–40)

The species chosen to produce this landscape have varied, however. Since the sixteenth century, German silviculturists have advocated the planting of conifers to maintain a source of wood.[85] The French, on the other hand, have preferred to plant oaks and beeches. Not only the extent of forests, but their composition now differs largely because of these practices. In Germany by the 1960s, 77 percent of the forests were conifers, compared with France's 35 percent, which included vast plantings of pines in the southern Landes and the more natural stands of fir, spruce, and larch in the mountains. The French choice of species favored coppice structure more than did the German: French forests in the 1960s were 57 percent coppice, while the German were only 5 percent. The same physical conditions and essentially similar natural forest composition resulted in very different forest structure after millennia of human use.

In the Himalayas, amid fear of depleting the forest resources in the mid–nineteenth century, the British-Indian Forest Service used fire to trans-

form mixed monsoon forest to pure stands of *Shorea robusta,* a more economically valuable tree.[86] The altering of species composition was not always
successful, however. In Brazil, planting of the native rubber tree (*Hevea
brasiliensis*) in monocultures for rubber production was unsuccessful because of a fungus that attacked these stands.[87] Research continues around
the world to discover what species will be most productive to plant, with the
intention of replacing entire communities of native plants and animals.

The value of forests other than for producing timber, game, and other forest products has long been recognized. Many nations have established forest
reserves not only to preserve the forest resource but also to protect water
supplies and the habitats of rare species, to offer opportunities for education,
and to attract tourists.[88] These efforts preferred managed to unmanaged
forests; after all, a managed forest grows faster and is more attractive than
an old, so-called overmature forest.

In the twentieth century, the United States witnessed the epic battle between preservation of natural resources, epitomized by Gifford Pinchot and
resulting in the establishment of the National Forest System, and preservation of untouched wilderness and scenic beauty, epitomized by John Muir
and Frederick Olmsted, Jr., and resulting in the establishment of the National
Park System.[89] Whereas the National Forests were in principle dedicated
to sustained production, the U.S. National Parks and many other lands
acquired for conservation were dedicated to preserving "natural" systems,
those not sullied by human disturbance. The belief was that these lands could
just be left alone and would thus, in the absence of human interference,
return to or remain in a pristine condition. The history of human impact was
irrelevant.

These sites do, however, all have a history. In some it is a history of sustained human use, such as agriculture in the Great Smoky Mountains and
changed fire frequency and grazing pressure in many western parks. Some
rare species depend on some disturbance; if the "natural" disturbance regime
has been altered, new, human-caused disturbance regimes may have to be
substituted. In English parks, for example, many species like oxlip (*Primula
elatior*) depend on coppice rotations. When coppice management is abandoned, these species disappear (fig. 7.6).[90] There is even a hypothesis that the
massive roosting sites and spectacular annual migrations of monarch butterflies (*Danaus plexippus plexippus*) in the southwestern United States are the
result of population and range expansions of this species after major deforestation following European colonization.[91] The history of human use of a
forest cannot be ignored even for management of naturalistic landscapes.

Figure 7.6. Abandoned hornbeam (*Carpinus*) coppice in southern England. (Photo by the author, spring 1985)

## Conclusion

Forests throughout the world have undergone changes owing to human impact at different times and rates. Indirect and direct effects of hunter-gatherer cultures were worldwide and most likely subtle, until the dawn of agriculture ten millennia ago. As civilizations based on agriculture grew and flourished, impacts on the forest intensified and spread, first in the Mediterranean and Near Eastern regions, then north, west, east, and south. The insatiable demand for open land, fuel, and timber led to vast deforestation in these regions over the succeeding millennia, until by the eleventh century much land in Europe and the Far East was either deforested almost completely or composed mainly of forests that were under intensive management. At that time, however, there still existed vast reaches of forests, chiefly in the Americas, Australia, and the tropics of Africa and Southeast Asia, that were subject only to the impacts of hunting, gathering, and shifting and low-intensity agriculture. The eighteenth and nineteenth centuries saw major deforestation in the Americas and Australia, and the process continues in the twentieth in remote regions of the Americas and in the tropics.[92] The motivations are in many areas not very different from those in the past, trade and other economic incentives, but the rates are greatly accelerated by use of fossil fuel energy.

From a time machine in space, as the glaciers melted, most of the northern hemisphere would have appeared covered with dense forest, which changed in temperate areas from winter-green to winter gray as deciduous species replaced conifers in response to warming climate. Large mammals and the effects of their demise would probably have been undetectable. But then bare patches appeared in spots, accompanied by increased smoke and fires. These spread from their centers, in the Near East, for example, with the dark green tree cover replaced by lighter green or brownish grasses, shrubs, and crops. The continuous forest cover would have changed to scattered patches of woodlots. This discoloration would spread slowly out until it had covered most of Europe and Asia between the evergreen zone of coniferous forest to the north and the evergreen tropics and pale deserts to the south. Then at an accelerated pace, it would jump the Atlantic Ocean and spread to temperate forest zones of North America broken already by some patches of cleared land. Regreening would appear unevenly as forests recaptured some farmland. In the twentieth century, the change from tree cover to scrub spread into the tropics, especially in Southeast Asia, and accelerated in the high mountains and remote regions of the Americas. The pace would have continued to accelerate, though tree cover had not completely disappeared. Patches spread and coalesced in some areas, while in others they were overrun by gray urban centers.

In this scenario, I have ignored the consequences of urbanization in the tropical regions of South America and many other important details of forest change. Nevertheless, the overall process of a change from more or less continuous forest cover minimally affected by human populations (though not unaffected), to a highly dissected forest cover with high human impact, to either total deforestation or urbanization or reforestation summarizes the trends that have been outlined in this chapter. No forests are unaffected; humans have been a part of the ecosystem over the past ten centuries of major climatic change, so that all forests have developed under some kind of human influence, although its intensity has varied greatly over time and space. This influence must be accounted for as an important part of any study of forest structure and dynamics. As D. Walker and Y. Chen have suggested with reference to tropical rain forests, "It might be better to begin by assuming the forest to have been subject to human selection pressure for a very long time unless positive contrary evidence is available."[93]

# Agriculture and Its Residual Effects

Was the discovery of agriculture "the worst mistake in the history of the human race" or "the greatest single step forward in the history of mankind," a step up from the "'robber' economy of savagery" that constituted the hunting, fishing, and gathering economy?[1] Most people would identify more with the positive view, which corresponds with the attitude that life before agriculture was, in the words of Thomas Hobbes, "nasty, brutish, and short." On the other hand, it seems possible that hunter-gatherers may have more, rather than less, leisure time than farmers and that the hunter-gatherer ancestors of the earliest farmers may have had a more varied diet and been healthier than their farming descendents.[2] Ecologically, the impact of farmers was orders of magnitude greater than that of hunter-gatherers, regardless of farming's direct effects on people. It accelerated introduction of non-native species and deforestation, both for land and for wood products, led to erosion and salinization, changed fire frequencies, and produced the surpluses necessary for industrialization; in ecological terms, it may have been the worst mistake in the history of the human race. It certainly had the most far-reaching consequences.

Cutting down of trees is frequently a prelude to agriculture. A farmer, however, follows this by intentionally disturbing the soil to cultivate plants that do not grow spontaneously locally. Ditches, walls, and banks are constructed to rearrange the hydrology and microtopography, and ecosystems are further altered by the unintentional importing of species and by applications of fertilizers, herbicides, and pesticides. Domesticated grazing animals preferentially remove palatable species and can damage the surface of the soil, leading to erosion. If the farmer abandons the fields, these past agricultural activities leave distinctive traces in the regenerated ecosystem.

The effects of these activities on the natural world range from the obvious—a forest cleared to make way for an agricultural field, say—to the subtle—nutrient depletion, perhaps. By actively manipulating plant and animal populations, farmers have changed habitats and species distributions in major ways, many inadvertent. Both "weed" plants and crops have evolved at an accelerated pace. Agriculture has in addition led to increased productivity, which has allowed the concentration of people in cities. These and other effects mark a major step beyond the modification of the natural world by fire and inadvertent species introductions and herald population and cultural changes that have resulted in modern industrial civilizations. The effects on ecosystems have been so far-reaching that it is often difficult to distinguish them from the effects of major changes in climate.

Because the creation of farms most often requires clearing trees from the land destined to become a farm or garden, the history of forest removal is inextricably linked to the history of agriculture. But the patterns and processes of forest use for the products of the forest itself, including those needed for farming, cause effects distinct from the decrease in forest area caused by agriculture. Agriculture potentially changes a forested landscape from a matrix of forest interrupted in places by clearings caused by windthrow or fire to a matrix of fields interrupted by small copses of trees or linear wooded features like stream banks or hedges. Even if agriculture is eventually abandoned in such a landscape, this structural change may affect the subsequent regeneration of seminatural vegetation. But the impacts of these innovations have fallen unevenly, both in time and space. Why did people farm where and when they did? What caused them to abandon agriculture in so many places?

## Preconditions for the Origins of Agriculture

As glaciers began their erratic retreat about fourteen thousand years ago, climates fluctuated throughout the world. For example, dry and wet periods alternated in the Amazonian basin of South America, and summer and winter monsoons shifted in central China.[3] Changes in ocean currents most likely caused cooling in the waters off South Africa.[4] In parts of the

Near East, oak forest became more widespread, probably in response to warmer and moister climate.[5] In northern Europe, brief (century-long) severe cold periods alternated with brief warmer episodes.[6] It is against this background of climate change at the end of the most recent glacial period that people began cultivating crops. Before then, there appears to have been no intentional cultivation of plants or domestication of animals. Many kinds of archeological and palynological evidence point to the independent development of agriculture around 10,000 B.P. in a wide geographical range, including the Middle East, north China, and Central America.[7] Because today's climate has developed at the same time as the spread of farming and other intense human activities in many parts of the world, it is very difficult to discern the composition of plant and animal communities before agriculture.

Although climatic change and concomitant changes in vegetation may have been important in the development of agriculture, other factors played a major role as well. After all, no animals besides humans evolved such a system for ensuring food supplies in the future. As climate ameliorated, at least in the view of *Homo sapiens,* human population began to increase. Some authors attribute the discovery of agriculture to an increase in population to a level that overwhelmed hunting and gathering for food, forcing people to adopt intentional cropping.[8] Others have argued that agriculture did not originate in a growing or chronic shortage of food; such a condition is not conducive to the kind of time-consuming and uncertain experimentation that must have characterized the first stages of the domestication of crops. It has also been argued that human mental and cultural development had reached a level at which experimenting with growing crops was a natural progression, which in turn afforded enough food for populations to grow.[9]

The intentional manipulation of plants and animals to ensure a predictable source of food and other useful products encompassed a wide variety of activities, among them growing annual crops, herding animals, and planting perennial trees, shrubs, and herbs. Its origins are obscure and spread out over many millennia, but of all the continents inhabited by people, only Australia escaped some kind of indigenous agriculture.

A model of the "human ecosystem" (fig. 8.1) incorporates the interrelations among the factors that led to the growth of agriculture.[10] For example, collecting (a form of subsistence) may have brought about some experimentation with growing crops on purpose (technology), which in turn stimulated population growth. As population grew, it became obvious that the way to feed the increased numbers was by expanding this system. A subtle positive feedback seems logical between population increase, which allowed some leisure time for experimentation but did not place a severe strain on food

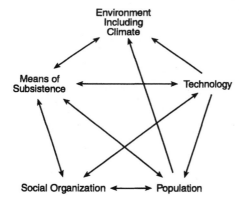

Figure 8.1. Model of the human ecosystem leading to agriculture. (Modified from Stoltman and Baerreis, The evolution of human ecosystems, fig. 16.1. Copyright 1983 by the University of Minnesota.

supplies, and a further increase in population fed by the surplus food produced by experimental cultivation. As more food became available, more people could be supported, so that inadequate food supplies would no longer hold population growth in check. As population increased further, the cultivated food would become a necessity and further population increases probable.[11] On the other hand, the environment may have also acted as a forcing factor, for example, aridification could have forced people to move to moister river valleys, where the increased population density may have stimulated experimental crop cultivation.[12]

Lack of precisely dated, accurate population figures makes it difficult to choose between these scenarios. The changes in cultivation and population were naturally so slow that they not only are imperceptible in the archeological record, but also were undetectable to those who were experiencing them; we cannot designate a specific century as the turning point between preagricultural cultures and agricultural ones, even in one locale.[13] What we can discern is a gradual shift from collecting to cultivation with continued reliance on hunting and gathering to full-blown reliance on agriculture as the major source of nutrition.

Such a chain of events took place independently in many parts of the world and under many ecological conditions; furthermore, it had divergent ecological consequences (fig. 8.2). Current climates in two of the earliest seats of domestication, the Middle East and Central America, are warm and dry, while that of the third, north China, is cool, with monsoonal rainfall.[14] The climates have changed since the origin of agriculture, but it appears that earliest agriculture was practiced neither in dense forests nor in grassland. Rather, it originated in thin woodland on slopes above rich floodplains, where native vegetation was easier to clear.[15] The tools available to prototypical agriculturalists, stone axes and fire, would have sufficed for opening

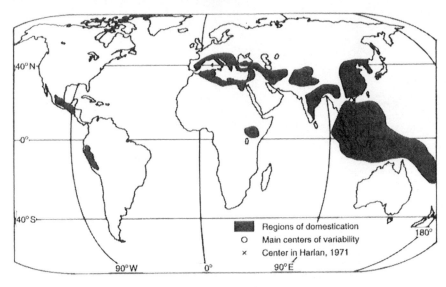

Figure 8.2. Interpretations of the centers and regions of domestication of agricultural plants. (Modified from Isaac, *Geography of Domestication*, fig. 4, and Harlan, *Agricultural origins*)

up woodland soils so that they could plant seeds, but not for breaking heavy grassland sod. From the centers of domestication, agriculture extended broadly over the succeeding millennia.

In some areas, for example, the Sahara and the Andes, finding a "center" is problematic; agriculture seems to have arisen by a slowly diffused process throughout a large region.[16] In Saharan Africa archeological and palynological evidence suggests that the beginning of agriculture corresponded with a time of increased rainfall about 6000 B.P., which led to a Mediterranean type of vegetation. Subsequently, cultivation spread south during a dryer period that started about 5000 B.P. Relating shifts in climate to the origins of agriculture in most of the rest of the world, however, is a complex task.[17]

About two thousand years ago, most of the land suitable for agriculture, except that in North America and Australia, was being cultivated or had been cultivated and abandoned (fig. 8.3). In most of the regions where there was no farming in A.D. 1, there is today at most nomadic pastoralism or ranching.[18] Within these regions, however, at a finer scale, agricultural land use was generally more dispersed and patchy two thousand years ago than it is today, so the patterns of impact have varied not only over time, but also over space within each region. There is still much to be learned about the

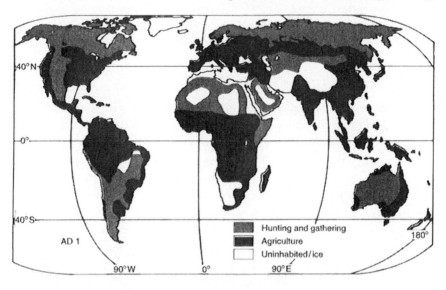

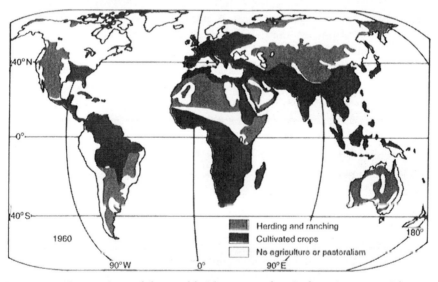

Figure 8.3. Comparison of the worldwide extent of agriculture in A.D. 1 with that in A.D. 1960. (Modified from *The Cambridge Encyclopedia of Archaeology*, A. Sherratt, ed. [Cambridge University Press, Cambridge, 1980], 64.26, reprinted with permission of Cambridge University Press, and Anonymous, *Hammond's Atlas*, 5, copyright Hammond Incorporated, Maplewood, N.J.)

spatial, environmental, and cultural conditions that led to agriculture or that, as in North America and Australia, slowed its spread.

### Processes of Domestication

In some areas, people were harvesting and processing wild grains before they domesticated crops. The Natufians in Palestine had elaborate tools such as sickles for harvesting wild grains as long ago as 13,000 B.P.[19] It is a short step from that to planting crops, but it does not seem that there would be much incentive to do so if there were already large fields of seed plants growing wild. In general, however, it appears that plant and in some cases also animal domestication occurred in cultures that were fairly sedentary, often relying on fish for their main protein source.[20] Three phases of the transition from a hunter-gatherer tradition to an agricultural one can be distinguished through the use of precisely dated remains of cultivated plants.[21] First, some species were brought under cultivation or were domesticated. This took much time and experimentation, and in the case of animals apparently had a religious rather than an economic impetus to start. Although it may seem easier to herd than to kill animals in the wild, that is partly because we visualize herding in terms of docile domestic livestock. Wild animals like cattle would have been difficult to contain and certainly to breed in captivity. Young animals, however, can be raised as pets and ceremonial animals, and this practice may have preceded breeding for such economic uses as meat, milk, hides, and wool.[22] All evidence for early domestication, except possibly for dogs, comes in conjunction with farming, either at the same time (in the case of the Middle East) or later. Where there is no history of farming, there seem to have been no domestic livestock.[23]

In some sites in the Middle East there was a gradual shift from wild progenitors of cultivated crops to such cultigens as barley, einkorn and emmer wheats, peas, lentils, flax, vetch, and chickpeas, implying a gradual domestication of the wild species. Remains of domesticated sheep, goats, pigs, and maybe cattle are found with the remains of these crops, which indicates that domestication of livestock accompanied that of plant crops. Within the general area, trade, especially in obsidian, may have diffused the ideas of cultivation.[24]

In the second phase of agricultural development, domestic crops came to furnish a significant proportion of the food supply. This step was associated with the use of more tools and more complex economic and cultural systems. The third phase, the shift to monocrop systems, took place later and in many cultures did not occur at all. In North America this shift has been recognized by a change in the carbon 13 ratio in human bones, caused by the consumption of maize, a "C-4" plant that uses carbon in a different ratio than the more widespread "C-3" plants.[25] The rates, timing, and details of these stages varied widely from region to region.

Even these simple advances imply several changes in resource use from living only by hunting, fishing, and gathering. Farmers must plan ahead, and so be more or less sedentary. On the other hand, declining productivity of a site after several years would require moving to a new site, until perhaps they observed that where animals had dropped dung, crops would remain productive for more cycles. Selection focused attention on the most useful genetic stock, eliminating some that was less desirable for its productivity.

Pollen of agricultural weeds, for example, plantains, dock (*Rumex*), and various members of the aster family, appears in pollen diagrams from many parts of the world at the same time that archeological research indicates the beginnings of agriculture (fig. 8.4).[26] The pollen record of trees and shrubs changed as well, showing decreases in the amounts of shade-tolerant forest trees like elm, followed by increases in shrubs and trees like birch that colonize open habitats. We suppose that this sequence reflects clearing and abandonment of agricultural fields, though the lengths of the cycles and the amount of land cleared apparently varied over time and space and may have been complicated by the occurrence of disease or climate change or both.[27]

Pollen analysis suggests some of the impacts this process had on the forests of southern Scandinavia and western Europe. In many areas of this region, the pollen of grasses, including cultivated ones, and such weeds as plantain and goosefoot (*Chenopodium*) appeared in pollen deposits at about 4500 B.P., as forest tree pollen became less common. Later, the crop and weed pollen disappeared, replaced by that of trees like willow (*Salix*) and hazelnut (*Corylus*). Eventually forest tree pollen recovered, though elm (*Ulmus*) and linden (*Tilia*) never regained their importance. This landnam episode (see chapter 4) was one of the first pollen sequences to be attributed to human activities rather than to climate, in recognition that humans had had major effects on vegetation at least since the beginning of agriculture.

But we may wonder whether Stone Age people really could have cleared a mature forest. To test this, J. Iversen and colleagues used flint axes to cut down trees on two acres of Danish forest, finding that they could easily cut down trees up to thirty centimeters in diameter and could girdle the larger ones so that light reached the forest floor. After letting the slash dry on the ground for a year, they were able to burn it thoroughly. They then planted primitive varieties of wheat in both the burned area and in an unburned control. On the burned plot the wheat grew luxuriously, illustrating that

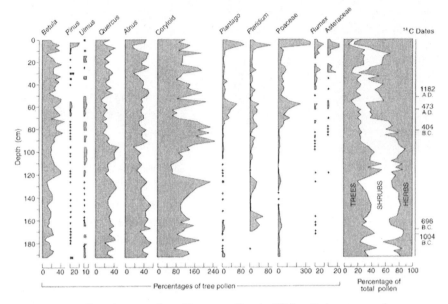

Figure 8.4. Pollen diagram from Tregaron Bog in Wales. Percentages of individual taxa are calculated based on tree pollen, so the total for all is much greater than 100 percent. Note the large amounts of weed pollen (*Plantago* and *Pteridium*) and grasses between 400 B.C. and A.D. 400. This and later episodes of agriculture are accompanied by changes in the proportions of the trees and shrubs, shown on the left. (Modified from Turner, Post-neolithic disturbance, fig. 3.)

primitive tools and fire were sufficient to clear well-established forest and grow crops.[28]

In addition to domesticating crops, agriculturally based cultures elaborated means of processing them. Wheat and other grains needed to be ground and baked, which called for the use of ovens, wood, grinding stones, and bowls. Grains such as rice that had to be boiled required pottery vessels as well as long-lasting cooking fires. The cultivation of yeast for bread, beer, and wine also required vessels for fermentation, though gourds could be used as well as pottery for this low-heat procedure.[29] Most of these processes were fueled by wood, so that even early agriculture had impacts on forests beyond the clearing of fields.

Only the most salient changes brought about by early agriculture are decipherable from the archeological and fossil records, so that the beginnings can never be fully uncovered. We are only beginning to sort out the effects of climatic change on agricultural expansion and do not understand the factors that intensified agriculture in some parts of the world, for example, Europe and Central America, while elsewhere, as in northern North America, native agriculture expanded only locally or late.

### Intensification of Agriculture

As cultivated plants and domestic animals became a major portion of the food supply in some areas, there was insufficient land to move to as crops depleted the soil, and there was less unoccupied good land. Farming moved up into the hills and down onto the floodplains. As forests that had held the soil on slopes were cut down, soil began to erode into waterways, and floods in all likelihood became more frequent. Terracing to control soil erosion and to direct water on slopes may have been devised as early as the sixth millennium B.C., just two millennia after the beginning of cultivation, both in the Old World and the New. Soil that washed down from upper levels of terraces was often carried laboriously back up to higher terraces.[30] On the other hand, control of water also meant irrigation and drainage. From South and Central America to northern Africa, southwestern Asia, and Afghanistan, millennia of irrigation had changed the hydrology and microtopography of land by A.D. 1 and sustained large populations even in regions where rainfall was minimal for nonirrigated agriculture.[31]

Other technical developments accompanied the cultivation of permanent fields and the move to less easily cultivated soils. Some preagricultural people fashioned native metals like copper and gold into ornaments. It appears, however, that only in communities characterized by sedentary agriculture, like those in the Near East and the Balkans, did people invent ways to smelt metals from their ores and to cast and alloy them to make strong, sharp tools. It is possible that the techniques used for casting pottery were adapted for metallurgical methods.[32] The shift from stone to metal tools, especially in due course to the use of iron, led to major changes in the use of land, including extensive mining of ore deposits, logging, and generally the ability to work faster and more efficiently, for example, with iron axes and plowshares.

The invention of plows brought with it changes in design, materials, and motive force. Simple scratch plows that could be pulled by a single ox worked well in the light soils of the Middle East and Mediterranean as much as five thousand years ago. From there their use diffused north into western Europe by three thousand years ago and east as far as Japan a little more than one thousand years ago.[33] Heavier moldboard plows that required more oxen and a strong plowshare could turn heavy clay soils, thereby permitting many more areas to be cultivated but also calling for more domestic livestock.[34] The use of domestic animals to help prepare the soil necessitated production of feed for them and yielded manure to keep soils fertile. With the invention of horseshoes and the horse collar, horses replaced oxen in many areas in the eleventh and twelfth centuries, allowing land to be plowed more quickly, perhaps in response to increased demand from growing urban centers.[35] These developments accompanied the intensification of agriculture. Their impact may be hinted at by the microtopography called ridge and furrow that was created by medieval plowing and that persists in fields today (see fig. 3.2).

Beyond these generalizations about the origins of agriculture lies a wide range of specific patterns. People in different places domesticated different crops, some of which eventually became widely adopted, while others fell into disuse. For example, North Americans domesticated squash (*Cucurbita pepo*), sumpweed (*Iva annua*), sunflower (*Helianthus annua*), and goosefoot (*Chenopodium berlandieri*) from 4000 to 3000 B.P., basing their food-producing economies primarily on these crops by 2200–1800 B.P.; but about 1200 B.P. they shifted their major concentration to maize, which was introduced from the south.[36] Especially in Mexico, cultures based primarily on maize agriculture developed large population densities using extensive irrigation systems, which had major effects on native vegetation.[37] In the northeastern part of the continent, however, maize cultivation never extended far beyond fertile river valleys, and cultivated plants provided only about half the total diet before the advent of European colonists.[38] Amerindians probably used less than 1 percent of the potentially arable land for shifting cultivation.[39]

Intensive land use in western Europe followed yet a different pattern. For example, drainage of coastal lands for pasture and crops began as early as the fifth to eighth centuries A.D. in the coastal marshes near the Mont-St. Michel in France.[40] At that time, monks owned most large estates, and they used the cultivation techniques of the Mediterranean, including draining of marshes and plowing only of the lighter soils of the uplands.[41] At the same time, Germanic tribes from the east, using heavier iron plows, had more influence on peasant agriculture.[42]

In England, by the time of the Norman conquest in 1066, most land that could be easily cultivated was in farms, as revealed by the surveys made for the Domesday Book and the increase of pollen of cultivated crops in sediments (see fig. 8.4).[43] Expansion in the succeeding two centuries was in more marginal areas such as the forests of the midlands, reclaimed marshes, and chalk downs. Plowed fields encroached on grazing lands.[44] The expansion was thus not even and demanded the use of different farming techniques from those that had been the custom before Norman rule. Climate at that time as inferred from pollen analysis and other techniques was also warmer than before, which would have encouraged farming at higher elevations.[45]

## Agriculture in the Age of Discovery and Beyond

The great age of exploration in the sixteenth and seventeenth centuries resulted in the colonization of many areas in which primitive agriculture still reigned. The transport of agricultural techniques, tools, and crops as well as extensive trade and commercial interests across the oceans constituted a new stage in agricultural transitions. In many areas colonists completely displaced local people, though the displacers adopted many local crops, such as maize, potatoes, and squash in the Americas. North America, a land of mainly forest with scattered temporary clearings became a land of fields and pastures within a few centuries. In parts of Argentina and Chile, grazing of domestic livestock and rabbits quickly changed the local vegetation into thorny scrublands and shrub-grasslands.[46] The pace and intensity of change of landscapes had accelerated.

The use of steam power and fossil fuel in the late nineteenth and twentieth centuries hastened this course of events by making it possible to till recalcitrant soils and to ship products farther to market. The marriage of science and technology produced so-called artificial manures, or fertilizers, and pesticides, which freed farmers from reliance on animal fertilizers and natural pest controls. The invention of barbed wire allowed more intensive use of land in areas where fencing materials were in short supply, such as the shortgrass plains and semideserts of the North American west.[47] In industrialized nations, the influence of machines and modern chemistry distanced agriculture from its roots in the natural world.

## Residual Effects on Ecosystems

Ecologists, anthropologists, and others can study today the interactions between current agricultural activities and ecosystems. But what of residual effects from past agriculture? Agricultural activities starting with the domestication of wild plant and animal species have accelerated extinctions, erosion, salinization, soil depletion, eutrophication (enrichment of water with nutrients), and landscape modification. Ecological study is carried out today against a background of these pervasive impacts.

The first extinctions were probably of the wild progenitors of many domesticated species, such as olives and squashes, partly through the domestication process and partly through the eventual cultivation of all the land on which they originally grew.[48] We know little of other taxa that grew in the areas of earliest intensive agriculture. Although current theory predicts that fewer plant species grew on fertile, productive soils than on poor ones,[49] it is to be expected that cultivation of large expanses of prime soils brought about the extinction of some plant and animal species, of which we now have no record. Agriculture was also conducive to major reductions in the ranges of many species, including wolves and mountain lions. Plowing, introduced species, and drainage as well as severe erosion have further modified ecosystems.

### EROSION

Evidence for water and wind erosion and consequent deposition in floodplains, deltas, and lakes is overwhelming. Blowing soil has buried whole cities. While some people were convinced centuries ago that cutting of forests on hillsides led to highly destructive erosion, others maintained that the real cause of erosion and deposition was climatic change. Evidence that agriculture has been the main cause of changes in sediment transport can be found through field studies of sites where erosion has taken place and those where the eroded material has been deposited. A change in sediment type occurring at the same time as an increase in indicators of agriculture seems to point to a connection (fig. 8.5).

In 1938 and 1939, W. C. Lowdermilk of the United States Department of Agriculture toured the world to study areas that had experienced soil erosion after centuries or millennia of cultivation. He hoped to learn lessons that would help the United States in its struggle to rejuvenate the devastated Dust Bowl and the gullied southeast. He visited Egypt, the Sinai peninsula, Syria, Lebanon, Cyprus, Tunisia, Algeria, Holland, England, and north China. In pondering the fate of Mesopotamia (in present-day Iraq), he concluded that siltation from the waters of the Tigris and Euphrates rivers, which had provided vital irrigation water for agriculture in this dry climate, not loss of soil fertility, had set in motion the downfall of this civilization and its lack of recovery. In most other areas, however, while continuing to blame soil erosion for the death of agriculture, he contended that it was not agriculture alone that was responsible, but rather that invading nomads neglected to maintain terraces and irrigation. This idea echoed the contention of George Perkins Marsh that there was no forest vegetation in the Sahara and Arabian deserts because of grazing by goats and camels.[50]

These observations emphasize differences between agriculturalists and pastoralists. Early agriculturalists seem to have believed in a bounteous earth that rewarded good husbandry with good crops and punished wastrels.[51] Wise

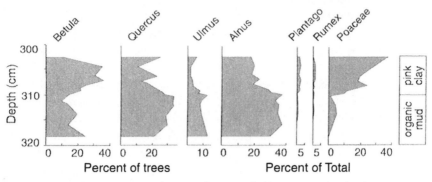

Figure 8.5. Pollen percentage diagram from Barfield Tarn, England. Changes in the importance of major taxa, especially the Poaceae, correspond with change in the lithology of the sediment. (Modified from Pennington, Vegetation history, fig. 11. Reprinted with permission of Cambridge University Press)

farmers generally treated the gods of the earth, who were usually productive females, well. Pastoralists, on the other hand, who husbanded their resources less carefully, generally had male gods who were not as closely tied to the earth as female deities.[52] One might expect pastoralists to be less concerned about preventing erosion because they were less directly dependent on local soils.

The material eroded from the hillsides itself caused major problems, not only silting in drainage ditches, but also flooding of major rivers like the Huang Ho in north China, which overflowed its banks and destroyed much land. Lowdermilk lauded the draining of the Pontine Marshes in Italy, a "former pestilential area . . . drained and rid of malaria and . . . now divided into farms." He called for an "Eleventh Commandment" requiring people to "inherit the Holy Earth as a faithful steward, conserving its resources and productivity from generation to generation."[53]

This fascinating report mirrored the ideas of its time, while foreshadowing the future. Lowdermilk was no more concerned than others of his time with the survival of "natural" ecosystems or species diversity. People should be stewards of natural resources, in particular of the productive soils that give us food. It is the responsibility of people to use these resources wisely, not to squander them. If they fail in this task, their just punishment is that "the land of the fruitful fields shall become sterile stony ground and wasting gullies, and thy descendants shall decrease and live in poverty or perish from off the face of the earth."[54] Attitudes like this may have encouraged people to hold a biased opinion of the nomads, whose life-style was so different from that of more settled farmers.

The sequence of clearing and farming of sloping land followed by erosion and the downfall of civilizations has repeated itself in many areas. The rise of Crete, which began with the cultivation of olive trees about 6000 years ago, culminated about 4500–3500 years ago in prosperous trade in olive oil and timber, especially with Egypt. But as olive trees replaced the native forest over larger areas, soil erosion grew unabated, contributing to the demise of trade and prosperity.[55] A similar pattern is visible in much of the Mediterranean, which is subject to heavy winter rains. These cumulative changes resulted in shrub vegetation and rock outcrops that bear little similarity to the forests and native communities that predated extensive cultivation.

Although most of us are familiar with these examples of erosion in the Old World, especially of the arid and semiarid seats of Egyptian, Greek, and Roman civilizations, erosion and deposition have characterized other parts of the world as well. For example, in Papua-New Guinea remains of extensive drainage systems date at their earliest from about 9000 B.P. These oldest drainage ditches are partly filled with light-gray silt, attributed to erosion from upland areas.[56] In northeastern North America, the sudden advent of European agriculture led to an increase in sediment accumulation in many lakes, especially where there was intensive agriculture. An increase of 1.6 to 1.4 times the pre-European rate is undoubtedly a conservative estimate; an increase of up to 6 times has been noted even for the Chesapeake Bay.[57] The scattered, shifting agriculture of the pre-European farmers in the region left no clear signal in the sediment load, consistent with the lack of signal in the pollen record.

Worldwide, agriculture has continued to cause severe erosion. According to a United Nations soil survey (1992), nine million hectares worldwide can no longer support vegetation because of erosion, while an additional one billion hectares need reclamation. The report attributes 35 percent of the erosion to livestock overgrazing and 30 percent to deforestation, while blaming other poor agricultural practices for 28 percent of the world's damaged soil.[58] The major attribution of erosion to grazing confirms Lowdermilk's observations of more than a half-century ago. Such soil degradation permanently alters the conditions for regeneration of natural vegetation, probably making the recovery of dense vegetation and some endemic species impossible.

CHANGING LANDSCAPE PATTERNS

Even where agriculture has not occasioned irreversible soil damage, it has had many other persistent effects on the landscape. In natural communities, transitions are usually gradual, following latitude, elevation, soil conditions, and other environmental variables. Except where there are sharp contacts, such as outcrops of serpentine rock, one community grades into the next. Communities usually interdigitate as well, producing uneven transitions. When an agricultural field is maintained next to a mature forest, however, there is a sharp boundary between the field and the surrounding forest. In time, a transition zone develops as more light-tolerant species are able to survive in the borders of the forest.[59]

Trees and shrubs, both planted and spontaneous, that characterize the boundaries between fields have unique attributes and affect reforestation of abandoned fields.[60] They often include such non-native taxa as black locust (*Robinia pseudoacacia*) north of its native range in northeastern North America, which can affect secondary succession when the fields are abandoned. Hedges differ in distribution and structure, however, depending on the kind of farming, which in turn is influenced by soil conditions as well as by demand for products and land distribution systems. For example, where soils developed from clay meet those developed from limestone in Wiltshire, England, there is an abrupt transition from small, irregular pastures separated by well-developed hedges with trees to large, rectilinear plowed fields separated by low hedges or none at all (fig. 8.6).[61] The ecology of these hedges is affected not only by their structure but also by the variations in the soils in which they occur and by different farming practices on these soils.

The pattern of land clearance is a further aspect of agriculture that alters ecological conditions differentially. For example, Dutch settlers along the upper Hudson River in New York State cleared the rich floodplain soils in the early eighteenth century. Later in the century, farmers from New England settled the upland areas, so that by 1777, scattered ten- to fifteen-acre clearings dotted the upland forest, some with standing dead, girdled trees, while the floodplain was more uniformly cleared.[62] Within less than half a century after the American Revolution, most of the remaining forest had fallen to the axe, leaving only scattered woodlots (fig. 8.7). Farms were diversified, with a variety of crops and livestock, but especially sheep. By the early twentieth century, the decline of demand for wool and other forces led to farm abandonment or retrenchment, which allowed forest once again to gain a foothold. The recovering forest, however, differed from the one that had preceded agricultural clearing. Some species, such as pitch pine (*Pinus rigida*), did not recolonize the agricultural lands. In areas of poor drainage and along hedgerows, American elm (*Ulmus americana*) flourished, only to be killed by an introduced disease.[63] The numbers of whitetail deer (*Odocoileus virginianus*) soared, as cover and forage proliferated, keeping tree reproduction low.[64] Many fields of 1900, separated by rows of trees or shrubs, had become a vast shrubland by 1990, with scattered trees. Herbaceous species typical of mature forests were scarce in this shrubland (only two were counted, less than 10 percent of the total), although abandoned fields that lay adjacent to old woodlots had far more (seven species, 30 percent of the total). Birds

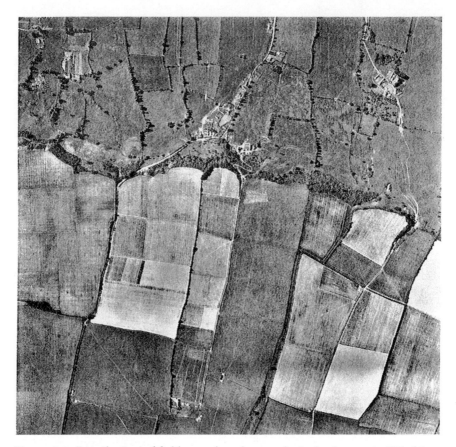

Figure 8.6. Distribution of field types based on geological substrate in Wiltshire, England. Large, mostly plowed fields in the lower part of the photograph are on limestone while the smaller irregular pastures in the top third of the photograph are on clay. Note the hedge trees along boundaries separating the pastures. (Photo courtesy of Hunting Aerofilms Ltd.)

characteristic of shrublands and forests began to replace those of open fields.[65] The history of farming and the pattern of abandonment continued to exert an influence on forest regrowth long after agricultural use had waned.

### PATTERNS OF ABANDONMENT AND REGENERATION

Why farms were abandoned is important in interpreting processes of revegetation; abandonment because of soil exhaustion or climatic change would produce different patterns of regeneration from abandonment for political or technological reasons. Assessing the causes is difficult, however,

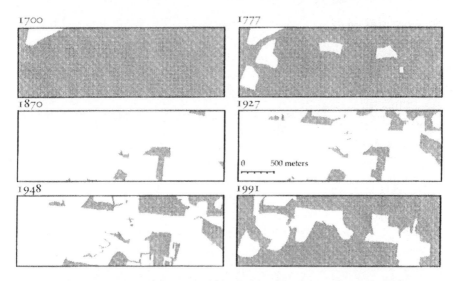

Figure 8.7. Distribution of forest and cleared land in the northern part of Saratoga National Historical Park, Saratoga County, New York. In general the eastern half of the area is underlain by clays and the west by till. The unforested area inferred for 1700 is a fairly steep shale outcrop with very shallow soil. Cleared areas in 1770 are taken from a map prepared for the British military in 1777, which showed cleared farms and other open areas. Data for 1870 are from woodlots reported in the 1870 or 1880 United States agricultural census data for individual farms. Data for land shown cleared for 1927, 1948, and 1991 come from aerial photographs. The pattern of forest and cleared land in 1991 resulted from management of the park to reconstruct the vegetation in 1777. Earlier changes reflect regional vegetational patterns. (All maps were digitized using the GIS GRASS at the Rutgers University Remote Sensing Laboratory, by the author)

because they commonly leave little direct evidence. For example, in the Mayan areas of Guatemala, the accumulation of products of erosion, especially phosphorus and inorganic matter, in lake sediments suggests soil depletion, but there is no clear correlation between this and population collapse about four hundred years ago.[66]

Recurring cycles of clearing, abandonment, and reforestation typified many areas of Western Europe in the Middle Ages. It is easy to blame abandonment on soil exhaustion, yet in many cases even as early as the ninth century A.D. the causes were more apt to be cultural. The advent of the moldboard plow and the horse harness in France, which permitted heavier soils to be cultivated, made the more easily cultivated but less productive soils less appealing. The founders of planned new towns and settlements between A.D. 1000 and 1320 offered attractive inducements to lure peasants from older settled areas to the new settlements.[67] In addition, often because of poor planning, some areas not appropriate for farms were settled, only to be abandoned later. By the twentieth century many of these, including the upper Marne plateau of Langres, which is now largely in timber, and the marshlands of the Artois, retained little direct evidence of former clearance.[68] Discerning details of just where villages stood and where fields were, even in recent centuries, is problematic.

A medieval record from several counties in England affords some fascinating detail of patterns of land use then. Tax data called the Nonarum Inquisitiones assessed the value of corn, wool, and lambs in 1342 and required an explanation of differences from data reported in 1291. Many parishes reported declines in these crops, caused by abandonment of arable land. Because parishes were well defined, it is possible to assess the relative amount of abandonment on different kinds of soils and to summarize the data by county. In Bedfordshire, light upland soils were abandoned rather than the heavier clay soils of the valleys, whereas in Cambridgeshire, the upland clays were abandoned rather than chalk or lowland fens. In Buckinghamshire there was no correlation between abandonment and soil type.[69] In other words, one cannot assume that physical attributes of the land were the major determinants of which fields were abandoned.

Widespread abandoned agricultural land has provided an ideal habitat for the dispersal of intentionally introduced species. In many areas of the eastern United States, for example, such non-native shrubs as multiflora rose (*Rosa multiflora*), autumn olive (*Elaeagnus umbellata*), and a variety of bush honeysuckles (*Lonicera* spp.) abound in some, but not all, abandoned agricultural fields. In the 1950s and 1960s the United States Department of Agriculture encouraged farmers to plant these species to offer cover for wildlife in "odd areas" on farms and to serve as living fences (fig. 8.8).[70] Where they have become naturalized, their patterns of spread are often related to whether they originated from plantings in fields, from hedgerows, or from shrub borders planted next to woodlots, as well as to the means of dispersal.[71] Discovering the route of introduction may help investigators understand the current dynamics of distribution.

The soil conservation service also recommended planting native vines such as bittersweet (*Celastrus scandens*) as wildlife habitat. Today, the non-native Japanese bittersweet (*C. orbiculatus*) commonly blankets trees on forest edges and in gaps or young stands, while the native species has become rare. Gardening books and plant nursery catalogues recommended Japanese bittersweet as a ground cover and "porch vine."[72] Because Japanese bittersweet

Figure 8.8. The benefits to a farm of non-native hedgerows and wildlife: (*top*) A healthy farm includes pheasants and domesticated plants even in noncultivated areas. All of these, as well as non-native earthworms and honeybees, interact in a positive way. (*bottom*) Multiflora rose hedge increases beneficial insects (non-native ladybird beetles), nesting birds, and beneficial small animals and decreases harmful insects and small animals. (W. L. Anderson, Making land produce useful wildlife, Farmers' Bulletin #2035, U.S. Department of Agriculture, 1960)

was easy to obtain, planting of it rather than of the native species presumably contributed to its spread and crowding out of the *C. scandens.*

Abandonment of agriculture, especially traditional agriculture, may lead to less diverse communities. From alpine meadows of Switzerland and grassy mountain balds of North America's Great Smoky Mountains to northern Israel, abandoning of traditional agriculture in the name of conservation allows brush to encroach on rich herbaceous plant communities, extirpating the very species for which these sites were preserved.[73] The same is true of the eastern edge of the prairie region of North America. Substituting more intensive agricultural methods for traditional hay meadows decreases the diversity of these very diverse communities.[74] In all of these cases, characteristic species appear to have been maintained at least in part by a specific agricultural use of the land, usually grazing or mowing or both, and to have been lost when this use ceased. How these species were maintained and in what densities before agriculture are unknown, but there is a good chance that they frequented disturbed sites and may well have been rarer in the distant, preagricultural past than in more recent times.[75] Elsewhere, agricultural alterations of the land and climate change may have irreversibly altered the conditions under which previous, possibly diverse, communities thrived.

Testing the similarity of regenerated ecosystems to those that predated agricultural modifications is hampered by the lack of fossils of many species and of written documentation. Pollen analysis from a wide range of areas, from the tropics of South America and Equatorial Africa to temperate grasslands and forests, does, however, record a consistent increase in species characteristic of disturbance after the appearance of pollen of agricultural species.[76] In lowland Ecuadorian Amazonia, the first appearance of maize pollen in lake sediment is followed by a major increase in the disturbance indicator *Cecropia* and the disappearance of pollen of the Bombaceae, characteristic of mature forests.[77] With later agricultural abandonment the amount of *Cecropia* decreased to only slightly more than before agriculture, as mature forest recovered. Studies conducted in Uganda suggest that forests cleared for agriculture some three thousand years ago originally resembled present-day *Prunus* zone forests, characterized by *Alchornea hirtella.* As these trees were cut, understory shrubs became more common or flowered more profusely, while trees of the kind found on less fertile upper slopes, including *Olea* and *Podocarpus,* were uncut. Species characteristic of greater disturbance such as *Dodonaea* and *Justicia* proliferated, probably where soil erosion was especially severe. Further intensification and expansion of agriculture led to loss of the *Olea* and *Podocarpus* forests as well.[78]

Irrigation has fostered salinization and waterlogging in many regions, obviously greatly altering the potential of the system to return to its pre-agricultural state. Twentieth-century use of pesticides has changed the balance of invertebrates and birds as well as other organisms in ways that are not well understood. Drainage and subsequent fires in highly organic soils have changed the potential for abandoned wetlands to regenerate.[79] Introduced, non-native species replace native ones in disturbed areas and even invade more mature ecosystems. Agricultural uses of fire have altered soils and changed ignition sources for adjacent unmanaged communities, while recent improvements in fire control have decreased the area a naturally ignited fire may burn.

Nowhere has there been a simple sequence beginning with cutting of forest trees to make a farm, farming for a few years, abandonment of the farm, followed finally by growth on the abandoned land of a forest like the original one. Shifting patterns of land use, changing agricultural practices, and other cultural transformations have led to a constant, though often very slow, shifting mosaic of agricultural land. The potentialities of the land and the climate have limited the kind of agriculture that could be practiced, but cultural developments have determined the details of agricultural systems within these limits. Climate has changed over the period during which agriculture has been a common activity of human populations, but so has agricultural technology. Historical studies of the patterns of change in a region should yield more evidence of the cultural framework in which agriculture grew, and thus what some of the climatic as well as cultural factors may be in determining the vegetation. The lingering effects both of former agriculture and of the process and timing of changes may influence the ecology of both abandoned agricultural lands and those in which light grazing or mowing persist. We cannot assume that just because active management has ceased, some preexisting "natural" community will reassert itself. Even the eliminating of non-native species or the reintroducing of native and natural processes cannot erase the effects of centuries or even millennia of human impact.

# 9

## *Historical Patterns of Human Settlement and Their Ecological Consequences*

As agricultural productivity allowed an ever larger proportion of the population to become more distant from intimate reliance on the natural world, patterns of human settlements and laws became ever more divorced from natural landscape features. Political boundaries bisected such biomes as the tropical rain forest of southeast Asia, the temperate deciduous forest of western Europe, and the grassland of North America. Each of these great complexes of vegetation extends across several nations or states, each with its own history of land divisions, legal systems, and population agglomerations. Although the lands within one biome, for example, grassland or deciduous forest, may have similar susceptibility to fire and invasion by exotic species, similar suitability for exploitation of natural resources and agriculture, the expression of these characteristics differed after millennia or even centuries of domination by different political systems.

Extensive trade allowed those living in one part of the world to appropriate the natural resources of another. The Judaeo-Christian tradition in the West emphasized that the deity had put natural resources on the earth for the (wise) use and perfection by humanity. If people were not making appropriate use of their land, they did not deserve it, so that those who would put it to better use were fully justified in acquiring it, by force if needed.

In North America, William Cronon has argued that the major factor distinguishing land use by the Amerindians from use by European settlers was a shift from treating land as territory that did not belong to any one person or group of persons and was not thus an item of trade to treating it as a commodity.[1] Furthermore, although native Americans derived their livelihood from the land, they apparently did not perceive that they had any responsibility to change it. Right to land was not tied to some manipulative use of it. This difference in the conception of the human relation to the environment allowed the European settlers both to justify appropriating native territory and to alter it for their own use. Unchanged land represented unfinished business.

### Dividing up the Land

In much of the world political and subsistence systems have developed over millennia, and the reasons for current patterns of land subdivision are well buried in the past. In more recently disrupted regions, such as the Americas and Australia, human invaders have imposed new systems of land allocations with little or no regard for entrenched indigenous customs. The consequences are dramatic and often bizarre, bearing little or no relation to topography. In South Australia, for example, it has been suggested that the "survey was the first, the greatest, and probably the most enduring imprint of man on the land."[2] In tracing changes in the landscape brought about by land subdivision one adds a temporal dimension to landscape analysis that may help explain anomalous characteristics in the resulting ecosystems.

These patterns are discernible, however, without reference to history; the history of the patterns adds depth to the analysis. First, it can tell us something of the age of the pattern, which affects the amount of influence the pattern exerts on current ecosystem structure and processes. Second, the rationale for locating divisions between properties affects their relation to soil quality and other features of the land that influence ecosystems. Why, for example, were woodlots left where they were? Why were some farms abandoned earlier than others?

Colonial land allocation in the state of New Jersey illustrates the diversity of systems and some possible impacts on the resulting ecosystems. In 1664 Charles II of England granted land including what is now New Jersey and New York to James, Duke of York. James then split what was to become New Jersey into two parts, East and West Jersey. The dividing lines separating these grants were straight lines drawn on rather poorly surveyed maps (fig. 9.1). This led to major problems in settling both the boundary between New Jersey and New York and that between East and West Jersey.

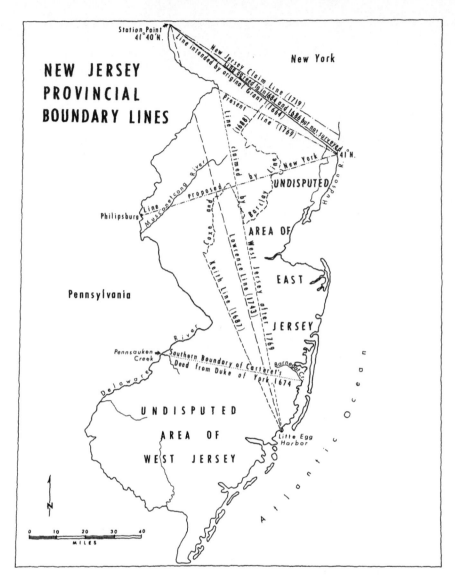

Figure 9.1. Provincial boundaries of New Jersey. Lack of agreement on these lines contributed to very irregular patterns of settlement. (Figure from P. O. Wacker, *Land and People*, courtesy of P. O. Wacker and Rutgers University Press)

In addition, magnetite in the bedrock of northern New Jersey led to erroneous compass readings in lines surveyed on the ground.[3] Boundary disputes resulted in uncertain titles to land. Absentee landownership also led to illegal clearing and timber cutting where the demand for land was low and there was a high cost to getting a clear title.[4] Some eighteenth-century visitors observed that because of the uncertainty of titles only lawyers could get rich.[5] All of this contributed to haphazard settlement patterns and poor stewardship of the land.

Actual settlement patterns under this confused regulatory nonsystem were quite varied. Proprietors encouraged settlers to establish villages by advertising with detailed plans of settlements consisting of carefully arranged house and farm plots, with no vacant land left between them. Such farmlots often had woodlots in distant swamps or mountains.[6] Farther from these aggregations of surveyed lots, however, the arrangement of farms was much more casual. Farmers cleared and fenced fertile, level land with or without legal title, leaving no woodlots on the better soils. Later surveys found these lots to be highly irregular and to exclude poorer, steep areas, which were used for common grazing and as sources of wood.[7] The relation of such varied systems of settlement and clearing to the location of remnant patches of uncultivated land and to patterns of field abandonment has not yet been elucidated. Both pressure on woodlots for grazing, timber, charcoal, and other products and soil or microclimatic characteristics varied with time and system of settlement and have continued to vary. These factors have influenced both the composition and structure of remnant and reforested stands.

The actual patterns of the subdivisions were thus related to natural features and to culture alike. In areas of North America originally settled by the French, for example, parts of Quebec, northern Wisconsin, and New Orleans, very long, thin lots prevailed (fig. 9.2).[8] Areas settled by the Dutch were also divided into long lots, but these were very large and usually subdivided into smaller farms. The lines dividing these lots, surveyed in the eighteenth century, still formed farm boundaries in the twentieth century (fig. 9.3).

The best studied of the survey systems is the United States General Land Office Survey (GLOS), which made a neat checkerboard of even highly dissected land surfaces (fig. 9.4). After the American Revolution, states ceded most of their extensive, unsettled western territory to the new federal government. The federal Ordinance of 1785 imposed a "rational," rectilinear surveying system on this land in keeping with the philosophy of the Enlightenment. The basic unit was the section, of 640 acres, or 1 square mile, which was often divided into four quarters for sale. This system transformed an unknown wilderness into a rational, familiar geometry, ignoring water rights, location

Figure 9.2. Farm lots along Bayou Lafourche, Assumption Parish, Louisiana. Intensive agriculture characterizes this area. Levees along the river cause drainage to be away from the river; forest is concentrated in the wet area in the lower part of the photograph away from the river, rather than as small woodlots. (Marschner, *Land Use,* plate 137)

of woodlots, topography, or any other natural features of the land.[9] Land was treated even more clearly as a commodity to be traded than it had been under colonial rule.

The major concern of the government was to get the land into private hands. The system it adopted led to widespread speculation in land, in which individuals gained title to large numbers of sections that they hoped to sell for a profit. Squatters often cleared land, acquiring title only later, so that there was a disjunction between the surveys and actual settlement.[10] Nevertheless, as these areas developed, farmsteads were usually to be found near the boundaries of the sections or quarters, with often a woodlot left in the center of the quarter. The locations of the woodlots were frequently determined not by the quality of the soil or steepness of the terrain, but by the distance from the farmstead. In other areas, woodlots were left near home-

Figure 9.3. Farm landscape, Saratoga County, New York, 1948. Arrows indicate the locations of boundaries between large lots as surveyed in 1750. Farm divisions within the large lots can also be traced back to the eighteenth century. (Photo courtesy of Saratoga National Historical Park)

steads or planted there to afford convenient access to wood products and to serve as a windbreak. It is often difficult to determine today the history of such woodlots, whether they are relics of the preclearance forest or second growth on cleared land. In either case, farmers would have relied heavily on them for wood products, but their composition and dynamics may differ. Planting, for example, for maple sugar production, affected the structure of many woodlots. In the prairie, where there were few trees, the entire parcel

Figure 9.4. Crop fields on the Columbia Plateau, Spokane County, Washington. The topography here is rugged, with an average gradient of about eighty meters per kilometer. Note the straight field lines crossing ridges and valleys. (Marschner, *Land Use*, plate 93)

was usually cultivated, creating heavy pressure on the few trees that grew along watercourses.

In each township, the government reserved four half-section lots for public purposes, such as to support a school or minister. None was reserved to preserve native natural resources. Many of these were unused, but they contributed to a highly dispersed arrangement of undeveloped lands in many townships.[11] Other lots were granted to railroads as sources of timber for fuel and ties, and these too had a different history from the nearby lots in private hands. In 1882, F. B. Hough noted the inappropriateness of a rectilinear survey in mountainous lands, where lots could well contain land on both sides of a mountain range, so that one side of the ridge would be cleared and used but the other not cleared because of the difficulty of access.[12]

This subdivision of the land on paper, with no attention to the nature of the landscape, thus led to a pattern of settlement that bore little resemblance to what would develop by the natural spread of cultivation across the land. Speculation and the allocation of reserved lots also contributed to a patchwork of development that bore little relation to the quality of the resources. Straight

Figure 9.5. Farming landscape in Clinton County, central Indiana. The irregular pattern of light and darkish patches caused by soil variability in this slightly rolling region contrasts with the straight-sided dark woodlot patches, field edges, and roads. (Marschner, *Land Use*, plate 42)

lines separating sections have often also separated different kinds of land management, such as row cropping and pasture, and also separate cultivated from uncultivated land.[13] If these fields are later abandoned, their future will depend on which side of the line they were on as well as on natural features, especially if soil erosion was more severe on one side than the other. Straight boundary lines that have become buried in forest regrowth are clues to these past uses and to probable lingering effects, both of the past uses and of the consequences of straight as compared with uneven, more natural boundaries.[14]

In a level landscape subject to the GLOS, almost all woodlots are square or rectangular and fairly evenly distributed across the landscape (fig. 9.5). Hedgerows are rare. In a level area first settled in the 1730s, on the other

Figure 9.6. Farming landscape in Addison County, Vermont, on the east shore of Lake Champlain. Field edges are generally straight, though the angles are irregular. Many woodlots have very irregular boundaries and are concentrated along watercourses. (Marschner, *Land Use,* plate 4)

hand, forest patches tend to have curved edges and few right angles (fig. 9.6). Hedgerows connect many of the woodlots. Although field and woodland patterns resulting from such surveys or other methods of land allocation often remain visible for centuries, their impact on natural resources is more subtle. Narrow, elongated fields with hedgerows may lead to better seed dispersal than more isodiametric fields, for example, or sinuous woodland edges may provide more habitat for edge-dwelling species than straight edges, thereby increasing the chance of these species moving from edge to interior of the forest.[15]

### Regulating Land Use

In addition to laying out the land and encouraging or directing settlement, governments have exerted control by regulating what people could do with their land. The motives for regulation have varied, from maximizing profit to caring about depletion of the resources. The first consideration in regulating land use, whether by custom or by law, is the perception of whether there is an adequate supply of land for subsistence. Those who practice shifting agriculture know that when one piece of land becomes overworked, they can move to another. They do not need to try to maintain the fertility of the soil because there is enough that they can use somewhere else. From the tropics of Central America to the chilly, temperate climates of western Europe and China, wherever population has become too dense to supply enough suitable land, so that farmers must remain in one place, they have learned to maintain soil fertility for generations. Terracing to hold soil and water, irrigating to distribute water, fertilizing with organic wastes from humans and domestic livestock, and other techniques have maintained agriculture in one place in a wide variety of habitats. Planting of trees, coppicing, and other methods of growing wood have conserved the supply of wood. Governments have regulated many of these practices, even though knowledge of the best methods has often been lacking, and even when the knowledge was there, enforcement has been problematic. Until the twentieth century, these regulations were usually designed to protect a specific resource, such as wood for the navy or agricultural productivity, not rare species or habitats. Endangered species have often been recognized as endangered only when their populations have fallen too low to survive, for example, the heath hen in North America.

The French ordinance for waters and forests of 1669 ensured that there were big trees available for the navy by regulating the rotation of cutting and maintenance of standards in coppices in the royal forests.[16] This ordinance embodied most of the characteristics of laws governing the use of natural resources and thus affecting the structure of the ecosystems. It had a direct relation to the resource that was needed, for example, leave standards in the coppices, and cut them at certain intervals, and it affected only lands that had not yet been alienated from public control. The kind of forest this system created could be understood only by reference to the kind of management that was imposed on it, most likely a variation on that stipulated by the regulations.

In England, one of the most controversial sets of regulations affecting large parcels of land was that of the enclosure movement in the eighteenth and nineteenth centuries. The aim of these enclosures was to ensure that land was used in the way best suited to its soil and climate.[17] Villages had been enclosing common lands at least since the fifteenth century, but the pace accelerated in the eighteenth, especially in the Midlands, where enclosure was by

Act of Parliament. Large open fields were divided into smaller fields with varying uses. The effects on the landscape were dramatic, as hedgerows and stone walls separating individual holdings broke up wide open spaces. Whereas the earlier enclosures had produced small fields with irregular boundaries, the later ones, reflecting the ideals of the U.S. GLOS, produced larger fields with straight lines drawn by surveyors. This proliferation of hedges, stone walls, and smaller fields, with arable land being converted to pasture and vice versa depending on the conditions, changed the potential for vegetational development in unplanted pastures at the same time that it created new, unanticipated habitats in the hedges and walls as a result of government actions.[18] In the late twentieth century, heavy machinery and other incentives have led to grubbing out of old hedges, again changing the landscape pattern. The ages of these hedges, and thus their effects on the landscape patterns, thus vary greatly depending on the local history of enclosure by regulation or local practice.

Differences across national borders highlight the importance of historic land use and regulation on current vegetation patterns. Until the 1890s, the border between Mexico and the United States was unfenced. The photographs of monuments erected as part of the survey of the border in the 1890s document a landscape denuded by overgrazing and drought, although the presence of construction crews erecting the monuments in all likelihood exaggerated the devastation of the vegetation as seen in the photographs.[19] In 1976 a survey of vegetation on both sides of the border at twelve boundary monuments found 28 percent more grass cover on the U.S. side than the Mexican and 30 percent less barren ground. Contrasting government regulations since the 1890s, superimposed on the conditions when the border was fenced, account for these differences. The United States Forest Service regulates grazing on the U.S. side by limiting stocking. In Mexico, however, the emphasis is on maximum stocking, so that overgrazing continues to be more serious. Tree density in 1976 was the same on both sides of the line, however, in part because of the lack of demand on the wood products on the U.S. side and prohibition of cutting green wood on the Mexican side. To understand the dynamics of change in these ranges, one has to look at the history and to realize that the changes noted since the establishment of the monuments, which is the earliest date for which there is good evidence of the ground cover, relate to already greatly modified vegetation.

In some places the role of past government policies on vegetation has been much more subtle. In central New Jersey, an area of more than one hundred hectares of Virginia pine (*Pinus virginiana*) constitutes the northernmost stand of this species in the state, many kilometers disjunct from another Virginia pine stand. Ecologists began noticing it in the 1970s when an interstate highway cut through its edge. Because of its irregular shape and the varied sizes of the trees, they assumed that it was a naturally occurring stand on highly eroded red shale. On searching the history of the stand, however, I found that it had been planted in the 1930s as part of the government's efforts to revegetate badly eroded soils. The trees had thrived and even begun seeding into recently abandoned fields along with local red cedar. This potential range extension of the species in this state can be understood only with reference to the combination of farming, erosion, and government policy. Analysis of the current conditions under which it is growing would not explain its presence there.

## Conflict: Wars

Land hunger and government policies have also contributed to armed conflicts. The internecine struggles that have characterized the history of most parts of the world have had major repercussions not just on the people involved in the conflicts but on the environment as a whole. Battles require weapons and the amassing of people and beasts of burden. Weapons, until recently, were fashioned mainly from products of the forest. Siege apparatus required tremendous amounts of wood, including huge old trees used as battering rams. During the Thirty Years War in the early seventeenth century, Germany used its forests as a source of wood for canon carriages, fortifications, and campfires, for tannins needed to prepare leather for the cavalry, and later for rebuilding burned buildings. Forests that regenerated after this onslaught included more alders, birches, and aspens than the more long-lived oaks and beeches. Depopulation from the depredations of the war meant that there were fewer animals grazing in the forests and fewer loggers cutting down trees than before. The impetus for experimental forestry and silviculture languished, as the attention of the government turned elsewhere.[20] Forests regenerated under very different conditions than they had before the war, when major efforts had been made to plant and manage new plantations.

Winter encampments of armies required large supplies of wood for building lodgings and for cooking and heating fires. Near Morristown, New Jersey, George Washington's troops encamped one winter during the Revolutionary War in a site chosen in part because of the large supply of wood in uncut forests. The troops leveled these forests, some of which were turned into farmland after the war, but most of which were left to regenerate because the soil was poor and rocky and the slopes steep. It is likely that they differ from other forests in the region that were clear-cut repeatedly for charcoal and often burned.

During the First World War, the last of the Tabor oak forest of Israel was cut to supply fuel for the railroad and wood for defense works.[21] In Switzerland during the Second World War, much remaining forest land was converted to farm fields to ensure self-sufficiency.[22] In other words, war led to the cutting of wood on land that might not have otherwise been cleared. The ecology of these recently cleared lands may differ from that of lands cleared longer ago in part because of the varying lengths of time since they have been cleared and diverse postclearing management.

In preparing for battle, soldiers have also cut trees to ensure a clear line of fire and a view of approaching enemies. They have constructed fortifications from wood and dirt and dug trenches. Subsequent agriculture and plowing flattened many of these, but some have persisted for centuries, or at least decades, where the forest was not cut and plowed. Foxholes dug during the First World War persist in the forest of Fontainebleau near Paris, and banks can be seen at many Revolutionary War sites in the United States. These alter drainage locally and are microsites for a variety of species to survive. They are sometimes nearly indistinguishable from other human constructions.

Bombs and chemicals have wreaked havoc during the last century. Plants characteristic of bombed-out sites have even received common names commemorating that habitat preference, for example blitz-weed, a common name for *Epilobium angustifolium* in England. Tanks moving across the land in western France in the Second World War cut across ancient hedgerows, breaking the continuity of habitat.[23] Defoliation of large areas of tropical forests in Indochina during the Vietnam War left saturated soils and disturbed areas that have been colonized by such grasses as *Imperata*. Forests have been slow to recover.[24]

Battles and wars have had indirect effects too. Depopulation is one, both because of local destruction and because of the death of men in war. The effects of such depopulation are evident in the vegetational history of England after the Norman Conquest, in France after the Hundred Years War in the fourteenth and fifteenth centuries, and in Germany after the Thirty Years War. Depopulation led to regeneration of seminatural vegetation on land that was abandoned, often on the poorer quality soils, and to less intensive use of much of the remaining land, including forests. Recovery resulted in changed patterns of use, related to the knowledge, organization, and technology that characterized the postwar period. Reallocation of land after war can also change land use patterns. After the American Civil War of the mid–nineteenth century, the rate of forest clearing in the southeastern United

States decreased because now landowners, deprived of slave labor, had to pay laborers for their work.[25] In three counties in north-central North Carolina, for example, the amount of woodland in farms increased after 1870.[26] The proliferation of small tenant farms may also have led to increased soil erosion, as farmers concentrated on the labor intensive but soil destructive crop, tobacco.[27] Analysis of these historical data, however, is complicated by the aftermath of the war, as data collected by the Census Bureau in the decades immediately after the war were not easily comparable to those before because of changes in tenancy and ownership of land.

Wars produce records of the ground cover that are often much more detailed than any records made for civilian purposes. To fight a battle effectively, it is necessary to know the terrain, including topography and the distribution of forests and fields. Maps of the eastern United States made for the Revolutionary and Civil wars furnish much information about the ground cover of at least local areas at these times. Even the infamous march of Gen. William T. Sherman through Georgia, during which he visited tremendous destruction on people, crops, and buildings, has bequeathed us a series of remarkably accurate maps of the terrain and land cover, and these can be compared with more recent maps to study the changes through time.[28] Aerial photography was developed for use in warfare, to spy out the disposition of the enemy. The photographs that have been unclassified are excellent records of past land cover, starting in some cases as early as the 1920s. A photomosaic from 1927 of vertical aerial photographs of the site of the revolutionary battle of Saratoga, in New York State, is one of these early photographs that documents the locations of woodlots, field boundaries, and other features of the ground cover. Wars have left documents in addition to scars.

## Trade and Transportation

A more benign contact between groups of people is trade, which has been going on for millennia, and the concomitant patterns of transportation routes. Transportation obviously moves species around, some on purpose and some by mistake, but it also affects the patterns of settlement, and by itself affects the environment. Earliest transport was obviously by foot and was consequently slow and somewhat limited in distance. The impact on distribution of species and on the land used in the transport routes was probably slight. As beasts of burden came into use, one could go longer distances with more goods. The beasts required forage along the way, and the people who were with them needed food.[29] The impact could be very large: in the early nineteenth century a route from Tennessee through North Carolina into South Carolina may have carried as many as 150,000 hogs a season, requiring up to 84,000 bushels of corn.[30] This transportation pattern affected the systems of clearing and agriculture in this region, perhaps more than other market or land use factors.

Much earlier, preindustrial transportation focused on waterways. Water carried people and products with much less effort than did animals, though the routes were more constrained. Population concentrations grew up near navigable waterways, and transportation allowed areas to specialize in different produce.[31] Preindustrial Holland and Flanders, for example, could specialize in dairying and market gardening, while they imported grain and timber from the Baltic states.[32] Transportation thus allowed greater concentration of people in Holland than the land could support and increased the impact of people on the forests of the Baltic states. Local population was not a good predictor of the kinds of influences on the land.

The arduousness of inland transport led to a pattern of land use that might be described as "nibbling around the edges." This was especially true in areas that supplied timber rather than served as sites of agricultural settlement. In regions as diverse as Tanganyika and northern New York State, timber cutting near navigation routes left the interior more or less forested, while the edges were deforested (fig. 9.7).[33] Study of the structure of remaining forests may reveal an imprint of this extensive edge effect.

The demand for better shipping, however, led to changes in transportation and access to more land. Early-nineteenth-century canal building in North America opened up much of the interior to the logging and mining industries as well as generally opening the region to settlement. Canals also provided a way for fish to migrate beyond their natural boundaries, with the result that alewives and sea lamprey appeared in the lower Great Lakes, for example. The warmer, siltier water caused by erosion following logging further improved conditions for these fish, which flourished in their new habitats.[34] The advent of steam engines made shipping even more attractive by lowering the prices substantially. The cost of shipping three hundred liters of wheat from southern Russia to Britain decreased from 8s6d in 1872 to 2s3d in 1900, while the cost of shipping wool from Australia to Britain was halved between 1873 and 1896 because of the increased speed of steamboats over sailboats. As railroads replaced ox- and horse-drawn wagons, overland shipping became cheaper too. In Argentina rail freight was one-twelfth that of oxcart, and in New South Wales, Australia, rail shipment of butter cost one-ninth that of wagon shipment.[35] These reduced prices for shipping were strong

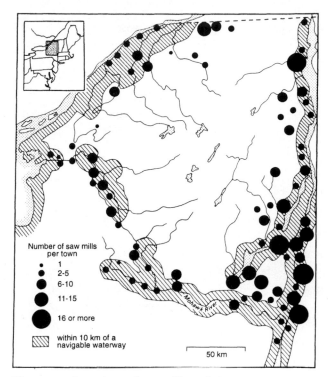

Figure 9.7. Locations of sawmills and river
transport corridors in the Adirondack Mountain
region of northern New York, ca. 1810. (From
M. Williams, *Americans and Their Forests*. Original figure courtesy of M. Williams, reprinted
with permission of Cambridge University Press)

incentives for further specialization and stimulated specialized and intensive
uses of land and water.

The interplay between improved transportation and demand for transportation is complex. In most cases the demand exists before the improved
transportation, as in the cases of canals and railroads.[36] However, once the
improved transport is in place or a new system of transportation such as
steam engines is developed, they can be used to increase demand as well as
to satisfy existing demand. The opening of new roads into hitherto inacces-
sible places by governments who want to be able to tap the resources of the
interior of their countries brings development into areas where the demand

did not exist prior to the building of the road.[37] Decisions are made on the basis of potential profit, either to the individual entrepreneur or to the government, not necessarily on the suitability of the resources to sustain development. Unlike older systems of transportation, which connected already established settlements, newer systems of transport have often opened up previously unreachable areas far from any settlement, thus accelerating the process of change in these remote areas. Much deforestation in the Brazilian Amazon basin, for example, follows transport routes.[38] Analysis of the rates and effects of deforestation should include changes in proximity of the forests to these routes as well as their cumulative effects on fragmenting the forest.

Railroads required so much wood for the replacement of ties that special congressional committees were set up in the early part of the twentieth century in the United States to consider how to deal with the upcoming shortage of wood for ties.[39] At about twenty-nine hundred ties per mile (1.6 kilometers), each with an average life of about six years, the almost eighty thousand miles of rail lines in the United States in 1877 would have required more than sixty million hardwood ties every year, each tie being about eight to ten feet (2.5 to 3 meters) long and six by seven or eight inches (15 by 18 or 23 centimeters) in profile. The railroads also consumed wood to produce steam, though as early as the 1870s many had switched to coal, using wood only as kindling.[40] Many railroad companies started tree plantations in order to stop erosion on steep road cuts, provide wood, and serve as an example of tree-planting to ameliorate the climate of the open, treeless prairies. Between 1872 and 1873 the Saint Paul and Pacific Railroad planted or sowed about 4 million trees along their rights-of-way in Minnesota, mainly willows, ash, box-elder, oaks, and maples. The effort flagged, however, in the ensuing years, when the company changed hands and embarked on a "short-sighted scheme of economy."[41] In Nebraska, the Burlington and Missouri Railroad Company planted 460,000 trees on 186 acres (75 hectares) along 28½ miles (45 kilometers). These included honey-locust, soft maple, box-elder, sugar maple, white elm, laurel-leaved willow, cottonwoods, and "evergreens." Norway spruce was not a success, but the others grew rapidly, offering evidence that trees could survive the conditions on the windswept prairies.[42] The progeny of these trees continues to affect the species composition of these and nearby woodlots.

Railroads and other roadways exerted a direct effect on the lands through which they passed. Sparks from locomotives were a major source of forest and grassland fires in the late nineteenth and early twentieth centuries, and many other fires started from careless use of fire by travelers.[43] Roads and railroads used land: as early as 1875, some 2.6 percent of the land area in Massachusetts was devoted to roads and railroads.[44] Trees planted along roads for beautification and shade—sugar maples and elms in the East—served as seed sources for forest regeneration when the adjacent farms were abandoned. When roads were moved, the line of old, open-grown trees often continued to mark the location of the old roadbed.

All forms of transport allowed species to be distributed farther than they could have gone on their own. Canals served as distribution corridors for aquatic and other wetland plants in addition to fish and other aquatic animals.[45] Railroads carried grain contaminated with weeds like *Bromus tectorum*.[46] Automobiles carried weed seeds, insect egg cases, and other stowaways in their tires and other parts.

The ability of humans to move quickly and travel far by means of transportation other than their own legs has developed through the years as an additional means of transport for many species as well as a way of intensifying and extending the impact of humans on the land. To trace the rate of spread of organisms one must incorporate the variable rates at which they have been carried by people and their intrinsic potential rates of spread.

### Urban Agglomeration

A logical consequence of convenient transportation and trade has been the concentration of people in towns and cities. The independent development of urban areas has been as widespread as the rise of agriculture and has a long history, from the great cities of Asia Minor, Mesopotamia, and Babylonia by 1500 B.C. to those of the Maya of Guatemala by 250 B.C.[47] Such cities required production and transport of food surpluses and building materials together with other products. They included permanent shelters, storage pits and bins, refuse heaps, burial mounds, and roads. Refuse from the city fertilized local fields, increasing their productivity.[48] To some living in cities the natural world became divorced from their everyday subsistence, coloring their perception of it. They also have had the time to develop intellectual curiosity about the world about them and to ponder the workings of the natural world.

Plants and animals that grew in the cities, for example, chickens and garden flowers, were either purposely grown there for the use or pleasure of the residents or were those that flourish in close proximity to people or frequent disturbance, such as rats and weeds. Early cities like Mesopotamia included land for gardens, both for beauty and for food.[49] The residents continued to have some direct contact with the land and growing things. In fact, city and

other home gardens usually have very high productivity because of the concentrated effort spent on them.[50] Cities provide unique, new habitats and
growing conditions, as lots fertilized by human wastes are abandoned and
the wide diversity of species that have been introduced by trade meet and
mingle in revegetating vacant land.

A comparative study of the plant communities in gardens and uncultivated
areas reveals some of the complexity of the ecology of these kinds of urban
sites. The city of Bariloche in northwestern Patagonia was built a century ago
in an area without a history of permanent agriculture. Weeds found there are
mainly exotics. On the other hand, the weeds found in gardens in Mexico
City, which has a very long history in a previously agricultural region, are
mainly native species. Around Mexico City, there was a substantial decrease
in the number of noncultivated species per hectare along a gradient from suburbs to downtown, while the opposite pattern, an increase with nearness to
a city, characterized Hertfordshire, England. The reasons for these differences are related to the different kinds of plants that have been cultivated in
the different regions as well as to the effect of intensive agriculture on species
diversity in England.[51] General patterns of species diversity in an urbanizing
area can be derived only by studying the species diversity within the historical and cultural context.

In addition to gardens and vacant lots, urban/suburban areas usually
include woodlots or forest areas that have been preserved for various reasons, usually for recreation. A study of nine forest stands along a gradient
from New York City to Connecticut indicated several consequences for forests
of proximity to cities. The stands were all at least sixty years old, occurred
on similar geological substrates, and were dominated by species of oaks.
Although the forests were smaller the closer they were to the city, rates of litter decomposition and potential nitrogen mineralization were also higher
close to the city, most likely because of the inputs of nitrogen from the urban
environment.[52] The history of these sites, in addition to their similar minimum age, might reveal further explanations for differences. Forests closer to
the city were more apt to have had a longer influence of urban disturbances
and to have been free of farm uses like pasturing or collecting wood longer
than those located farther into the countryside. Introductions of exotic
species, as described in the studies of species diversity along rural-urban gradients in Mexico and England, may differ among them. Fire frequencies may
have differed as well. Incorporating such historical factors into these studies
will explain otherwise enigmatic relations along this gradient.

The attitudes of city and suburban residents affect plant and animal communities under their influence. Many city-dwellers have an "illusion of self-

sufficiency and independence [from nonhuman nature] and of the possibility of physical continuity without conscious renewal."[53] The forces of nature, storms and droughts, for example, are not as clearly relevant to life as they are for farmers. The current western attitude that one is in control of nature developed in medieval Europe as cities grew, beginning in the twelfth century.[54] Where food supplies and other necessities of life arrive abundantly into a city, city-dwellers are little aware of their dependence on the produce of the land. As the city spreads from its small original perimeter, it engulfs fertile agricultural soils, with little regard for the loss of potential productivity. Many cities themselves are located on rich alluvial soil, while others expand over drained marshland. The nonbuilt landscape becomes part of the "other," to be enjoyed but treated as a kind of museum, frozen in time and kept available for leisure activities. Land is perhaps treated less as a commodity than as a museum, neither for active use nor for change. If someone moves from the city to the surrounding land that is focused on the city, it is to enjoy this more natural environment, with little regard for the consequences of more people doing the same thing. The buying of property for its amenity value, dissociated from more natural bonds with its productivity, leads to suburbanization, as more people leave the city, facilitated by increasing convenience of transportation.[55]

As long as their life is not tied to the land in some direct way, there is no natural check on overpopulating the land. Suburban dwellers want to see "nature" but are unaware that by building close to it, they are destroying the very thing that attracted them in the first place. These activities lead to different kinds of treatment of the land than does active exploitation, with varying results for ecosystems. For example, in 1988, fully 75 percent of the owners of parcels of forest in rural northern New Jersey were white-collar workers or retirees. Forty-five percent came from communities with populations greater than fifteen thousand, while only about 20 percent came from a rural background. In 1972, about 12 percent had harvested trees from their forest land, but by 1988, almost all had cut timber. The change was related both to international events such as an oil embargo, which led people to cut firewood, and to local infestation of a non-native insect, the gypsy moth, which led to salvage cutting.[56] This example is illustrative of the volatility of land use decisions by those who do not depend on the land for survival. They can change their use quickly to respond to different conditions, leading to a very discontinuous history of impacts on the land over time. And this history continues right up to the present day.

Distinct effects of cities on the surrounding, nonbuilt land are also important. City-dwellers place a large demand on water supplies, both for human use and for manufacturing. When a city is near the sea, such demand often leads to pumping the water table down so that saltwater intrusion contaminates wells. Wastes produced by people and industry pollute surface water, so cities must turn to water supplies far from their locales. Roman cities built large aqueducts to carry water from the countryside or mountains to the cities, the cities of southern Germany rely on water from Lake Constance, and the cities of coastal California rely on water from the distant Sierra Nevada Mountains.

Reliance on distant water supplies may lead to efforts to protect the water supplies as well as to a depletion of the supply in the source areas. Water supplies for the cities of Newark, New Jersey, and New York City come from large forested areas west and north of the cities. Protection of the watersheds of these water supplies is in the interest of the city-dwellers, even if those who live in the vicinity of the watersheds may prefer other uses for the land. The mayor of the city of Newark has claimed that governmental action is appropriate to "save the best stands of intact forest in the New York metropolitan area before they are lost to sprawl."[57] The goal of management of these forests is preservation of a good water supply, which has led to management that concentrates on preventing erosion, rather than on use of the timber resources, thus obscuring and reversing a long history of logging for industrial purposes, such as production of charcoal and tanbark.

The impact of cities on local aquatic systems is not so benign. Studies of urban effects on aquatic environments suggest major impacts, impacts that may not be obvious. In Guatemala, a decline of the pollen of forest taxa relative to herbaceous taxa about 3000 B.P. signals Mayan agriculture and urbanization. A combination of archeological and stratigraphic studies suggests that there was major erosion of local riparian soils at the same time, leading to transport of soil as well as phosphorous probably derived from both human waste and the surface of the soil.[58] The phosphorous-loading of the lakes did not lead to their eutrophication, possibly because the amount of suspended silt in the water decreased light penetration sufficiently to prevent overproductivity.[59] At the same time, the accumulation rate of inorganic material in the sediment increased as much as ten times. Similar kinds of impacts have occurred in many parts of the world, leaving a legacy of lakes that are greatly modified by past human activities.[60]

Marshes have long been regarded as entirely negative environments, to be drained and filled or used as dumping grounds for wastes produced by cities. Few coastal marshes near cities do not have drainage canals, built for a variety of purposes, from mosquito control to pasture or hay production to feed the large herds of cattle needed to supply milk and other products to the nearby cities. On the Nile delta large lagoons were drained and converted to agriculture as early as Hellenistic times, especially in the vicinity of the city of Alexandria, and by the first millennium B.C. the large number of river channels in the delta had been reduced to two by excavation, changing the shape of the coast.[61] The large concentrations of people in cities create new demands on the land, which require more intensification of use. Even when the use changes, these former activities leave distinctive marks on the ecosystems they have disturbed.

Many human imprints on the land have been only indirectly influenced by nonhuman resources. The causes of these imprints have changed over time, but the effects of the past are still being felt in the present, even where the reasons for the activities or even the activities themselves have been forgotten. If these are ignored in studies of current landscapes and ecosystems, they may introduce confounding factors that complicate results. On the other hand, they provide in themselves exciting areas for research into the factors that control processes and patterns of ecosystems.

# PART III

*Case Studies: Contributions of Historical Ecology to the Understanding of Ecological Issues*

In the past few chapters, I have illustrated how alterations of the environment by human activities in the past have contributed to the complexity of ecosystems in the present. To some this may smack too much of "natural history," curious but not really consequential in the uncovering of underlying patterns and forces governing natural systems. I would like to turn now to a consideration of how historical ecology can play an important role specifically in addressing some of the conceptual issues that drive and have driven ecological research. I shall also discuss the importance of these studies to confronting and defining practical issues

The examples I discuss relate to three issues: human modifications of lake ecosystems; decrease in biodiversity caused by species extinctions; and the concept of sustainability of the biosphere. I treat the critical role of historical ecology in understanding and potentially resolving each of these issues.

# 10

## Human Modifications of Lake Ecosystems

Lakes have long been favored as dwelling sites that offer many advantages: fresh water and food, transportation, and recreation. In addition, lakes are aesthetically appealing because they are perceived as beautiful, restful, refreshing. In recent years, however, we have become aware of many threats to these qualities. Some lakes have acquired too many undesirable fish or have lost desirable ones. Some have become greatly enriched, turning into stews of blue-green algae (cyanobacteria), while others have become almost sterile as their waters acidified beyond the tolerances of most organisms.

Lakes have also long fascinated ecologists. In 1887, Stephen Forbes introduced the concept of the lake as a "microcosm," the forerunner of the more general concept of an ecosystem. His extensive studies of populations of organisms in Illinois lakes had convinced him that it was impossible to "[study] any form out of relation to other forms,"[1] in other words, one had to consider the entire system in order to comprehend the parts. It was not possible to reason directly from individual parts to the whole. He concluded that natural selection acting on the community of organisms in a lake led to stability, in which prey and preyed upon had arrived at a mutually advantageous condition. He found lakes to be the best examples of this principle because, he contended, they were independent of the surrounding land and "had remained substantially unchanged from a remote geological period."[2]

By the 1930s and 1940s the emphasis in lake studies had shifted to the changing productivity of the organisms living in lakes over time. According to these theories, lakes start life in an unproductive (oligotrophic) condition, then develop to a productive (eutrophic) one. They remain in this fairly stable eutrophic state of quasi-climax for a long time, but the lake basin eventually fills with sediment, becoming a marsh and finally dry land.[3]

Because for much of the year lake water is thermally stratified, the process of the sedimentary filling of the lake basin reduces the volume of the deep water (hypolimnion), so that less oxygen is available to animals living there. In addition, as organisms die and sink to the bottom of the lake, their decay uses up the oxygen in the deeper parts of the lake. Phosphorus is more soluble in anoxic (that is, deficient in oxygen) water, so as decay and the respiration of deepwater animals exhaust the oxygen supply, the recycling of phosphorus from the sediments accelerates. The lake can thus be enriched in this limiting nutrient even with no increased input from the land.[4]

Focus on the lake itself, what goes on in the water, and perhaps on the sediments is only one part of understanding the dynamics of lake ecosystems. Lakes are intimately connected with their surroundings, which serve as sources of water, dissolved and suspended nutrients, and organisms. To understand the dynamic structure of a lake ecosystem we must consider the flux of materials, most of which originate outside the lake basin, by integrating "(1) the lake, (2) the surrounding terrestrial ecosystems, and (3) the human society of the paralimnion [a more inclusive term than *watershed*]."[5]

Absent a historical perspective, the present condition of a lake may be mistakenly seen as a long-standing equilibrium, as Forbes saw it. Recent changes would be interpreted as aberrations from this well-established, pristine equilibrium. On the other hand, a simplistic historical approach may view recent changes merely as the culmination of natural eutrophication or acidification. It turns out that the dynamics are much more complex than either of these scenarios allows for. For example, in some lakes productivity may have fluctuated greatly in the past, with no apparent human cause; in others, conditions appear to have been fairly stable until human intervention. A change in the past decade or so is superimposed on preexisting conditions and thus reflects them as well as more recent perturbations.

The combined characteristics of lakes make them ideal subjects for testing of ecological theories. Their sediments include an accumulated, sequential record of past conditions, and the sources and sinks of these sediments are reasonably well defined. Superimposed on these advantages is the great variety of changing human impacts over time. Logging, agriculture, industrial uses, urbanization, fish introductions, and various direct and indirect inputs of pollutants have affected lakes over the last few millennia. Whether such changes have pushed the lake ecosystem into an unstable, unpredictable state, Deevey's "realm of dragons" about which we can predict little or nothing, is a major question, one that has both theoretical and practical implications.[6] I shall discuss several examples of lake studies that, by placing current conditions in a historical context, have led to greater understanding of lake system dynamics as well as to a determination of the causes of recent changes. The historical perspective emphasizes the importance of incorporating a broader view of lake ecosystems in order to anticipate future conditions.

## Sediment Chemistry in Brief

Organisms in a lake respond to changes in the lake water chemistry, leaving a record, albeit tantalizingly abstruse, in the sediment. Some inorganic components of the sediment are part of the allochthonous (that is, coming from outside the boundaries of the lake proper)[7] fraction. They enter the lake water and settle to the bottom without undergoing much change. In many lakes, the chemistry of this fraction of the sediment, especially in terms of sodium, potassium, and magnesium, closely reflects the chemistry of the soils of the watershed rather than fluxes of materials within the water column.[8]

Complex processes drive the recycling and deposition of other minerals in the sediment. Iron and manganese form insoluble hydroxides in well-oxygenated water and precipitate to the bottom, picking up phosphorus from the water column as they sink. If the hypolimnion is aerobic, they remain precipitated and are incorporated into the sediment. Deeper in the sediment, however, reducing conditions occur, so the minerals are redissolved and may be redistributed to the surface, where they again precipitate. This leads to a misleading higher concentration in the surface sediment, which reflects sediment processes rather than changes in the chemistry of the water column. However, if the surface sediment becomes anoxic, the minerals are returned to the water, thus depleting the sediment. As they become mixed throughout the lake in spring or fall overturn they again reach oxygenated water and again precipitate, or, if the lake has a rapid flushing rate, they may be washed out of the lake. These models of mineral deposition and redissolution from the sediment indicate the complexity of interpreting the chemistry of lake water from the chemistry of the sediment.[9]

In one empirical study, the amount of phosphorus in the sediment closely reflected the inputs to the lake, over a period of about fifty years, suggesting that when inputs are large enough they override these theoretical restrictions. Lake Washington in the United States Pacific Northwest experienced a dramatic decline in water quality between 1941 and 1963 as the city of Seattle and its suburbs built sewage treatment plants that discharged directly into the lake. The lake responded to the increase in phosphorus by increased productivity, especially in the form of the cyanobacterium *Oscillatoria rubescens*. Between 1963 and 1968 the sewage effluent was progressively diverted from the lake, resulting by 1969 in a return of the phosphorus level to what it had been in 1933. The mean amount of chlorophyll in the summer, used to measure the productivity of algae in the lake, had also returned to approximately the level of 1933.[10] A direct relation between the measured input of phosphorus to the sediment and the amount of phosphorus coming into the lake[11] suggests that increases in that element in sediment may be a good indicator of its input into a lake, and that this indicator corresponded with the period of eutrophication. Long-term studies correlating changes in phosphorus and phytoplankton were necessary to make this connection.

## Sedimentary Studies of Cultural Eutrophication

A lake choked with cyanobacteria and characterized by murky, smelly water and frequent fish kills offends our sensibilities. This is especially true when we remember the lake as having been in the past fairly clear and non-odoriferous with good fishing and swimming. Certainly in this state the water is not fit for drinking; even with extensive treatment to render it safe it still smells of decaying algae and fish. As a practical matter, we would like to know how this problem came about and whether it is reversible. Some answers are obvious; sewage input can often be correlated with the onset of the unpleasant conditions, and altering of this input may reverse them, as it did in Lake Washington.

Cultural eutrophication is, however, often more subtle, both in cause and in potential cure. When we do not directly know the causes of eutrophication, we can try to relate the sedimentary record to historical documentation of changes in the watershed, and possibly airshed, to give us clues to the causes of changes in the recent past.

### LINSLEY POND

Linsley Pond, Connecticut, is one of the classic studies in lake history. Limnological studies in the 1940s inferred from the sedimentary record that this originally oligotrophic pond had gone through a period of fairly rapid

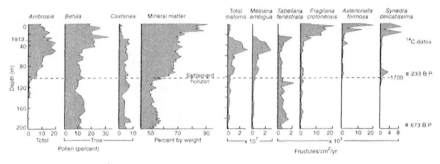

Figure 10.1. Diagram of pollen, diatoms, and mineral content in sediment core from Linsley Pond, Connecticut. (Modified from Brugam, Human disturbance, figs. 2, 6)

eutrophication several thousand years ago, to a moderately eutrophic state that had persisted until the advent of European settlers on its shores.[12] These inferences were based on changes found in taxa preserved in sediments and current distribution of these taxa in lakes of different trophic levels as well as on chemical analyses of the sediments. Rapid cultural eutrophication was apparent beginning about 1960.

Further analysis of pollen, diatoms, zooplankton, midge larvae, and chemistry in the most recent nine hundred years of sediment, precisely dated with lead 210 and carbon 14, correlated well with documented changes in land use around the lake (fig. 10.1).[13] A major increase in a group of diatoms associated with eutrophic lakes, including *Fragilaria crotonensis, Asterionella formosa,* and *Synedra delicatissima,* and a decline in *Melosira ambigua* signaled eutrophication beginning about 1915 (see fig. 4.2). Descriptions of the lake in the 1940s included these three major diatoms as well as blooms of cyanobacteria.

A peak in the dinoflagellate *Staurastrum gracile,* larvae of two midges that reflect eutrophic conditions, and especially high peaks of *A. formosa* and *F. crotonensis* occurred after 1960. This date marks a rapid suburbanization in the watershed after a developer bought land there. The houses built at that time all had individual septic fields.

The sedimentary record also revealed other, unexpected changes after local land clearance. Increased mineral matter and a decrease in the diatom *Tabellaria fenestrata* in the century following local settlement probably reflected the earliest clearing and pasturing of cattle in the watershed. A tripling of the influx of diatoms to the sediment, mostly *Melosira ambigua,* reflected the nineteenth-century construction of a dairy farm and house on the shore of the pond and operation of a gristmill and an axe factory. That is, the species that declined most precipitously in response to recent enrichment of the water had become much more common, at least in the sedimentary record, after local clearance.

In the midwestern United States, *M. ambigua* is common in lakes with a pH between 6.4 and 7.15,[14] so it may have responded at first to some change in pH caused by disturbance of soils in the watershed, although one species cannot by itself be used to infer past pH. Two of the currently dominant diatom taxa, *A. formosa* and *S. delicatissima,* were not present in the prehistoric period but appeared only at low levels above the cultural horizon. Thus the changes that characterize this century occurred against a background of disequilibrium that postdated agricultural activities in the area.

### EUTROPHICATION AT OTHER TIMES AND PLACES

Some of the historical patterns of eutrophication in Linsley Pond are typical of lakes from a wide geographical range. Across North America, from Vermont to Washington, major increases in *A. formosa* and *F. crotonensis* in sediments appear to indicate increasing cultural eutrophication.[15] This new phytoplankton community resembles no prior community recorded in the sediment. Current taxa are predominantly planktonic, suggesting that conditions at the sediment surface, deep in the lake, are no longer appropriate for growth of benthic species. Increased cyanobacteria and algae, including diatoms, caused by enrichment of the water in limiting nutrients most likely intercept light in the water column. As these algae decompose, they deplete the oxygen in the hypolimnion, leading to a profusion of midges. The major input of mineral matter to the sediment may also have clouded the water and had deleterious effects on preexisting fauna and flora on the lake bottom.

In Harvey's Lake, Vermont, peaks in the pigments oscillaxanthin, characteristic of the cyanobacterium *Oscillatoria,* and myxoxanthophyll, characteristic of cyanobacteria in general, occurred in sediment after 1945, along with other elements of eutrophication (fig. 10.2). Analysis of these pigments can provide more direct evidence of cyanobacterial blooms than the indirect evidence derived from diatoms. (Cyanobacteria do not have fossilizable structures.) Although the amount of chlorophyll in the sediment corresponds with overall production in the water column, an alternation between oscil-

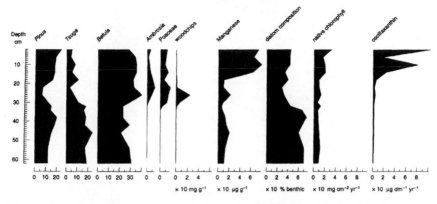

Figure 10.2. Composite diagram of sedimentary features at Harvey's Lake, Vermont. Woodchips, including hemlock and white pine, are waste from a sawmill. Decomposition of finer sawmill waste depleted the oxygen in the deep water. (Data for this figure courtesy of D. R. Engstrom)

laxanthin and amounts of the diatom *Stephanodiscus hantzchii* implies some form of interspecific competition during this period of high production.[16]

In other parts of the world as well, human activities, especially farming and urbanization, have had similar impacts on past lake development. In Blelham Tarn, England, *Asterionella formosa* and *Fragilaria crotonensis* have become important in the recent sediment, when drainage and nutrient input from sewage enriched the water, as they have in North American lakes. *Stephanodiscus astraea,* which indicated eutrophication in Lake Sallie, Minnesota,[17] also increased in the recent sediment of Blelham Tarn. These increases, along with other changes such as a decrease in several species of *Cyclotella,* appear to have begun in the mid to late nineteenth century, when the input streams to the tarn were channeled. The building of more houses in the watershed, houses with piped water, apparently exacerbated eutrophication. Construction of a sewage treatment plant also increased nutrient input by channeling treated sewage, detergents, and fertilizers to the lake.[18]

An increase in *Asterionella formosa* and a decrease in species of *Cyclotella* in two connected lakes, Llyn Padern and Llyn Peris in Wales, about 2500 B.P. corresponded with a decrease in tree pollen and an increase in grass, suggesting local deforestation and agriculture (fig. 10.3). Earlier there also appears to have been a reciprocal relation between the amounts of several

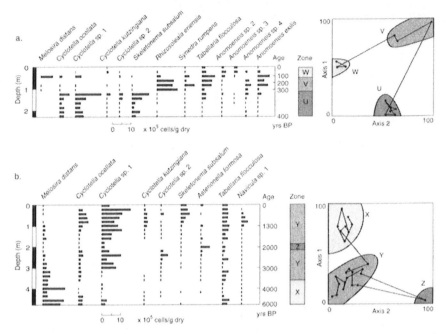

Figure 10.3. Concentration of major diatom species in two cores from Wales and reciprocal averaging of diatom data by sample: (*a*) Llyn Peris; (*b*) Llyn Padern. (Modified from Elner and Happey-Wood, Paleoecology of two Welsh lakes, figs. 10, 11, 16, 17)

species of *Cyclotella* and grass. The *Cyclotella* species recovered higher in the core, whereas *Asterionella* almost disappeared until the top sample, at which point the *Cyclotella* again decreased. In Llyn Peris, local mining caused a major shift in the dominant diatoms from *Cyclotella* to *Rhizosolenia eriensis, Synedra rumpens,* and *Tabellaria flocculosa.*[19] These changes appear to have been abrupt. The changes in phytoplankton, caused most likely by human impact on the watershed, have not been reversed.

Pollen analysis conducted to reconstruct the vegetation of the watershed suggests abrupt vegetational changes around Llyn Padern, where the effects of clearing are used to explain changes in the diatoms. Vegetational changes near Llyn Peris, where mining caused the alterations in phytoplankton, were less distinct. Further research is needed to understand, however, why the timing of changes in the diatoms, that is, the lake itself, and the vegetation do not coincide for Llyn Padern. Such disjunctions emphasize that the relation between responses by the biota of a lake and vegetational change in a watershed is a complex one, involving adjustments over long periods of time.

Regardless of the complications, major changes in the concentration of minerals in the sediment often accompany biotic indicators of anoxia. Changes in the lake biota thus reflect changes in the flux of materials as well as energy in the lake ecosystem. The mineral content of sediments has furnished evidence of human impact on lakes in many parts of the world. The sediments of Lake Miragoane in Haiti, for example, record an increase in eroded minerals that corresponds with an increase in pollen of weeds tentatively attributed to the arrival of European settlers who cleared forests for farms. A brief recovery, with less mineral input and less weedy pollen, corresponds with the period after Haiti gained independence from France and large plantations were abandoned. The watershed around the lake in 1927, for example, was a "jungle," which included "lignum vitae and logwood trees." A renewed input of eroded material near the surface of the sediment comes from the more recent deforestation of the surrounding steep slopes.[20]

Sediment and lake water chemistry have also recorded recovery from human disturbance in the more distant past. In the Petén lowlands of Guatemala, the collapse of the Maya population and reforestation of the watersheds decreased phosphorus loading and sediment input, though not to pre-Maya levels. Lake productivity, which had been depressed during maximum population, apparently recovered.[21] Cultural eutrophication has involved not only increased productivity, but also unprecedented shifts in species assemblages in many lakes. In most cases, both the rates and the patterns of changes are unique to human interactions with the lake systems.

## Acidification

Recent acidification of lakes has resulted in the loss of fisheries and major shifts in the biota in many lakes. According to some, "On a global scale, acidification is one of the major issues of freshwater pollution."[22] Although the causes of eutrophication are usually more or less apparent—inputs of sewage (treated or not), fertilizer runoff, or other forms of nutrient enrichment—the causes of acidification are obscure, often not related to any obvious changes in the local watershed. Like a eutrophic lake, an acidified, fish-free lake reflects past and present human impact superimposed on past, nonhuman mediated ecosystem processes. Clearing followed by recovery of forests and acidified precipitation, for example, will have different effects on a lake formed in limestone than on one formed in granite. The age and volume of a lake also will have affected its susceptibility to acidification. Historical research has elucidated many of these relations, with some new twists related to the complexity of factors causing changes in pH and the many correlated variables. Like eutrophication, acidification has resulted in many cases from human activities and is not simply a natural consequence of century- or millennia-old processes.

pH AND LAKE PROCESSES

Understanding acidification requires some basic understanding of the factors that affect pH of lake water. The pH of lake water varies both spatially and seasonally. In many lakes, the carbon dioxide, carbonate, bicarbonate system buffers acidity. Because photosynthesis of organisms in the water uses carbon dioxide while respiration produces it, the balance between these two phenomena can cause changes in the concentration of carbon dioxide in the water. As photosynthesis lowers carbon dioxide, the pH of the lighted zone rises, while respiration in the deeper waters, especially in poorly buffered lakes with an anoxic hypolimnion, lowers pH. Measurements of the pH of water at varying depths can produce different measurements at the same time as such a difference develops over the season. This stratification in pH, temperature, dissolved oxygen concentration, and other qualities of the water column is lost in the fall overturn in dimictic lakes (that is, lakes that are thermally stratified in summer and winter and mixed in fall and spring), averaging the pH throughout the lake.[23]

In addition, the input of water from the watershed influences water pH. Meltwater from snow can lower pH if the snow includes mineral acids like sulfuric or nitric acid. This sudden input of strong acids may temporarily depress the pH of the water, which recovers later in the season as buffers have time to act. The soils and bedrock of the watershed also affect pH of lake water. Highly leached soils and sphagnum-dominated bogs or fens will contribute acidified water to the lake, with little input of buffers like carbonate salts. In newly disturbed soils, in which fresh, unweathered materials are brought to the surface, more highly buffering materials leach out, raising the pH of the lake. Highly weathered soils release mainly organic acids, while salts produced from plants also act as buffers. Organic acids, on the other hand, can contribute to pH's as low as 3.[24]

Thus, in glaciated regions, one would expect lake waters to have been well buffered for a few millennia after the retreat of the glaciers, as basic salts weathered out of surrounding rocks.[25] Where the bedrock was crystalline, containing few basic salts, the buffering system would soon shift to carbonates and/or organic acids and their salts. Thus the lake waters would slowly acidify over time. Disturbance of the watershed soils by agriculture, most likely by European colonists, would perhaps have elevated the pH somewhat by releasing newly weathered buffering minerals. Abandonment of agriculture then allowed the forest vegetation and the soils to became reestablished. Especially in areas where the vegetation consisted of conifers, the soil would again become depleted in buffering minerals, and the pH of the lake water would again decrease. The pH of the water is thus closely tied to events in the watershed.

Adding such strong mineral acids as sulfuric or nitric acid essentially titrates the buffering capacity of the lake water, which is referred to as alkalinity. Once the buffering capacity is saturated, pH of the lake may drop rapidly in response to further hydrogen ion additions. Adding extraneous buffers like lime may temporarily raise the pH, but because there is no continuous input of buffer, this, too, will become saturated, allowing pH again to drop.

The pH of a lake is therefore governed by a balance between the buffers present in the watershed and washed into the lake and the rate of input of acids from both the watershed and other sources, for example, rainwater and metabolism of lake organisms. As long as the input does not overwhelm the buffering capacity, the pH stays within a fairly well constrained range, with variation around a central value due to metabolism and mixing. Brief excursions, for example, from rapid photosynthesis in carbonate-dominated ecosystems in the summer or from input of mineral acids in meltwater in the spring, may affect the biota if they exceed tolerances.

Lake pH covaries with many other characteristics of lake water. Alkalinity is an obvious covariant; others include concentrations of sulfate, zinc, aluminum, and often dissolved organic matter and transparency of the water.[26] Zinc and aluminum are often complexed and rendered insoluble in less acid waters, especially those high in dissolved organic matter, but may be released as ions if the water is acidified or the organic buffering system is overwhelmed by mineral acids. Aluminum solubility depends strongly on pH, rising abruptly below pH of 5. This can account for increased input of aluminum to lakes with acidified watershed soils and possibly for leaching of aluminum from sediments in lakes where the pH falls below 5. This leaching will not show up in analysis of the sedimentary chemistry, however, because of the large reservoir of aluminum in the sediments.[27] The pH of the water and watershed soils also influences the solubilities of iron, manganese, and phosphorus.[28] The complex interactions of pH and these other features of water quality make it difficult to tie any specific changes in the biota directly to pH, but changing pH clearly affects the biota in a variety of ways.

### THE EFFECT OF ACIDITY ON LAKE ORGANISMS

In a classic study of lakes in Java, Sumatra, and Bali in 1937–39, F. Husted determined that pH was a major environmental factor influencing the diatom flora.[29] Although many taxa had a wide tolerance range, others were most prevalent only at a restricted range of pH. He used these relations to classify species, ranging from the alkalibiontic forms that were found almost exclusively at pH greater than 7 to the acidobiontic forms that were most common at pH less than or equal to 5. From this classification, he devised a scale for estimating pH of a lake's water.[30] Because diatom forms are very widely distributed, this scale applied also to lakes in other parts of the world. Limnologists use modified versions of this scale to infer the pH of lake waters in the past from the diatoms found in sediments.[31] Large calibration sets of diatom data from surface sediments in many lakes in a region have resulted in indices tailored to quirks in the local distribution of different taxa. For example, two species correlated with pH in many geographic regions and used for paleoecological reconstruction of pH, *Cyclotella stelligera* and *C. kutzingiana,* are associated with depth of lakes on the Canadian shield of ancient rocks in Ontario, rather than with pH.[32]

The most widely reported concern about acidification of lakes is the loss of fish. This appears to result not directly from low pH, but rather from the toxic effects of aluminum and possibly other metals made more soluble by the acidity.[33] The lakes are not "dead." They support populations of acid-tolerant taxa. They are, however, changed from what is perceived as their natural state and thus cause concern about human impact.[34] The broader preoccupation is our ability to alter systems by remote action. If the acidification is actually due to the long-distance transport of pollutants, even across international boundaries, the potential is great for altering ecosystems in ways and places that are at best very difficult to predict.

### SEDIMENTARY STUDIES OF ACID LAKES

Large, interdisciplinary research projects in the 1980s addressed these and other questions about lake acidification, using sedimentary evidence. Because acidification has been most marked in Scandinavia and northeastern North America, I shall concentrate on results from studies done there.

Although we can map lakes that are very acid, say, pH less than 5.5, and sources of air pollutants, especially sulfates and nitrates, any correlations tell us nothing about the genesis of the low pH. Have these lakes been acid for most of their past, or have they only recently become so? Can changes in past acidity be correlated with land use changes in the watershed, thus implicating these rather than long-distance transport of pollutants in the changes? A pamphlet published by Environment Canada expressed the popular attribution of acidification to the effects of acid precipitation: "The Adirondacks are . . . victims of the most serious environmental problem we face today—acid rain. It has already caused tragic and irreparable damage to this scenic paradise and will continue to destroy it—and many other parts of the world—unless this deadly pollution is stopped."[35] It has required paleolimnological studies, however, to document where acid precipitation is the culprit, and at the same time to reveal a diversity of changes in the pH of lake water over time.

From Finland to New England, many lakes in glaciated terrain started life less acidic than they are today. Most acidified slowly in the few thousand years after they were formed, most likely after carbonates had leached out of the developing soils and as forests grew in the watersheds.[36] The development of acid wetlands in the watersheds, especially in Scandinavia, also contributed to lowering pH.[37] Some lakes, however, remained nearly neutral or slightly alkaline, for example, Mirror Lake in New Hampshire.[38] Human activity may have begun to alter the pH of some lakes in Scandinavia seventy-five hundred years ago. For example, about 7500 B.P. the inferred pH of a lake in Finland rose from 4 to about 6.6 over a fairly short period, possibly owing to slash-and-burn cultivation in the watershed.[39] In southern Sweden, too, Iron Age and later cultural practices like clearing, burning, and forest grazing corresponded with an increase in lake pH from about 5.5 to about 6.5 from approximately 2300 B.P. to A.D. 1900.[40] Similarly, in the nineteenth century, increases in pH accompanied forest clearance by logging in northeastern North America.[41]

The most rapid change in pH inferred from many studies across Scandinavia and New England is the decrease in the recent sediment, generally reversing other culturally induced increases. The change is much more rapid than those that had occurred earlier, and in many cases is more or less synchronous within a region. Within the limits of dating specificity, past fluctuations have not been synchronous. This leads to the hypothesis that these recent changes are due to some modern, novel process that has not been acting on these lakes in the long-term past. It seems reasonable to attribute this process to some human activity, perhaps changes in disturbance in the watersheds that have led to acidification and leaching of acids into the lake or input from acidified precipitation or both. For at least the past two hundred years, pH has not declined in some other lakes, most often those with pH greater than about 6 (for example, Mirror Lake), but also some like Cone Pond in New Hampshire with a pH of about 4.6–4.8.[42]

Comparisons among a suite of Finnish lakes with diverse histories of land use afforded a ground for distinguishing between watershed contributions and acid precipitation as causes of recent acidification. For some, abandonment of agriculture in the watershed may account for the recent acidification. For example, slash-and-burn agriculture and pasturing seem to be responsible for the inferred pH increase from about 6 to 6.8 about a thousand years ago in one lake, and the abandonment of cultivation and possibly pasturing for a more recent acidification. In other lakes, however, decline in pH in the past twenty to thirty years does not correlate with any known human activity or change in the watershed vegetation. Historical documentation is insufficient to allow us to read past patterns of field abandonment, but it appears that the cause of the recent acidification was acidified precipitation.[43]

A study comparing pH changes inferred from diatoms in Norway and New England further suggested the complexity of causes of recent acidification. In Norway, pH decreased 0.6–0.8 units in the three lakes (of nine studied) that currently have pH less than 5.0 (fig. 10.4). In three other lakes, inferred pH decreased only slightly, while it remained constant in the remaining three. Fish disappeared from the three most acidified lakes in the 1940s and 1960s, though the acidification began much earlier. Even before acidification began, the concentrations of the heavy metals lead, zinc, and copper increased in the sediment at most of these lakes. In New England, inferred pH decreased somewhat in ten of twelve lakes.[44] Of the two with a recent slight increase in pH, the watershed of one had recently been subjected to heavy logging. Fish were still present in at least nine of the lakes in 1980, although the pH was less than 5 in five of them. As in Norway, the amounts of lead, zinc, and copper in the sediments increased well before the decrease in pH. In several of the lakes in Norway and in New England alike the amount of zinc in the sediment decreased again near the tops of the cores.[45]

How can these data help us understand recent changes in these lakes? First, pH decreases seem to have been greater in lakes with lower current pH. Diatoms and cladocera (minute crustaceans) responded to changes in the chemistry of the water, as inferred from the sediment, before fish did and after the initial inputs of heavy metals to the lakes. This result agrees with observations made in experimental manipulations of lake chemistry in Canada, in which small, rapidly reproducing and widely dispersed taxa like diatoms and small cladocera are the first to respond to stress.[46] Heavy metals can come from airborne pollution in even the earliest stages of industrialization. For example, an increase in lead in the sediments of several Swedish lakes began in 2600 B.P. and is correlated with airborne pollution from Roman mining of lead. Medieval activities apparently caused a further

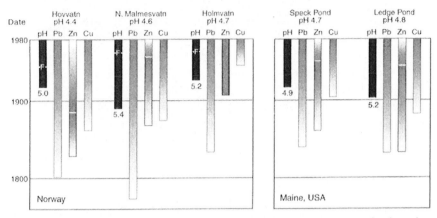

Figure 10.4. Inferred decreases over time in pH and increases in zinc, lead, and copper concentrations in several Norwegian and New England lakes. The date of disappearance of fish in three is indicated by "F." (Modified from Davis et al., Paleolimnological reconstruction, figs. 6, 7, with permission of Kluwer Publishers)

increase starting about 1000 B.P.[47] Mobilization in the sediments, especially if there were changes in the acidity and/or redox potential of interstitial and sediment surface waters, may have altered heavy metal concentrations, especially that of zinc. The inputs of these heavy metals, however, were most likely accompanied by inputs of acidifying anions, such as oxides of sulfur and nitrogen but the diatom communities showed no immediate evidence of these inputs, probably because the lake water was buffered.[48] Experimental research linked with paleoecological inference should serve both to elucidate the processes responsible for the inferred changes and to help us understand better the relations between lake water and sediment chemistry.

The question of the origin of the pollution remains. Because there are no refineries or mines in the watersheds of most of the acidified lakes, the heavy metal contamination may have come from the air. Acid anions likely arrive by air as well, and others are washed into the lake from the watershed when it is subjected to acidified precipitation. Modifications in the watersheds of many of these lakes may have played a part in the recent changes, but these could have been complicated and exacerbated by changing chemistry of precipitation.[49]

Two German lakes that lost their fish populations in the 1960s have also become acidified recently, as reconstructed from the sediments. There is no evidence of alterations in forest composition around the lakes for the past 150 or so years. (Both are in the Bavarian Wood, a mixed forest of *Picea abies, Abies alba,* and *Fagus sylvatica.*) Chromium, nickel, lead, and cadmium have increased in one, the Grosser Arbersee, since 1915, while cadmium and zinc have increased in the nearby Kleiner Arbersee. These increases may be related to local mining and smelting of heavy metals, but there are no local watershed changes, so regional inputs of heavy metals and anions from precipitation are a credible cause.[50]

The causes of recent acidification are thus not easy to pinpoint, but at least in some cases they are most directly related to acidic precipitation, coming from a distance. At the least, acidic precipitation helps mobilize acidic anions from watershed soils in which vegetation and the soil itself are recovering from past disturbances.

The sedimentary record thus documents a history of eutrophication and acidification in many lakes over millennia. Human activities appear to have accelerated and altered these processes, changing lake water chemistry in a century or less. Such rapid and new fluctuations in the lake environment may best be described as "stress." The first organisms to react to the stress are small, rapidly reproducing taxa such as diatoms; species composition shifts quickly to those that can tolerate the new conditions. It appears from the sedimentary record that the response to the stress of hydrogen ion loading does not occur just when it is applied, but somewhat later, as the buffering system is overwhelmed. Response to nutrient loading, on the other hand, is more rapid, especially when the nutrient is a limiting one such as phosphorous. Recovery if the stress is removed appears also to be more complete and quick if the stress is nutrient loading rather than acidification, although the recovered system may still bear the imprint of human influence. Study of these systems can take many forms, some oriented toward understanding processes, others oriented more toward applications. An understanding of the fundamental processes, through experimental as well as historical approaches, can afford a solid basis for intervention. In the absence of historical reconstructions, it is impossible to determine whether the current condition has been caused by some specific, recent human activities or is the culmination of a series of events that started millennia ago, for example, with the retreat of the glaciers. The extent to which a system can be strained before it moves into a "realm of dragons" has yet to be established.[51] What is certain is that systems are being pushed beyond states that they have experienced in the known past.

## Fishes and Fishing

Fishing is a more direct manipulation of a lake than is changing its chemistry. It also seems to be a "natural" use of a lake; after all, many other animals, bears and ospreys to mention just two, catch fish, and people have been catching and eating fish for millennia. People, however, have devised more efficient means of removing fish from lakes than have other animals and have also decided to add certain fish to lakes to increase the pleasure or profit in removing them. These practices, combined with changing productivity of many lakes, have combined to make the fish populations of many (most?) lakes highly manipulated ones. People add desirable fish to lakes, set regulations to try to keep these fish in the lake, and, at the extreme, in some small lakes periodically kill all the fish to eliminate undesirable ones. Some fish, for example, in parts of New Jersey, are even known as "put and take" fish; they are put in the rivers and lakes during the week to be fished (taken) out the following weekend or at the latest before the winter. There is no expectation that they will reproduce. They do, however, compete for food with any remaining, naturally reproducing fish.

Fish function as very effective high order consumers, so that their predation has cascading ramifications for the lake's productivity. Large populations of fish-eating fish (piscivores) reduce the populations of their prey, smaller fish that eat the larger zooplankton (zooplanktivores). If there are fewer zooplanktivores, their prey, for example, daphnids, flourish. Daphnids consume a lot of cyanobacteria, so if there are more of them, there will be smaller crops of cyanobacteria and thus less anoxia caused by their biomass decomposing in deep parts of the lake.[52] In these ways the balance of predatory fish species helps regulate the amount of algae in a lake and the oxygen content of the deep waters.

Human activities have directly and indirectly affected this balance over time. In Frains Lake, Michigan, the sediments record the presence of daphnids from about eight thousand years ago to the time of the *Ambrosia* increase in the sediment, that is, when Europeans colonized the area. At that time, the daphnids disappeared from the sediment, replaced by smaller zooplankton.[53] The hypothetical chain of events that led to this change is that clearing for agriculture produced more clay and nutrient input to the lake, resulting in more near-shore vegetation. This vegetation provided cover for zooplanktivorous fish, which preyed on the larger zooplankton, including daphnids. The agricultural inputs of sediment and nutrients also reduced both the volume of deep water, as the lake filled with sediment, and the oxygen content of the deep water because of decaying algae. These conditions were deleterious to the deepwater fish. In addition, people caught the larger piscivores. Because there were fewer of these, there were more of their prey, the planktivores, so their prey, the larger daphnids, suffered. Experimental manipulations confirmed that large daphnids flourish only in the presence of few planktivorous fish. If there are more planktivorous fish, the smaller zoo-plankton do better.

The history of Lake Mendota, Wisconsin, followed a somewhat different path but confirms the importance of fish as regulators of water clarity. Daphnid and other cladoceran populations were apparently low but fairly stable for several centuries before European clearing of the watershed for agriculture. The explanation was undoubtedly that there were a lot of zooplanktivorous fish in the lake, especially cisco, which ate the cladocera. Increased nutrient input from agricultural runoff initially caused very little change in the numbers of daphnids, probably because of the continued importance of the cisco. Daphnid populations, however, rose dramatically near the turn of the century. A likely cause was increased anoxia in the hypolimnion, which restricted the volume of water available to cold-water fish like cisco. Newspapers reported major die-offs of fish at that time. Subsequent fluctuations of daphnids and cisco responded to changing inputs of nutrients, such as sewage diversion in the 1960s. The daphnids apparently can control cyanobacteria when there are large inputs of nutrients. For example, two years of heavy rains and other factors led to major inputs of nutrients to the lake, but the lake water remained clear. A sudden die-off of ciscos just before this time seems to have allowed large daphnia populations to thrive, and these controlled the blooms of cyanobacteria.[54] Introduced large piscivorous fish like walleye and northern pike have kept the cisco populations low more recently, helping to keep the water clear by sparing the daphnids. Fishing pressure has to be controlled, however, to maintain high populations of these large fish in order to keep the water clear.[55]

Studies such as these shed additional light on the questions raised by paleoecological investigations of lake ecosystems. Changes in planktonic species apparently relate not only to changes in nutrient inputs and pH and other correlated factors, but also to changes in their predators. Larger plankton affect the populations of smaller plankton, both by predation and shading. The losses of fish in many acidified lakes (for example, Cone Pond, New Hampshire; Lake Blâmissusjön, Sweden; Valkealampi and Grosser and Kleiner Arbersee, Germany; Big Moose Lake and many other lakes in the Adirondack Mountain region of New York)[56] were also associated with prior manipulations of fish populations. In some of these lakes, people had been introducing favored fish species and poisoning others for many years. In the 1960s, Cone Pond was treated with rotenone to kill the resident populations of brown bullhead, chain pickerel, and yellow perch, for example, prior to introducing brook trout. This and a repeat treatment in 1963 killed only a few large yellow perch; the others had already disappeared from the lake. Subsequent introductions of brook trout from 1968 to 1970 were unsuccessful.[57] Sometime before 1960 *Salmo gairdneri* introduced from North America replaced the native populations of *Salmo trutta* f. *fario* in the Grosser and Kleiner Arbersee in Germany.[58] Integration of the consequences of such manipulations of fish populations to other features of the lake ecosystem may allow a better understanding of the dynamics of these systems.

These examples suggest several tentative conclusions regarding the value of historical research in the attempt to understand the dynamics of lakes: (1) Most lakes that have experienced recent cultural eutrophication were previously somewhat eutrophic or mesotrophic, while those that have become overly acid were previously acidic. (2) Recent eutrophication or acidification does not just continue natural processes in these lakes; it includes different taxa in very different concentrations from what existed in the past and changes at least an order of magnitude more rapid. Comparisons with lakes that have not had heavy human impact are valuable in understanding current dynamics. (3) Very recent changes in biota and chemistry have occurred against a background of changes taking place over past centuries or even millennia of human-induced changes in the lakes. (4) The connection between changes in the watersheds (with the exception of direct input of such nutrients as phosphorous) and reactions by the biota is very complex and depends on past conditions, the chemistry of watershed soils, the shape of the lake basin, and other factors still to be elucidated. (5) Current dynamics of lakes are often considerably altered from the past, so are most likely not in equilibrium, either in terms of mass transfer or energetics.

Modern techniques have greatly enhanced the interpretation of the sedimentary record. Precise dating of sediments and multiple cores per lake track the reactions of the lakes to changes in human activities. In several lakes multiple cores have revealed different patterns or different dating or both because of complex processes of sediment resuspension and focusing that may make data from one core not representative of the lake as a whole.[59] In addition, separation of allochthonous and autochthonous portions of the sediment allows us to disentangle the reciprocal influences of erosion and lake chemistry.

By combining sedimentary and documentary evidence we can establish reasonable causal connections between human activities and changes in lake chemistry. In some cases, obvious cultural changes may have little effect, while in others, obvious changes—the eutrophication of Linsley Pond in the early twentieth century, for example—have no obvious causes. Some activities may have delayed effects.

Aquatic systems are excellent records of the consequences of past human activities. Terrestrial systems, on the other hand, leave poorer records than aquatic, and their limits are less easily defined. Patterns in the long-term interactions of people with lake ecosystems provide insight into the possible effects of people on ecosystems in general. For example, early stages of strain in an aquatic ecosystem often do not manifest themselves in easily measured characteristics of acute toxicity like fish kills or in ecosystem processes like changes in standing crop, productivity, or decomposition.[60] They are more manifest in altered population dynamics of rapidly reproducing plankton, morphological abnormalities of sediment-dwelling organisms, and losses of some short-lived species that are especially sensitive to pollution.[61] The studies discussed here indicate that the precursors of major changes often predate the first obvious indicators of problems by decades at least. If these changes are reversible, such a delay may be acceptable, but if they are not, it is critical to be aware of them immediately. Much basic research is needed to accumulate baseline data on changes that have already occurred, to provide the background to study current stresses. Patterns derived from such studies afford insights that can be applied to terrestrial systems, much as the early ideas of lakes as ecosystems have led to better understanding of terrestrial ecosystems.

# Diversity and Species Extinctions

One indicator of stress is loss of species, a reduction in diversity. Human activities tend both to diminish and to augment diversity. Agriculture, tree plantations, and urbanization have all reduced the variety of habitats and species in local ecosystems as well as reducing population sizes of many native species. As early as the late eighteenth century, the Comte de Buffon noted that human civilization disrupts previously flourishing populations of such diverse animals as elephants, beavers, ants, and bees and locally may completely extirpate such large animals as elephants. He even deduced from the continuing diminution in the numbers of animals like lions and elephants that human population had increased since the Roman period. Some of the species described by Buffon, for example, lions, were deliberately eliminated, but others, such as sloths, disappeared because they did not thrive near human habitations.[1] This kind of observation foreshadowed twentieth-century concerns about loss or reduction of species indirectly by habitat change.

In the mid–nineteenth century, George Perkins Marsh pointed out that hunting had eliminated animals and large bird species in many areas, for example, bears and wolves in Great Britain and ostriches in Asia Minor and Syria. The reasons for overhunting were often indirect. For example, he blamed overenthusiastic shooting of small birds in part to the repeal of game laws in France and other countries after the French Revolution. Game laws had restricted hunting to the privileged few, while the new regime opened it to all. Whether this can be proven or not, the destruction of small birds was appalling; in the Tuscan province of Grosseto, whose area was just under five thousand square kilometers, about three hundred thousand thrushes were being brought to market annually.[2] Some species like beavers in North America, however, recovered somewhat after such heavy depredations. When fashion shifted from beaver hats to silk, hunting pressure on the almost extirpated beavers decreased, allowing at least some populations to expand.

On the other hand, while agriculture and logging eliminated many habitats favored by native species, they introduced new habitats and landscape patterns favored by species that thrive in transitional environments. Importation of non-native taxa at least temporarily increased local numbers of species. Figure 11.1 illustrates the inferred effect of changed habitat and species introductions since the Neolithic period in Central Europe, in terms of increasing numbers of habitat types. Again, Marsh made cogent observations on this phenomenon: "Though the first operations of the settler are favorable to the increase of many species, the great extension of rural and of mechanical industry is, in a variety of ways, destructive even to tribes not directly warred upon by man."[3] This subsequent decrease in diversity is illustrated in figure 11.1 by the decrease in diversity after the mid–eighteenth century, when both the landscape and the variety of species became more monotonous.[4] Eventually, as human-dominated landscapes replace ancient, native ecosystems, the biota becomes more homogeneous.[5]

In the past few decades the accelerated decrease in diversity caused by extinction has sparked widespread concern. Even species that are not yet extinct but whose populations have been severely limited have less genetic diversity than their progenitors and thus probably have less ability to respond to environmental changes. International agreements banning the export and import of rare species as well as national laws to protect endangered species testify to international awareness of the potential losses. The consequences of these losses are, however, mostly unpredictable.

If we had been living during the Carboniferous period, for example, we could not have predicted the evolution of dinosaurs, mammals, or flowering plants.[6] Neither could we have predicted the great late-Permian extinction of perhaps 95 percent of all living species, 83 percent of all genera, and 57 percent of all families of organisms.[7] Other major extinctions of which we would have had no hint involved 30–85 percent of all species, and 15–60 percent of all genera in nine major extinctions between 439 and 35 million years ago.[8] Reradiation of species after each extinction was slow, and each

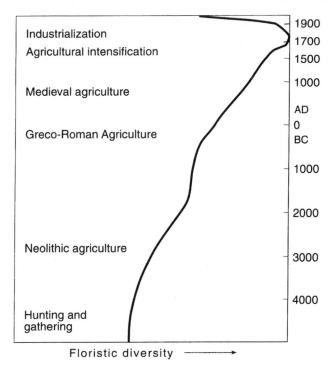

Figure 11.1. Inferred changes in numbers of
plant species versus time in Central Europe.
(Modified from F. Jukarek et al., *Pflanzenwelt
der Erde*, [Urania-Verlag, Leipzig, 1980])

changed the living world forever. Each extinction event no doubt lasted millions of years, although the one at the end of the Cretaceous period may have
lasted only for millennia or less. Why, then, are we concerned about extinctions now? They have occurred in the past and life has continued. But there
is a hitch: life has continued but in a greatly changed form.[9] And a more
rapid time frame for extinctions may lead to even slower recovery. If most
of the life forms we know become extinct, the successors will undoubtedly
be different and quite possibly will not include *Homo sapiens*. We count on
perpetuating life as we know it.

In addition, we feel responsible. Past extinctions have almost certainly
been initiated by physical events beyond the control of organisms. It is
almost inconceivable that one species modified conditions so much that
many others and even they themselves perished forever, even though species
interactions may have been the cause of secondary extinctions.[10] If we cause

massive extinctions equivalent to the great extinctions of the geological past, not only will we lose our sense of place, if we survive, but we will also be responsible for it.[11] Ethically, this is appalling to many people. Even Buffon in the eighteenth century, for example, was saddened by the indiscriminate destruction of wildlife, commenting that carnivores were harmful only because they competed with people, not because of some inherent evil nature.[12] Today, we have the hope, and the hubris, that we can control our actions sufficiently to save the rest of the living world from ourselves. We see ourselves thus not only as the cause but also possibly as the mitigators of massive extinctions.[13]

Historical analyses have formed a major part of studies of extinction, especially in cataloguing the past existence and distributions of species. History, however, not only allows us to study diversity in the past, to compare with the present, but also places a region or an individual site within a temporal framework, from which we gain insight into the importance that changing diversity has for ecosystem processes.

## What Is Diversity?

The concept of diversity is intuitively obvious. The greater the variety of entities, the more diverse the system. We can easily recognize that an old-growth forest or even a prairie grassland is more diverse than a cornfield. At its simplest, biological diversity can be defined as the number of species, or species richness, of some defined space (even the entire earth) at a specific time (alpha diversity). It can also refer to level of difference in species composition between habitats (beta diversity). Both measures will change from one time to the next, by evolution, extinction, and migration, all of which are operating constantly. If additions by evolution or immigration equal extinctions, the absolute number of species will stay the same, though the mix of species and thus communities and ecosystems will change.

The defining of diversity becomes a slippery issue beyond simple species counts per unit area or per political unit. Ecologists have grappled with the problem and offer several approaches.[14] Two communities may have the same number of species, but in one the individuals may overwhelmingly consist of only one species, with the rest quite rare, while in the other several species may be more or less equally common. Indices of diversity would rank the first community as less diverse than the second. These indices are very sensitive to small changes in population sizes, however, potentially skewing comparisons,[15] so many global studies rely instead on the simpler counts of species, which tend to be correlated with the indices.[16]

This leaves the question of what species to count, and whether diversity expressed as higher taxonomic categories, such as families or orders, affords better comparative data. Often species cannot be counted because they have not been identified, for example, insects of tropical regions or bacteria in soils. Ecologists have to rely in these cases on extrapolations from known distributions if they want to count these taxa in their estimates of biological diversity.

These measures provide an estimate of alpha diversity. Beta diversity is measured by the turnover of species over space, either from one habitat to another, where habitats are distinct, or in the area inhabited by a species. These are both components of gamma, or regional, diversity. In the tropics, for example, each community has high alpha and high beta diversity, that is, there are many species, each inhabiting only a small number of habitats or a small area. This produces high gamma diversity. In boreal areas, on the other hand, there are few species per habitat, and many species occur over very large regions, producing low alpha, beta, and gamma diversities.

Obviously, species are not just equivalent beads in a jar. Individuals of different species interact with each other and their nonliving environments in many ways, forming a wide range of associations. Again, these assemblages and interactions change over time. Assemblages with abundant sedges (Cyperaceae) and spruces (*Picea* spp.) eighteen thousand to twelve thousand years ago in central North America, for example, experienced interactions quite distinct from those of the same region today with still abundant sedges but no spruces,[17] even with no global extinctions of any of the major species. Loss of large carnivores in much of the developed world has created new animal communities, though the species continue to exist in other, less developed places and the total number of species may have stayed the same or even increased. That is, local extinctions or reductions in diversity have had major impacts on the earth's biota. But what factors ultimately have influenced diversity?

The earliest explanations relied on evolutionary and biogeographic processes, in which each species spread from its place of origin, spawning new species, which spread in their turn. The older an area was, the more species would have evolved there and spread there from other centers, and the older a species was, the greater an area it would cover. A geologically old area would thus have the greatest diversity of species.[18] Subsequent research in evolution, plate tectonics, and biogeography replaced these ideas with a theory based on the partitioning of a habitat into a series of unique niches, each occupied by its unique species.[19] Further modifications have focused on the patterns by which species interact locally and over time within the broad confines imposed by regional diversity.[20]

Thus, the long sweep of evolutionary, migrational, and climatic history has shaped regional diversity.[21] Even within one kind of biome, differences in diversity can be large: there are 124 species of trees, in 5 families, in the moist temperate forests of Europe, while a similar area of temperate forest in east-central Asia contains 729 tree species, in 9 families. The greater number of tree species in Asia than in Europe has resulted not only from varied climate history and migration routes over the last few thousands of years, but also from evolution over many millions of years, when Asia had much broader connections to subtropical diversity than did Europe.[22] Focus on contemporary distributions and environments alone could not explain these patterns. The current gene pool was created over eons of evolution and migration, influenced by changing climates and migrational corridors.

On a continental scale, diversity generally increases with decreasing latitude; arctic and boreal systems have fairly low alpha and beta diversity, while both measures of diversity are greater in the tropics. For example, the Northwest Territory of Canada, 3.3 million square kilometers, has 400 species of flowering plants, while Panama has 7,500 species in only 82,000 square kilometers.[23] In general, flowering plant family diversity increases linearly with an increase in absolute minimum temperature.[24] Such differences present at least two major questions: first, what are the causes?; and, second, what are the consequences for stability and resilience of the systems?

Local conditions further influence alpha diversity at the community scale. From the Ghanian rain forest to the North American prairie, the species or generic diversity is generally at its highest at lower levels of biomass, soil fertility, and soil moisture.[25] For example, along an elevational gradient in the Santa Catalina Mountains in Arizona, high diversity corresponds with low biomass, low productivity, and low moisture index (fig. 11.2).[26] If taxa are separated according to life form, however, the patterns may be different. In Australia, sclerophyllous genera are most numerous at low levels of soil phosphorus, while rain forest species increase to an asymptote along the phosphorus gradient (fig. 11.3).[27] Diversity is often lowest at very low fertility or water availability. Although distinguishing the importance of such other factors as microclimate or exposure in these studies is difficult, the similarity of the results over a large range of habitats using many measures of fertility or moisture content suggests that this is a common pattern: local species diversity does not increase monotonically along a gradient of favorable habitat. The most fertile, well-drained habitats do not usually have the largest number of species. Models predict that competition should play a

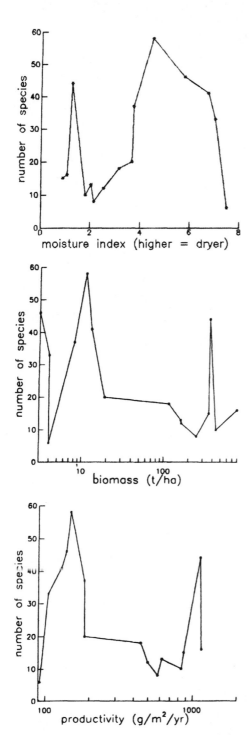

Figure 11.2. Change in plant species richness with change in biomass, moisture, and productivity along an elevational gradient in the Santa Catalina Mountains. (Data from Whittaker and Niering, Vegetation of the Santa Catalina Mountains)

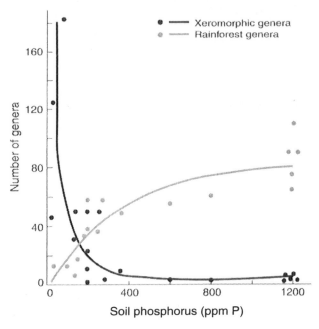

Figure 11.3. Contrast between responses of a
diversity of rain forest genera and xeromorphic
genera along a gradient of soil phosphorus in
Australia. (Modified from Beadle, Soil phosphate, fig. 2)

major role in this pattern. Under excellent nutrient and moisture conditions,
a few species are able to capture a large proportion of the resources, driving
out others.[28]

The consideration of past human impact, especially in changing the disturbance regime, has been critical in many studies of these relations.[29] The
impact of past human disturbance is critical even in studies that do not
explicitly take it into account. The Santa Catalina Mountain site, for example, had a history of grazing, which had ceased about twenty-five or thirty
years before the study. The authors made the assumption that the communities had returned to a stable condition, although they noted that it was not
the "climatic climax" described by F. E. Clements.[30] The Australian study
did not mention human impact, but the one picture shows a landscape in
which "the tall shrubs . . . are dying from the effects of overgrazing and
drought."[31] Grazing could reduce dominant species in some communities,
thus offering space and resources for more species and thereby increasing

diversity. It could also decrease diversity by changing nutrient cycling as well as by eliminating some favored, uncommon species. The relations between diversity and measures of site conditions may be skewed by prior human disturbance. However we measure diversity, the systems in which we measure it have been altered in some ways by human activities, so these subtle (or not-so-subtle) effects color our perceptions of patterns and causes.

## History as a Catalogue of Extinction and Evolution

The concept of extinction is easy to grasp: if species *a* exists at time *t* and does not exist at time *t+n,* it has become extinct in the intervening time *n,* locally or globally, depending on the area in which it has disappeared. Empirical documentation of extinction, however, is often problematical. No one has described or named a large number of species in existence now, so their extinction can only be estimated. Extreme rarity and absence are often difficult to differentiate. Many plant species, for example, remain dormant as seeds or tubers for years, appearing to be extinct, only to reappear when some critical conditions are met.[32] Some species like the California condor (*Gymnogyps californianus*) and franklinia (*Franklinia altamaha*) may survive only under domestication; they are not extinct in terms of having ceased to exist but are extinct in terms of their role in natural communities. Some species, such as the European bison, have been preserved only under domestication at least since the nineteenth century.[33]

Extinction diminishes both the total gene pool and the diversity of species and niches. The genes of such species as the condor and franklinia are not yet lost. Gene banks and cultivation can preserve the genetic material of rare species that are on the brink of extinction, with the possibility that sometime in the future it can be used for enriching still-extant genetic diversity.[34] As for their roles in natural ecosystems, however, these species are currently extinct; their loss has simplified the ecosystems to which they contributed.

There are several stages in global extinction. A species may first become increasingly rare, restricted to very limited habitats in less of its range; that is, it becomes locally extinct.[35] Extinction is usually accelerated when changes in habitat outpace the ability of the species to adapt. As climate changes, for example, a species must either have the phenotypic plasticity or the genetic diversity to survive under the new conditions or it must migrate to habitats that remain favorable. Species that can adapt successfully survive this "loss" of habitat.[36] Analyses that trace patterns of descent suggest that the rare and endemic species are often those in nonradiating lines, most likely on the way to extinction, while often more widespread, "weedy" species are in lines that are actively radiating and less likely to disappear in the near future.[37]

Species may be rare, however, at the early stages of range expansion as well as during range reduction. Reports in the 1940s of deer populations in New Jersey and eastern New York document a species worthy of note because of its rarity.[38] By the 1980s this species was common enough in these areas to be regarded by many as a pest. Wild turkeys were rare in the 1980s in New Jersey, but by the mid-1990s were becoming common. Both species had become extinct in much of their former range, but because populations survived elsewhere and communities similar to those they had inhabited earlier reappeared, repopulation was possible, although with a somewhat different genetic stock.

On the other hand, common species with large ranges may also become rare or extinct: the passenger pigeon, American chestnut,[39] and bison in North America are three examples. Interestingly, it is thought that at least two of these, the passenger pigeon and the chestnut, became more common under early impact of major land disturbance, before their precipitous declines.[40]

A less spectacular example is the running Buffalo clover (*Trifolium stoloniferum*), which was first described in 1813 as abundant in several areas of the Ohio Valley and in other parts of the south-central United States. By the late nineteenth century, its populations were scattered and local, and by the late twentieth century only one or two known populations persisted.[41] The variety of potential causes of its decline points to the difficulty of determining why species disappear, even those that have vanished in the recent past. The clover's preferred habitat seems to have been bison-maintained openings, characterized by frequent disturbance and high fertility soils; bison themselves perhaps dispersed and scarified seeds. These habitats disappeared with the disappearance of the bison. Much of the clover's range was cleared and planted with non-native grasses and broad-leaved herbaceous plants, including white clover (*T. repens*). There is also some evidence that white clover may have introduced a viruslike disease that affected the buffalo clover. The white clover also brought with it a nitrogen-fixing rhizobium, which may have out-competed the rhizobium specific to the buffalo clover. Plants grown under cultivation are lacking in nitrogen-fixing nodules, suggesting possible loss of the rhizobium. Historical research correlating changes in the species distribution and such changes as decreases in buffalo herds, spread of agriculture, and introduction of non-native clovers might give further insights into the causes of its reduction. This kind of research offers a unique view of some of the potentially critical factors in the processes that lead to extinction.

## History as Prologue to the Present

Today, we can document all around us species on the brink of extinction and habitats modified beyond recognition, as a result of human actions. Forty percent of the native mammals and birds of France are threatened, and 4 percent are threatened even in sparsely settled Canada.[42] Homogeneous agricultural fields and plantations, to say nothing of cities and transportation corridors, have replaced diverse natural forests, grasslands, and heaths. Endemic native species yield place to more competitive, world travelers like dandelions and eucalyptus. Can analysis of the recent past, leading to the present, yield clues to the importance of these changes and to the potential to stem them? Much of the variation among communities under very similar microclimate, topography, soils, and moisture conditions results in large part from their history. The extraction of general laws governing the organization of these communities requires that we strip away the features that result from historical factors in order to focus on the more basic structure and function.

It is almost axiomatic in ecology that higher diversity makes a community more resilient and better able to recover from disturbance. Testing this axiom depends in part on defining diversity, recovery, and disturbance. Less diverse forests of the temperate zones have been able to recover to some semblance of their former composition after major disturbance in the eighteenth and nineteenth centuries, while highly diverse forests of the tropics appear less resilient in the face of major disturbance. Other characteristics of the habitat, such as soil fertility and dispersal ability of propagules, in all likelihood play an important role in this anomaly.[43] Beta as well as alpha diversity is much higher in the tropical stands than in the temperate ones. If there is a greater turnover of species over space, when species are removed from a specific area there may not be as great a pool of individuals to recolonize. An understanding of the specific patterns of disturbance as well as beta and gamma diversity is needed to predict responses to changes in the future.[44]

The species composition of forest islands, patches of forest isolated in a sea of fields, may result as much from the length of time they have been isolated, the characteristics of the fields, and the conditions under which they were left as forest or regenerated as forest as from more immediate factors such as size or distance from other such forest patches.[45] Hunting pressure in the surroundings may have reduced the numbers of herbivores, for example, white-tailed deer or cottontail rabbits, thereby changing the patterns of survival of plant species in the forest. On the other hand, lack of hunting and change in habitat to favor herbivores may also shift the survival potential of these species.

A recent study of the recovery of several stands of grassland after severe drought supports the hypothesis that alpha diversity confers an advantage in terms of resistance and to some extent recovery.[46] Four grassland stands figured in the study: one was a prairie opening in native savanna, and the other three had been abandoned twenty, thirty-one, and fifty-four years, respectively, prior to 1988 (presumably after agricultural use). Plots with fewer than eleven species had the greatest decrease in biomass during the drought. Four years after the drought, plots with three or more than five species had recovered their predrought biomass, while those with only one, two, four, or five species had not. Plots in the native prairie recovered most quickly. Plots in the most recently abandoned field recovered most slowly, followed in order by those in the two older successional fields. The consequences of past land use appear to have been expressed via species richness, that is, the factor causing the differences in resilience was species richness, which was itself directly related to past land use and time since abandonment. The conclusions reached in the study apply, then, to communities of plants that have undergone significant impacts of human land use, since only the most species-rich plot had had minimal impact. The others, which were most affected, had suffered the greatest human impact. The plots differed not only in species diversity, but also in their history. The history of the sites appears to have been the underlying cause of the differences in species diversity and hence resilience.

Recent paleoecological research posits that communities are never at an equilibrium or stable state for long; change, possibly a dynamic equilibrium, is more the rule than stasis.[47] Each species has physiological tolerance limits and optima, but the collection of species that make up a community varies with time, so that the interactions also vary. Models of forest change over time abstract equations for dynamic equilibrium, which allow them to predict with some level of accuracy the changes that have been seen for a specific forest area.[48] The predictions become more problematical, however, when these models are applied to other forests, which have necessarily had a different history. They often fail too in their predictive value. For example, models of forest growth for the Hubbard Brook Forest, which have been well tested against prior conditions, predicted continued growth into the future, but growth in biomass has ceased several decades before it was predicted. Is this because some previously unanticipated conditions have arisen or because the model was time-bound in the first place? Taking ecological systems out of their historical context removes a major factor in controlling their structure and function.

## Susceptibility and Change: A Variety of Examples

Most people *like* exotic species, such as pets, garden plants, game animals, and fast-growing trees. And exotics add to the alpha diversity of most habitats. For example, when first studied, Clear Lake in California had twelve native fish species, but because of introductions it now has twenty, though only five are native.[49] (I have seen no report on the numbers of species of other organisms in the lake, however.) People also like disturbed or heavily managed environments: neat lawns surrounded by well-tended flowerbeds, golf courses, weed-free fields, neat woodlands. Management may also concentrate native diversity, by planting native wildflowers, for example, providing habitat for species eliminated by other human activities in the past.

The historical development of current patterns of diversity in a variety of regions illustrates that there is no one cause of the loss of diversity and no easy answer to maintaining it. The history of the community to be preserved is at least as important a factor in programs designed to maintain diversity as are the current distribution and characteristics of the ecosystems.

### ECOSYSTEMS IN WHICH DIVERSITY HAS
### BEEN MAINTAINED BY DISTURBANCE

The New Jersey Pine Barrens are an expanse of about half a million hectares of pine and oak forest interspersed with white cedar and hardwood swamps growing on a very sandy substrate with a high water table. Soils are either overly well drained or poorly drained and of very low fertility. The vegetation is fire-prone, and fires are frequent. During Quaternary glacial periods, lowered sea level exposed the continental margin to the east, probably opening a migration corridor both north and south along the coast. Rising sea level must have interrupted species ranges, leaving disjunct populations. That and other accidents of paleogeography left this landscape with a large number of disjunct species as well as species at the northern and southern edges of their ranges.[50]

We know little of the disturbance regimes here before European colonization. The presence of large stands of pitch pine and other fire-dependent vegetation implies that it had long been subject to frequent hot fires. There is even less evidence for other kinds of disturbance, such as windthrow, but being near the Atlantic coast along the route of major hurricanes, major windthrow has undoubtedly been part of its past. The extent to which native Americans disturbed the vegetation and increased fire ignitions is also unknown, although abundant evidence of local occupation for millennia[51] points to augmented fire frequencies during their presence. Beavers must have been another source of disturbance in wet habitats.

European colonists found as early as the eighteenth century that buried in the soils of the Pine Barrens were deposits of iron ore, which they processed through the use of charcoal made from local trees. Charcoal also fueled glass factories. The pine trees supplied rich stores of pitch and tar for the nearby naval fleets. Hunting of beaver for their pelts had eliminated them very early, probably by 1700, but certainly by 1820.[52] Although the soils were poor for most kinds of agriculture, they were ideal for cranberry and blueberry culture, both native plants. Farmers diked depressions and planted them with cranberries, which could be flooded to protect them from late frosts and to float berries for harvest. Peatmoss was also harvested and sold for horticultural and other uses.

Thus, although the land was not productive in a conventional sense, it yielded a wide variety of products for which the forests were cut over repeatedly in the eighteenth and nineteenth centuries.[53] In the late nineteenth and early twentieth centuries, large fires, many of which were started by sparks from locomotives, were also common, no doubt more so than before that time, although there are no data with which to compare the frequencies.[54] Pollen analyses have not yet yielded good charcoal data, and the historical records are sketchy.

Many of the rare species of the region flourish in disturbed habitats, including those disturbed by recent human activities. After peat is mined from a fen and white cedars logged, an open wetland with sandy soil often develops, with small cedars growing on scattered hummocks (fig. 11.4). These wetlands support many species, among them three kinds of sundews (*Drosera rotundifolia, D. filiformis,* and *D. intermedia*), pitcher plants (*Sarracenia purpurea*), golden club (*Orontium aquaticum*), and the globally rare curly-grass fern (*Schizaea pusilla*), which grows preferentially on hummocks at the bases of regenerating white cedar saplings on old cut stumps.[55] The less disturbed fens generally contain a less diverse set of species. Thus the major human disturbances, mining and logging, have improved the habitat for these species. Perhaps beavers provided the appropriate disturbed habitats before they were extirpated. Human-ignited fires are most likely responsible for the continued dominance of pines in this area and for the success of other rare species like *Scirpus longii* (see chapter 5). People have thus both eliminated past disturbances that maintained species and added new ones that may substitute for the natural ones. Some of the species currently restricted to disturbed areas were most likely even rarer in the precolonial

Figure 11.4. Diverse vegetation at Webbs Mill Bog in the Pine Barrens of New Jersey. This site was mined for peat, so that the current substrate is sand. (Photo by the author, spring 1983)

period. To preserve them in their current extent will require continued human intervention.

Another ecosystem that is maintained in its current diversity by continued active management is the coppice woodlands of England. Many of these woodlands, which have been described earlier (see chapter 7), have been maintained over centuries by regular cycles of clear-cutting. Species of plants, butterflies, and birds adapted to this regime are common there and not elsewhere. Where management has ceased and the woodlands have been allowed to grow unattended, these characteristic species have begun to disappear.[56] The pre-coppice distribution of these species is unknown, but many are not found today outside actively managed coppices, so the continuation of this habitat is predicated on continuance of this activity. Human activity here again perpetuates diversity, although it is diversity that may not predate the human activity.[57]

Hay meadows long used as parts of farms also frequently include diverse plant and animal communities. J. Hughes and B. Huntley have observed that "hay meadows provide some of the most diverse communities in Britain, not only in terms of plants but also of invertebrates. These, in turn, support a

large number of increasingly uncommon mammals and birds."[58] Such meadows demand constant management to prevent the encroachment of taller
shrubs and trees, which would eliminate the highly diverse meadow communities. Similar meadows exist in old cultural landscapes throughout western Europe and Scandinavia, for example, in Switzerland and Norway.[59]
These are ecosystems that require the continuation of historic disturbances
in order to maintain their current diversity.

### Historic Dimensions of Island Diversity

The human role in modifying biological diversity is nowhere as distinctive as it is on islands, especially those with a very high proportion of
endemic species. Two especially notable examples are Madagascar and the
Hawai'ian Islands. Both have a very long history of isolation from the mainland. Madagascar separated from the ancient southern continent of Gond-
wanaland in the mid-Cretaceous period, more than one hundred million
years ago, having remained in contact at the latest with India. The Hawai'ian
Islands originated through the eruption of volcanos caused by sea-floor
spreading in the midst of the Pacific Ocean, more than three thousand kilometers from the nearest mainland. People settled in both areas less than two
thousand years ago; in Madagascar these early settlers have remained the
dominant people on the island, while in Hawai'i a second, distinct pulse of
human settlement followed a few centuries ago, largely displacing the original inhabitants.

Charles Darwin used the unique properties of the biota of remote islands
to support his theory of the evolutionary origin of species.[60] Islands had
fewer species than equal areas of mainland, they were rich in endemic species
in a few taxonomic groups, they entirely lacked some major taxa, and their
biotas were most closely related to those of the nearest mainland. (In Madagascar, this encompasses India as well as Africa because of the geological history.) Darwin explained these features by chance colonization from the
mainland by species that crossed deep bodies of water and subsequently
diversified. Later studies of island biogeography led to generalization of these
observations with relation to animal species: the number of species on an
island was related positively to its age and area and negatively to its distance
from the nearest mainland.[61] Later studies suggested that these species were
especially liable to extinction by new introductions, probably because of long
isolation from certain kinds of competition and predation; such reasoning
accounts for the high rates of extinction on islands when they were colonized
by humans, who brought with them large numbers of alien organisms.[62]

The relation between human colonization and extinction, resulting in loss of biological diversity, is thus particularly close on islands. Mainland plants and animals have evolved in a rough and tumble world of competition, herbivory, and predation. They are, in principle, most able to resist takeover by alien aggressors. The issues and processes are not simple on islands, either, though.

The current levels of endemism on Madagascar and the Hawai'ian archipelago can be seen in table 11.1, based on the number of extant species within each taxonomic category. The many endemic species that have already become extinct, for example, many species of lemurs in Madagascar and passerine birds in Hawai'i, are not included in this table. Because the sources disagree about which species are actually extinct and about taxonomy, the figures merely suggest orders of magnitude. Levels of endemism were at least as high before any human contact, and there were more species in both regions.

At least twenty-five species of animals, including at least fifteen species of lemurs, all larger than their surviving near relatives, became extinct on Madagascar soon after the arrival of people between two thousand and fifteen hundred years ago.[63] Bird species, especially the large, flightless ones, were decimated at the same time when people arrived on the Hawai'ian Islands and also on Madagascar.[64] Elimination of the large birds and mammals suggests that hunting played a major role in their demise. We may speculate that this changed species dynamics in remaining native habitat, but so far we have no evidence for these changes.

Both groups of people modified the native habitats through fire, hunting, and agriculture. They also brought domesticated animals and cultivated plants, along with unintentional passengers like rats and weeds. They cleared vegetation to make farms, using fire in both regions. Theories of changed habitat in Madagascar have long blamed people for the spread of fire-prone vegetation in a land lacking fire before human colonization. Recent sedimentologic evidence, however, indicates that fires and fire-adapted vegetation predated human colonization.[65] While human activities led to a major expansion of fire-adapted habitats, they did not initiate them. Drying climate also likely contributed to the spread of drought-tolerant vegetation at that time.

In Hawai'i, a few native species, such as pili grass (*Heteropogon contortus*) and koa (*Acacia koa*), are adapted to fire, but most are not. The widespread use of fire in the lowlands for clearing farms and the propagating of pili for use as thatch undoubtedly eliminated many fire-sensitive species from these areas.[66] Most of the vegetation did not carry fire well, however, so fires were localized to fields.

*Table 11.1. Endemism in several taxonomic groups on the island of Madagascar and the archipelago of Hawai'i.*

| Taxonomic group | Total number of species | Number endemic | % endemic |
|---|---|---|---|
| Madagascar | | | |
| Carnivora | 8 | 7 | 88 |
| (in Jolly et al.) | 7 | 7 | 100 |
| Tenrecidae (Insectivora) | 30 | 29 | 97 |
| Aves | 250 | 106 | 42 |
| Reptilia | 245 | 233 | 95 |
| (in Jolly et al.) | 260 | 247–257 | 95–99* |
| chameleons | 59 | 59 | 100 |
| Anura | 144 | 142 | 99 |
| (in Jolly et al.) | ca. 150 | 148 | 99 |
| Palmae | 112 | 110 | 98 |
| Magnoliophyta | ca. 8000 | 6400 | 80 |
| (in Jolly et al.) | 12000 | 10200 | 85 |
| Primates | 29 | 27 | 93 |
| Hawai'i (% from Peters and Lovejoy, most numbers from Vitousek or Cuddihy and Stone) | | | |
| Insecta | | | ca. 100 |
| Aves | 27 | 30? | 98 |
| Magnoliophyta | ca. 1400 | 1300 | 93 |
| Filicophyta | 168 | 110 | 65 |

*Many new species described from 1973 to 1976—still more to be found.

*Sources:* R. A. Mittermeier, Primate diversity and the tropical forest. Case studies from Brazil and Madagascar and the importance of megadiversity countries. In *Biodiversity,* E. O. Wilson and F. M. Peter, eds. (National Academy Press, Washington, D.C., 1988), 145–54; A. Jolly, P. Oberlé and R. Albignan, eds., *Key Environments. Madagascar* (Pergamon Press, Oxford, 1984); and Richard and Dewar, Lemur ecology, for Madagascar; and R. L. Peters and T. E. Lovejoy, Terrestrial fauna. In *The Earth as Transformed by Human Action* (Cambridge University Press, Cambridge, 1990), 353–69; P. M. Vitousek, Diversity and biological invasion of oceanic islands. In Wilson and Peter, *Biodiversity,* 181–89, and L. W. Cuddihy and C. P. Stone, *Alteration of Native Vegetation* for Hawai'i.

These islands represent two regions—one large and old geologically and the other small and young—that supported unique biota that had developed in the absence of people. The arrival of the new species *Homo sapiens* forever altered these ecosystems. To arrive at an understanding of the ecology, and thus of the survival potential, of many species that remain, for example, lemurs in Madagascar, one must integrate the effects of changes in the past with observations of species today. For example, some extant lemurs are active both at night and in the daytime. An anatomical characteristic, the development of a reflective layer in the retina, does not, however, correspond with this activity pattern, as would be expected. One possible explanation is that since the extinction of the large species, nocturnal and diurnal species have expanded their activities temporally.[67] In other words, one cannot explain the current patterns of activity without reference to fairly recent changes brought about by people; to try to explain them by current physiology and ecosystem dynamics may lead to erroneous interpretations. The extinction of large lemurs may have had as yet undetermined impacts on the dispersal of plant species as well.[68] One cannot just catalogue the losses of habitat and species and then study current systems as if they were stable. Losses may not always be evident: forests may appear in terms of tree species diversity to be fully functioning but may have suffered changes in their fauna or soil that limit their potential for continued survival.

On the islands of Hawai'i, a second wave of human colonization followed the first, about three hundred years ago. The new colonists introduced more domesticated animals and plants, more inadvertent passengers, and more intensive and extensive use of the land. They converted almost all of the lowlands to such agricultural uses as monocultures of pineapples and bananas (see fig. 1.2). Much larger fields replaced the indigenous agriculture in the lowlands. Large areas of uplands were converted to pastures. On the island of Hawai'i, such introduced plants as *Opuntia* and non-native spreading grasses overran much of the northern regions, which lie in the rain shadow of the major volcanic peaks. Goats roamed everywhere, destroying reproduction of such rare species as silversword (*Argyroxiphium sandwicense*). The dynamics of the systems were, however, complex. A successful effort to remove the goats from Volcanos National Park reduced the grazing pressure but allowed grasses, a ready supply of fuel for large fires, to spread. Uncontrollable fires in these grasses have destroyed some persisting stands of the fire-sensitive tree *Metrosideros* (see fig. 6.4). The spread of a non-native, nitrogen-fixing tree, *Myrica faya*, is changing the nutrient relations of primary succession on lava flows.[69] Some plant species seem to have lost important dispersers, which may have led to their current restricted distributions.[70]

The consequences of the human occupation of Madagascar and Hawai'i have been dramatic; many endemic species have been lost and replaced by non-native species in the last two millennia. The intensity of human disturbances in these relatively small, isolated landscapes may throw into relief the consequences of these disturbances, in ways that are not obvious in larger landscapes with a longer history of human impact. Studying them may help us understand not only their distinctive systems, but also, by extrapolation, potential impacts in larger areas.

Ecosystems that exist today are a single node in the continuing evolution and migration of species. They have been shaped not only by the prehuman processes of evolution and migration, but also by such human impacts as human-caused extinctions and modification of habitats. In most of the world, ecosystems contain novel associations of species brought together through human agency in habitats that have been altered by human activities. Because of this, the maintenance of native species diversity calls for a major input of effort (energy) to counteract human-dispersed species and modified habitats. Although climate change may favor these native systems, it is more likely that it will render them even more labile in their competition with wide-ranging introduced species with wide environmental tolerances. Not only have species formed changing associations over time when subjected to climate change, but also insurmountable barriers to migration have led to the extinction of species that could not adapt quickly enough to extremes of climate. We may be placing such barriers, in the shape of very resistant non-native communities or human-modified habitats, in the way of species migrations in reaction to climatic warming, which will lead to extinctions.

Regardless, the historical record shows that communities have constantly changed, over all timescales from evolutionary and geologic down to seasonal. Human-induced changes are superimposed on those forced by climate, plate tectonics, evolution, and geomorphology. It may be reasonable to assume, because of the slow rate of change, that ecosystems are in some kind of equilibrium with nonhuman forces, but it is not reasonable to assume that they are in equilibrium with rapid, human-induced changes. Current ecosystems carry with them the baggage of human-induced modifications over the past millennia or at least the past centuries. Assuming otherwise—that is, assuming that they are in equilibrium with conditions that can be measured now—will almost surely lead to erroneous conclusions about the relation between current conditions and processes that drive the systems.

*Biospheric Sustainability*

Can the earth continue to support life as we know it for the foreseeable future? This is the most basic question addressed by the concept of biospheric sustainability. It presents questions of theoretical, practical, and philosophical importance and subsumes concerns about eutrophication, acidification, and decreased biodiversity. Within this context, eutrophication and acidification represent the loss of a desirable, sustainable state, and biodiversity is a potentially critical factor in sustaining systems. To maintain an ecosystem or the biosphere, we must understand the ecology of the systems and apply this basic knowledge to their management. Because the use of resources changes them as well as irreversibly depleting some, making decisions about the limits of acceptable change or substituting renewable for nonrenewable resources requires the assigning of relative values to the resources.[1]

Conscious concern that humans are running out of room and resources is not new. In A.D. 200, for example, Tertullian, a Carthaginian Christian writer, observed that "our numbers are burdensome to the world, which can hardly supply us from its natural elements."[2] People had explored everywhere and exploited everything. Wilderness areas had become estates and forests cultivated fields. Swamps had been drained, deserts planted, and wild beasts replaced by domestic herds. Nature was failing to provide its usual sustenance.[3] The theme of overpopulation recurred sporadically through the centuries, but the dire predictions were fulfilled only locally. After decimation by major wars, famines, or diseases, population usually rebounded to even higher levels, spurred by new techniques of production. Immigration to lightly settled regions relieved local population pressure, so that the real limits for global population did not ever appear to be reached. Some people mourned the loss of "natural" beauty where human populations became dense, yet most applauded the taming of wilderness.

Early apprehension about sustainability focused on resources, especially food and forest products. As populations grew, the demand on agriculture to produce adequate supplies of food and fiber and on forestry to produce adequate wood products grew apace. Even where agriculture produced surpluses, wind and water erosion threatened future productivity in many areas.[4] People devised a wide range of techniques to perpetuate the productivity of agriculture, such as terraces to hold soil, and fertilizers, including human and livestock manure and other waste, to replenish nutrients removed by crops or eroded away. Shifting agriculture relied on soil processes to return nutrients to depleted soil. In dry, windy areas, windbreaks helped to protect the earth from wind erosion. In the mid–nineteenth century, major trade developed in materials used for fertilizer, for example, bones, guano, and oil seed cake, fed to livestock mainly for its value in producing excellent manure. About the same time, the nascent chemical industry introduced the first major manufactured fertilizer, superphosphate.[5]

With chemical fertilizers, it became possible to increase productivity quickly and greatly. These, combined with technological advances in pest and weed control, new crop varieties, and larger equipment, led to more intensive and extensive use of land, with major short-term increases in productivity. Less emphasis was placed on such long-term benefits as holding topsoil or improving soil. In reaction against this attitude, there was renewed interest in growing crops in ways that would be "sustainable" over the long term. These methods improved rather than degraded the quality of the soil, minimized erosion, and in general helped assure productivity into the future. They copied some features of natural systems, for example, mixing crops and encouraging natural predator control of pests.[6] These were, however, still agroecosystems, designed for producing food and fiber. Species composition was planned and carefully monitored and controlled. Inputs of nutrients responded to measured requirements of specific crop plants. Continued productivity defined sustainability, although there was also a desire for minimizing impact on the surrounding, more natural ecosystems.

Heavy demands for wood products led to the planting and managing of trees as well. The ancient coppice woodlands of England, for example, survived many centuries of continuous cropping.[7] Plantations of fast-growing, often non-native species, especially *Eucalyptus* and conifers, also furnished a constant supply of wood, although they, too, replaced naturally reproducing forests.

Space exploration inspired quite a different concept of sustainability. People generally had accepted the concept, based on theory and exploration, that the earth was finite, but this concept crystallized when satellites sent back pictures of the earth floating in a sea of space. We became conscious that we really are like Antoine de Saint-Exupéry's Little Prince, tending our planet, which will no longer support us if we do not keep the destructive elements under control. Even more, we began to realize that we have the ability to alter the entire planet, not just little parts of it, and that altering one bit, or component, will very likely have indirect impacts on many others.

The earth as we know it is the result of billions of years of change. Not only the species that constitute the biosphere, but also the physical life-support systems of earth, water, and atmosphere have developed through eons of evolution. The rapid changes that we see today appear to be retrograde, and the possibility of natural adaptation, migration, or evolution to mitigate them appears remote. The message of sustainability of the biosphere is, then, that it is up to humans to redirect their energies to learning to live within the limits imposed by current tolerances of the living and nonliving earth and actively to manage ecosystems where necessary to keep them from deleterious alterations.[8] In the terminology of economics, use of the environment should not deplete its capital.[9] As the title of a recent book by several ecologists says, the future is *In Our Hands*.[10] That such self-determination might not be possible in the face of an increasing population was suggested by Thomas Malthus in the mid–nineteenth century, when he observed that whereas population increases at a geometric rate, productivity increases only at an arithmetic rate, so will inevitably be overwhelmed—but the limits can probably be stretched.

Sustainability thus has meaning mainly in terms of its implications and expectations for the future.[11] If sustainability means maintaining the requisite conditions for life to continue more or less as we know it, it implies a dynamic system that changes within certain boundaries, within which fluctuations are damped to avoid total destruction. Sustainability cannot mean maintaining some status quo ante, for example, some hypothetical system that may have existed in the past in a world without people. It also cannot mean maintaining a static system because climate and culture will continue to change. Projecting current processes to the future is instructive but can represent only a small portion of the potential consequences of altered conditions because the biosphere, and certainly the biosphere plus people, is an open system, one that will change unpredictably.[12]

The concept of sustainability thus suffers from a loss of specificity when it is removed from the realm of sustaining specific resources. Sustaining of ecosystem services, for example, cycling carbon dioxide and nutrients and maintaining hydrologic regimes, is a laudable goal, but until we know more about how these function, including their regional and temporal variability and resilience, we can only insist, not unreasonably, that any change is for the worse. According to a report on world conservation strategy for sustainable development, for example, forest resources should be managed according to principles of stewardship "to maintain in perpetuity ecological processes, watersheds, soils and genetic diversity."[13] We know little, however, about how to maintain processes or species, either individually or in assemblages. We do know that climatic change will require that species alter their ranges and most likely their associations, as has happened since the end of the last glaciation, if they are to survive.[14] We do not know which species will be able to do this and which will not, and what the consequences of losing those that cannot will be.

The usefulness of historical study in evaluating potential change and formulating policy may be illustrated with a specific example: problems of sustaining the oak-dominated forests of the northeastern United States. "Recent evidence . . . has accumulated to the point where there is no longer any question that oak will be displaced on many sites" in its range in North America.[15] In part because this is regarded as a major silvicultural problem ("one of the most serious silvicultural problems in the eastern United States"),[16] foresters and ecologists have devoted considerable research to trying to understand its causes. The use of historical study, both to assess the vegetation of the area before major deforestation in the last few centuries and to interpret changes in factors responsible for oak regeneration, constitutes a model for applying historical analyses to current ecological questions. Sustainability is often viewed today with reference to potential future environmental changes, for example, global warming, but first we must be able to do the easier job, to sustain systems under current conditions. This research raises many questions about sustainability as it refers to preserving seminatural ecosystems, processes, and genetic diversity.[17] Among them are

1. What community do we want to maintain?
2. When a community is changing, how do we know which changes are temporary and which signal future loss of the community?
3. How have past human impacts affected the potential to maintain the community, whether by nonintervention or by active management?

*Table 12.1. Commercial timberland in the eastern United States.*

| Forest type | Hectares (millions) | Percent of total |
|---|---|---|
| Oak-hickory | 44 | 26.8 |
| Maple-beech-birch | 15 | 9.0 |
| Oak-pine | 14 | 8.5 |
| Oak-gum-cypress | 11 | 6.6 |
| Elm-ash-cottonwood | 9 | 5.5 |
| Aspen-birch | 8 | 4.7 |
| Other | 64 | 39.0 |

*Source:* Millers et al., *History of Hardwood Decline.*

## Critical Features and Changes in Oak-dominated Forests

Oaks are synonymous with the forest vegetation of large areas of eastern North America.[18] Other kinds of trees like hemlock, beech, sugar and red maples, and pines are common on some sites, but various species of oak dominate remaining mature forests (table 12.1).[19] Advance regeneration in many of these stands, however, consists of the more shade-tolerant and mesic species—eastern hemlock, beech, and sugar maple—or the fast-growing species characteristic of more open sites—red maple, black gum, and black birch. The maintenance of this forest type is important for two reasons: first, it was widespread when European settlers arrived on this continent, so it embodies the natural biodiversity and typical ecosystem processes of the region; and, second, oak is currently more valuable as lumber than its replacements.[20]

Three categories of forest stands contain clues about changes in these forests: old growth stands, which contain many very old trees; successional stands that have grown after the abandonment of farming; and younger forests that have grown after logging operations. None of these is an exclusive category; overlaps are common. For example, many stands that include very old trees have been grazed and selectively logged. Finally, the composition of any of these stands can be compared with that inferred for precolonial forests to indicate changes in the interim.

Almost all extensive stands have regenerated after repeated logging or abandonment of agricultural land as well as being subject to such natural disturbances as hurricanes. In such stands in Connecticut in 1907, more than 90 percent of the trees had originated about 1870–75 as sprouts that had overtopped the numerous but slower-growing seedling trees (table 12.2).

Table 12.2. *Average number of trees per acre in three different forest associations in the Housatonic Valley of Connecticut.*

| | Chestnut | Chestnut oak | White oak | Red oak | Black oak | Hickories | Sugar maple | Red maple | Other | Total | % | Average age (years) |
|---|---|---|---|---|---|---|---|---|---|---|---|---|
| **Chestnut slope** | | | | | | | | | | | | |
| Sprouts | 411 | 22 | 24 | 46 | 4 | 67 | 61 | 97 | 138 | 732 | 97 | 28 |
| From seed | 3 | 0 | 3 | 4 | 0 | 6 | 2 | 2 | 39 | 20 | 3 | |
| Total | 414 | 22 | 27 | 50 | 4 | 73 | 63 | 99 | 177 | 752 | | |
| **Mixed slope** | | | | | | | | | | | | |
| Sprouts | 157 | 124 | 53 | 135 | 13 | 110 | 146 | 153 | 232 | 891 | 96 | 32 |
| From seed | 3 | 8 | 4 | 12 | 1 | 6 | 4 | 3 | 64 | 41 | 4 | |
| Total | 160 | 132 | 57 | 147 | 14 | 116 | 150 | 156 | 296 | 932 | | |
| **Oak ridge** | | | | | | | | | | | | |
| Sprouts | 29 | 272 | 99 | 148 | 45 | 251 | 21 | 72 | 133 | 937 | 96 | 38 |
| From seed | 0 | 14 | 5 | 12 | 0 | 8 | 2 | 1 | 16 | 42 | 4 | |
| Total | 29 | 286 | 104 | 160 | 45 | 259 | 23 | 73 | 149 | 979 | | |

*Source:* Schwarz, The sprout forests.

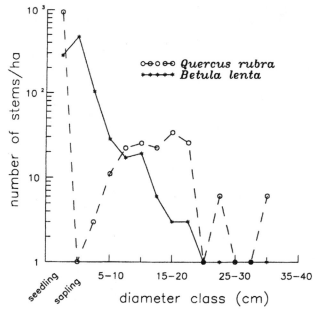

Figure 12.1. Size-class distribution of two tree
taxa in a previously logged forest in New Jersey.
(Data from E. W. B. Russell, Vegetational change
in northern New Jersey since 1500 A.D.: a palynological, vegetational and historical synthesis
[Ph.D. diss., Rutgers University, 1979])

Seedlings in these stands also suffered from burial by heavy litter, fires, and
browsing by squirrels, rabbits, and mice. Although they could sprout back
from such damage several times, they gradually lost vigor and died, lasting
maybe as long as thirty years. In these sprout forests it appeared in the early
to mid–twentieth century that oaks would maintain dominance for some
time to come but mainly from sprout reproduction.[21] In the mid to late twentieth century, however, studies in many oak forests in the northeastern
United States encountered very few oak saplings in such sprout-dominated
forests. Oak seedlings might be numerous, but other species were more common as small trees (fig. 12.1).[22]

Not only is reproduction apparently insufficient to replace older oak trees,
but drought, frost, outbreaks of fungi, and insect pests, often exacerbating
each other's effects, have killed mature trees prematurely throughout their
range in the past few centuries. Hard hit, for example, have been stands in
the Appalachian Mountains, where mortality has been associated with

*Table 12.3. Relative abundance of potential canopy tree species in Hutcheson Memorial Forest in New Jersey.*

| Species | Trees | Saplings | Seedlings |
|---|---|---|---|
| *Acer negundo* | 0.7 | 2.3 | 0.3 |
| *Acer platanoides*\* | 3.4 | 5.7 | 5.3 |
| *Acer rubrum* | 8.9 | 25.2 | 4.6 |
| *Acer saccharum* | 0.7 | 6.5 | 10.2 |
| *Ailanthus altissima*\* | 0.3 | 0.5 | 0.0 |
| *Betula lenta* | 0.0 | 0.0 | 0.0 |
| *Carya* spp | 10.5 | 2.6 | 2.1 |
| *Fagus grandifolia* | 0.9 | 4.4 | 0.8 |
| *Fraxinus americana* | 15.0 | 44.7 | 21.9 |
| *Nyssa sylvatica* | 0.0 | 0.0 | 2.1 |
| *Prunus avium*\* | 9.2 | 3.9 | 4.3 |
| *Prunus serotina* | 0.3 | 0.0 | 2.4 |
| *Quercus alba* | 30.5 | 2.1 | 1.1 |
| *Quercus rubra* | 9.5 | 0.8 | 0.0 |
| *Quercus velutina* | 8.8 | 0.3 | 42.7 |
| *Sassafras albidum* | 1.2 | 1.0 | 1.8 |
| *Ulmus* spp | 0.0 | 0.0 | 0.3 |

\*Non-native species.

*Source:* Forman and Elfstrom, Forest structure comparison.

droughts since 1980, insect defoliation, and perhaps high ozone concentrations.[23] Uniform age, low diversity, and sprout origin are other factors contributing to the problem.[24]

On the other hand, old growth stands have never been clear-cut, so they constitute a very small remnant carrying the tenuous thread of continuity from the aboriginal forest into the present. Human activities have altered them all, however, to a greater or lesser extent; the continued existence of "pristine old growth" is indeed a myth.[25] The few unlogged oak woodlands are small and isolated and have been subject to heavy use for firewood and grazing as well as to changed disturbance regimes; ongoing changes are apparent in most. The dominant white oaks in an old, twenty-four-hectare unlogged stand in New Jersey, for example, probably originated as seedlings, but in the late twentieth century there was little evidence of replacement from seedlings or saplings (table 12.3). White ash dominated the (sparse) sapling layer, while the seedlings were mainly black oak, white ash, and sugar maple. Beech and red maple as well as white and black oaks dominated younger

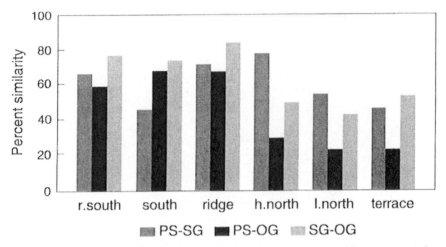

Figure 12.2. Comparison of forests on six different site types in Illinois. On each site type (ridge south, south-facing slope, ridge top, high and low north-facing slopes, and terrace) paired comparisons are made between prehistoric composition derived from survey data (PS), old growth stands (OG), and successional stands (SG). (Data from Fralish, Comparisons of forests in Illinois.)

stands in the region, and in these there were more beech and red and sugar maple than oak saplings and seedlings.[26] In other areas such as east-central Indiana, other species are also apparently replacing oaks in old-growth oak-dominated woodlots.[27]

The differences between the composition of old-growth oak forests and precolonial forest, as reconstructed by survey data, suggest the possible effects of human impact in the past several centuries. In one such stand in Pennsylvania in 1992, some 87 percent of the stems were chestnut oaks, red maples, and black and yellow birches, some of the chestnut oaks being at least three hundred years old. In the eighteenth century, however, these four species accounted for only 9 percent of the 513 witness trees tallied for the area, while 80 percent of the trees were black and white oaks, chestnut, and hickory. Most of the saplings and seedlings were red maple and yellow birch in 1992, with some chestnut oak, implying yet a further change in composition.[28] In Illinois, one-hundred- to two-hundred-year-old forest stands on south-facing and ridgetop sites were fairly similar to forests reconstructed from precolonial surveys on similar sites, but north-facing stands had more sugar maple and beech trees than the reconstructed presettlement forests (fig. 12.2).[29]

In New Jersey, the divergence from eighteenth-century forest composition in part reflects different past land use (table 12.4). Stands that were clear-cut once in the late eighteenth century and subsequently cut selectively include

*Table 12.4. Comparison of prehistoric and twentieth-century forest vegetation in New Jersey.*

|  | Prehistoric (relative density) | Area 1 (relative density) | Area 2 (relative basal area) | Area 3 (relative density) |
|---|---|---|---|---|
| Oak | 60–65 | 35 | 70 | 51 |
| Hickory | 1–20 | 4 | + | 11 |
| Chestnut | 1–20 | 0 | 0 | 0 |
| Maples | 1–6 | 6 | 17 | 11 |
| Ash | 1–5 | 2 | + | 16 |
| Beech | 0–5 | 13 |  | 1 |
| Walnut | 1–12 |  |  | + |
| Elm |  |  |  | 0 |
| Birch | 1–5 | 28 | 10 | 0 |
| Yellow poplar |  | 10 |  | 0 |
| Norway maple |  |  |  | 10 |

Area 1. One area of larger forest clearcut in eighteenth century, selectively cut thereafter.*

Area 2. One area of larger forest cut several times for charcoal in the nineteenth century.**

Area 3. Old-growth woodlot, twenty-four hectares.†

*Data summarized from J. G. Ehrenfeld, History of the vegetation and the land of Morristown National Historical Park, New Jersey, since 1700, *Bulletin of the New Jersey Academy of Science* 27:1–19, 1982.

**E. W. B. Russell, Vegetational change in northern New Jersey since 1500 A.D.: a palynological, vegetational and historical synthesis (Ph.D. diss., Rutgers University, New Brunswick, N.J., 1979).

†R. T. T. Forman and B. A. Elfstrom, Forest structure.

more beech, birch, and yellow poplar than eighteenth-century forests. An area somewhat farther north and west but on similar geologic substrate was repeatedly cut for charcoal, and here the late-twentieth-century vegetation included about the same amount of oak as earlier forests but more red and sugar maples and birch. Hickory had become less common under both regimes, while oak dominance had shifted from white and black oak to chestnut oak in both. For an old-growth, uncut forest, the figures are closer to those found in the surveys for oak and hickory, but there is much more ash, native maples (red and sugar), and the non-native Norway maple (*Acer platanoides*). The old-growth forest remained a better model of the older, prehistoric forests than the more extensive cut-over stands.

Few rare or endangered species of plants or animals are restricted to these oak-dominated forests, although some are undoubtedly more common there than elsewhere. On the other hand, many formerly common species have been eliminated from this region over the past several hundred years, including wolves, mountain lions, passenger pigeons, and chestnut trees. Some currently regionally rare species, for example, small whorled pogonia (*Isotria medeoloides*), American ginseng, and bald eagles, were formerly much more common in these forests. Others like deer and beavers were almost eliminated by the late nineteenth century or even earlier but have rebounded because of changed habitat and reintroductions by people. The ranges of many others, such as birds that live in forest interiors, have been greatly limited by the reduction in forest cover and the fragmentation of remaining forests.[30]

How important was the loss of chestnut to the remaining species composition and functioning of forests? In most areas, it appears that species that were formerly important in the forests are replacing the chestnut, perhaps shifting the composition somewhat toward such earlier successional species as black birch and red maple, but in general having minor impact.[31] On the other hand, a forest modeling experiment indicates that the loss of chestnut will lead to long-term changes in forest function as indicated by biomass and leaf area index as well as composition.[32] Forests in which the chestnut trees died decades ago and which now have a closed canopy may still be responding to this loss well in the past.

The reintroduced white-tailed deer may eliminate most vegetation less than a meter tall except species that they do not prefer, such as the prolific non-native Japanese barberry (*Berberis thunbergii*) and native white snakeroot (*Eupatorium rugosum*) (see fig. 6.3). Especially where hunting is not allowed, changed habitat and extermination of most predators (except cars!) have contributed to the sizes of deer herds. Where deer browsing is not very intense, such non-native vines as Japanese honeysuckle and oriental bittersweet inhibit regeneration of trees, while the non native tree, Norway maple, often flourishes. The complex interactions of changing past and present land use, hunting, and species interactions contribute to the changing composition of these forests.

To summarize, although there are still extensive oak-dominated forests in this region, the structure and diversity of these has been greatly changed by people over the past several centuries. These forests have value for such uses as timber production, recreation, and watershed protection. Foresters seem to agree that the value is highest if they are maintained as oak forests, yet it is possible that they might serve the other functions even if their composition were to change. Loss or severe further reduction in a major forest type, however, would entail a decrease in the diversity of the regional vegetation, possibly reducing its ability to respond to further perturbations. The question then becomes, Do we know enough to sustain such a forest? Can it sustain itself or have people modified conditions so much that continued active management will be necessary to maintain it? And, finally, just what kind of forest do we want? These questions may seem trivial in the face of the major losses of species and old-growth forests in tropical regions, but answers for this well-studied exemplar may provide some directions for research and management in complex tropical systems.

## The Contributions of History to Elucidating Causes of Changes

Oak is a widely distributed genus of tree; it is found in North and South America, Eurasia, and North Africa and has 450 or more species, all of which formed part of a variety of assemblages during the Tertiary period.[33] In North America oak probably grew with other broad-leaved trees like chestnut, walnut (*Juglans*), alder, willow (*Salix*), water elm (*Planera*), hackberry (*Celtis*), elm, holly, and maple.[34] As the climate alternated between glacial and interglacial during the Quaternary period the differences among species in their tolerances of changed climate and their migration rates led to a shifting mosaic of plant and animal communities. Because more time was spent in glacials than in interglacials, it is unlikely that the relations that characterize the interglacials, such as the one that we are currently experiencing, are highly evolved.[35] In addition, during the last millennia of the last glacial advance humans arrived in North America.

It is against this backdrop that we must evaluate the stability and dynamics of this forest vegetation. According to pollen records, oak migrated north rapidly in North America as the glaciers retreated, reaching its northern limit by about 8000 B.P.[36] We can only conjecture what the interactions of people were with these plant and animal communities. As large herbivores like mastodons and giant beavers became extinct, along with their predators, did other smaller herbivores increase in density to substitute for them, changing the kinds of plants eaten? What other adjustments followed their demise?

In addition, the people who immigrated to North America were adept at using fire; otherwise they could never have survived their long, arduous trek from Asia and the harsh cold of their early years on the continent. Their arrival in an area must have brought an increase not only in use of resources, but also in fire ignitions. Populations waxed and waned and cultures developed, causing varied impacts on the biota. With the advent of agriculture in the region, shifting agricultural clearing, sometimes extensive and at least semiper-manent, introduced yet other potential impacts on the vegetation and fauna.

Although the overall pattern of oak dominance in the region was fairly stable after about eight thousand years ago, locally the proportion of oak fluctuated.[37] Local disturbances or short-term changes in climate may have caused these variations, but such human activities as the setting of fires and local clearing may have been important too. When these practices are superimposed on the overall pollen record for the region, however, the pattern that emerges is still one of overall oak dominance that lasted for many millennia. Unfortunately, the record does not allow us to assess the contributions of different species of oak, many herbaceous plants, and insect-pollinated taxa. It does, however, indicate a wide range of conditions, from cool areas with hemlock and beech to warm ones with hickory, from wet areas with alder to dry ones with pine.

The amount of fire in the region, indicated by fossil charcoal, varied both regionally and over time. Near the prairie border to the west, it appears that oak was common upwind of local firebreaks, with mesic species downwind, on similar soils.[38] There was a major increase in the number of fires in the northeast, for example, after a major decline in the amount of hemlock in the forests about 5000 B.P. Human populations also became larger then.[39] The causal relations here are, however, difficult to disentangle. Oaks provide more food for people than hemlocks do; they are also more fire prone than hemlocks. Did the higher human population density contribute to more fire, thus helping perpetuate the oak forests, or did increased fire and oaks predate human population increase? Careful crossdating of fire histories and human population levels will help elucidate these complex interactions.

Seventeenth- and eighteenth-century colonists in eastern North America faced a daunting task: vast forests stood in the way of their planting of crops they needed to sustain their lives. Some were able to exploit fields previously cleared by Amerindians, but most had to remove large trees to make fields.[40] Deforestation was a goal to be achieved as quickly as possible. After farmers removed or killed the trees, they plowed the soil, planted crop plants, pastures, orchards, and, inadvertently, weeds and sent their livestock into remaining forests for forage. Where soils were poor or hillsides too steep for crops, they cut trees for fuel. This process of deforestation was rapid and drastic. For example, in one agricultural region of New York State, a few small fields had been cleared by 1777, totaling perhaps 7 percent of the area. Dense forest surrounded these fields. About a hundred years later, in the mid–nineteenth century, more than 90 percent of the land was cultivated (see fig. 8.7). In north-central North Carolina, farmland covered 80–90 percent of the land by the mid to late nineteenth century. The general picture is clear: major deforestation for agriculture took place within a century or so of the arrival of European settlers. The effect on the vegetation was equivalent to that of a major climatic change.[41]

In agricultural areas, native trees remained in scattered woodlots, as small trees regenerating along field edges and as plantings along roads and around buildings. Agricultural fields isolated most of these from other woodlots (see figs. 9.3, 9.6),[42] although some hedgerows and stream-bank trees formed more or less continuous, though narrow, corridors. Farm use of these woodlots for fuel, building materials, litter for fertilizer, and wood ashes was intense.[43] Farmers collected hickory nuts and chestnuts and hunted small game and deer, reenacting the activities of a hunting and gathering culture. They eliminated some animals through overhunting, habitat reduction, and deliberate attempts to reduce the threat to domestic livestock and other resources. Passenger pigeons, for example, were killed in their roosts, both because they were edible and because their large concentrations damaged the forest trees. In their major roosting sites during migration they had provided a major source of fertilizer to the forest floor.[44]

Many forested areas, however, were not suitable for agriculture. Massive harvesting of wood from these never eliminated the forest completely but did change its structure. By 1900 in New Jersey, for example, forests covered only 10–20 percent of the land in fertile valleys, but extended over 80–100 percent of upland areas with rocky soils on steep slopes. The average age of the upland forests was only about thirty years, while woodlot trees were often much older. Such a pattern of land use favored species that sprouted easily and those that thrive in open areas, for example, birch, replacing seedling-grown oaks and chestnuts.[45]

Starting in the late nineteenth century and continuing into the twentieth, farmland in this region was abandoned, and heavy, destructive cutting of forests for charcoal ceased. Abandoned farms became young forest stands, usually with no active management. Most of the sprout forests also grew back without active management. Many of these would be a hundred years old by 1990, with much of their disturbance history, caused by human activities, hidden in the past, although some grazing and selective logging continued.

In the late nineteenth century, surveys that catalogued the forest resources of the individual states generally concluded that the resources had been severely abused in the past and recommended future management to maintain the stock of timber and to protect watersheds.[46] For example, in 1900 the New Jersey State geologist commented that the "superior quality of water from . . . wooded districts, over that gathered in a cleared farming country, makes it desirable that the forests in the Highlands should be kept, and not be cleared and put in farms."[47] Forests were also valuable for education, because "there trees, shrubs and herbaceous plants are found in their native *habitat*, and their relations to one another are there studied to the best advantage." In addition, "it would be a public misfortune to lose any of our characteristic species or their natural grouping, as now existing, or to have our rich botanical heritage marred by general deforestation of the State."[48] Such forests should be managed wisely for timber, especially chestnut, probably as coppice.

The most serious threats to forest vegetation were thought to be clearing for farmland, fires, grazing, and overcutting.[49] Removing the thick understory and dead, dying, and diseased trees and preventing forest fires and grazing would allow natural forces to produce healthy forests.[50] Nature needed a little help from people but would basically do the job alone. The assumption was that increased disturbance by humans was upsetting the natural balance of the forests. The role of forest managers was to prevent this disturbance in order to let natural processes return to the forests.

Pollen analysis confirms this pattern of a fairly stable forest before European colonization, followed by major changes due to human disturbance. By about 1900, under the onslaught of deforestation for agriculture, negligent logging, and increased fires indicated by charcoal in sediments, most remaining forests had less beech and hemlock and more birch, red maple, pine and probably chestnut than the precolonial forests.[51]

A shift in attitude about management of forests, from nonintervention to the reintroduction of disturbance, has characterized the second half of the twentieth century. It has been argued that the only factors likely to have altered forest composition over such a large region are changed fire regimes and climate.[52] For example, changes in old-growth forests in Illinois have been blamed on the eliminating of disturbance, especially fire and possibly buffaloes: "Our present old growth forest is an artifact of near total protection while presettlement forest developed under a fire regime."[53] To maintain this forest type with its typical herbaceous understory, the management of oak forests may require the reintroduction of "disturbance at the level found in presettlement forest."[54] In Pennsylvania too, fire was assumed to have been the major disturbance responsible for presettlement dominance of oak. Since then, however, in addition to the removal of disturbance, selective logging in the 1930s and 1940s is assumed to have accelerated succession to more mesic trees, by releasing those that were in the understory (successful there because of the absence of fire). In the absence of major disturbance, this stand is assumed now to be heading for dominance by mesic hardwoods.[55]

This assumption focuses on disturbances that have decreased in the past several centuries, ignoring the consequences of greatly increased disturbance regimes in the interim. The reintroduction of fire does not seem to mimic the conjectured role of fire in the prehistoric forests.[56] Patterns of logging, especially in terms of favoring trees that sprout and the sprouting habit, have had widespread, major repercussions on forest growth. Selective logging, for example, has been blamed both for increasing the amounts of the light-demanding species such as red maple and black birch and for accelerating succession to sugar maple.[57] Chestnut and chestnut oak sprout prolifically even when they are large, but white oak does not sprout well when it is more than forty centimeters in diameter at breast height, so the original cutting had most likely led to a decrease in white oak.[58]

More subtle causes for the change in species dominance can be inferred, and their possible impacts tested by incorporating them into models of forest growth. For example, some experiments hint that tree species respond differently to various levels of soil nutrients, especially nitrogen. It appears that low levels of nitrogen may, for example, favor sugar maple over red and chestnut oaks.[59] The impact of industrial air pollutants and diverse kinds of land use on the available nitrogen in soils may help account for the current increase in sugar maple and other changes in species composition. In addition, microsites for seedling establishment are different after a site has been clear-cut or burned than after a blowdown.[60]

Other changed conditions caused by human impact have played a role in changing these forests. Seas of cultivated farmland that isolated woodlots inhibited the transport of animal-dispersed seeds from one woodlot to another, while favoring the dispersal of species such as birch, yellow poplar, and maple, with windblown seeds. Hedgerows favored species spread by birds.[61] The absence of passenger pigeons may have inhibited long-distance dispersal of large seeds, even though blue jays may have partly filled this niche.[62] In England, defoliation by caterpillars that drop from the canopy and then feed on young seedlings is blamed in part for the lack of oak regeneration under oak canopy.[63] Perhaps the increase in non-native herbivorous insects such as gypsy moths is important in North America. Deer undoubtedly are also having an impact in many forests.

The processes and composition of these forests are not only the consequences of factors that can be measured and analyzed currently. They also reflect logging history, changed disturbance regimes and landscape patterns, and altered soil processes over the life of the trees (and perhaps even longer). Imaginative research is beginning to tease out the details of these differences and their historical causes, and only starting to elucidate some of their consequences for the regenerating of stable oak forests. Assuming that the landscape will return to some pristine, revirginized condition if left to its own devices flies in the face of the evidence by ignoring critical intervening factors. The sustainability of this landscape must be defined in light of these factors.

### Prediction and Management for Sustainability

The dynamics of ecosystems make it difficult to predict how changing climate and human activities will affect biodiversity and ecosystem stability or resilience. In the words of one group of researchers, "In most places, the forests of 1975 have changed since . . . 1955 and, by the time we learn to accommodate to the damage, it will be 1995 and more changes will have taken place."[64] Vegetational changes predicted under conditions of global climate change are often drastic.[65] Could we have predicted two centuries ago the changes that have occurred up to the present even without major climatic change? A century ago? Fifty years ago? Are current changes consistent with previous predictions? Why not? All of these questions affect decisions made in regard to sustainability, which implies the possibility of predicting the effects of current and future management or lack of management.

It is self-evident that one could not have predicted the current structure of the forests of the Northeast from the dynamics and structure of those of the eighteenth century. Even if there had been ecologists in the eighteenth century who were able to decipher all of the processes that were active at the time, prediction would have been impossible. They would have had to foresee the effects of peripheral land clearing, grazing, a changed fire regime, and timber cutting. They may have anticipated a dearth of seed sources, edge effects that would penetrate the borders of the forest, and the impacts of domestic livestock. They could have observed the decline in deer browsing as deer populations plummeted, and perhaps changes in other small game species that were hunted, such as squirrels and rabbits. They could not have predicted the invention of the locomotive with concomitant increases in fire ignitions, the explosive increase in deer herds in the twentieth century, or which exotic species would invade the forests. The chestnut blight and the destructive use of hemlock for bark used to tan imported hides would also have been beyond the realm of reasonable expectations. These hypothetical eighteenth-century ecologists would have no doubt predicted expanded agriculture in the region and seen no reason for the pressure on the local forest products to decrease. Presumably such surprises lie in our future as well.

What are the consequences of such insights for the questions of sustainability? First, we do not know the composition of vegetation at any particular historical period. Even in North America, where conservation often aims to reconstruct or maintain ecosystems as they were before the advent of European colonists only a few centuries ago, the details are hazy, and, of course, such an observation is even more pertinent to the study of historic vegetation in regions settled by dense populations even farther back in time. Second, climate is only one of a complex of factors that influence vegetation. Disturbances, both "natural" and human-mediated, play major roles in determining the structure and composition of plant and animal communities. The magnitudes and kinds of such disturbances have changed in the past and can be expected to change unpredictably in the future. Most current ecosystems are likely not in a steady state, so if the goal of sustainability is to maintain systems as they exist today, complex disturbance regimes will probably be necessary. It has been observed with relation to oak forests of England that "if the objective of management is to produce something approaching mature forest then the management prescription should be unequivocally one of non-intervention. This will necessarily produce an ecosystem of zero net-productivity, probably a woodland of low aesthetic value and one which possibly would provide some surprises for ecologists in the final composition of its tree canopy!"[66] We may not agree with this observation, but it is becoming ever more obvious that most ecosystems that we value have a long history of human intervention, both intentional and nonintentional, and to maintain them will require continued intervention.

Decisions affecting sustainability include mitigating the effects of undesirable changes that have already occurred and eliminating causes of future changes perceived as deleterious. Dealing with the first level implies local solutions, both private and public, about managing land and ecosystems. Dealing with the second implies political solutions, convincing people and governments that some sacrifice now will pay off in the future. Both of these decisions imply the acquiring of potentially critical habitat in order to accommodate ecosystems that will be eliminated by climate change where they now exist. But do we know how to manage even those lands that have been acquired to preserve their current biota?

In addition, it will be necessary to make management recommendations for much privately owned property if we are to maintain any semblance of natural ecosystems for the long term. This will require some basis for prediction. Any expectation of the future is a model, based on the extrapolating of past experience into the future. Formal mathematical models based on hypotheses and assumptions about relevant processes form the basis for the most precise predictions and also pinpoint processes that are critical in determining outcomes. When the models are tested against experiments and past analogues, specific elements are modified where predicted results do not agree with observed results, as tested against historical trends or experiments.[67] This process allows us to focus on those factors that are most important in altering outcomes in these historical reconstructions and experimental manipulations. It generally ignores, or downplays, the openness of the system that is being modeled.[68] It is in essence ahistorical, even where it uses past conditions for testing, because it cannot incorporate unanticipated contingencies or conditions that are novel, which history documents.

History also records the uniqueness of events caused by the juxtaposition of culture, climate, and other factors at a specific time. Models, however, are tested by multiple runs, producing a central tendency, which is the most likely outcome, based on the common elements that run through history. In the real world, however, the system will run only once, and even though the central tendency is the most likely result, no extreme outcome can be ruled out. This in no way invalidates the model, just as an erroneous weather report does not invalidate the model on which it was made. History documents such contingencies, indicating some of the range of possibilities for change and how difficult they are to predict. The understanding of this range may afford additional information for decision-making, especially for indicating to the public what the uncertainties of the models are and why the models need not be ignored just because they are uncertain.[69] We approve budgets for future income and expenditures, even though actual income and expenditures rarely conform to the expected because of unanticipated contingencies. A budget fraught with uncertainties is better than no budget at all, even though it only roughly approximates the future. By comprehending the range of past conditions we can make more realistic models for the future.

Some suggestions for sustainable development in the tropics involve using the products of the intact rain forest, such as fruits, for income. This is a use that encourages maintaining the forests rather than cutting them down, and in this sense is clearly the lesser of the evils. However, one can envision past proposals for making a living in the oak, hickory, and chestnut forests also by using the resources of the forest, for example, nuts and valuable herbaceous species like climbing fern (*Lygodium palmatum*). Even if this had been sufficient to support local human populations, it would have depleted the herbaceous resources. Collecting has depleted populations of climbing fern and other valued forest herbs like ginseng and many orchids. The entirely unexpected chestnut blight eliminated a major source of fruits. The removal of large numbers of fruits also removes them from forest food webs. In other words, all activities have impacts.

Forests in many parts of eastern North America are less fragmented and abused today than they were a century or even fifty years ago. These young or recovering stands are growing on soils that have a history of disturbance, lack of old mound and pit topography, increased air pollution, high levels of carbon dioxide and available nitrogen, non-native diseases and pests, high levels of herbivory, absence of such formerly abundant species as passenger pigeons and large chestnut trees, and other changed conditions known and unknown. That they are as similar as they are to precolonial forests suggests the critical, basic role of species availability, climate, topography, and some essential soil characteristics, all of which are amenable to conventional forest modeling. Most important tree species in this region are, however, already under the onslaught of disease or pests: gypsy moth, chestnut blight, beech bark disease, Dutch elm disease, and most recently hemlock wooly adelgid, among others. In the face of these, the assumption that an unmanaged forest will develop in some "natural" way to maintain the diversity that existed before human intervention is a will-o'-the-wisp. Without knowing the history of an ecosystem, how it got to its present state, we have no way of guessing what kind of management is necessary either to deflect it from its current trajectory or to maintain the status quo. History teaches us that management for sustainability will always have to be flexible in the face of changing human impacts.

# 13

## Toward the Future: Research and Applications

Historical ecology delves into the perplexing realm between mechanistic, experimental science and descriptive "natural history." To most people, the ideal of the natural world conjures up images that are eternal and unchanging. Add humans to this world, however, and it becomes dynamic and even precarious.[1] Although we realize that the world independent of humans changes over time, the pace of such change has usually been slow, except for catastrophic events like volcanic eruptions. Mechanistic science based on the premise that the laws that govern both static and dynamic relations in this world are constant and knowable has yielded much practical information, confirming the basics of the premise. Subject poinsettias to a certain light regime and they will flower; replace the terminal buds of flowers with auxins (a plant growth hormone) and lateral buds will remain inhibited. We may not understand all the details of these processes, but we do know that they follow certain laws and can be predicted, and we expect that they will work the same a century from now as they do now.

On the other hand, we cannot predict the potential activities of people in the future, except in a gross sense. Although all people have similar requirements for food, shelter, and reproduction, cultural developments have led to an enormous variety of systems for fulfilling these requirements and many others. These adaptations cannot have been predicted from basic, constant laws, even those that include dynamic equilibria, just as future adjustments cannot be predicted. In addition, this changeability in adaptations means that observations of current human activities cannot allow one to reconstruct the past or to predict the future.

Ecosystems fall somewhere between these extremes. Ecologists act under the assumption that there are basic laws that control the essential patterns of ecosystems, for example, that productivity of lower trophic levels limits that of higher ones. Superimposed on these are, however, the outcomes of evolutionary and climatic history and sporadic past disturbances, both human and nonhuman. The human-mediated changes are those least amenable to understanding according to general laws (although prediction is also questionable for evolutionary changes). The recurrence and consequences of hurricanes can be generalized and, within certain limits, predicted. The pattern of recovery of a forest after a hurricane can likewise be predicted within limits. However, changing culture prevents our predicting future human actions. Some have criticized ecological studies that incorporate humans for continuing to treat humans as distinct from the rest of "nature," but this may be inevitable. It is by distinguishing the unique contributions of humans to current ecosystems that we can disentangle them from what can be more easily accounted for by general laws. These laws may govern the sequence of species that recolonize bare soil, but the kind of human disturbance that created the bare land may interfere with this regular pattern, or newly introduced species may disrupt it. Some laws may be robust in the face of the variety of human activities, for example, productivity or biomass accumulation may proceed the same regardless of prior conditions, but others may not hold constant, for example, prior grazing or plowing may alter nutrient cycling. Prior conditions may confound experiments carried out on sites that differ not only in current conditions, but also in history.

Human history is not repeatable (neither is any historic circumstance exactly repeatable) and is generally not reversible, yet by learning the contributions of history to present systems we can narrow the field of study necessary for prediction and management. In addition, past human activities act as experiments from which we can deduce general laws, laws that would be much more difficult to understand if we had to rely on the usually slow workings of changing natural conditions.

The contributions of historical study to the present are perhaps best understood in terms of considering history as analogue and history as prologue. Using history as analogue, we search for patterns that are repeated and use these to interpret the present and predict a range of options for the future.[2] This assumes some degree of constancy or dynamic equilibrium. Using history as prologue, we emphasize the mutability of changes and their unique contributions to the present. Those who use history as analogue commonly strive to avoid human contribution, whereas those who see history as prologue seek to partition the impacts of the past into categories that can shed light on their potential contributions to current conditions and to predictions.

### Incorporating Historical Research into Basic Ecological Studies

If the current vegetation of a formerly grazed site differs from that of a nearby plowed site, how can we determine the importance of the past use on the current system and thus incorporate this in models to interpret and predict the consequences for varying types of vegetation? The difference in past use may have been the result of subtle site characteristics that are not obvious today or may have even been obliterated by the uses. On the other hand, they may have been dictated mainly by cultural forces largely independent of the site itself. Current vegetation may affect the reaction of the system to various disturbances, but past use may also have residual effects that confound these results. Describing past human impacts qualitatively in mutually exclusive categorical terms—for example, grazed versus not grazed, clear-cut versus not clear-cut—and quantitatively—for example, ten cows per hectare versus one cow per hectare, removal of $x$ tons biomass per hectare versus removal of $y$ tons per hectare—can provide important independent variables along with more obvious variables like current vegetation, topography, and soils. Incorporating these variables into basic field experiments will add a new dimension to predicting dependent variables.

When historical analyses can reveal quantitative details of past site use, especially if there is a gradient of impact, these past uses may often be the major independent variable studied, to reveal the importance of the past activity on current systems and to model the consequences of such behaviors. These studies can be compared with studies of gradients of current stresses for analyses of the long-term consequences of the activities.[3]

The importance of quantifying past impacts lends urgency and excitement to historical ecological studies. For example, to state that fires were critical to maintaining a vegetation pattern in the past is vague and almost useless for understanding the importance of fire in affecting regeneration of vegetation. What kinds of fires? what season? how often? Such critical questions must be answered if the historical data are to be useful for comprehending the systems and for applying the knowledge to management.

In a larger conceptual context, we come back to what questions we are asking and why. The overall similarity of temperate forests in eastern Asia, eastern North America, and western Europe suggests that there are overarching physiological and evolutionary factors responsible for determining these patterns. These regions have very different histories of disturbance, but similar vegetation because of climate, soils, and adaptations of deciduous trees. The diversity of the communities is very different, being much higher in Asia than in North America and higher in North America than in Europe, largely for reasons of evolution and glacial history. These factors, however, go only part way in explaining the differences in the systems. The effects of the variable lengths and intensities of human habitation on the three continents have had major consequences for the landscape, from the human-dominated landscapes of Asia and Europe to the less obvious impacts in much of eastern North America.

These differences have made themselves felt in the development of ecological studies in the different regions: in North America ecologists until very recently tried to avoid human impact, while in Europe, human impact was assumed to be universal. Thus not only the kinds of systems that we study, but even the factors that we consider to be important are influenced by the past.

Regardless of the region, however, historical studies of past community patterns have indicated that most systems are in flux; as climate has changed, species distributions have also changed, with different species tracking climatic change with different lag times.[4] Periods of relative stability have been interspersed with periods of rapid change, sometimes referred to as times of disassembly and reassembly of communities, when climate is changing too rapidly for species to adjust quickly.[5] Although on a scale of several centuries and thousands of square kilometers the species may track climate closely, at the finer scales of time and space in which most ecologists work and species interactions take place, this equilibrium may not be apparent.[6]

Human-induced changes afford an ideal set of experiments for evaluating the relative stability of communities because they occur rapidly, can be well defined, and can to some extent be reversed. These suggest some measure of stability, and thus climatic control, of some kinds of communities and lack of resilience of others. The overall patterns of forest dominants have remained stable in northeastern North America even after a variety of human disturbances, for example, which suggests that these patterns are robust and not just chance assemblages of species that are in flux. Not only biomass and cover, but even species, or at least generic, dominance have so far been resilient in the face of unprecedented disturbance. On the other hand, the prairie-forest border has apparently shifted eastward, suggesting that the forces that control it are not only climatic, that it has been in a state of flux over the past few centuries. The use of sedimentary evidence to compare rates and directions of change over the past few centuries or millennia will help us evaluate the resiliency of these stands from a longer temporal perspective than is available through the study of contemporary stands.

Which systems have been able to remain productive and diverse after various kinds of human impacts and which have not? Which features have been most susceptible to irreversible change and which least? What kinds of human impacts have created the most irreversible changes? What kinds of human activities have increased productivity or diversity or both in a variety of ecosystems? Focusing on questions such as these will broaden our understanding of the resilience of ecosystems and communities and of the basic characteristics that determine their structure and functioning. Research to date has just begun to answer these questions, based on historical conditions.

For example, disturbance of the substrate seems to have the most permanent effects on both aquatic and terrestrial ecosystems. Climate alone does not control these systems. The importance of migration, evolution, and species interactions in regulating communities is amply documented by the disruptions caused by the introduction of non-native species. These species are often adapted to the climate and substrate but were not present in the past because of migrational barriers. Their sudden introduction to an ecosystem has caused major dislocations among species already present. Systems that have been recently disrupted, for example, successional stands, are more susceptible to invasion than are more mature systems, suggesting some degree of community coherence in resisting invasion. Do certain kinds of past disturbance lead to different susceptibility to invasion or to different patterns of recovery? What are the consequences for productivity and other ecosystem characteristics of having replaced native species by non-native ones?

Historical analyses are a basic component of the answers to all of these questions. It is routine to include physical attributes and geological history of a study site in analyses, and, if such studies are to yield results of use in detecting underlying consistent patterns, it should become routine to include site history and human impact as well. They are also necessary for using the results of research for managing seminatural ecosystems.

### Incorporating Historical Research into Management of Natural Areas

Why do people commit money and effort to preserving natural areas, interfering with conventional economically remunerative uses of these lands? The answers to this question are deeply rooted in human perceptions of their role in the natural world. In the Western tradition from which the modern industrial world developed, the nonhuman world is distinctly other, to be used, perfected, or otherwise manipulated by people.[7] Nature is at the same time crude, uncivilized, and dangerous and pure and beautiful, an example of God's creation untainted by sin and corruption. This ambivalence is reflected in contrasting attitudes of destructive manipulation of nature for human use and the attempt to rearrange it to emphasize its beauty.[8] Running through these attitudes, however, is the continuous thread of thought that nature is God's creation for the use of humans and that they have the right and responsibility to use and perfect it.[9] Those who modify the natural world are called "developers," not "destroyers."

Conservation is a form of such development, with the goal of protecting or recapturing the good qualities of nature. Some land is preserved for saving rare species, some for protecting water supplies, some for propagating wildlife for hunting, some just for people's enjoyment of open, nonbuilt spaces. The goal dictates the type of management, but both goals and ways to achieve them change through time. In the mid–twentieth century, most "managers" of natural areas in North America would probably have said that their main job was to prevent human intervention in the systems that they managed, allowing nature to take its course. This would lead to a natural system, in essence a climax community, a "wilderness."[10] But the systems that developed in the absence of intervention often did not resemble the ideal for which they had been preserved. The recent past of the systems was exerting an influence that seemed not to be easily negated by ignoring it. Some assumed that the reason the systems were not developing in the desired direction was that prehistoric human disturbance had been removed; replacing it, especially in terms of fire, would put the site back on the path toward the goal, which was prehistoric systems, not systems with no human influence. Additional "active management," a form of human disturbance, was necessary to correct changes wrought by past uses and current changes, such as the spread of non-native species. By imposing such a new, directed disturbance regime on the system, one could reestablish and maintain prehistoric ecosystems, though now not strictly "natural" because of the need for human interaction. Although there was the hope that eventually one could erase the problems of the past and of the present surroundings and thus no longer have to manage in such an active way, the aim as a rule was not to remove management but to establish the ideal system. An ideal that corresponded to some time in the past and legitimated efforts required to reestablish it was posited. The ends justified the means.

In Europe, on the other hand, the most diverse and interesting communities often result from centuries, if not millennia, of human actions, for example, coppice woodlands in England and pasture systems in Scandinavia and the Alps. In the last century, economic benefits from these systems declined, and for this reason and others the centuries-old disturbances ceased. The systems that developed in the absence of human impact were less diverse than those that had been there and did not have the appeal for which they were being preserved, so active management had to be reinstituted.[11] Again, these were not "natural" systems that could continue in the absence of human intervention. The historical intervention had to be continued to maintain the features of interest. Management had to be informed not only by the expected outcome, but also by the conditions imposed by previous use. The boundary between managing the habitat of a rare species that requires frequent disturbance and managing an English coppice has narrowed over the past few decades, as managers of both have recognized the importance of human-imposed disturbance to maintaining the systems.

The importance of management mirrors our ambivalent attitude toward nonhuman nature: some native North American forests, for example, those dominated by hemlock, have fairly low diversity, while highly disturbed sites such as bombing ranges have very high diversity. Which is preferred? Trees proliferate in an unburned savanna, quickly overrunning typical prairie species. Is it more appropriate to allow nonhuman forces to operate, or should one set fires to keep the site open? There are no scientific answers to these questions. We strive to preserve rare species, which may exist only in a very few sites, while we have not found evidence that the extinction of such major species as passenger pigeons, moas, or chestnut trees in the forest canopy has had major ecological consequences. Can historical research indicate the consequences of these losses? Or is our interest in preserving rare species (apart for their possible individual value in supplying people with unique products) more a matter of values, ethics, and aesthetics? Do they tell us a more satisfying story?[12]

There is a long history of preserving remnants of natural systems, from ancient sacred groves to contemporary nature preserves and wilderness areas. Both the sacred groves and nature preserves are islands in a sea of cultivated or built landscapes. In small islands such as Chinese naturalistic gardens, careful design creates a landscape in which every point of view gives a naturalistic impression. In large islands, such as large wilderness areas in North America, the aim is to avoid any evidence of human intervention.[13] The goal of an urban woodlot may be simply to provide urban residents with a glimpse into a system with minimal human disturbance, while that of a nature preserve may be to maintain the conditions necessary for the survival of one or a suite of rare species. Sacred groves, gardens, and urban woodlots are often surrounded by intensively used land, have concentrated, heavy use, and often were set aside for protection while the land around them was being built. The very fact that they were preserved presumes that conflicting uses are occurring around them, so that past conditions will not continue unchanged. In addition, the past always includes some human impact that has had some effects. It is not necessary to regard all human impacts as negative.[14] Management decisions that ignore past land use both of the preserves and of surrounding areas are apt to be derailed by unexpected residual impacts as well as by those caused by changes in the future.

### Global Change

The concept of global change includes diverse human-mediated changes that affect the entire globe, among them increases in carbon dioxide, pesticides, and other anthropogenic chemicals in the atmosphere, decreases in stratospheric ozone, and a decrease in the number of species present on the earth. While it occurs against a background of nonhuman-mediated changes in climate and evolution, it seems to overwhelm these. It implies a past as well as a present and a future. Historical ecology has contributed to predicting the consequences of global change mainly by providing analogues of the responses of systems to change in the past.[15] These will continue to suggest possible rates and directions of change in the future, although as with all analogues, there are many factors that will differ between the actual situation and the analogue.

By becoming aware of how culturally conditioned our attitudes are and have been we can begin to understand their effects and integrate them into ecological studies.[16] In 1967, Lynn White argued in his provocative article "The Historical Roots of Our Ecologic Crisis" that we must seriously weigh the fundamental causes of our ecologic problems if we are to avoid making serious errors in trying to solve them. According to White, the roots of the problems lie in modern Western science and technology, which have developed from the Christian dogma that people have the right to assert their mastery over nature. His focus on the historical roots of perceived contemporary problems is cogent, although devastated Eastern landscapes belie his emphasis on the crucial role of Christian religion.

In the past, much human-mediated change was regarded as good. Humans tamed the wilderness, irrigated barren deserts, reclaimed malarial marshes—accomplishments that marked the advance of human civilization.[17] In Australia in the mid–nineteenth century lands that European settlers were not using were referred to as "waste lands" that should be "rescued from a state of nature."[18] Now, the salvaging of remaining wilderness, deserts, and marshes is a keystone of wise use of land. This emerging paradigm, which values the nonbuilt environment, is in conflict with the old one, which sees no problems with using nature mainly to satisfy concrete human needs.[19] Some see an inherent conflict between the pursuit of increased productivity and the preservation of nature.[20] Historical analyses show, however, that the effects of the pursuit of productivity can destroy the basis of that productivity when the pursuit is heedless of historic evidence of earlier damage. Drained marshes may increase the amount of land available for hay or building and decrease the habitat of some disease-causing organisms, but eventually they lead to decreased productivity of adjacent waters and to increasing floods, which threaten the landscapes built on the drained land. History holds evidence of good and bad reclamation, which can direct the future. It can also show where current problems are exacerbated by past "improvements" (witness the flooding of the United States Midwest during the summer of 1993, which was made worse by levees built to control water). The lessons learned from the clearing of forest for farms on poor soils in the Great Lakes area of North America should be applied to similar efforts in the tropics.

General concern about global change must be linked to specific concerns, which are in turn determined not only by the actual changes, but also by the perceptions, such as whether the change is perceived as natural or human-caused. Our perception of the major problem of the time has shifted over the past few decades, from pesticide residues to acid precipitation to global warming and losses of biodiversity. Other critical preoccupations will undoubtedly appear in the future. Solutions to one problem may not apply to others, and the old problems usually do not disappear as attention shifts elsewhere. Historical research may reveal overall patterns that merit study, for example, the effect of human modifications of ecosystems, by whatever means. People simplify landscapes by replacing diverse ecosystems with cultivated fields, but in terms of landscape patchiness, development of new successional pathways, and increase in species numbers, human activities have made ecosystems more complex. Perhaps human activities render ecosystems less coherent—that is, the more human actions change them, the farther removed they are from a position in which they can remain somewhat stable in the face of stresses. The specific human activity may not be as important as the extent to which it diverts an ecosystem from some preexisting state. The amount of energy necessary to maintain "natural" systems in nature preserves alone implies that the systems have been so diverted.

The evolution of photosynthesis caused the greatest change ever in the atmosphere of the earth, from a reducing environment to an oxidizing one, and required enormous evolutionary adaptations, leading to life on land—but the pace was exceedingly slow. One of Darwin's greatest contributions was to emphasize the slowness of this ponderous process, an insight he coupled with a recognition of the unimaginable length of time that has elapsed since the first appearance of life on earth. Changes wrought by people in the past few millennia and especially in the past few centuries have accelerated the pace immeasurably as they piggyback on each other.

Even if we do not pass judgment on whether a speeded up rate of change is good or bad, we must admit that it is happening and that it is unprecedented in the evolutionary history of life on earth. By considering the long sweep of history we are able to place what we are doing in this context and to evaluate some potential consequences. It already appears that modifying of the physical substratum has been especially destructive to the ability of systems to recover after disturbance. Will this also be true of modifying climate and the atmosphere? Historical analyses will make a crucial contribution to generalizing this observation so that we will no longer have to react to each new crisis but instead can proactively posit reasonable limits to disrupting the very systems that have led to life as we know it.

# Notes

## Chapter 1. History Hidden in the Landscape

1. P. W. Richards, Africa, the "Odd Man Out." In *Tropical Forest Ecosystems in Africa and South America,* B. Meggers, E. S. Ayensu, and D. Duckworth, eds. (Smithsonian Institution Press, Washington, D.C., 1973), 24.

2. At least two recent books are titled "Historical Ecology": L. J. Bilsky, ed., *Historical Ecology: Essays on Environment and Social Change* (Kennikat Press, Port Washington, N.Y., 1980), and C. L. Crumley, ed., *Historical Ecology, Cultural Knowledge and Changing Landscapes* (School for American Research Advanced Seminar Series, Santa Fe, N.M., 1994). Bilsky's book discusses past ecological crises in terms of learning to deal with those of the present, while Crumley's primarily focuses on the reciprocal responses of human communities and environmental changes. That is, both focus more on the human aspect of environmental change than I do here.

3. R. J. Lincoln and G. A. Boxshall, *The Cambridge Illustrated Dictionary of Natural History* (Cambridge University Press, Cambridge, 1987), 127.

4. G. Utterström, Climatic fluctuations and population problems in early modern history, *Scandinavian History Review* 3:3–47, 1955 (reprinted in *The Ends of the Earth,* D. Worster, ed. [Cambridge University Press, Cambridge, 1988], 39–79).

5. J. L. Vankat, *The Natural Vegetation of North America* (John Wiley and Sons, New York, 1979).

6. W. H. Schlesinger et al., Biological feedbacks in global desertification, *Science* 247:1043–48, 1990.

7. L. W. Cuddihy and C. P. Stone, *Alteration of Native Hawaiian Vegetation* (University of Hawaii Cooperative National Park Resources Studies Unit, Honolulu, Hawai'i, 1990).

8. S. W. Trimble, The Alcovy River swamps: the result of culturally accelerated sedimentation. In *The American Environment: Interpretations of Past Geographies,* L. M. Dilsaver and C. E. Colten, eds. (Rowman and Littlefield, Lanham, Md., 1992), 21–32 (originally published in the *Bulletin of the Georgia Academy of Sciences* 28:131–41, 1970).

9. For example, see collected volume *Villages Désertés et Histoire Economique, XIe–XVIIIe siècles* (Ecole Pratique des Hautes Etudes, Paris, 1965); another good example in North America is Martha Furnace, a thriving furnace town in southern New Jersey in the nineteenth century, now reduced to some foundations in the midst of pine forest.

10. Aldo Leopold, quoted in S. Flader, *Thinking Like a Mountain* (University of Missouri Press, Columbia, 1974), 79.

11. E. L. Braun, *Deciduous Forests of Eastern North America* (Blakiston Co., Philadelphia, 1950), 248–52, 238; E. W. B. Russell, Pre-blight distribution of *Castanea dentata* (Marsh.)Borkh., *Bulletin Torrey Botanical Club* 114:183–90, 1987.

12. C. F. Korstian and P. W. Stickel, The natural replacement of blight-killed chestnut in hardwood forests of the northeast, *Journal of Agricultural Research* 34:631–48, 1927.

13. A. B. Parmelee and Son, Malone, New York, quoted in F. B. Hough, *Report on Forestry to the United States Department of Agriculture* (Government Printing Office, Washington, D.C., 1882), 3:157.

14. M. Williams, *Americans and Their Forests: A Historical Geography* (Cambridge University Press, Cambridge, 1989).

15. M. Kudish, Vegetational history of the Catskill High Peaks (Ph.D. diss., SUNY College of Environmental Science and Forestry, Syracuse, 1971).

16. W. Pennington, Vegetation history in the north-west of England: a regional synthesis. In *Studies in the Vegetational History of the British Isles,* D. Walker and R. G. West, eds. (Cambridge, Cambridge University Press, 1970), 41–79; K. E. Behre, The rôle of man in European vegetation history. In *Vegetation History,* B. Huntley and T. Webb III, eds. (Kluwer Academic Publishing, Dordrecht, Netherlands, 1988), 633–72.

17. C. H. Gimingham and J. D. De Smidt, Heaths as natural and semi-natural vegetation. In *Man's Impact on Vegetation,* W. Holzner, M. J. A. Werger, and I. Ikusima, eds. (Dr W. Junk Publishers, The Hague, 1983), 185–99.

18. A. Goudie, *The Human Impact on the Natural Environment,* 3d ed. (MIT Press, Cambridge, 1990), 56–59.

19. B. Green, *Countryside Conservation,* Resource Management Series 3 (George Allen and Unwin, London, 1981).

20. J. Terborgh, *Where Have All the Birds Gone? Essays on the Biology and Conservation of Birds that Migrate to the American Tropics* (Princeton University Press, Princeton, 1989).

21. Ibid.

22. Williams, *Americans and Their Forests*; for an example of changing forest patterns, see comparison of 1900 and 1954 in E. W. B. Russell, The 1899 New Jersey State Geologist's report: a call for forestry management, *Journal of Forest History* 32:205–11, 1988, and B. E. Smith, P. L. Marks, and S. Gardescu, Two hundred years of forest cover changes in Tompkins County, New York, *Bulletin Torrey Botanical Club* 120:229–47, 1993.

23. C. C. Vermeule, The forests of New Jersey. In *Annual Report of the State Geologist for the Year 1899: Report on Forests* (Geological Survey of New Jersey, Trenton, 1900), 13–172, 16; R. H. Ferguson and C. E. Meyer, *The Timber Resources of New Jersey*, USDA Forest Resource Bulletin NE-34 (Upper Darby, Penn., 1974).

24. The lack of precision is caused by the difficulty in comparing the data in the two surveys, 1899 and 1972, in which different definitions were used for forest land, and counties appear to have different total areas. County areas also differ between the reports of 1972 and 1987.

25. D. M. DiGiovanni and C. T. Scott, *Forest Statistics for New Jersey—1987*, USDA Forest Resource Bulletin NE-112 (Radnor, Penn., 1990).

26. E. W. B. Russell et al., Recent centuries of vegetational change in the glaciated northeastern United States, *Journal of Ecology* 81:647–64, 1993.

27. R. N. Mack, Invasion of *Bromus tectorum* L. into western North America: an ecological chronicle, *Agro-Ecosystems* 7:145–65, 1981; N. E. West, Intermountain deserts, shrub steppes, and woodlands. In *North American Terrestrial Vegetation*, M. G. Barbour and W. D. Billings, eds. (Cambridge University Press, Cambridge, 1988), 209–30; W. D. Billings, *Bromus tectorum*, a biotic cause of ecosystem impoverishment in the Great Basin. In *The Earth in Transition: Patterns and Processes of Biotic Impoverishment*, G. M. Woodwell, ed. (Cambridge University Press, Cambridge, 1990), 301–32.

28. Harold C. Fritts, *Reconstructing Large-Scale Climatic Patterns from Tree-Ring Data: A Diagnostic Analysis* (University of Arizona Press, Tucson, 1991), 130, 132.

29. Anonymous, People vs. the ecosystem, *Science* 255:155, 1992.

30. National Research Council Report quoted in Anonymous, People vs. the ecosystem.

31. J. R. Benjamin, *A Student's Guide to History*, 4th ed. (St. Martin's Press, New York, 1987), 1.

32. L. R. Iverson, Land-use changes in Illinois, USA: The influence of landscape attributes on current and historic land use, *Landscape Ecology* 2:45–61, 1988.

33. B. F. Hough, *Report upon Forestry* (Government Printing Office [Department of Agriculture], Washington, D.C., 1878), Vol. 1.

34. Elbert L. Little, Jr., Important forest trees of the United States. In *Trees, Yearbook of Agriculture*, USDA (Government Printing Office, Washington, D.C., 1949), 763–814; R. B. Davis and T. Webb III, The contemporary distribution of pollen in eastern North America: A comparison with the vegetation, *Quaternary Research* 5:395–434, 1975; C. J. Bernabo and T. Webb III, Changing patterns in the Holocene Pollen Record of Northeastern North America: A mapped summary, *Quaternary Research* 8:64–96, 1977; R. M. Godman and K. Lancaster, *Tsuga canadensis* (L.)

Carr. Eastern hemlock. In *Silvics of North America,* vol. 1, R. M. Burns and B. H. Honkala, eds., Agriculture Handbook 654 (USDA Forest Service, Washington, D.C., 1990), 604–12.

35. L. F. Ellsworth, *Craft to National Industry in the Nineteenth Century: A Case Study of the Transformation of the New York State Tanning Industry* (Arno Press, New York, 1975).

36. Anonymous, On the processes of tanning, leather-dressing, and dying, &c. from Eakin's Dictionary of Chymistry, *Journal of the Franklin Institute* 1:117–20, 143–46, 1926; Ellsworth, *Craft to National Industry,* 28.

37. M. Williams, *Americans and Their Forests.*

38. Ellsworth, *Craft to National Industry.*

39. W. A. Walsh, *Philosophy of History. An Introduction,* rev. ed. (Harper Torchbooks, New York, 1967), 31.

40. J. Opie, Environmental history: pitfalls and opportunities. In Bailes, *Environmental History,* 22–35; D. Worster, The vulnerable earth: toward a planetary history. In Worster, *The Ends of the Earth,* 3–20.

41. K. E. Bailes, Critical issues in environmental history. In *Environmental History: Critical Issues in Comparative Perspective,* K. E. Bailes, ed. (University Press of America, Lanham, Md., 1985), 1–21, 6.

42. Quotation from A. W. Crosby, The past and present of environmental history, *American Historical Review* 100:1189, 1995; W. Cronon, *Changes in the Land: Indians, Colonists, and the Ecology of New England* (Hill and Wang, New York, 1983); J. F. Richards, Land transformation. In *The Earth as Transformed by Human Action: Global and Regional Changes in the Biosphere over the Past 300 Years,* B. L. Turner II et al., eds. (Cambridge University Press, Cambridge, 1990), 163–78; M. Williams, Forests. In Turner et al., *The Earth as Transformed,* 179–201.

43. C. O. Sauer, Forward to historical geography, *Annals of the Association of American Geographers* 31:1–24 (Presidential Address, Dec. 1940); S. R. Eyre and R. J. Jones, Introduction. In *Geography as Human Ecology: Methodology by Example* (Edward Arnold, London, 1966), 1–29, 24.

44. Ibid., 7.

45. J. P. Radford, Editorial, *Journal of Historical Geography* 16:1–2, 1990.

46. G. P. Marsh, *Man and Nature* (1864; repr. Belknap Press of Harvard University, Cambridge, 1965).

47. Attributed by Marsh to H. Bushness, *Sermon on the Power of an Endless Life* (Marsh, *Man and Nature,* 1).

48. M. Somerville, *Physical Geography.* New American edition from the 3d rev. London edition (Blanchard and Lea, Philadelphia, 1853).

49. W. C. Lowdermilk, Conquest of Land through 7000 Years: Dr. Lowdermilk's Trip after the Dustbowl. USDA, *Agricultural Information Bulletin* #99, 1975; A. F. McEvoy, *The Fisherman's Problem: Ecology and Law in the California Fisheries, 1850–1980* (Cambridge University Press, Cambridge, 1986), 163 on fisheries.

50. F. E. Clements, Nature and structure of the climax, *Ecology* 24:252–84, 1936.

51. A. W. Küchler, *Potential Natural Vegetation of the Conterminous United States,* Special Publication #36 (American Geographical Society, New York, 1964).

52. O. Rackham, *Ancient Woodland: Its History, Vegetation and Uses in England* (Edward Arnold, London, 1980).

53. A. G. Tansley, *Practical Plant Ecology* (Dodd, Mead, New York, 1923), 23.

54. G. E. Hutchinson, Concluding remarks, *Population Studies: Animal Ecology and Demography. Cold Spring Harbor Symp. on Quantitative Biol.* 22:415–27, 1957.

55. McEvoy, *The Fisherman's Problem*, 15–16.

56. R. F. Heizer, Primitive man as an ecologic factor, *Kroeber Papers* 13:1–31, 1955.

57. G. E. Likens and M. B. Davis, Postglacial history of Mirror Lake and its watershed in New Hampshire, USA: an initial report, *Verhandlungen der Internationaler Vereinigung für Theoretischen und angewandte Limnologie* 19:982–93, 1975.

58. S. P. Hamburg and R. L. Sanford, Jr., Disturbance, *Homo sapiens,* and ecology, *Bulletin Ecological Society of America* 67:169–71, 1986.

59. N. L. Christensen, Landscape history and ecological change, *Journal of Forest History* 33:116–25, 1989.

60. W. L. Thomas, Jr., ed., *Man's Role in Changing the Face of the Earth* (University of Chicago Press, Chicago, 1956); Turner et al., eds., *Earth as Transformed.*

61. G. P. Nicholas, Introduction: Human behavior and Holocene ecology. In *Holocene Human Ecology in Northeastern North America,* G. P. Nicholas, ed. (Plenum Press, New York, 1988), 1–7.

62. M. B. Davis, Climatic instability, time lags, and community disequilibrium. In *Community Ecology,* Jared Diamond and T. J. Case, eds. (Harper and Row, New York, 1986), 269–84.

63. E. S. Deevey, Coaxing history to conduct experiments, *BioScience* 19:40–43, 1969.

## Chapter 2. The Written Record

1. E. Le Roy Ladurie, *Times of Feast, Times of Famine* (New York, 1971).

2. S. Olson, *The Depletion Myth* (Harvard University Press, Cambridge, 1971); R. Robbins, *Our Landed Heritage: The Public Domain, 1776–1970,* 2d ed. (University of Nebraska Press, Lincoln, 1976).

3. S. Cramp, Toxic chemicals and birds of prey, *British Birds* 56:124–39, 1963.

4. G. L. Jacobson, Jr., H. Almquist-Jacobson, and J. C. Wynne, Conservation of rare plant habitats: insights from the recent history of vegetation and fire at Crystal Fen, northern Maine, USA, *Biological Conservation* 57:287–314, 1991.

5. J. R. Benjamin, *A Student's Guide to History,* 4th ed. (St. Martin's Press, New York, 1987); M. Bloch, *The Historian's Craft* (Vintage Books, New York, 1953); W. Gray, *The Historian's Handbook* (Houghton Mifflin, Boston, 1959).

6. H. Nickerson, *The Turning Point of the Revolution Or Burgoyne in America* (Houghton Mifflin, Boston, 1928).

7. A. van der Donck, Remonstrances of New Netherlands, 1649. In *Documents Relative to the Colonial History of the State of New York,* E. B. O'Callaghan, ed. (Weed Parsons, Albany), 1:276; A. van der Donck, *Vertoogh van Nieu Nederland,* Henry C. Murphy, trans. (New York, [n.p.], 1854), 145–46.

8. R. E. Loeb, Reliability of the New York City Department of Parks and Recreation's forest records, *Bulletin of the Torrey Botanical Club* 109:537–41, 1982.

9. M. Bloch, *Land and Work in Medieval Europe,* trans. J. E. Anderson (University of California Press, Berkeley, 1967), 48.

10. A point made by Richard White, in his talk "Interpreting the historical environment," Ecological Society of America Meeting 1989, abstract in *Bulletin of the Ecological Society of America* 71(2):367, 1989.

11. Sworn testimony, signed by Justice John Budd on May 1, 1732, deposed by John Hayward, published in the American Weekly Mercury, June 8–15, 1732, printed in *Documents Relating to the Colonial History of the State of New Jersey,* W. Nelson, ed. (Paterson, N.J., 1895), 11:280–81.

12. R. T. T. Forman and E. W. B. Russell, Evaluation of historical data in ecology, *Bulletin of the Ecological Society of America* 64:5–7, 1983.

13. C. C. Vermeule, The Forests of New Jersey. In *Annual Report of the State Geologist for the Year 1899, Report on Forests* (Geological Survey of New Jersey, Trenton, 1900), 13–108.

14. J. D. Black, *The Rural Economy of New England* (Harvard University Press, Cambridge, 1950), chap. 4.

15. J. Shapiro and E. B. Swain, Lessons from the silica "decline" in Lake Michigan, *Science* 221:457–59, 1983.

16. M. J. R. Healy and E. L. Jones, Wheat yields in England, 1815–1849, *Journal of the Royal Statistical Society,* ser. A, 125:474–79, 1962.

17. Governor Dobbs, 17 June 1755, letter "to the Board" in *Colonial Records of North Carolina* 5:361.

18. G. P. Marsh to C. S. Sargent, 20 July 1882, Marsh Collection, University of Vermont, written three days before he died, quoted by editors of *Man and Nature,* G. P. Marsh (Belknap Press of Harvard University Press, Cambridge), 261n223.

19. Marsh, *Man and Nature,* 260.

20. H. C. Darby, *A New Historical Geography of England before 1600* (Cambridge University Press, Cambridge, 1976), 52–53.

21. F. F. Kreisler, Domesday Book. In *Dictionary of the Middle Ages,* J. R. Strayer, ed. (Charles Scribner's Sons, New York, 1984), 4:237–39.

22. Peter Kemble, Mt. Kemble, N.J., Diary, April 21, 1780–Dec. 25, 1785, 24 pages, Special Collections, Alexander Library, Rutgers University, New Brunswick, N.J.

23. M. Clawson and C. L. Stewart, *Land Use Information: A Critical Survey of U.S. Statistics Including Possibilities for Greater Uniformity* (Resources for the Future, Washington, D.C., 1965).

24. Samuel Rogers, Estate Inventory, Saratoga County (N.Y.) Clerk's office, Ballston Spa, 21 February 1823.

25. E. A. Bourdo, Jr., A review of the General Land Office Survey and of its use in quantitative studies of former forests, *Ecology* 37:754–68, 1956; P. L. Marks, S. Gardescu, and F. K. Seischab, Late Eighteenth Century Vegetation of Central and Western New York State on the Basis of Original Land Survey Records, *New York State Museum Bulletin,* no. 484, Albany, 1992.

26. Military Tract—New York State, Original Survey Records, Township of Locke, #18 (lots 7–40), surveyed 1790. Data transcribed by P. L. Marks.

27. Military Tract—New York State, Original Survey Records, Dryden Township, #23, surveyed by John Konkle 1790 & 1791, thicket in lot #16. Data transcribed by P. L. Marks.

28. For example, see P. G. Guthorn, *American Maps and Mapmakers of the Revolution* (Philip Freneau Press, Monmouth Beach, N.J., 1966), and P. G. Guthorn, *British Maps of the American Revolution* (Philip Freneau Press, Monmouth Beach, N.J., 1972), for examples of how surveyors were schooled and what protocols they followed.

29. W. C. Wilkinson, The encampment & position of the Army under His Excy. Lt. Gl. Burgoyne at Swords and Freeman's Farms on Hudsons River near Stillwater, 1777.

30. E. W. B. Russell, The 1899 New Jersey Geologist's Report: a call for forest management, *Journal of Forest History* 32:205–11, 1988.

31. P. W. Dunwiddie, Forest and heath: the shaping of the vegetation on Nantucket Island, *Journal of Forest History* 33:126–33, 1989.

32. R. R. Humphrey, *Ninety Years and 535 Miles: Vegetation Changes along the Mexican Border* (University of New Mexico Press, Albuquerque, 1987).

33. M. Klett, E. Manchester, J. Verburg, G. Bushaw, R. Dingus, and P. Berger, *Second View: The Rephotographic Survey Project* (University of New Mexico Press, Albuquerque, 1984).

34. T. E. Avery, *Interpretation of Aerial Photographs,* 3rd ed. (Burgess Publishing, Minneapolis, 1977).

35. Edward Howell, Harrisonville, N.J., Account Books, 1828–31, Special Collections, Alexander Library, Rutgers University, New Brunswick, N.J.

36. Ingvild Austad, Tree-pollarding in western Norway. In *The Cultural Landscape— Past, Present and Future,* H. H. Birks et al., eds. (Cambridge University Press, Cambridge, 1988), 11–29.

37. P. O. Wacker, *Land and People: A Cultural Geography of Preindustrial New Jersey: Origins and Settlement Patterns* (Rutgers University Press, New Brunswick, N.J., 1975), 362, 264, 408.

38. A. Leopold, *Game Management* (Charles Scribner's Sons, New York, 1933).

39. D. Daube, The self-understood in legal history, *The Juridical Review,* n.s. 18:126–34, 1973.

40. O. Rackham has used primarily historical documents to show changes in the vegetation of the British Isles through the Middle Ages, in *The History of the Countryside* (J. M. Dent and Sons, London, 1986); G. G. Whitney has compiled a compendium of forest change for parts of North America in *From Coastal Wilderness to Fruited Plain: A History of Environmental Change in Temperate North America, 1500–Present* (Cambridge University Press, Cambridge, 1994).

## Chapter 3. Field Studies

1. M. Bell and M. J. C. Walker, *Late Quaternary Environmental Change: Physical and Human Perspectives* (Longman Scientific and Technical and John Wiley and Sons, New York, 1992).

2. G. B. Emerson and C. L. Flint, *Manual of Agriculture for the School, the Farm and the Fireside* (Brewer and Tileston, Boston, 1862); H. G. Schmidt, *Rural Hunterdon: An Agricultural History* (Rutgers University Press, New Brunswick, 1946), 72–75; J. T. Curtis, The modification of mid-latitude grasslands and forests by man. In *Man's Role in Changing the Face of the Earth,* W. L. Thomas, Jr., ed. (University of Chicago Press, Chicago, 1956), 721–62; R. L. Burgess and D. M. Sharpe, Introduction. In *Forest Island Dynamics in Man-Dominated Landscapes,* R. L. Burgess and D. M. Sharpe, eds. (Springer-Verlag, New York, 1981), 1–5; J. W. Ranney, M. C. Bruner, and J. B. Levenson, The importance of edge in the structure and dynamics of forest islands. In *Forest Island Dynamics,* Burgess and Sharpe, eds., 67–96.

3. G. E. Bard, Secondary succession on the Piedmont of New Jersey, *Ecological Monographs* 22:195–215, 1952.

4. E. W. B. Russell and A. E. Schuyler, Vegetation and flora of Hopewell Furnace National Historic Site, eastern Pennsylvania, *Bartonia* 54:124–43, 1988.

5. O. Rackham, *Ancient Woodland: Its History, Vegetation and Uses in England* (Edward Arnold, London, 1980).

6. Ibid.; E. W. B. Russell, *Cultural Landscape History. Saratoga National Historical Park,* Report to Saratoga National Historical Park, 1991.

7. S. Limbrey, *Soil Science and Archaeology* (Academic Press, London, 1975).

8. R. J. P. Kain and J. M. Hooke, *Historical Change in the Physical Environment: A Guide to Sources and Techniques* (Butterworth Scientific, London, 1982).

9. I. L. Martin and T. C. Bass, *Erosion and related land use conditions on the Lake Michie Watershed, near Durham, North Carolina* (USDA, Washington, D.C., 1940); W. C. Lowdermilk, Conquest of Land through 7000 Years: Dr. Lowdermilk's Trip after the Dustbowl. USDA, *Agricultural Information Bulletin* #99, 1975; G. W. Olson, *Soils and the Environment* (Chapman and Hall, New York, 1981), 105–08, 113–14.

10. R. L. Sanford et al., Amazon rain-forest fires, *Science* 227:53–55, 1985; J. S. Clark, J. Markt, and H. Mullers, Post-glacial fire, vegetation and human history on the northern alpine forelands, southwestern Germany, *Journal of Ecology* 77:897–925, 1989.

11. S. W. Buol, F. D. Hole, and R. J. McCracken, *Soil Genesis and Classification,* 2d ed. (Iowa State University Press, Ames, 1980), 31–36.

12. E. M. Bridges, *World Soils* (Cambridge University Press, Cambridge, 1970), 51; Olson, *Soils,* 38; E. C. Krug and C. R. Frink, Acid rain on acid soil: a new perspective, *Science* 221:520–25, 1983.

13. A. Goudie, *The Human Impact on the Natural Environment,* 2d ed. (MIT Press, Cambridge, 1986), 130–31.

14. H. H. Birks et al., Recent paleolimnology of three lakes in northwestern Minnesota, *Quaternary Research* 6:249–72, 1976; R. B. Davis, Paleolimnological diatom studies of acidification of lakes by acid rain: an application of Quaternary science, *Quaternary Science Reviews* 6:147–63, 1987.

15. M. W. Binford et al., Ecosystems, paleoecology and human disturbance in subtropical and tropical America, *Quaternary Science Reviews* 6:115–28, 1987.

16. J. Quilter et al. Subsistence economy of El Paraíso, an early Peruvian site, *Science* 251:277–83, 1991.

17. D. L. Wigston, Ecological Society of America Meeting, August 1993, Madison, Wisconsin.

18. D. C. Clark, Edaphic and human effects on landscape-scale distributions of tropical rain-forest palms, *Ecology* 76:2581–94, 1995.

19. E. W. B. Russell, *Vegetation study of Hopewell Furnace National Historic Site,* Report to Hopewell Furnace NHS, 1988, 16.

20. C. D. Piggott, personal communication; Rackham, *Ancient Woodland.*

21. G. G. Whitney and D. R. Foster, Overstorey composition and age as determinants of the understorey flora of woods of central New England, *Journal of Ecology* 76:867–76, 1988.

22. H. J. D. Swan and J. M. A. Swan, Reconstructing forest history from live and dead plant materials—an approach to the study of forest succession in southwest New Hampshire, *Ecology* 55:772–83, 1974; C. D. Oliver and E. P. Stephens, Reconstruction of a mixed-species forest in central New England, *Ecology* 58:562–72, 1977.

23. H. C. Fritts, *Reconstructing Large-scale Climatic Patterns from Tree-Ring Data: A Diagnostic Analysis* (University of Arizona Press, Tucson, 1991).

24. W. W. McCaughey, Understory tree release following harvest cutting in spruce-fir forests of the Intermountain West, U.S. Department of Agriculture Forest Service Research Paper INT-285, 1982; C. G. Lorimer, Methodological considerations in the analysis of forest disturbance history, *Canadian Journal of Forest Research* 15:200–13, 1985.

25. F. James, D. A. Wiedenfeld, and C. E. McCulloch, Geographic variation in population trends of wood warblers, *Bulletin of the Ecological Society of America* 74(2) suppl:292, 1993.

26. S. T. A. Pickett, Space-for-time substitution as an alternative to long-term studies. In *Long-Term Studies,* G. E. Likens, ed. (Springer-Verlag, New York, 1989), 110–35.

27. H. J. Oosting, An ecological analysis of the plant communities of Piedmont, North Carolina, *American Midland Naturalist* 28:1–126; Bard, Secondary succession.

28. L. M. Hoehne, The groundlayer vegetation of forest islands in an urban-suburban matrix. In Burgess and Sharpe, eds., *Forest Island Dynamics,* 41–54.

29. A. F. Hough, A twenty-year record of understory vegetational change in a virgin Pennsylvania forest, *Ecology* 46:370–73, 1965.

30. A. D. Hall, *The Book of the Rothamsted Experiments* (New York, 1905).

31. L. R. Taylor, Objective and experiment in long-term research. In Likens, ed., *Long-Term Studies,* 20–70.

32. R. J. Frye II, Structural dynamics of early old-field succession on the New Jersey Piedmont: A comparative approach (Ph.D. diss., Rutgers University, New Brunswick, N.J., 1978); S. T. A. Pickett, The absence of an *Andropogon* stage in old-field succession at the Hutcheson Memorial Forest, *Bulletin of the Torrey Botanical Club* 110:533–35, 1983.

33. H. C. Bormann and G. E. Likens, *Pattern and Process in a Forested Ecosystem* (Springer-Verlag, New York, 1979).

34. D. B. Botkin, Causality and succession. In *Forest Succession: Concepts and Application,* D. C. West, H. H. Shugart, and D. B. Botkin, eds. (Springer-Verlag, New York, 1981), 36–55.
35. Taylor, Objective and experiment.
36. L. K. Ramey-Gassert and J. R. Runkle, Effect of land use practices on composition of woodlot vegetation in Greene County, Ohio, *Ohio Journal of Science* 92:25–32, 1992.
37. M. G. Turner and C. L. Ruscher, Changes in landscape patterns in Georgia, USA, *Landscape Ecology* 1:241–51, 1988.
38. James et al., Geographic variation.
39. H. H. Shugart, D. C. West, and W. R. Emanuel, Patterns and dynamics of forests: an application of simulation models. In West, Shugart, and Botkin, eds., *Forest Succession,* 74–94.

## Chapter 4. The Sedimentary Record

1. O. K. Davis, *Aspects of Archaeological Palynology: Methodology and Applications,* American Association of Stratigraphic Palynologists Contribution Series 29, AASP Foundation, Dallas, 1994
2. Details of sediment sampling, processing, and analysis can be found in such textbooks as B. Kummel and D. M. Raup, *Handbook of Paleontological Techniques* (W. H. Freeman, San Francisco, 1965); *Handbook of Holocene Palaeoecology and Palaeohydrology,* B. E. Berglund, ed. (John Wiley and Sons, Chichester, 1986); K. Faegri, P. E. Kaland, and K. Krzywinski, *Textbook of Pollen Analysis,* 4th ed. (John Wiley and Sons, Chichester, 1989); P. D. Moore, T. A. Webb, and M. E. Collinson, *Pollen Analysis* (Blackwell Scientific Publications, Oxford, 1991).
3. I. C. Prentice, Forest-composition calibration of pollen data. In Berglund, *Handbook,* 799–816;
4. M. B. Davis, On the theory of pollen analysis, *American Journal of Science* 261:897–912, 1963; Prentice, Forest-composition calibration, 799–816.
5. D. Walker and Y. Chen, Palynological light on tropical rainforest dynamics, *Quaternary Science Reviews* 6(2):77–92, 1987.
6. K. Heide and R. Bradshaw, The pollen-tree relationship within forests of Wisconsin and upper Michigan, USA, *Review of Palaeobotany and Palynology* 36:1–24, 1982; E. W. B. Russell, Early stages of secondary succession recorded in soil pollen on the North Carolina piedmont, *American Midland Naturalist* 129:384–96, 1993.
7. G. L. Jacobson, Jr., and R. H. W. Bradshaw, The selection of sites for paleovegetational studies, *Quaternary Research* 16:80–96, 1981.
8. P. A. Delcourt, H. A. Delcourt, and J. L. Davidson, Modern Pollen-vegetation relationships in southeastern United States, *Review of Palaeobotany and Palynology* 39:1–45, 1983; P. A. Delcourt, H. R. Delcourt, and T. Webb III, Atlas of mapped contributions of dominance and modern pollen percentage for important tree taxa in eastern North America, American Association of Stratigraphic Palynologists Contribution Series 14, 1984; R. H. W. Bradshaw and T. Webb III, Relationships

between contemporary pollen and vegetation data from Wisconsin and Michigan, USA, *Ecology* 66:721–37, 1985.

9. I shall refer to these remains as "fossils" for want of a better term, though for much of the time period under consideration here they are not actually fossilized.

10. H. H. Birks, Modern macrofossil assemblages in lake sediments in Minnesota. In *Quaternary Plant Ecology,* H. J. B. Birks and R. G. West, eds. (Blackwell Scientific Publications, Oxford, 1973), 173–89; S. A. Elias, *Quaternary Insects and Their Environments* (Smithsonian Institution Press, Washington, D.C., 1994).

11. W. A. Watts, Late-glacial plant macrofossils from Minnesota. In *Quaternary Paleoecology,* E. J. Cushing and H. E. Wright, Jr., eds. (Yale University Press, New Haven, 1967), 89–97.

12. W. Pennington, Vegetation history in the north-west of England: a regional synthesis. In *Studies in the Vegetational History of the British Isles,* D. Walker and R. G. West, eds. (Cambridge University Press, Cambridge, 1970), 41–79.

13. D. R. Engstrom and H. E. Wright, Jr., Chemical stratigraphy of lake sediments as a record of environmental change. In *Lake Sediments and Environmental History: Studies in Palaeolimnology and Palaeoecology in honour of Winifred Tutin,* E. Y. Haworth and J. W. G. Lund, eds. (University of Minnesota Press, Minneapolis, 1984), 11–67.

14. G. Brush and F. W. Davis, Stratigraphic evidence of human disturbance in an estuary, *Quaternary Research* 22:91–108, 1984.

15. R. W. Batterbee, J. P. Smol, and J. Merilainen, Diatoms as indicators of pH: an historical review. In *Diatoms and Lake Acidity: Reconstructing pH from Siliceous Algal Remains,* J. P. Smol et al., eds. (Dr. W. Junk, Dordrecht, Netherlands, 1986), 5–14; R. B. Davis, Paleolimnological diatom studies of acidification of lakes by acid rain: an application of Quaternary science, *Quaternary Science Reviews* 6:147–63, 1987.

16. R. W. Batterbee, Diatom analysis. In Berglund, *Handbook,* 527–70.

17. See P. L. Smart and P. D. Frances, eds., *Quaternary Dating Methods—A User's Guide,* Quaternary Research Association, Technical Guide No. 4 (Quaternary Research Association, Cambridge, 1991), for detailed discussion of the various methods used to date Quaternary sediments.

18. I. U. Olsson, Radiometric dating. In Berglund, *Handbook,* 273–312. See especially calibration curve, 278.

19. A. M. Davis, Dating with pollen: methodology, applications, limitations. In *Quaternary Dating Methods,* W. C. Mahaney, ed. (Elsevier, Amsterdam, 1984), 283–97; K. L. Van Zant et al., Increased *Cannabis/Humulus* pollen, an indicator of European agriculture in Iowa, *Palynology* 3:227–33, 1979.

20. M. B. Davis and E. S. Deevey, Jr., Pollen accumulation rates: estimates from late-glacial sediment of Rogers Lake, *Science* 145:1293–95, 1964.

21. M. B. Davis, R. E. Moeller, and J. Ford, Sediment focusing and pollen influx. In Haworth and Lund, *Lake Sediments,* 261–93.

22. H. J. B. Birks and A. D. Gordon, *Numerical Analysis in Quaternary Pollen Analysis* (Academic Press, London, 1985), discusses most of those used in palynology, as do Faegri et al., *Textbook of Pollen Analysis,* and Moore et al., *Pollen Analysis.*

23. T. Webb III, Corresponding patterns of pollen and vegetation in lower Michigan: a comparison of quantitative data, *Ecology* 55:17–28, 1974; I. C. Prentice, Multivariate methods for data analysis. In Berglund, *Handbook,* 775–97.

24. T. Webb III, A comparison of modern and presettlement pollen from southern Michigan (USA), *Review of Palaeobotany and Palynology* 16:137–56, 1973.

25. S. T. Andersen, The relative pollen productivity and representation of North European trees, and correction factors for tree pollen spectra, *Danmarks Geologiske Undersøgelse,* Raekke II, 96 (99 pp.), 1970.

26. J. T. Overpeck, T. Webb III, and I. C. Prentice, Quantitative interpretation of fossil pollen spectra: dissimilarity coefficients and the method of modern analogs, *Quaternary Research* 23:87–108, 1985.

27. A. D. Gordon and H. J. B. Birks, Numerical methods in Quaternary palaeoecology. 1, Zonation of pollen diagrams, *New Phytologist* 71:961–79, 1972; H. J. B. Birks, Numerical treatment of biostratigraphical data. In Berglund, *Handbook,* 743–74.

28. D. G. Green, Time series and postglacial forest ecology, *Quaternary Research* 15:265–77, 1981.

29. B. Huntley and H. J. B. Birks, *An Atlas of Past and Present Pollen Maps for Europe: 0–13 000 Years Ago* (Cambridge University Press, Cambridge, 1983).

30. M. B. Davis, Holocene vegetational history of the eastern United States. In *Late-Quaternary Environments of the United States. Vol. 2. The Holocene,* H. E. Wright, Jr., ed. (University of Minnesota Press, Minneapolis, 1983), 166–81.

31. K. D. Bennett, The spread of *Fagus grandifolia* across eastern North America during the last 18 000 years, *Journal of Biogeography* 12:147–64, 1985; M. B. Davis et al, Dispersal versus climate: expansion of *Fagus* and *Tsuga* into the Upper Great Lakes region, *Vegetatio* 67:93–103, 1986.

32. F. Firbas, Der pollenanalytische Nachweis des Getreidebaus, *Zeitschrift für Botanik* 31:447–78, 1937.

33. J. Iversen, Land occupation in Denmark's Stone Age, *Danmarks Geologiske Undersøgelse,* Raekke II, 66:1–68, 1941.

34. H. J. B. Birks, Late-Quaternary biotic changes in terrestrial and lacustrine environments, with particular reference to north-west Europe. In Berglund, *Handbook,* 3–65.

35. E. W. B. Russell et al., Recent centuries of vegetational change in the glaciated north-eastern United States, *Journal of Ecology* 81:647–64, 1993.

36. Davis, Holocene vegetational history.

37. I. D. Campbell and J. H. McAndrews, Forest disequilibrium caused by rapid Little Ice Age cooling, *Nature* 366:336–38, 1993.

38. K. Faegri, *Textbook of Pollen Analysis,* 177–78.

39. G. W. Dimbleby, *The Palynology of Archaeological Sites* (Academic Press, London, 1985), 112.

40. Webb, Corresponding patterns; I. C. Prentice, Pollen representation.

41. Overpeck et al., Quantitative interpretation.

42. T. Webb III, The Reconstruction of climatic sequences from botanical data, *Journal of Interdisciplinary History* 10:749–72, 1980; M. B. Davis, Climatic instability, time lags, and community disequilibrium. In *Community Ecology,* J. Diamond and

T. J. Case, eds. (Harper and Row, New York, 1984), 269–84; T. Webb III, Is vegetation in equilibrium with climate? How to interpret late-Quaternary pollen data, *Vegetatio* 67:75–91, 1986; H. R. Delcourt and P. A. Delcourt, *Quaternary Ecology: A Paleoecological Perspective* (Chapman and Hall, London, 1991), 21–60.

43. L. J. Graumlich and M. B. Davis, Holocene variation in spatial scales of vegetation pattern in the Upper Great Lakes, *Ecology* 74:826–39, 1993.

## *Chapter 5. Fire: Mimicking Nature*

1. Fire Research Institute, *International Bibliography of Wildland Fire,* advertised in International Bulletin of Wildland Fire 1(1):8, 1992 (published by the Fire Research Institute, Roslyn, Washington).

2. M. J. Schroeder and C. S. Buck, *Fire Weather . . . A Guide for Application of Meteorological Information to Forest Fire Control Operations,* USDA Forest Service, Agriculture Handbook 360, 1970.

3. A. R. Taylor, Ecological aspects of lightning in forests, *Tall Timbers Fire Ecology Conference Proceedings* 13:455–82, 1974; A. Goudie, *The Human Impact on the Natural Environment,* 3d ed. (MIT Press, Cambridge, 1990), 30.

4. R. W. Mutch, Wildland fires and ecosystems—a hypothesis, *Ecology* 51:1046–51, 1970.

5. A. M. Gill, J. R. L. Hoare, and N. P. Cheney, Fires and their effects in the wet-dry tropics of Australia. In *Fire in the Tropical Biota: Ecosystem Processes and Global Challenges,* J. G. Goldammer, ed. (Springer-Verlag, Berlin, 1990), 159–77.

6. J. E. Keeley, Resilience of Mediterranean shrub communities to fires. In *Resilience in Mediterranean-type Ecosystems,* B. Dell, A. J. M. Hopkins, and B. B. Lamont, eds. (Dr W. Junk, Dordrecht, Netherlands, 1986), 95–112.

7. A. E. Schuyler and J. L. Stasz, Influence of fire on reproduction of *Scirpus longii, Bartonia,* 51:105–07, 1985.

8. G. J. Retallack, D. P. Dugas, and E. A. Bestland, Fossil soils and grasses of a middle Miocene East African grassland, *Science* 247:1325–28, 1990.

9. R. L. Specht, Changes in the eucalypt forests of Australia as a result of human disturbance. In *The Earth in Transition: Patterns and Processes of Biotic Impoverishment,* G. M. Woodwell, ed. (Cambridge University Press, Cambridge, 1990), 177–98.

10. A. P. Kershaw, Australasia. In *Vegetation History,* B. Huntley and T. Webb III, eds. (Kluwer Academic Publishers, Dordrecht, Netherlands, 1988), 237–306.

11. D. A. Burney, Late Quaternary stratigraphic charcoal records from Madagascar, *Quaternary Research* 28:274–86, 1987.

12. M. L. Heinselman, Fire intensity and frequency as factors in the distribution and structure of northern ecosystems. In *Fire Regimes and Ecosystem Properties,* H. A. Mooney et al. eds., USDA Forest Service, General Technical Report WO-26, 1981, 7–57; N. L. Christensen, Fire regimes in southeastern ecosystems. In Mooney et al., *Fire Regimes,* 112–36.

13. W. L. Loope, Interrelationships of fire history, land use history, and landscape pattern within Pictured Rocks National Lakeshore, Michigan, *Canadian Field Naturalist* 105:18–28, 1991; J. S. Clark and P. D. Royall, Transformation of a northern

hardwood forest by aboriginal (Iroquois) fire: Charcoal evidence from Crawford Lake, Ontario, Canada, *The Holocene* 5:1–9, 1995.

14. W. P. Patterson III and K. E. Sassaman, Indian fires in the prehistory of New England. In *Holocene Human Ecology in Northeastern North America,* G. P. Nicholas, ed. (Plenum Press, New York, 1988), 107–35.

15. C. K. Brian and A. Siller, Evidence from the Swartkranz cave for the earliest use of fire, *Nature* 336:464–66, 1988.

16. W. Hough, Fire as an agent in human culture, *United States National Museum Bulletin,* 139, Washington, 1926.

17. O. C. Stewart, Fire as the first great force employed by man. In *Man's Role in Changing the Face of the Earth,* W. L. Thomas, Jr., ed. (University of Chicago Press, Chicago, 1956), 115–33.

18. G. M. Day, The Indian as an ecological factor in the northeastern forest, *Ecology* 34:329–46, 1953; Stewart, Fire; C. O. Sauer, *The Early Spanish Main* (University of California Press, Berkeley, 1966).

19. A. Woeikof, De l'influence de l'homme sur la terre, *Annales de géographie* 10:97–114, 193–215, 1901.

20. Hough, Fire; C. O. Sauer, *The Early Spanish Main*; M. Williams, *The Making of the South Australian Landscape* (Academic Press, London, 1974), 5; J. Carver, *Three years travels through the interior parts of North America* (Key and Simpson, Philadelphia, 1796), 187; P. M. Lindeström, *Geographia Americae, with an account of the Delaware Indians,* trans. A. Johnson, written 1691 from notes made in 1654–56 (Swedish Colonial Society, Philadelphia, 1925).

21. W. Blane, A tour in southern Illinois in 1822. In *Pictures of Illinois One Hundred Years Ago,* M. M. Quaife, ed. (R. R. Donnelley, Chicago, 1918), 74–76. This is an excerpt from Blane's "An excursion through the United States and Canada during the years 1822–1823."

22. H. T. Lewis, Fire technology and resource management in aboriginal North America and Australia. In *Resource Managers: North American and Australian Hunter-Gatherers,* N. M. Williams and E. S. Hunn, eds., AAAS Selected Symposium 67 (Westview Press, Boulder, Colo., 1982), 45–68.

23. Z. S. Eldredge, *The March of Portolá and the Discovery of the Bay of San Francisco,* California Promotion Committee, San Francisco, 1909, note made November 7, 1769; Hough, Fire.

24. Stewart, Fire, 128; A. A. Brown and K. P. Davis, *Forest Fire Control and Its Use,* 2d ed. (McGraw-Hill, New York, 1973), 10.

25. Williams, *The Making,* 5; Lewis, Fire technology.

26. S. Pyne, *Burning Bush: A Fire History of Australia* (Holt, New York, 1991), 61.

27. M. Hall, Man's historical and traditional use of fire in southern Africa. In *Ecological Effects of Fire in South African Ecosystems,* P. deV. Booysen and N. M. Tainton, eds. (Springer-Verlag, Berlin, 1984), 39–52.

28. B. H. Walker, *Management of Semi-arid Ecosystems* (Elsevier Scientific, New York, 1980).

29. E. C. Grimm, Fire and other factors controlling the Big Woods vegetation of Minnesota in the mid-nineteenth century, *Ecological Monographs* 54:291–311, 1984.

30. H. M. Chittendon, *Letters and Travels of Father Pierre-Jean de Smet, S.J., 1801–1873* (Francis P. Harper, New York, 1905), 4:1347.
31. Blane, A tour.
32. H. A. Gleason, The relation of forest distribution and prairie fires in the Middle West, *Torreya* 13:173–81, 1913.
33. B. B. McInteer, The barrens of Kentucky, *Transactions of the Kentucky Academy of Science* 10:7–12, 1942.
34. E. W. B. Russell, Indian-set fires in the forests of the northeastern United States, *Ecology* 64:78–88, 1983.
35. L. E. Heusser and J. E. King, North America. In Huntley and Webb, *Vegetation History,* 192–236.
36. E. W. B. Russell, R. B. Davis, R. S. Anderson, T. E. Rhodes, and D. S. Anderson, Recent centuries of vegetational change in the glaciated north-eastern United States, *Journal of Ecology* 81:647–64, 1993.
37. K. J. Narr, Early food-producing populations. In Thomas, ed., *Man's Role,* 134–51.
38. H. J. B. Birks, Late-Quaternary biotic changes in terrestrial and lacustrine environments, with particular reference to north-west Europe. In *Handbook of Holocene Palaeoecology and Palaeohydrology,* B. Berglund, ed. (John Wiley and Sons, Chichester, 1986), 20.
39. J. S. Clark, J. Merkt, and H. Müller, Post-glacial fire, vegetation, and human history on the northern alpine forelands, southwestern Germany, *Journal of Ecology* 77:897–925, 1989.
40. R. L. Sanford, J. Saldarriga, R. F. Clark, C. Uhl, and R. Herrera, Amazon rain-forest fires, *Science* 227:53–55, 1985; S. P. Horn, Prehistoric fires in the Chirripó highlands of Costa Rica: Sedimentary charcoal evidence, *Revista de Biología Tropical* 37:139–48, 1989.
41. S. Boyden, *Western Civilization in Biological Perspective* (Clarendon Press, Oxford, 1987), 61.
42. J. T. Overpeck, D. Rind, and R. Goldberg, Climate-induced changes in forest disturbance and vegetation, *Nature* 343:51–53, 1990.
43. M. Saarnisto, Annually laminated lake sediments. In Berglund, *Handbook,* 341–70.
44. M. Kerkkonen, *Peter Kalm's North American Journey: Its Ideological Background and Results* (Helsinki, 1959), 17.
45. W. A. Whitehead, Answer to letter inquiring about former forest between Newark and New York, *Proceedings New Jersey Historical Society,* 2d ser., 6:145–47, 1881.
46. F. B. Hough, *Report upon Forestry,* USDA (Government Printing Office, Washington, D.C., 1882), 3:130–55.
47. Ibid., 206–07.
48. W. Sarvis, An Appalachian forest: Creation of the Jefferson National Forest and its effect on the local community, *Journal of Forest and Conservation History* 37:169–78, 1993.
49. M. F. Buell, H. F. Buell, and J. A. Small, Fire in the history of Mettler's Woods, *Bulletin of the Torrey Botanical Club* 81:253–55, 1954.
50. N.J. State Geologist report 1903, 51.

51. A. van der Donck, *A Description of the New Netherlands,* T. F. O'Donnell, ed. (Syracuse University Press, Syracuse, 1968), 20–21 (originally published in *Collections of the New-York Historical Society,* 2d ser., 1:125–242, 1841); T. Dwight, *Travels in New England and New York,* B. M. Solomon, ed. (Harvard University Press, 1969), 4:38–40 (originally published in 1841, printed by the Author, New Haven, Conn.).

52. N. S. Shaler, *Kentucky: A Pioneer Commonwealth* (Houghton Mifflin, New York, 1884), 29.

53. H. Maxwell, The use and abuse of the forests by the Virginia Indians, *William and Mary College Quarterly Historical Magazine* 19:73–103, 1910.

54. H. E. Wright, Jr., and M. L. Heinselman, Introduction to the ecological role of fire in natural conifer forests of western and northern North America, *Quaternary Research* 3:319–28, 1973.

55. Hough, *Report,* 60.

56. Ibid., 206–07. This report includes extensive detail about the fires that were reported as well as a summary of laws regulating fires in the various states.

57. G. Pinchot, The effects of fire. In *Report of the State Geologist for the Year 1899* (Geological Survey of New Jersey, Trenton, 1900), 108

58. F. C. Clements, *Plant Succession: An Analysis of the Development of Vegetation,* Carnegie Institute of Washington Publication #242, 1916.

59. R. T. T. Forman and R. E. Boerner, Fire frequency and the Pine Barrens of New Jersey, *Bulletin of the Torrey Botanical Club* 108:34–50, 1981.

60. A. A. Brown, Progress, but still a problem. In *Trees, The Yearbook of Agriculture 1949,* A. Stefferud, ed., USDA (Government Printing Office, Washington, D.C., 1949), 477–79.

61. A. W. Hartman, Fire, friend and enemy: Fire as a tool in southern pine. In Stefferud, *Trees,* 517–27.

62. R. F. Hammatt, Bad business; your business. In Stefferud, *Trees,* 479.

63. W. A. Niering and R. H. Goodwin, Ecological studies of the Connecticut Arboretum natural area. I. An introduction and a survey of vegetation types, *Ecology* 43:41–54, 1962; L. H. Ohmann and M. F. Buell, Forest vegetation of the New Jersey highlands, *Bulletin of the Torrey Botanical Club* 95:287–98, 1968.

64. J. R. Brown, The role of fire in altering the species composition of forests in Rhode Island, *Ecology* 41:310–16, 1960.

65. W. A. Niering, R. H. Goodwin, and S. Taylor, Prescribed burning in southern New England: introduction to long-range studies, *Proceedings of the Annual Tall Timbers Fire Ecology Conference* 8:267–86, 1970; C. Chandler, P. Cheney, P. Thomas, L. Trabaud, and D. Williams, eds., *Fire in Forestry.* Vol. 1. *Forest Fire Behavior and Effects* (John Wiley and Sons, New York, 1983).

66. Niering et al., Prescribed burning.

67. Forman and Boerner, Fire frequency.

68. R. A. Minnich, Fire mosaics in southern California and northern Baja California, *Science* 219:1287–94, 1983; T. Swetnam, Fire history and climate change in Giant Sequoia groves, *Science* 262:885–89, 1993.

69. D. J. Parsons et al., Natural fire management in National Parks, *Environmental Management* 10:21–24, 1986; N. L. Christensen et al., Interpreting the Yellowstone fires of 1988, *BioScience* 39:678–85, 1989.

70. L. W. Cuddihy and C. P. Stone, *Alteration of Native Hawaiian Vegetation: Effects of Humans, Their Activities and Introductions* (University of Hawaii Cooperative National Park Resources Studies Unit, Honolulu, Hawai'i, 1990).

71. D. J. Parsons, Objects of ecosystems: Giant Sequoia management in national parks, *USDA Forest Service Gen. Tech. Rep.* PSW-51, 1994.

72. M. Williams, *Americans and Their Forests: A Historical Geography* (Cambridge University Press, Cambridge, 1989), 228-37.

## Chapter 6. *Extending Species Ranges*

1. Charles Darwin, *On the Origin of Species*. A Facsimile of the First Edition, with introduction by Ernst Mayr (Harvard University Press, Cambridge, 1966), 380–81.

2. C. S. Elton, *The Ecology of Invasions by Animals and Plants* (Methuen, London, 1958).

3. R. J. Groves and J. J. Burden, eds., *Ecology of Biological Invasions* (Cambridge University Press, New York, 1986).

4. J. A. Drake, H. A. Mooney, F. diCastri, R. H. Groves, E. J. Kruger, M. Rejmànek, and M. Williamson, eds., *Biological Invasions: A Global Perspective,* SCOPE volume 37 (John Wiley and Sons, New York, 1989).

5. H. A. Mooney and J. A. Drake, eds., *Ecology of Biological Invasions of North America and Hawaii* (Springer-Verlag, New York, 1986).

6. Webster's *New Unabridged Universal Dictionary,* 2d ed., 1979.

7. Elton, *Ecology of Invasions,* 33.

8. M. B. Davis, Holocene vegetational history in the eastern United States. In *Late-Quaternary Environments of the United States,* Volume 2. *The Holocene,* H. E. Wright, Jr., ed. (University of Minnesota Press, Minneapolis, 1983), 166–181; T. Webb III, Eastern North America. In *Vegetation History,* B. Huntley and T. Webb III, eds. (Kluwer Academic Publishers, Dordrecht, Netherlands, 1988), 385–414.

9. M. B. Davis, K. D. Woods, S. L. Webb, and R. P. Futyma, Dispersal versus climate: expansion of *Fagus* and *Tsuga* into the Upper Great Lakes region, *Vegetatio* 67:93–103, 1986.

10. G. H. Orians, Site characteristics favoring invasions. In Mooney and Drake, *Ecology of Biological Invasions,* 133–48.

11. D. R. Snow, *The Archaeology of New England* (Academic Press, New York, 1980).

12. J. R. Dorney, The impact of native Americans on presettlement vegetation in southeastern Wisconsin, *Wisconsin Academy of Science, Arts and Letters* 69:26–36, 1981.

13. J. Turner, Post-Neolithic disturbance of British vegetation. In *Studies in the Vegetational History of the British Isles,* D. Walker and R. G. West, eds. (Cambridge University Press, Cambridge, 1970), 97–116.

14. A. Goudie, *The Human Impact on the Natural Environment* (MIT Press, Cambridge, 1990), 17.

15. M. Bates, Man as an agent in the spread of organisms. In *Man's Role in Changing the Face of the Earth*, W. L. Thomas, Jr., ed. (University of Chicago Press, 1956), 788–804.

16. B. Huntley and H. J. B. Birks, *An Atlas of Past and Present Pollen Maps for Europe: 1–13,000 Years Ago* (Cambridge University Press, Cambridge, 1983), 413; K-E. Behre, The rôle of man in European vegetation history. In Huntley and Webb, *Vegetation History,* 633–67.

17. H. C. Darby, *A New Historical Geography of England before 1600* (Cambridge University Press, Cambridge, 1976), 98; J. Sheail, The rabbit, *Biologist* 31:135–40, 1984.

18. G. B. Corbet, The importance of oak to mammals. In *The British Oak: Its History and Natural History,* M. G. Morris and F. H. Pering, eds. (E. W. Classey, Farringdon, Berkshire, 1974), 312–23.

19. Elton, *Ecology of Invasions,* 118; I. Garrard and D. Streeter, *The Wild Flowers of the British Isles* (Macmillan, London, 1983), 248.

20. A. W. Crosby, *The Columbian Exchange, Biological and Cultural Consequences of 1492* (Greenwood Press, Westport, Conn., 1972).

21. Ibid., 175.

22. D. B. Wingate, The restoration of Nonsuch Island as a living museum of Bermuda's precolonial terrestrial biome. In *The Earth in Transition,* G. M. Woodwell, ed. (Cambridge University Press, Cambridge, 1990), 133–50.

23. L. W. Cuddihy and C. P. Stone, *Alteration of Native Hawaiian Vegetation: Effects of Humans, Their Activities and Introductions* (University of Hawaii Cooperative National Park Resources Studies Unit, Honolulu, Hawai'i, 1990), 40.

24. Sheail, The rabbit.

25. C. Lever, *Naturalized Mammals of the World* (Longman, London, 1985), 401–06.

26. H. G. Schmidt, *Agriculture in New Jersey: A Three-Hundred-Year History* (Rutgers University Press, New Brunswick, N.J., 1973); E. W. B. Russell, Vegetational change in northern New Jersey since 1500 A.D.: a palynological, vegetational, and historical synthesis (Ph.D. diss., Rutgers University, New Brunswick, N.J., 1979).

27. K. L. Van Zant, T. Webb III, G. M. Peterson, and R. G. Baker. Increased *Cannabis/Humulus* pollen, an indicator of European agriculture in Iowa, *Palynology* 3:227–33, 1979.

28. Letter from Peter Collinson to John Bartram, April 6, 1738, quoted in H. G. Cruickshank, ed., *John and William Bartram's America* (Devin-Adair, Greenwich, Conn., 1990), 73–74.

29. Letter from Bartram to Collinson, June 24, 1760, quoted in Cruickshank, *Bartram's America,* 85–86.

30. W. K. Martin, *The Concise British Flora in Colour* (Ebury Press and Michael Joseph, Norwich, 1965).

31. D. E. Fairbrothers, personal communication; F. A. J. von Wangenheim, *Beschreilbung einiger nordamerikanischen Holz und Busharten, mit Anwendung auf deutsche Forsten* (Gottingen, Prussia, 1781).

32. M. Landa, Ecological changes in the history of forestry and game management in Czechoslovakia, especially southern Bohemia. In *Human Influence on Forest*

*Ecosystems Development in Europe,* F. Salbitano, ed. (Pitagora Editrice, Bologna, 1988), 287–99.

33. E. Power, *The Wool Trade in English Medieval History* (Oxford University Press, London, 1941), 53.

34. N. S. B. Gras, *The Economic and Social History of an English Village (Crawley, Hampshire),* A.D. *909–1928* (Harvard University Press, Cambridge, 1930), 18.

35. Power, *The Wool Trade,* 47.

36. Van Zant et al., Increased *Cannabis/Humulus* pollen.

37. F. Densmore, *How Indians Use Wild Plants for Food, Medicine and Crafts* (Dover Publications, New York, 1974) (unabridged republication of "Uses of plants by the Chippewa Indians," 44th Annual Report of the Bureau of American Ethnology [Government Printing Office, Washington, D.C., 1928], 275–897).

38. A. W. Crosby, *Ecological Imperialism: The Biological Expansion of Europe, 900–1900* (Cambridge University Press, Cambridge, 1986), 155.

39. A. C. Clark, The impact of exotic invasion on the remaining New World mid-latitude grasslands. In Thomas, *Man's Role,* 737–62.

40. C. D. Darlington, *The Evolution of Man and Society* (Simon and Schuster, New York, 1969), 652; P. H. Wood, The impact of smallpox on the native population of the 18th century South, *New York State Journal of Medicine* 87:30–36, 1987.

41. Ibid. Variolation was a vaccination procedure widely practiced among the Africans, though regarded by the Europeans as a "heathen" custom not to be used by Christians.

42. Orians, Site characteristics.

43. Cuddihy and Stone, *Hawaiian Vegetation,* 50.

44. Orians, Site characteristics.

45. Cuddihy and Stone, *Hawaiian Vegetation,* 76–77.

46. Ibid., 84–85.

47. O. Polunin and B. E. Smythies, *Flowers of South-West Europe: A Field Guide* (Oxford University Press, New York, 1973), 177.

48. D. McClintock and R. S. R. Fitter, *Guide des Plantes à Fleurs de l'Europe occidentale* (Delachaux et Niestlé, Neuchatal, Switzerland, 1964), 91; I. Garrard and D. Streeter, *Wild Flowers,* 243; David Fairbrothers, personal communication.

49. P. B. Dean and A. de Vos, The spread and present status of the European hare, *Lepus europaeus hybridus* (Demarest), in North America, *The Canadian Field Naturalist* 79:38–48, 1965.

50. Elton, *Ecology of Invasions,* 73.

51. Ibid., 88; Clark, The impact of exotic invasion; A. F. Mark and G. D. McSweeney, Patterns of impoverishment in natural communities: case history studies in forest ecosystems—New Zealand. In Woodwell, *The Earth in Transition,* 151–76; Goudie, *The Human Impact,* 106.

52. Lever, *Naturalized Mammals,* 193–203; G. Caughley, *The Deer Wars: The Story of Deer in New Zealand* (Heinemann, Auckland, 1983), 13–22.

53. F. M. Packard, Wildlife and aspen in Rocky Mountain National Park, Colorado, *Ecology* 23:478–82, 1942; Anonymous, *New Jersey's White-Tailed Deer: A Report*

on *New Jersey's Deer Management Program for Fiscal Year 1975–1976,* New Jersey Division of Fish, Game and Shellfisheries, 1976, and ibid., 1976–1977, 1977; P. R. Ratcliffe, The control of red and Sika deer populations in commercial forests. In *Mammals as Pests,* R. J. Putman, ed. (Chapman and Hall, London, 1989), 98–115; F. H. Wagner and C. E. Kay, "Natural" or "healthy" ecosystems: are the U.S. National Parks providing them? In *Humans as Components of Ecosystems: The Ecology of Subtle Human Effects and Populated Areas,* M. J. McDonnell and S. T. A. Picket, eds. (Springer-Verlag, New York, 1993), 257–76.

54. G. D. Waugh, Fish and fisheries. In *The Natural History of New Zealand: An Ecological Survey,* G. R. Williams, ed. (A. H. and A. Reed, Wellington, 1973), 251–84.

55. P. B. Moyle, Fish introductions into North America: patterns and ecological impact. In Mooney and Drake, *Ecology of Biological Invasions,* 27–43.

56. Elton, *Ecology of Invasions,* 26–27.

57. Moyle, Fish introductions.

58. Ibid.; J. F. Kitchell and S. R. Carpenter, variability in lake ecosystems: complex responses by the apical predator. In McDonnell and Pickett, *Humans as Components,* 125–40.

59. M. G. Hadfield and S. E. Miller, Ecology and conservation of endemic Hawai'ian tree snails (subfamily Achatinellinae), *Bulletin Ecological Society of America* 73(2):196, 1992.

60. Elton, *Ecology of Invasions,* 75–76; Moyle, Fish introductions.

61. R. U. Swingle, R. R. Whitten, and E. G. Brewer, Dutch elm disease. In *Trees: The Yearbook of Agriculture,* A. Stefferud, ed., United States Department of Agriculture (Government Printing Office, Washington, D.C., 1949), 451–52; Goudie, The Human Impact, 62, 74.

62. N. Good, A study of natural replacement of chestnut in New Jersey (Ph.D. diss., Rutgers University, New Brunswick, N.J., 1965).

63. R. C. Bigalke, Present-day mammals of Africa. In *Evolution of African Mammals,* J. J. Maglio and H. B. S. Cooke, eds. (Harvard University Press, Cambridge, 1978), 1–16.

64. N. L. Britton, *A Preliminary Catalogue of the Flora of New Jersey,* Geological Survey of New Jersey, New Brunswick, 1881.

65. H. A. Gleason and A. Cronquist, *Manual of the Vascular Plants of Northeastern United States and Adjacent Canada* (New York Botanical Garden, New York, 1991).

66. Orians, Site characteristics.

67. Gleason and Cronquist, *Manual,* 64; personal observations in eastern Pennsylvania and New Jersey.

68. C. M. D'Antonio and P. M. Vitousek, Ecosystem consequences of alien grass invasion, *Bulletin Ecological Society of America* 73(2):153, 1992.

69. G. E. Bard, Secondary succession on the Piedmont of New Jersey, *Ecological Monographs* 22:195–215, 1952.

70. Haleakalâ, *Hosmer Grove Trail Guide,* Haleakalâ National Park, National Park Service, U.S. Department of the Interior, 1990.

## Chapter 7. The Forest as a Resource

1. G. F. Peterken, *Natural Woodland: Ecology and Conservation in Northern Temperate Regions* (Cambridge University Press, Cambridge, 1996), 12–19 and *passim*.

2. E.g., for the United States, see discussions in M. Williams, *Americans and Their Forests: A Historical Geography* (Cambridge University Press, Cambridge, 1989).

3. M. Williams, Thinking about the forest: a comparative view from three continents. In *The Great Lakes Forest: An Environmental and Social History,* S. L. Flader, ed. (University of Minnesota Press and Forest History Society, 1983), 253–73.

4. M. K. Anderson, California Indian horticulture, *Fremontia* 18(2): 7–14, 1990.

5. M. Devèze, Forêts françaises et forêts allemandes, *Revue Historique* 236:47–68, 1966.

6. O. Rackham, *Ancient Woodland: Its History, Vegetation and Uses in England* (Edward Arnold, London, 1980), *passim*.

7. J. R. Flenley, *The Equatorial Rain Forest: A Geological History* (Butterworth, London, 1979), *passim*; J. H. McAndrews, Human disturbance of North American forests and grasslands: the fossil pollen record. In *Vegetation History,* B. Huntley and T. Webb III, eds. (Kluwer Academic Publishers, Dordrecht, Netherlands, 1988), 673–97; L. Sponsel, The environmental history of Amazonia: natural and human disturbance, and the ecological tradition. In H. K. Steen and R. P. Tucker, eds., *Changing Tropical Forests: Historical Perspectives on Today's Challenges in Central and South America* (Forest History Society, n.p., 1992), 233–51; E. W. B. Russell, R. B. Davis, R. S. Anderson, T. E. Rhodes, and D. S. Anderson, Recent centuries of vegetational change in the glaciated north-eastern United States, *Journal of Ecology* 81:647–64, 1993.

8. D. W. Dragoo, Some aspects of eastern North American prehistory: a review 1975, *American Antiquity* 41:3–27, 1976.

9. C. S. Kidwell, Science and ethnoscience: native American world views as a factor in the development of native technologies. In K. E. Bailes, ed., *Environmental History: Critical Issues in Comparative Perspective* (University Press of America, Lanham, Md., 1985), 277–87; S. Boyden, *Western Civilization in Biological Perspective* (Clarendon Press, Oxford, 1987), 59–82.

10. C. O. Sauer, *Seeds, Spades, Hearths and Herds* (MIT Press, Cambridge, 1969), 10–11; A. Goudie, *The Human Impact on the Natural Environment,* 3d ed. (MIT Press, Cambridge, 1990), 26–28, 107–11.

11. A. J. Sutcliffe, *On the Track of Ice Age Mammals* (Harvard University Press, Cambridge, 1985), 206.

12. P. S. Martin, Prehistoric overkill: the global model. In *Quaternary Extinctions: A Prehistoric Revolution,* P. S. Martin and R. G. Klein, eds. (University of Arizona Press, Tucson, 1984), 354–403.

13. Sutcliffe, *On the Track of Ice Age Mammals,* 181, 199.

14. Ibid., 181–85.

15. Ibid.; Paul S. Martin, Prehistoric overkill: Pleistocene extinctions, *Proceedings VIIth Congress of INQUA,* 6:75–120, 1967. Martin has continued to develop this theme, but he introduced it formally in this paper.

16. R. Bonnichsen et al., The environmental setting for human colonization of northern New England and adjacent Canada in Late Pleistocene time, *Geological Society of America, Special Paper* 197, 1985, 151–59; H. J. B. Birks, Late-Quaternary biotic changes in terrestrial and lacustrine environments, with particular reference to north-west Europe. In *Handbook of Holocene Palaeoecology and Palaeohydrology* (John Wiley and Sons, Chichester, 1986), 3–65, 49.

17. I. G. Simmons, *Changing the Face of the Earth: Culture, Environment, History* (Blackwell, New York, 1989), 59–60; F. Densmore, How Indians use wild plants for food, medicine and crafts (Dover Publications, New York, 1974), 314 (unabridged republication of "Uses of plants by the Chippewa Indians," 275–397 in *44th Annual Report of the Bureau of American Ethnology* [Government Printing Office, Washington, D.C., 1928]).

18. R. F. Heizer, Primitive man as an ecological factor, *Kroeber Anthropological Society Papers* 13:1–31, 1955.

19. P. Kalm, *Peter Kalm's Travels in North America,* The English Version of 1770, tr. and ed. A. B. Benson. Vol. 2 (Wilson-Erickson, New York, 1937).

20. G. P. Nabhan and M. K. Anderson, Gardeners in Eden, *Wilderness* 55(194):30.

21. R. A. Yarnell, Aboriginal relationships between culture and plant life in the Upper Great Lakes Region, *Anthropological Papers,* Museum of Anthropology, University of Michigan, Ann Arbor, #23, 1964.

22. Boyden, *Western Civilization,* 81n26, data taken from R. Clarke and G. Hindley, *The Challenge of the Primitives* (Jonathan Cape, London, 1975), 30–31.

23. A. G. Smith, The influence of Mesolithic and Neolithic man on British vegetation: a discussion. In *Studies of the Vegetational History of the British Isles,* D. Walker and R. G. West, eds. (Cambridge University Press, Cambridge, 1970), 81–96; F. M. Chambers and L. Elliott, Spread and expansion of *Alnus* Mill. in the British Isles: timing, agencies and possible vectors, *Journal of Biogeography* 16:541–50, 1989.

24. Remonstrance of New Netherland, 28 July 1649. In *New York Colonial Manuscripts* I, Holland Documents II, 276.

25. E. W. B. Russell, Vegetation of northern New Jersey before European settlement, *American Midland Naturalist* 105:1–12, 1981.

26. J. Perlin, *A Forest Journey: The Role of Wood in the Development of Civilization* (W. W. Norton, New York, 1989), *passim.*

27. J. L. Betancourt, J. S. Dean, and H. M. Hull, Prehistoric long-distance transport of construction beams, Chaco Canyon, New Mexico, *American Antiquity* 51:370–75, 1986.

28. H. R. Delcourt, The impact of prehistoric agriculture and land occupation on natural vegetation, *Trends in Ecology and Evolution* 2:39–44, 1987.

29. O. Rackham, *The History of the Countryside* (J. M. Dent and Sons, London, 1986), 16.

30. H. C. Darby, *A New Historical Geography of England before 1600* (Cambridge University Press, Cambridge, 1976), 52–53.

31. P. Young, Going to the goats, *Science News* 137:142, 1990, report on work by G. O. Rollefson and I. Kohler-Rollefson at the 1990 Annual Meeting of the American Association for the Advancement of Science.

32. Old Testament, 2 Chronicles II, 8, 18; W. C. Lowdermilk, *Conquest of Land Through 7000 Years: Dr. Lowdermilk's Trip After the Dustbowl*, USDA Agricultural Information Bulletin #99, 1975. The sources differ in identification of the trees used. Some include cypress and algum (?) (also translated as *almuggim*), but the main point is that there were many trees, primarily gymnosperms.

33. L. Sponsel, Environmental history of Amazonia.

34. S. Horn, Microfossils and forest history in Costa Rica. In Steen and Tucker, *Changing Tropical Forests*, 16–30.

35. A. M. Lambert, *The Making of the Dutch Landscape: An Historical Geography of the Netherlands* (Academic Press, London, 1971), 49–50.

36. D. Hooke, Woodland utilization in England, AD 800–1100. In *Human Influence on Forest Ecosystems Development in Europe*, F. Salbitano, ed. (Pitagora Editrice, Bologna, 1988), 301–10.

37. G. Duby, *The Early Growth of the European Economy: Warriors and Peasants from the Seventh to the Twelfth Century*, trans. H. B. Clarke (Cornell University Press, Ithaca, 1974), 24.

38. Darby, *A New Historical Geography*, 167.

39. I. Austad, Tree-pollarding in western Norway. In H. H. Birks, H. J. B. Birks, P. E. Kaland, and D. Moe, eds., *The Cultural Landscape—Past, Present and Future* (Cambridge University Press, Cambridge, 1988), 11–30; J. Hughes and B. Huntley, Upland hay meadows in Britain—their vegetation, management and future. In Birks et al., *The Cultural Landscape*, 91–110.

40. Rackham, *Ancient Woodland*.

41. G. F. Peterken, Long-term changes in the woodlands of Rockingham Forest and other areas, *Journal of Ecology* 64:123–46, 1976; K. J. Kirby, Conservation in British woodland—adapting traditional management to modern needs. In Birks et al., *The Cultural Landscape*, 79–89; O. Rackham, Trees and woodland in a crowded landscape—the cultural landscape of the British Isles. In Birks et al., *The Cultural Landscape*, 53–77.

42. H. Schmidt, *Agriculture in New Jersey: A Three-Hundred Year History* (Rutgers University Press, New Brunswick, 1973), 53, 66.

43. Ibid., 73; E. W. B. Russell, Vegetational change in northern New Jersey since 1500 A.D.: a palynological, vegetational and historical synthesis (Ph.D. diss., Rutgers University, New Brunswick, N.J., 1979).

44. Ibid.

45. K. H. Redford, The empty forest, *BioScience* 42:412–22, 1992.

46. A. Leopold, *Game Management* (Charles Scribner's Sons, New York, 1933), 420–23.

47. Devèze, Forêts françaises; Duby, *The Early Growth of the European Economy*, 20; G. P. Marsh, *Man and Nature* (1864; reprint, Harvard University Press, Cambridge, 1965), 240–44.

48. Darby, *A New Historical Geography*, 55.

49. Hooke, Woodland utilization.

50. Ibid., 273.

51. Devèze, Forêts françaises.

52. R. E. McCabe and T. R. McCabe, Of slings and arrows: an historical retrospective. In *White-tailed Deer: Ecology and Management* (Stackpole Books, Mechanicsburg, Penn., 1984), 19–72.

53. A. F. Hough, A twenty-year record of understory vegetational change in a virgin Pennsylvania forest, *Ecology* 46:370–73, 1965.

54. R. C. Anderson and O. L. Loucks, White-tail deer (*Odocoileus virginianus*) influence on structure and composition of *Tsuga canadensis* forests, *J. Applied Ecology* 16:855–61, 1979.

55. Devèze, Forêts françaises; Darby, *A New Historical Geography,* 65; Hooke, Woodland utilization.

56. Darby, *A New Historical Geography,* 65.

57. Devèze, Forêts françaises.

58. Darby, *A New Historical Geography,* 171, 228–29.

59. J. P. Métailié, J. Bonhote, and C. Frauhauf, A thousand years of forest history in the French Pyrenees Mountains: the Ariège example. In Salbitano, *Human Influence,* 159–67.

60. P. Piussi and S. Stiavelli, Forest history of the Cerbaie Hills (Toscona, Italy). In Salbitano, *Human Influence,* 109–20.

61. E. L. Braun, *Deciduous Forests of Eastern North America* (Blakiston Co., Philadelphia, 1950), 248–52, 238, 429.

62. T. Webb III, A comparison of modern and presettlement pollen from southern Michigan (USA), *Rev. Palaeobotany and Palynology* 16:137–56, 1973; E. W. B. Russell, Vegetational change in northern New Jersey from pre-colonization to the present: a palynological interpretation, *Bulletin of the Torrey Botanical Club* 107:432–46, 1980; M. B. Davis, History of the vegetation on the Mirror Lake watershed. In *An Ecosystem Approach to Aquatic Ecology: Mirror Lake and Its Environment,* G. E. Likens, ed. (Springer-Verlag, New York, 1985); J. H. McAndrews, Human disturbance of North American forests and grasslands: the fossil pollen record. In *Vegetation History,* B. Huntley and T. Webb III, eds. (Kluwer Academic Publishers, Dordrecht, Netherlands, 1988), 673–97; Russell et al., Recent centuries of vegetational change.

63. G. G. Whitney and W. C. Davis, From primitive woods to cultivated woodlots: Thoreau and the forest history of Concord, Massachusetts, *Journal of Forest History* 30:70–81, 1986.

64. Braun, *Deciduous Forests,* 338, 429.

65. J. H. Hanson, Extractive economies in a historical perspective: gum arabic in West Africa. In *Non-Timber Products from Tropical Forests: Evaluation of a Conservation and Development Strategy,* D. C. Nepstad and S. Schwartzman, eds., Advances in Economic Botany 9 (New York Botanical Garden, New York, 1992), 107–14.

66. Darby, *A New Historical Geography,* 273; F. B. Hough, *Report upon Forestry,* U.S. Forest Service. Vol. 3 (Government Printing Office, Washington, D.C., 1882), 68–128.

67. J. G. Lefèbvre, Les forêts de l'Europe et de l'Amérique: Etude sur le Régime des Forêts et leur Reconstruction (Paris and Havre, 1879), quoted in Hough, *Report upon Forestry,* 283

68. Lambert, *The Making of the Dutch Landscape,* 196–200.
69. Hough, *Report upon Forestry,* 305.
70. Lefèbvre, Les forêts de l'Europe; C. S. Sargent, *The Silva of North America,* vol. 9, *The Cupuliferae-Salicaceae* (Houghton-Mifflin, Boston, 1896), 59.
71. Williams, *Americans and Their Forests.*
72. Ibid., 393–424.
73. S. T. A. Pickett and P. S. White, Patch dynamics: a synthesis. In *The Ecology of Natural Disturbance and Patch Dynamics,* S. T. A. Pickett and P. S. White, eds. (Academic Press, Orlando, 1985), 371–84.
74. D. M. Sharpe, F. Stearns, R. Burgess, and W. C. Johnson, Spatio-temporal patterns of forest ecosystems in man-dominated landscapes. In *Proceedings Int. Congr. Neth. Soc. Landscape Ecol.,* Veldhoven, Netherlands, 1981:109–16; R. T. T. Forman and M. Godron, *Landscape Ecology* (John Wiley and Sons, New York, 1986), *passim*; W. C. Zipperer, R. L. Burgess, and R. D. Nyland, Patterns of deforestation and reforestation in different landscape types in central New York, *Forest Ecology and Management* 36:103–17, 1990; T. A. Spies, W. J. Ripple, and G. A. Bradshaw, Dynamics and pattern of a managed coniferous forest landscape in Oregon, *Ecological Applications* 4:555–68, 1994; D. O. Wallin, F. J. Swanson, and B. Marks, Landscape pattern response to changes in pattern generation rules: land-use legacies in forestry, *Ecological Applications* 4:569–80, 1994.
75. J. F. Franklin and R. T. T. Forman, Creating landscape patterns by logging: ecological consequences and patterns, *Landscape Ecology* 1:5–18, 1987.
76. A. Aubréville, Regeneration patterns in the closed forests of Ivory Coast, trans. S. R. Eyre. In *World Vegetation Types,* S. R. Eyre, ed., 40–55, 1971 (originally published in 1938).
77. E. A. Bourdo, The forest the settlers saw. In Flader, *The Great Lakes Forest,* 3–16.
78. J. R. McNeill, Deforestation in the araucaria zone of southern Brazil, 1900–1983. In J. F. Richards and R. P. Tucker, eds., *World Deforestation in the Twentieth Century* (Duke University Press, Durham, N.C., 1988), 15–32.
79. P. M. Chandler, The indigenous knowledge of ecological processes among peasants in the People's Republic of China, *Agriculture and Human Values* 8:59–66, 1991.
80. J. W. Hurst, The institutional environment of the logging era in Wisconsin. In Flader, *The Great Lakes Forest,* 137–55.
81. C. E. Ahlgren and I. F. Ahlgren, The human impact on northern forest ecosystems. In Flader, *The Great Lakes Forest,* 33–51.
82. Ibid.; M. D. Abrams and M. L. Scott, Disturbance-mediated accelerated succession in two Michigan forest types, *Forest Science* 35:42–49, 1989.
83. D. A. Marquis, Even-age development and management of mixed hardwood stands: Allegheny hardwoods, Paper presented at the Annual Silviculture Workshop, USDA Forest Service, Roanoke, Vir., 1981.
84. J. Gifford, Forestal conditions and silvicultural prospects of the coastal plain of New Jersey. In *Annual Report of the State Geologist for 1899. Report on Forests* (Geological Survey of New Jersey, Trenton, 1900), 292.
85. Devèze, Forêts françaises.

86. U. Schweinfirth, Man's impact on vegetation and landscape in the Himalayas. In *Man's Impact on Vegetation*, W. Holzner, M. J. A. Werger, and I. Ikusima, eds. (Dr. W. Junk, The Hague, 1983), 297–310.

87. W. Dean, *Brazil and the Struggle for Rubber: A Study in Environmental History* (Cambridge University Press, Cambridge, 1987), 5–6, 59.

88. Gifford, Forestal conditions; Devèze, Forêts françaises; E. W. B. Russell, The 1899 New Jersey State Geologist's Report: a call for forest management, *Journal of Forest History* 32:205–11, 1988.

89. C. Merchant, The women of the progressive conservation crusade. In Bailes, Environmental History, 153–75; N. T. Newton, *Design of the Land: The Development of Landscape Architecture* (Harvard University Press, Cambridge, 1971), 530.

90. R. C. Steele, Variation in oakwoods in Britain. In *The British Oak*, M. G. Morris and F. H. Perring, eds. (E. W. Classey, Faringdon, Berkshire, 1974), 130–37.

91. R. R. Vane-Wright, The Columbus hypothesis: an explanation for the dramatic 19th century range expansion of the Monarch butterfly. In *Biology and Conservation of the Monarch Butterfly*, S. B. Malcolm and M. P. Zalucki, eds. (Natural History Museum of Los Angeles County, Los Angeles, 1993), 179–87.

92. For example, see J. F. Richards and R. P. Tucker, *World Deforestation in the Twentieth Century* (Duke University Press, Durham, N.C., 1988).

93. D. Walker and Y. Chen, Palynological light on tropical rainforest dynamics, *Quaternary Science Reviews* 6(2):77–92, 1987.

## *Chapter 8. Agriculture and Its Residual Effects*

1. J. Iversen, Forest clearance in the stone age, *Scientific American* 194:36–41, 1956; W. Allan, *The African Husbandman* (Oliver and Boyd, Edinburgh, 1965), quoted in R. C. Bigalke, Present-day mammals of Africa. In *Evolution of African Mammals*, J. J. Maglio and H. B. S. Cooke, eds. (Harvard University Press, Cambridge, 1978), 13; J. Diamond, The worst mistake in the history of the human race, *Discovery*, May 1987:64–66.

2. Diamond, The worst mistake.

3. Z. S. An et al., Episode of strengthened summer monsoon climate of Younger Dryas age on the loess plateau of central China, *Quaternary Research* 39:45–54, 1993; Yechiele et al., Late Quaternary geological history of the Dead Sea area, *Quaternary Research* 39:59–67, 1993.

4. A. L. Cohen et al., A Holocene marine climate record in mollusc shells from the southwest African coast, *Quaternary Research* 38:379–85, 1992.

5. N. Miller, The origins of plant cultivation in the Near East. In *The Origins of Agriculture: An International Perspective*, C. W. Cowan and P. J. Watson, eds. (Smithsonian Institution Press, Washington, D.C., 1992), 39–58.

6. H. J. B. Birks, Late-Quaternary biotic changes in terrestrial and lacustrine environments, with particular reference to north-west Europe. In *Handbook of Holocene Palaeoecology and Palaeohydrology*, B. E. Berglund, ed. (John Wiley and Sons, Chichester, 1986), 3–65.

7. L. L. Cavalli-Sforza, P. Menozzi, and A. Piazza, Demic expansion and human evolution, *Science* 259:639–46, 1993.

8. E. Boserup, Environment, population and technology in primitive societies. In Worster, *The Ends of the Earth*, 23–38.

9. For a summary of ideas of the factors that caused the development of agriculture, see R. S. MacNeish, *The Origins of Agriculture and Settled Life* (University of Oklahoma Press, Norman, 1992), 3–33. Other discussions with different points of view include C. O. Sauer, *Agricultural Origins and Dispersals* (American Geographical Society, New York, 1952); C. D. Darlington, *The Evolution of Man and Society* (Simon and Schuster, New York, 1969), 70; E. Boserup, *The Conditions of Agricultural Growth: The Economics of Agrarian Change under Population Pressure* (Aldine, Chicago, 1965); M. N. Cohen, *The Food Crisis in Prehistory* (Yale University Press, New Haven, 1977), 42; Diamond, The worst mistake.

10. J. B. Stoltman and D. A. Baerreis, The evolution of human ecosystems in the eastern United States. In *Late-Quaternary Environments of the United States*, vol. 2, *The Holocene*, H. E. Wright, Jr., ed. (University of Minnesota Press, Minneapolis, 1983), 252–68.

11. S. Boyden, *Western Civilization in Biological Perspective* (Clarendon Press, Oxford, 1987), 89.

12. MacNeish, *Origins of Agriculture*, chap. 1.

13. B. D. Smith, Origins of Agriculture in Eastern North America, *Science* 246:1566–71, 1989; Stoltman and Baerreis, The evolution of human ecosystems.

14. Anonymous, *Hammond's Advanced Reference Atlas* (C. S. Hammond, Maplewood, N.J., 1961), 12, 32; J. P. Harlan, Agricultural origins: centers and non-centers, *Science* 174:468–74, 1971; Cavalli-Sforza, Demic expansion.

15. Sauer, *Agricultural Origins*, 21–22; A. C. Roosevelt, *Parmana: Prehistoric Maize and Manioc Subsistence along the Amazon and Orinoco* (Academic Press, New York, 1980), 251–52.

16. Harlan, Agricultural origins.

17. Ibid.

18. Anonymous, *Atlas*, 5.

19. E. Isaac, *Geography of Domestication* (Prentice-Hall, Englewood Cliffs, 1970), 61–62; Boyden, *Western Civilization*, 84–85.

20. Sauer, *Agricultural Origins*, 21–24; Isaac, *Geography of Domestication*.

21. Smith, Origins of agriculture. This kind of dating is made possible by AMS (Accelerator Mass Spectrometry) dating of small amounts of carbon.

22. Sauer, *Agricultural Origins*, 28–32; Isaac, *Geography of Domestication*, chap. 5; Boyden, *Western Civilization*, 88–89.

23. Isaac, *Geography of Domestication*, 4.

24. Harlan, Agricultural origins.

25. Smith, Origins of agriculture.

26. F. Firbas, Der pollenanalytische Nachweis des Getreidebaus, *Zeitschrift für Botanik* 31:447–78, 1937; J. Iversen, Land occupation in Denmark's Stone Age, *Danmarks Geologiske Undersøgelse*, II Raekke 66:1–68, 1941; P. D. Moore and E. H. Chater, The changing vegetation of west-central Wales in the light of human

history, *Journal of Ecology* 57:361–79; J. H. McAndrews, Human disturbance of North American forests and grasslands: the fossil pollen record. In *Vegetation History,* B. Huntley and T. Webb III, eds. (Kluwer Academic Publishers, Dordrecht, Netherlands, 1988), 673–97; B. Huntley and H. J. B. Birks, *An Atlas of Past and Present Pollen Maps for Europe: 0–13 000 Years Ago* (Cambridge University Press, Cambridge, 1983).

27. Iversen, Forest clearance; Birks, Late-Quaternary biotic changes; S. M. Peglar, The mid-Holocene *Ulmus* decline at Diss Mere, Norfolk, UK: a year-by-year pollen stratigraphy from annual laminations, *The Holocene* 3:1–13, 1993.

28. Iversen, Land occupation; Iversen, Forest clearance

29. Darlington, *The Evolution of Man,* 82–83.

30. W. C. Lowdermilk, Conquest of Land Through 7000 Years: Dr. Lowdermilk's Trip after the Dustbowl, *Agricultural Information Bulletin* 99, USDA, 1975; Darlington, *The Evolution of Man,* 85–86.

31. Isaac, *Geography of Domestication,* 45–46; I. G. Simmons, *Changing the Face of the Earth: Culture, Environment, History* (Basil Blackwell, New York, 1989), 93–97.

32. C. Renfrew, *Before Civilization: The Radiocarbon Revolution and Prehistoric Europe* (Cambridge University Press, Cambridge, 1979), 167–75.

33. A. Goudie, *The Human Impact on the Natural Environment,* 3d ed. (MIT Press, Cambridge, 1990), 19.

34. Boyden, *Western Civilization,* 91.

35. G. Duby, *Rural Economy and Country Life in the Medieval West,* trans. Cynthia Postan (University of South Carolina Press, Columbia, 1968), 109–10; A. Verhulst, The "agricultural revolution" of the Middle Ages reconsidered. In *Law, Custom and the Social Fabric: Essays in Honor of Bryce Lyon,* B. S. Bachrach and D. Nicholas, eds., Ghent University Studies in Medieval Culture 28 (Kalamazoo, 1990), 17–28.

36. Smith, Origins of agriculture.

37. McAndrews, Human disturbance.

38. H. L. Driver, *Indians of North America,* 2nd ed. (University of Chicago Press, Chicago, 1969), 64; C. M. Aikens, Environmental archaeology in the western United States. In *Late-Quaternary Environments of the United States,* vol. 2, *The Holocene,* H. E. Wright, Jr., ed. (University of Minnesota Press, Minneapolis, 1983), 239–51.

39. Driver, *Indians of North America,* 64.

40. H. D. Clout, ed., *Themes in the Historical Geography of France* (Academic Press, London, 1977), 188 ff.

41. G. Duby, *The Early Growth of the European Economy: Warriors and Peasants from the Seventh to the Twelfth Century,* trans. Howard B. Clarke (Cornell University Press, Ithaca, 1974), 16.

42. Ibid.

43. O. Rackham, *The History of the Countryside* (J. M. Dent and Sons, London, 1986), p. 75

44. D. Grigg, *The Dynamics of Agricultural Change: The Historical Experience* (St. Martin's Press, New York, 1982), 32–35.

45. H. H. Lamb, Climatic variation and changes in the wind and ocean circulation: The little ice age in the northeast Atlantic, *Quaternary Research* 11:1–20, 1979.

46. E. H. Bucher, Impact of European colonization on the chaco savannas of Argentina, *Bulletin Ecological Society of America* 69(2):86, 1988; J. A. Simonetti, Human disturbance and community patterns in central Chile, *Bulletin Ecological Society of America* 69(2):296, 1988.

47. H. D. McCallum and F. T. McCallum, *The Wire that Fenced the West* (University of Oklahoma Press, Norman, 1965), 115–215.

48. Darlington, *The Evolution of Man*, 75; Smith, Origins of agriculture.

49. D. Tilman and S. Pacala, The maintenance of species richness in plant communities. In *Species Diversity in Ecological Communities: Historical and Geographical Perspectives*, R. E. Ricklefs and D. Schluter, eds. (University of Chicago Press, Chicago, 1993), 13–25.

50. G. P. Marsh, *Man and Nature* (1864; reprint Belknap Press, Harvard University Press, Cambridge, 1965), 117; Lowdermilk, Conquest of Land.

51. J. Donald Hughes, Gaia: environmental problems in chthonic perspective. In Bailes, *Environmental History*, 64–78.

52. F. Turner, *Beyond Geography: The Western Spirit Against the Wilderness* (Viking Press, New York, 1980), 24.

53. Lowdermilk, Conquest of Land, 20.

54. Ibid., 30.

55. Darlington, *The Evolution of Man*, 52–53.

56. J. R. Flemley, *The Equatorial Rain Forest: A Geological History* (Butterworths, London, 1979), 126.

57. R. B. Brugam, Pollen indicators of land-use change in southern Connecticut, *Quaternary Research* 9:349–62, 1978; R. B. Davis and S. A. Norton, Paleolimnologic studies of human impact on lakes in the United States, with emphasis on recent research in New England, *Polskie Archiwum Hydrobiology* 25:99–115, 1978; G. S. Brush and F. W. Davis, Stratigraphic evidence of human disturbance in an estuary, *Quaternary Research* 22:91–108, 1984.

58. M. Stroh and J. Raloff, New UN soil survey: the dirt on erosion, *Science News* 141:215, 1992.

59. E. W. B. Russell and A. E. Schuyler, Vegetation and flora of Hopewell Furnace National Historic Site, eastern Pennsylvania, *Bartonia* 54:124–43, 1988.

60. M. J. McDonnell and E. W. Stiles, The structural complexity of old-field vegetation and the recruitment of bird-dispersed plant species, *Oecologia* 56:109–16, 1983.

61. J. G. Evans, *The Environment of Early Man in the British Isles* (Paul Elek, London, 1975), 162.

62. W. C. Wilkinson, "The Encampment & Position of the Army under His Excy. Lt. Gl. Burgoyne at Swords and Freeman's Farms on Hudsons River near Stillwater, 1777," Manuscript Map, Copy at Saratoga National Historic Park, Stillwater, N.Y.

63. E. W. B. Russell, Cultural landscape history, Saratoga National Historical Park, draft report, National Park Service, North Atlantic Regional Office, 1993.

64. H. B. Underwood et al., Deer and vegetation interactions on Saratoga National Historical Park, draft report, National Park Service, North Atlantic Regional

Office, 1989; K. A. Austin, Gray dogwood (*Cornus racemosa* Lam.) as a refuge from herbivory in old fields of Saratoga National Historical Park, New York (Ph.D. diss., State University of New York, College of Environmental Science and Forestry, Syracuse, 1992).

65. These data come from information presented at the George Wright Society Meeting in Jacksonville, Florida, in 1992 and the ESA meeting, Madison, Wisconsin, 1993.

66. Binford et al., Ecosystems.

67. Clout, *Themes,* chap. 4.

68. Ibid.

69. Grigg, *Dynamics,* 59.

70. W. L. Anderson, Making land produce useful wildlife, *Farmers' Bulletin* #2035, U.S. Department of Agriculture, 1960; Anonymous, *Invite Birds to Your Home,* PA-940, U.S. Department of Agriculture, Soil Conservation Service, 1969 (pamphlet).

71. M. J. McDonnell and E. W. Stiles, The structural complexity of old field vegetation and the recruitment of bird-dispersed plant species, *Oecologia* (Berlin) 56:109–16, 1983.

72. E. L. D. Seymour, *The Wise Garden Encyclopedia* (Grosset and Dunlap, New York, 1970), 237; Gurney's catalogue, 1992–93.

73. Z. Naveh and P. Kutiel, Changes in Mediterranean vegetation of Israel in response to human habitation and land use. In *The Earth in Transition: Patterns and Processes of Biotic Impoverishment,* G. M. Woodwell, ed. (Cambridge University Press, Cambridge, 1990), 259–99.

74. J. Hughes and B. Huntley, Upland hay meadows in Britain—Their Vegetation, Management and Future. In *The Cultural Landscape—Past, Present and Future,* H. H. Birks et al., eds. (Cambridge University Press, Cambridge, 1988), 91–110.

75. P. L. Marks, On the origin of the field plants of the northeastern United States, *American Naturalist* 122:210–28, 1983.

76. Flemley, *Equatorial Rain Forest,* 116–21; McAndrews, Human disturbance.

77. M. B. Bush et al., A 14,300-yr paleoecological profile of a lowland tropical lake in Panama, *Ecological Monographs* 62:251–75, 1992.

78. Flemley, *Equatorial Rain Forest,* 118.

79. E. W. B. Russell, Vegetational change in northern New Jersey from precolonization to the present: a palynological interpretation, *Bulletin of the Torrey Botanical Club* 107:432–46, 1980.

## Chapter 9. *Historical Patterns of Human Settlement*

1. W. Cronon, *Changes in the Land* (Hill and Wang, New York, 1983), 54–81.

2. M. Williams, *The Making of the South Australia Landscape* (Academic Press, London, 1974), 67.

3. P. O. Wacker, *Land and People. A Cultural Geography of Preindustrial New Jersey: Origins and Settlement Patterns* (Rutgers University Press, New Brunswick, N.J., 1975), chap. 4.

4. Ibid., 322–23.

5. A. Hamilton, Hamilton's Itinerarium . . . being a Narrative of a Journey . . . 1744, A. B. Hart, ed., privately printed, St. Louis, 1907. In *New Jersey in Travellers' Accounts, 1524–1971: A Descriptive Bibliography,* O. Coad, ed. (Scarecrow Press, Metuchen, N.J., 1972), 14; R. Rogers, *A Concise Account of North America . . . ,* (Printed for the Author, London, 1765), cited in Coad, *New Jersey in Travellers' Accounts,* 23–24.

6. H. G. Schmidt, *Rural Hunterdon: An Agricultural History* (Rutgers University Press, New Brunswick, N.J., 1946), 72–73.

7. Wacker, *Land and People,* 245–46.

8. J. R. Dorney, Increase A. Lapham's pioneer observations and maps of landforms and natural disturbances, *Wisconsin Academy of Science, Arts and Letters* 71:25–30, 1983.

9. R. M. Robbins, *Our Landed Heritage: The Public Domain, 1776–1970* (University of Nebraska Press, Lincoln, 1976); J. Opie, *The Law of the Land: Two Hundred Years of American Farmland Policy* (University of Nebraska Press, Lincoln, 1987).

10. Robbins, *Our Landed Heritage,* chap. 2; Opie, *The Law of the Land.*

11. L. C. Irland, Rufus Putnam's ghost: an essay on Maine's public lands, 1783–1820, *Journal of Forest History* 30:60–69, 1986.

12. F. B. Hough, *Report upon Forestry,* Vol. 3, U.S. Dept. Agriculture, Washington, D.C., 1882, 10.

13. H. B. Johnson, *Order Upon the Land: The U.S. Rectangular Land Survey and the Upper Mississippi Country* (Oxford University Press, New York, 1976), chap. 8.

14. M. J. McDonnell and E. W. Stiles, The structural complexity of old-field vegetation and the recruitment of bird-dispersed plant species, *Oecologia* 56:109–16, 1983; J. W. Ranney, M. C. Bruner, and J. B. Levenson, The importance of edge in the structure and dynamics of forest islands. In *Forest Island Dynamics in Man-Dominated Landscapes,* R. L. Burgess and D. M. Sharpe, eds. (Springer-Verlag, New York, 1981), 67–95.

15. R. T. T. Forman and M. Godron, Patches and structural components for a landscape ecology, *BioScience* 31:733–40, 1981.

16. M. Devèze, Forêts françaises et forêts allemandes, *Revue Historique* 236:47–68, 1966.

17. H. C. Darby, *A New Historical Geography of England before 1600* (Cambridge University Press, Cambridge, 1976), 25.

18. H. C. Darby, The age of the improver: 1600–1800. In *A New Historical Geography of England after 1600,* H. C. Darby, ed. (Cambridge University Press, Cambridge, 1976), 21–26.

19. C. J. Bahre and D. E. Bradbury, Vegetation change along the Arizona-Sonora boundary, *Annals of the Association of American Geographers* 68:145–65, 1978; R. R. Humphrey, *Ninety Years and 535 Miles: Vegetation Change along the Mexican Border* (University of New Mexico Press, Albuquerque, 1987).

20. Devèze, Forêts françaises.

21. Z. Naveh and P. Kutiel, Changes in Mediterranean vegetation of Israel in response to human habitation and land use. In *The Earth in Transition,* G. M. Woodwell, ed. (Cambridge University Press, Cambridge, 1990), 259–99.

22. F. Kienast, Analysis of the historic development of landscape ecological networks with GIS technology, Abstract, World Congress of Landscape Ecology, Ottawa, Canada, 1991, 62.

23. J. Baudry, personal communication.

24. I. G. Simmons, *Changing the Face of the Earth: Culture, Environment, History* (Basil Blackwell, New York, 1989), 315–16.

25. R. H. Taylor, Fertilizers and farming in the Southeast, 1840–1900, *North Carolina Historical Review* 30:305–28, 1953.

26. United States Federal Census, Agricultural Schedules, 1850–1960, Washington, D.C.

27. S. W. Trimble, Man-induced soil erosion on the southern Piedmont, 1700–1970 (Ph.D. diss., University of Wisconsin, Milwaukee, 1974).

28. D. J. de Laubenfels, Where Sherman passed by, *Geographical Review* 47:381–95, 1957.

29. E. L. Ullman, The role of transportation and the bases for interaction. In Thomas, *Man's Role,* 862–80.

30. A. Hollander, Historical geography of land use in western North Carolina—1850–1890, a proposal, term paper, Duke University, 1990.

31. Ullman, The role of transportation.

32. D. Grigg, *The Dynamics of Agricultural Change: The Historical Experience* (St. Martin's Press, New York, 1982), 143.

33. H. G. Schabel, Tanganyika forestry under German colonial administration, 1891–1919, *Journal of Forest and Conservation History* 34:130–41, 1990; Williams, *Americans and Their Forests: A Historical Geography* (Cambridge University Press, Cambridge, 1989), 97.

34. D. M. Gates, C. H. D. Clarke, and J. T. Harris, Wildlife in a changing environment. In *The Great Lakes Forest: an Environmental and Social History,* S. L. Flader, ed. (University of Minnesota Press and Forest History Society, 1983), 52–81.

35. Grigg, *Dynamics of Agricultural Change,* 14.

36. Ullman, The role of transportation.

37. P. M. Fearnside, Deforestation in Brazilian Amazonia. In Woodwell, *The Earth in Transition,* 211–38.

38. D. Skole and C. Tucker, Tropical deforestation and habitat fragmentation in the Amazon: satellite data from 1978–1988, *Science* 260:1905–10, 1993.

39. S. Olson, *The Depletion Myth: A History of Railroad Use of Timber* (Harvard University Press, Cambridge, 1971).

40. B. F. Hough, *Report Upon Forestry,* Vol. 1 (U.S. Department of Agriculture, Washington, D.C., 1878), 112–16.

41. Ibid., 122.

42. Ibid., 120.

43. Ibid., 206–07; R. T. T. Forman and R. E. Boerner, Fire frequency and the Pine Barrens of New Jersey, *Bulletin of the Torrey Botanical Club* 108:34–50, 1981.

44. Hough, *Report,* Vol. 3, 419.

45. M. L. Roberts and R. L. Stuckey, Distribution patterns of selected aquatic and wetland vascular plants in relation to the Ohio canal system, *Bartonia* 57:50–74, 1992.

46. R. N. Mack, Invasion of *Bromus tectorum* L. into western North America: an ecological chronicle, *Agro-Ecosystems* 7:145–65; W. D. Billings, *Bromus tectorum,* a

biotic cause of ecosystem impoverishment in the Great Basin. In Woodwell, *The Earth in Transition,* 301–22.

47. D. Kagan, S. Ozment, and F. M. Turner, *The Western Heritage* (Macmillan, New York, 1979), 17; C. Glacken, *Traces on the Rhodian Shore* (University of California Press, Berkeley, 1967), 117; E. S. Deevey et al., Mayan urbanism: impact on a tropical karst development, *Science* 206:298–306, 1979.

48. L. Mumford, The natural history of urbanization. In Thomas, *Man's Role,* 382–98.

49. Ibid.; Glacken, *Traces,* 126.

50. Simmons, *Changing the Face,* 271.

51. E. H. Rapoport, The process of plant colonization in small settlements and large cities. In *Humans as Components of Ecosystems: The Ecology of Subtle Human Effects and Populated Areas,* M. J. McDonnell and S. T. A. Pickett, eds. (Springer-Verlag, New York, 1993), 190–207.

52. M. J. McDonnell and S. T. A. Pickett, Ecosystem structure and function along gradients of urbanization: an unexploited opportunity for ecology, *Ecology* 71:1232–37, 1990; M. J. McDonnell, S. T. A. Pickett, and R. V. Pouyat, The application of the ecological gradient paradigm to the study of urban effects. In McDonnell and Pickett, *Humans as Components,* 175–89.

53. Mumford, The natural history, p. 387.

54. C. R. Bowlus, Ecological crisis in fourteenth century Europe. In *Historical Ecology: Essays on Environment and Social Change,* L. J. Bilsky, ed. (Kennikat Press, Port Washington, N.J., 1980), 86–99.

55. A. M. Solomon and D. F. Kroener, Suburban replacement of rural land uses reflected in the pollen rain of northeastern New Jersey, *Bulletin New Jersey Academy of Sciences* 16:30–44, 1971.

56. Highlands Study Team, New York-New Jersey Highlands Regional Study, n.p.[United States Forest Service], n.d. [1992].

57. G. Bishop, Newark mayor suggests urban-Highlands link, *New York Times,* Jan. 19, 1992, sec. 1:22.

58. M. W. Binford, M. Brenner, T. J. Whitmore, A. Higuera-Gundy, E. S. Deevey, B. Leyden, Ecosystems, paleoecology and human disturbance in subtropical and tropical America, *Quaternary Science Reviews* 6:115–28, 1987.

59. Ibid.

60. D. R. Engstrom and H. E. Wright, Jr., Chemical stratigraphy of lake sediments as a record of environmental change. In *Lake Sediments and Environmental History. Studies in Palaeolimnology and Palaeoecology,* E. Y. Haworth and J. W. G. Lund, eds. (University of Minnesota Press, Minneapolis, 1984), 11–64.

61. D. J. Stanley and A. G. Warne, Nile delta: recent geological evolution and human impact, *Science* 260:628–34, 1993.

## Chapter 10. Human Modifications of Lake Ecosystems

1. S. A. Forbes, The lake as a microcosm, *Bulletin of the Peoria Scientific Association,* 77–87, 1887. Reprinted in *Bulletin of the Illinois State Natural History Survey*

15:537–50, 1925. In *Foundations of Ecology. Classic Papers with Commentaries,* L. A. Real and H. A. Brown, eds. (University of Chicago Press, Chicago, 1991), 14.

2. Ibid.

3. G. E. Hutchinson and A. Wollack, Studies on Connecticut lake sediments II. Chemical analyses of a core from Linsley Pond, North Bransford, *American Journal of Science* 238:493–517, 1940; E. S. Deevey, Studies on Connecticut lake sediments III. The biostrotonomy of Linsley Pond, *American Journal of Science* 240:233–64, 313–24, 1942; R. L. Lindeman, The trophic-dynamic aspect of ecology, *Ecology* 23:399–418, 1942. This is the classic concept of hydrach succession, as developed by F. E. Clements (*Plant Succession: An Analysis of the Development of Vegetation,* Carnegie Institute of Washington Publication #242, Washington, D.C., 1916) and A. G. Tansley (The classification of vegetation and the concept of development, *Journal of Ecology* 8:118–49, 1920). The contrast made by limnologists was between ecosystems developed on concave surfaces, in which ecosystem processes led to development of a substrate that would eventually end the system, i.e., sedimentation, and those developed on convex surfaces, in which ecosystem processes led to a substrate that would sustain the system, i.e., soil genesis.

4. D. R. Engstrom and H. E. Wright, Jr., Chemical stratigraphy of lake sediments as a record of environmental change. In *Lake Sediments and Environmental History: Studies in Palaeolimnology and Palaeoecology in Honour of Winnifred Tutin,* E. Y. Haworth and J. W. G. Lund, eds. (University of Minnesota Press, Minneapolis, 1984), 11–67.

5. E. S. Deevey, Stress, strain, and stability of lacustrine ecosystems. In Haworth and Lund, *Lake Sediments,* 205; G. E. Likens and F. H. Bormann, An ecosystem approach. In *An Ecosystem Approach to Aquatic Ecology: Mirror Lake and Its Environment,* G. E. Likens, ed. (Springer-Verlag, New York, 1985), 8.

6. Deevey, Stress, strain and stability.

7. *Allochthonous* is contrasted with *autochthonous,* i.e., formed within the lake, though, of course, from components that derive from the surroundings of the lake.

8. F. J. H. Mackereth, Some chemical observations on post-glacial lake sediments, *Philosophical Transactions of the Royal Society of London (B)* 250:165–213, 1966; R. B. Brugam, Human disturbance and the historical development of Linsley Pond, *Ecology* 59:19–36, 1978.

9. C. H. Mortimer, The exchange of dissolved substances between mud and water in lakes, *Journal of Ecology* 29:280–329, 1941, and 30:147–201, 1942; Mackereth, Some chemical observations; R. Carignan and R. J. Flett, Postdepositional mobility of phosphorus in lake sediments, *Limnology and Oceanography* 26:361–66, 1981; Engstrom and Wright, Chemical stratigraphy.

10. W. T. Edmonson, Phosphorus, nitrogen, and algae in Lake Washington after diversion of sewage, *Science* 169:690–91, 1970.

11. W. T. Edmonson and J. T. Lehman, The effect of changes in the nutrient income on the condition of Lake Washington, *Limnology and Oceanography* 26:1–29, 1981.

12. Hutchinson and Wollack, Studies; Deevey, Studies; R. Patrick, The diatoms of Linsley Pond, Connecticut, *Proceedings of the Academy of Natural Sciences of Philadelphia* 95:53–110, 1947.

13. Brugam, Human disturbance.

14. K. E. Camburn and J. C. Kingston, The genus *Melosira* from soft-water lakes with special reference to northern Michigan, Wisconsin and Minnesota. In *Diatoms and Lake Acidity: Reconstructing pH from Siliceous Algal Remains in Lake Sediments*, J. P. Smol, R. W. Battarbee, R. B. Davis, and J. Meriläinen (Dr W. Junk, Dordrecht, Netherlands, 1986), 17–34.

15. D. R. Engstrom, E. B. Swain, and J. C. Kingston, A palaeolimnological record of human disturbance from Harvey's Lake, Vermont: geochemistry, pigments and diatoms, *Freshwater Biology* 15:261–88, 1985; J. P. Bradbury and R. O. Megard, Stratigraphic record of pollution in Shagawa Lake, northeastern Minnesota, *Geological Society of America Bulletin* 83:2639–48, 1972; Brugam, Human disturbance.

16. Engstrom et al., A palaeolimnological record.

17. H. H. Birks, M. C. Whiteside, D. M. Stark, and R. C. Bright, Recent paleolimnology of three lakes in northwestern Minnesota, *Quaternary Research* 6:249–72, 1976.

18. E. Y. Haworth, Stratigraphic changes in algal remains (diatoms and chrysophytes) in the recent sediments of Blelham Tarn, English Lake District. In Haworth and Lund, *Lake Sediments*, 165–90.

19. J. K. Elner and C. M. Happey-Wood (Mrs. D. G. E. Wood), The history of two linked but contrasting lakes in North Wales from a study of pollen, diatoms and chemistry in sediment cores, *Journal of Ecology* 68:95–121, 1980.

20. M. Brenner and M. W. Binford, A sedimentary record of human disturbance from Lake Miragoane, Haiti, *Journal of Paleolimnology* 1:85–97, 1988.

21. E. S. Deevey et al., Mayan urbanism: impact on a tropical karst environment, *Science* 206:298–306, 1979; M. W. Binford et al., Ecosystems, paleoecology and human disturbance in subtropical and tropical America, *Quaternary Science Reviews* 6:115–28, 1987; J. H. McAndrews, Human disturbance of North American forests and grasslands: the fossil pollen record. In *Vegetation History*, B. Huntley and T. Webb III, eds. (Kluwer Academic, Dordrecht, Netherlands, 1988), 673–97.

22. C. E. W. Steinberg and R. F. Wright, Introduction. In *Acidification of Freshwater Ecosystems: Implications for the Future*, C. E. W. Steinberg and R. F. Wright (John Wiley and Sons, Chichester, 1994), 1.

23. G. K. Reid and R. D. Wood, *Ecology of Inland Waters and Estuaries*, 2d ed. (D. Van Nostrand, New York, 1976), 203–09.

24. R. B. Davis, D. S. Anderson, and F. Berge, Palaeolimnological evidence that lake acidification is accompanied by loss of organic matter, *Nature* 316:436–38, 1985; R. B. Davis, personal communication.

25. E. Crompton, Soil formation. In *Selected Papers in Soil Formation and Classification*, J. V. Drew, ed. (Soil Science Society, Madison, Wis., 1967), 3–15.

26. R. B. Davis and J. P. Smol, The use of sedimentary remains of siliceous algae for inferring past chemistry of lake water—problems, potential and research needs. In Smol et al., *Diatoms and Lake Acidity*, 291–300.

27. Engstrom and Wright, Chemical stratigraphy.

28. Ibid.

29. F. Husted, 1937–1939. Systematische und ökologische Untersuchungen über den Diatomeenflora von Java, Bali, Sumatra, *Archiv für Hydrobiol.* (Suppl.) 15 & 16 [not seen]—reference in R. W. Batterbee, J. P. Smol and J. Meriläinen, Diatoms as indicators of pH: an historical review. In Smol et al., *Diatoms and Lake Acidity,* 5–14.

30. Batterbee et al., Diatoms as indicators.

31. Ibid.; Davis and Smol, The use of sedimentary remains; H. J. B. Birks, S. Juggins and J. M. Line, Lake surface-water chemistry reconstructions for palaeolimnological data. In *The Surface Waters Acidification Programme,* B. J. Mason, ed. (Cambridge University Press, Cambridge, 1990), 301–13.

32. R. B. Davis and P. M. Stokes, Overview of historical and paleoecological studies of acidic air pollution and its effects, *Water, Air and Soil Pollution* 30:311–18, 1986.

33. B. O. Rosseland and M. Staurnes, Physiological mechanisms for toxic effects and resistance to acidic water: an ecophysiological and ecotoxicological approach. In Steinberg and Wright, *Acidification,* 227–46.

34. D. W. Schindler, Changes caused by acidification to the biodiversity, productivity and biogeochemical cycles of lakes. In Steinberg and Wright, *Acidification,* 153–64.

35. Environment Canada (Environnement Canada), Downwind. *The Acid Rain Story,* Minister of Supply and Services Canada, En56–56/1981E, 1981.

36. R. B. Davis, Paleolimnological diatom studies of acidification of lakes by acid rain: an application of quaternary science, *Quaternary Science Reviews* 6:147–63, 1987; J. Ford, The recent history of a naturally acidic lake (Cone Pond, N.H.). In Smol et al., *Diatoms and Lake Acidity,* 131–48; Whitehead et al., Late-glacial and Holocene acidity changes in Adirondack (N.Y.) lakes. In Smol et al., *Diatoms and Lake Acidity,* 251–74.

37. Tolonen, Acidification in Finnish lakes.

38. John W. Sherman, Diatoms. In Likens, *An Ecosystem Approach,* 366–82.

39. Tolonen, Acidification in Finnish lakes.

40. I. Renberg, T. Korsman, and N. J. Anderson, A temporal perspective of lake acidification in Sweden, *Ambio* 22:264–71, 1993; I. Renberg, T. Korsman, and H. J. B. Birks, Prehistoric increases in the pH of acid-sensitive Swedish lakes caused by land-use changes, *Nature* 362:824–27, 1993.

41. R. B. Davis et al., Acidity of twelve northern New England (U.S.A.) lakes in recent centuries, *Journal of Paleolimnology* 12:103–54, 1994.

42. Ford, Cone Pond; Sherman, Diatoms.

43. Tolonen, Acidification in Finnish lakes.

44. Davis et al., Acidity.

45. R. B. Davis, S. A. Norton, T. Hess, and D. F. Brakke, Paleolimnological reconstruction of the effects of atmospheric deposition of acids and heavy metals on the chemistry and biology of lakes in New England and Norway, *Hydrobiologia* 103:113–23, 1983.

46. D. W. Schindler, Detecting ecosystem response to anthropogenic stress, *Canadian Journal of Fisheries and Aquatic Sciences* 44(SUPPL 1):6–25, 1987.

47. I. Renberg, M. W. Persson, and O. Emteryd, Pre-industrial lead contamination detected in Swedish lake sediments, *Nature* 368:323–26, 1994.

48. Davis et al., Paleolimnological reconstruction; R. Carignan, Quantitative importance of alkalinity flux from the sediments of acid lakes, *Nature* 317:158–60, 1985.

49. Davis and Stokes, Overview.

50. K. Arzet, D. Krause-Dellin, and C. Steinberg, Acidification of four lakes in the Federal Republic of Germany as reflected by diatom assemblages, cladoceran remains and sediment chemistry. In Smol et al., *Diatoms and Lake Acidity*, 227–50.

51. Deevey, Stress, strain and stability.

52. J. F. Kitchell and S. R. Carpenter, Variability in lake ecosystems: complex responses by the apical predator. In *Humans as Components of Ecosystems. The Ecology of Subtle Human Effects and Populated Areas* (Springer-Verlag, New York, 1993), 125–40; W. C. Kerfoot, Net accumulation rates and the history of Cladoceran communities, *Ecology* 55:51–61, 1974.

53. Kerfoot, Cladoceran communities.

54. J. J. Magnuson and R. C. Lathrop, Historical changes in the fish community. In *Food Web Management: A Case Study of Lake Mendota*, J. F. Kitchell, ed. (Springer-Verlag, New York, 1992), 193–231.

55. Kitchell and Carpenter, Variability in lake ecosystems.

56. J. Ford, Cone Pond; I. Renberg, A sedimentary diatom record of severe acidification in Lake Blåmissusjön, N. Sweden. In Smol et al., *Diatoms and Lake Acidity*, 213–19; H. Simola, Diatom responses to acidification and lime treatment in a clearwater lake: comparison of two methods of analysis of a diatom stratigraphy. In Smol et al., *Diatoms and Lake Acidity*, 221–26; K. Arzet, D. Krause-Dellin, and C. Steinberg, Acidification of four lakes in the Federal Republic of Germany as reflected by diatom assemblages, cladoceran remains and sediment chemistry. In Smol et al., *Diatoms and Lake Acidity*, 227–50.

57. Ford, Cone Pond.

58. Arzet et al., Acidification of German lakes.

59. M. B. Davis and M. S. (Jesse) Ford, Sediment focusing in Mirror Lake, New Hampshire, *Limnology and Oceanography*, 27:137–50; M. B. Davis and M. S (Jesse) Ford, Late-glacial and Holocene sedimentation, in Likens, *An Ecosystem Approach*, 346–66; Haworth, Stratigraphic changes.

60. D. W. Schindler, Detecting ecosystem response to anthropogenic stress, *Canadian Journal of Fisheries and Aquatic Sciences* (suppl.) 44:6–25, 1987.

61. Ibid.

## Chapter 11. Diversity and Species Extinctions

1. C. Glacken, *Traces on the Rhodian Shore* (University of California Press, Berkeley, 1967), 677–79.

2. G. P. Marsh, *Man and Nature* (1864; reprint Belknap Press of Harvard University Press, Cambridge, 1965) 76–77.

3. Ibid., 84.

4. F. Fukarek, *Pflanzenwelt der Erde* (Urania-Verlag, Leipzig, 1979), 77.

5. C. S. Elton, *The Ecology of Invasions by Animals and Plants* (Methuen, London, 1958).

6. N. Eldridge, *The Miner's Canary: Unraveling the Mysteries of Extinction* (Prentice-Hall, New York, 1991) 134.

7. D. Jablonski, Extinction: a paleontological perspective, *Science* 253:754–57, 1991; D. H. Erwin, *The Great Paleozoic Crisis: Life and Death in the Permian* (Columbia University Press, New York, 1993), 16. There is some question about the magnitude of the extinction at the end of the Paleozoic era, perhaps lowering the proportion of species that became extinct to 80 percent of all marine species, but this would still have been the most massive extinction event in the history of life (S. M. Stanley and X. Yang, A double mass extinction at the end of the Paleozoic Era, *Science* 266:1340–44, 1994).

8. Jablonski, Extinction.

9. Eldridge, *The Miner's Canary,* 1–12.

10. Stephen K. Donavan, ed., *Mass Extinctions: Processes and Evidence* (Columbia University Press, New York, 1989) (review by M. L. McKinney, *Science* 247:475–76, 1990).

11. M. Sagoff, Biodiversity and the culture of ecology, *Bulletin of the Ecological Society of America* 74:374–81, 1993.

12. Glacken, *Traces,* 678.

13. P. H. Raven, Defining biodiversity, *Nature Conservancy* 44(1):11–15, 1994.

14. See such basic ecology textbooks as P. Colinvaux, *Ecology* (John Wiley and Sons, New York), and M. G. Barbour, J. H. Burk, and W. D. Pitts, *Terrestrial Plant Ecology,* 2d ed. (Benjamin/Cummins, Menlo Park, Calif., 1987).

15. R. K. Peet, Relative diversity indices, *Ecology* 56:496–98, 1975.

16. D. Schluter and R. E. Ricklefs, Species diversity: An introduction to the problem. In *Species Diversity in Ecological Communities: Historical and Geographical Perspectives,* R. E. Ricklefs and D. Schluter, eds. (University of Chicago Press, Chicago, 1993), 1–10.

17. T. Webb III, The appearance and disappearance of major vegetational assemblages: long-term vegetational dynamics in eastern North America, *Vegetatio* 69:177–87, 1987.

18. J. C. Willis, *Age and Area: A Study in Geographical Distribution and Origin of Species* (Cambridge University Press, Cambridge, 1922).

19. G. E. Hutchinson, Homage to Santa Rosalia; or, why are there so many kinds of animals? *American Naturalist* 93:145–59, 1959.

20. H-K. Luh and S. L. Pimm, The assembly of ecological communities: a minimalist approach, *Journal of Animal Ecology* 62:749–65, 1993.

21. D. R. Brooks, Historical ecology: a new approach to studying the evolution of ecological associations, *Annals Missouri Botanical Garden* 72:660–80, 1985; D. Schluter and R. E. Ricklefs, Species diversity.

22. R. E. Latham and R. E. Ricklefs, Continental comparisons of temperate-zone tree species diversity. In Ricklefs and Schluter, *Species Diversity,* 294–314.

23. R. Good, *The Geography of the Flowering Plants,* 3d ed. (John Wiley and Sons, New York, 1964), 157.

24. F. I. Woodward, A review of the effects of climate on vegetation: ranges, competition, and composition. In *Global Warming and Biological Diversity,* R. L. Peters and T. E. Lovejoy, eds. (Yale University Press, New Haven, 1992), 105–23.

25. M. Huston, Biological diversity, soils, and economics, *Science* 262:1676–80, 1993; D. Tilman and S. Pacala, The maintenance of species richness in plant communities. In Ricklefs and Schluter, *Species Diversity,* 13–25.

26. R. H. Whittaker and W. A. Niering, Vegetation of the Santa Catalina Mountains, Arizona. V. Biomass, production, and diversity along the elevation gradient, *Ecology* 56:771–90, 1975.

27. N. C. W. Beadle, Soil phosphate and its role in molding segments of the Australian flora and vegetation with special reference to xeromorphy and sclerophylly, *Ecology* 47:991–1007, 1966.

28. Tilman and Pacala, Maintenance of species richness.

29. R. K. Peet, D. C. Glenn-Lewin, and J. W. Wolf, Prediction of man's impact on plant species diversity: A challenge for vegetation science. In Holzner et al., *Man's Impact,* 41–54.

30. Whittaker and Niering, Santa Catalina Mountains.

31. Beadle, Soil phosphate, 997.

32. D. B. Snyder, Extinct, extant, extirpated or historical? or, In defense of historical species, *Bartonia* 57 (suppl.):50–57, 1993.

33. Marsh, *Man and Nature,* 77.

34. M. Soulé, Conservation: tactics for a constant crisis, *Science* 253:744–50, 1991.

35. Some ecologists refer to this process as extirpation, as contrasted with total extinction throughout the range of the species, but because *extirpation* connotes active removal, *extinction,* which implies no causal mechanism, seems the better term.

36. E. C. Pielou, *After the Ice Age* (University of Chicago Press, Chicago, 1991), 263.

37. T. L. Erwin, An evolutionary basis for conservation strategies, *Science* 253:750–52, 1991.

38. Superintendents' reports, Morristown National Historical Park and Saratoga National Historical Park.

39. Chestnut is an interesting case, since it is extinct as a large, naturally regenerating tree but survives as small sprouts and in a few planted populations well outside its prehistoric range.

40. Marsh, *Man and Nature,* 78–79; Russell et al., Recent centuries of vegetational change.

41. J. F. Jacobs and R. L. Bartgis, The running buffalo clover. In *Audubon Wildlife Report 1987,* R. L. DiSilvestris, ed. (Academic Press, Orlando, 1987), 438–43.

42. "The Green League Table," *Science* 262:1815, 1993, table taken from a report by the New Economics Foundation in London.

43. D. C. Nepstad and C. Uhl, Environmental constraints to tree seedling establishment in abandoned Amazon pasture, *Program of the IV International Congress of Ecology,* State University of New York, Syracuse, 1986, 253.

44. R. L. Burgess, Community organization: effects of landscape fragmentation, *Canadian Journal of Botany* 66:2687–90, 1988; S. L. Pimm and J. L. Gittleman, Biological diversity: where is it? *Science* 255:940, 1992.

45. Burgess, Community organization. Also see more complete treatments of these topics in R. T. T. Forman and M. Godron, *Landscape Ecology* (John Wiley and Sons,

New York, 1986), and M. Turner, ed., *Landscape Heterogeneity and Disturbance* (Springer-Verlag, New York, 1987).

46. D. Tilman and J. A. Downing, Biodiversity and stability in grasslands, *Nature* 367:363–65, 1994.

47. M. B. Davis, Climatic instability, time lags, and community disequilibrium. In *Community Ecology*, J. Diamond and T. J. Case, eds. (Harper and Row, New York, 1986), 269–84.

48. D. B. Botkin, J. F. Janak, and J. R. Wallis, Some ecological consequences of a computer model of forest growth, *Journal of Ecology* 60:849–72, 1972; H. H. Shugart, D. C. West, and W. R. Emanuel, Patterns and dynamics of forests: an application of simulation. In *Forest Succession, Concepts and Application*, D. C. West, H. H. Shugart, and D. B. Botkin, eds. (Springer-Verlag, New York, 1981), 74–94.

49. E. Culotta, Biological immigrants under fire, News and Comment, *Science* 254:1444–47, 1991.

50. D. E. Fairbrothers, Endangered, threatened, and rare vascular plants of the Pine Barrens and their biogeography. In *Pine Barrens: Ecosystem and Landscape,* R. T. T. Forman, ed. (Academic Press, New York, 1979), 395–405.

51. Pinelands Commission, *Comprehensive Management Plan for the Pinelands National Reserve and Pinelands Area* (Pinelands Commission, New Lisbon, N.J., 1980), 98–103.

52. J. E. Applegate, S. Little, and P. E. Marucci, Plant and animal products of the Pine Barrens. In Forman, *Pine Barrens,* 25–36.

53. P. O. Wacker, Human exploitation of the New Jersey Pine Barrens before 1900. In Forman, *Pine Barrens,* 3–23.

54. R. T. T. Forman and R. E. Boerner, Fire frequency and the Pine Barrens of New Jersey, *Bulletin of the Torrey Botanical Club* 108:34–50, 1981; F. B. Hough, Report on Forestry, (USDA) (Government Printing Office, Washington, D.C.), 3:158–61.

55. D. E. Fairbrothers, Endangered plants.

56. G. F. Peterken, *Natural Woodland: Ecology and Conservation in Northern Temperate Regions* (Cambridge University Press, Cambridge, 1996), 410–13.

57. O. Rackham, *Ancient Woodland: Its History, Vegetation and Uses in England* (Edward Arnold, London, 1980).

58. J. Hughes and B. Huntley, Upland hay meadows in Britain—their vegetation, management and future. In *The Cultural Landscape—Past, Present and Future*, H. H. Birks et al., eds. (Cambridge University Press, Cambridge, 1988), 91–110.

59. L. Hauge, Galdane, Lærdal, western Norway—management and restoration of the cultural landscape. In Birks et al., *The Cultural Landscape,* 31–45.

60. C. Darwin, *On the Origin of Species (A Facsimile of the First Edition)* (Harvard University Press, Cambridge, 1966), 388–410.

61. R. H. MacArthur and E. O. Wilson, An equilibrium theory of insular zoogeography, *Evolution* 17:373–87, 1963.

62. S. J. Carlquist, *Island Biology* (Columbia University Press, New York, 1974).

63. A. F. Richard and R. E. Dewar, Lemur ecology, *Annual Review of Ecology and Systematics* 22:145–75, 1991; D. A. Burney, Late Quaternary stratigraphic charcoal records from Madagascar, *Quaternary Research* 28:274–86, 1987.

64. D. A. Burney et al., L'environnement au cours de L'Holocène et la disparition de la mégafaune à Madagascar: quel rapport avec la conservation de la nature? In *Priorités en matière de conservation des espèces à Madagascar,* R. A. Mittermeier et al., eds. (Antananarivo, Madagascar, 1987), 137–43; S. L. Olson and H. F. James, Fossil birds from the Hawai'ian Islands: evidence for wholesale extinction by man before western contact, *Science* 217:633–35, 1982.

65. D. A. Burney, Late Quaternary charcoal.

66. L. W. Cuddihy and C. P. Stone, *Alteration of Native Vegetation: Effects of Humans, Their Activities and Introductions* (University of Hawaii Cooperative National Park Resources Studies Unit, Honolulu, Hawai'i, 1990), 29–31.

67. Richard and Dewar, Lemur ecology.

68. Ibid.

69. P. Vitousek et al., Introduced species in Hawai'i: biological effects as opportunities for ecological research, *Trends in Ecology and Evolution* 2:224–27, 1987.

70. Richard and Dewar, Lemur ecology.

## Chapter 12. Biospheric Sustainability

1. D. Pearce, Sustainable futures: some economic issues. In *Changing the Global Environment: Perspectives on Human Involvement,* D. B. Botkin, M. F. Caswell, J. E. Estes, A. A. Urio, eds. (Academic Press, New York, 1989), 311–23; J. C. Aber, Modification of nitrogen cycling at the regional scale: the subtle effects of atmospheric deposition. In M. J. McDonnell and S. T. A. Pickett, eds., *Humans as Components of Ecosystems,* 163–74.

2. A. Cleveland Coxe, *Latin Christianity: Its Founder, Tertullian, Ante-Nicene Fathers* (Hendrickson, Peabody, Mass.), 3:210.

3. D. J. Herlihy, Attitudes toward the environment in medieval society. In *Historical Ecology: Essays on Environment and Social Change,* L. J. Bilsky, ed. (Kennikat Press, Port Washington, N.J., 1980), 103. Clarence Glacken provided a different translation of this passage from Tertullian, giving a different flavor to the observation that, according to Herlihy's translation, "now pleasant estates obliterate the famous wilderness areas of the past." Glacken's translation reads "most pleasant farms have obliterated all traces of what were once dreary and dangerous wastes," C. Glacken, *Traces on the Rhodian Shore* (University of California Press, Berkeley, 1967), 296

4. G. P. Marsh, *Man and Nature* (1864; reprint Belknap Press of Harvard University Press, Cambridge, 1965); F. B. Hough, *Report upon Forestry,* USDA, Washington, D. C., Vol. 1, 1878, Vol 2, 1880, Vol. 3, 1882; W. C. Lowdermilk, Conquest of Land through 7000 Years: Dr. Lowdermilk's Trip after the Dustbowl, *USDA Agricultural Information Bulletin* #99, 1975.

5. J. Caird, *English Agriculture in 1850–1* (LONDON, 1852); L. F. Haber, *The Chemical Industry during the Nineteenth Century* (Oxford University Press, Oxford, 1958), 61–62; F. M. L. Thompson, The second agricultural revolution, 1815–1880, *Economic History Review,* 2d ser., 21:62–77, 1968.

6. W. Jackson and J. Piper, The necessary marriage between ecology and agriculture, *Ecology* 70:1591–93, 1989.

7. O. Rackham, *Ancient Woodland: Its History, Vegetation and Uses in England* (Edward Arnold, London, 1980).

8. Lubchenko et al., The sustainable biosphere initiative: an ecological research agenda, *Ecology* 72:371–412, 1991.

9. Pearce, Sustainable futures.

10. J. Roughgarden et al., *In Our Hands* (Stanford University Press, Stanford, 1989).

11. R. Shearman, The meaning and ethics of sustainability, *Environmental Management* 14:1–8, 1990.

12. N. Oreskes, K. Shrader-Freshette, and K. Belitz, Verification, validation, and confirmation of numerical models in the earth sciences, *Science* 263:641–48, 1994.

13. International Union for Conservation of Nature and Natural Resources, *World Conservation Strategy. Living Resource Conservation for Sustainable Development,* IUCN-UNEP-WWF, n.p. [Gland, Switzerland], 1980, chap. 11, part 9.

14. M. L. Hunter, Jr., G. L. Jacobson, Jr., T. Webb III, Paleoecology and the coarse-filter approach to maintaining biological diversity, *Conservation Biology* 2:375–85, 1988.

15. C. G. Lorimer, The oak regeneration problem: new evidence on causes and possible solutions, *Forest Resources Analyses* #8 (Department of Forestry, University of Wisconsin, Madison, 1989), 3.

16. Ibid., 2.

17. D. J. Parsons, Objects or ecosystems? Giant Sequoia management in national parks, USDA Forest Service Gen. Tech. Rep. PSW-151, 1994.

18. E. L. Braun, *Deciduous Forests of Eastern North America* (The Blakiston Press, Philadelphia, 1950); J. L. Vankat, *The Natural Vegetation of North America* (John Wiley and Sons, New York, 1979).

19. J. C. Campbell, Gradients of tree species composition in the central hardwood region. In *Proceedings of the Central Hardwood Forest Conference* VI, R. L. Hay, F. W. Woods, and H. DeSelm, eds., Knoxville, 1987, 325–45; I. Millers, D. S. Shriner, D. Rizzo, *History of Hardwood Decline in the Eastern United States,* USDA Forest Service, General Technical Report NE-126, 1989, 3.

20. Lorimer, The oak regeneration problem.

21. G. F. Schwartz, The sprout forests of the Housatonic Valley of Connecticut, *Forestry Quarterly* 5:121–53, 1907; C. Keever, Distribution of major forest species in southeastern Pennsylvania, *Ecological Monographs* 43:303–27, 1973.

22. E. W. B. Russell and A. E. Schuyler, Vegetation and flora of Hopewell Furnace National Historic Site, eastern Pennsylvania, *Bartonia* 54:124–43, 1988; J. G. Ehrenfeld, *Vegetation of the Morristown National Historical Park, Ecological Analysis and Management Implications,* Report to U.S. Department of the Interior, National Park Service, Center for Coastal and Environmental Studies, Rutgers University, New Brunswick, N.J., 1980; M. F. Buell et al., The upland forest continuum in northern New Jersey, *Ecology* 47:416–32, 1966; H. J. Lutz, Trends of silvicultural significance of upland forest succession in southern New England, *Yale School of*

*Forestry Bulletin* 22:1–68, 1928; C. J. Mikan, D. O. Orwig, and M. D. Abrams, Age structure and successional dynamics of a presettlement-origin chestnut oak forest in the Pennsylvania piedmont, *Bulletin of the Torrey Botanical Club* 121:13–23, 1994.

23. Millers et al., *History of Hardwood Decline,* 46–48.
24. Ibid., 7–14.
25. B. V. Barnes, Old-growth forests of the northern lake states: a landscape ecosystem perspective, *Natural Areas Journal* 9:45–57, 1989.
26. G. E. Bard, Secondary succession on the piedmont of New Jersey, *Ecological Monographs* 22:196–215, 1952; R. T. T. Forman and B. A. Elfstrom, Forest structure comparison of Hutcheson Memorial Forest and eight old woods on the New Jersey Piedmont, *William L. Hutcheson Memorial Bulletin* 3:44–51, 1975.
27. G. R. Parker, D. J. Leopold, and J. K. Eichenberger, Tree dynamics in an old-growth, deciduous forest, *Forest Ecology and Management* 11:31–57, 1985.
28. Mikan et al., Age structure and successional dynamics.
29. J. S. Fralish et al., Comparison of presettlement, second-growth and old-growth forest on six site types in the Illinois Shawnee Hills, *American Midland Naturalist* 125:294–309, 1991.
30. R. F. Whitcomb et al., Effects of forest fragmentation on avifauna of the eastern deciduous forest. In *Forest Island Dynamics in Man-Dominated Landscapes,* R. L. Burgess and D. M. Sharpe, eds. (Springer-Verlag, New York, 1981), 125–205.
31. C. F. Korstian and P. W. Stickel, The natural replacement of blight-killed chestnut in hardwood forests of the northeast, *Journal of Agricultural Research* 34:631–48, 1927; N. Good, A study of natural replacement of chestnut in New Jersey (Ph.D. diss., Rutgers University, New Brunswick, N.J., 1965).
32. H. H. Shugart and D. C. West, Development of an Appalachian deciduous forest model and its application to the assessment of the chestnut blight, *Journal of Environmental Management* 5:161–79, 1977.
33. J. C. Willis (rev. by H. K. Airy Shaw), *A Dictionary of the Flowering Plants and Ferns,* 8th ed. (Cambridge University Press, Cambridge, 1973), 972; R. Good, *The Geography of the Flowering Plants* (John Wiley and Sons, New York, 1964), 85.
34. Braun, *Deciduous Forests,* 457.
35. M. B. Davis, Quaternary history and the stability of forest communities. In West et al., *Forest Succession,* 132–53.
36. Davis, Quaternary history; T. Webb III, The past 11,000 years of vegetational change in eastern North America, *BioScience* 31:501–06, 1981; P. A. Delcourt and H. R. Delcourt, Vegetation maps for eastern North America: 40 000 yr B.P. to the present. In *Geobotany II,* R. Romans, ed. (Plenum, New York, 1981), 123–66; T. Webb III, Late Quaternary pollen stratigraphy and isochrone maps for the northeastern United States. In *Pollen Records of Late-Quaternary North American Sediments,* V. M. Bryant and R. G. Holloway, eds., (AASP Foundation, Dallas, 1985), 247–80.
37. W. A. Watts, Late Quaternary vegetation of central Appalachia and the New Jersey coastal plain, *Ecological Monographs* 49:427–69, 1979; D. C. Gaudreau and T.

Webb III, Late-quaternary pollen stratigraphy and isochrone maps for the north-eastern United States. In Bryant and Holloway, *Pollen Records,* 247–80.

38. J. R. Dorney, The impact of native Americans on presettlement vegetation in south-eastern Wisconsin, *Wisconsin Academy of Sciences, Arts and Letters* 69:26–36, 1981; E. C. Grimm, Fire and other factors controlling the Big Woods vegetation of Minnesota in the mid-nineteenth century, *Ecological Monographs* 54:291–311, 1984.

39. W. A. Patterson III and K. E. Sassaman, Indian fires in the prehistory of New England. In *Holocene Human Ecology in Northeastern North America,* G. P. Nicholas, ed. (Plenum Press, New York, 1988); M. B. Davis, Holocene vegetational history of the eastern United States. In *Late-Quaternary Environments of the United States.* Vol. 2. *The Holocene,* H. E. Wright, Jr., ed. (University of Minnesota Press, Minneapolis, 1983), 166–81.

40. H. G. Schmidt, *Agriculture in New Jersey* (Rutgers University Press, New Brunswick, N.J., 1973), chap. 3; H. S. Russell, *A Long, Deep Furrow: Three Centuries of Farming in New England* (University Press of New England, Hanover, N.H., 1976), chaps. 3–4.

41. M. B. Davis, Phytogeography and palynology of northeastern United States. In *The Quaternary of the United States,* H. E. Wright and D. G. Frey, eds. (Princeton University Press, Princeton, N.J., 1965), 377–401.

42. J. T. Curtis, The modification of mid-latitude grasslands and forests by man. In *Man's Role in Changing the Face of the Earth,* W. L. Thomas, Jr., ed. (University of Chicago Press, Chicago, 1956), 721–62.

43. J. Gifford, Forestal conditions and silvicultural prospects of the coastal plain of New Jersey. In *Annual Report of the State Geologist for 1899. Report on Forests* (Geological Survey of New Jersey, Trenton, 1900), 261.

44. A. Wilson and C. L. Bonaparte, *American Ornithology; or, the Natural History of the Birds of the United States* (Porter and Coates, Philadelphia, n.d. [ca. 1880?]), 2:253–61.

45. E. W. B. Russell et al., Recent centuries of vegetational change in the glaciated north-eastern United States, *Journal of Ecology* 81:647–64, 1993.

46. J. T. Rothrock, Forests of Pennsylvania, *Proceedings of the American Philosophical Society* 33:114–33, 1894; C. C. Vermeule, The forests of New Jersey. In Geological Survey of New Jersey, *Report on Forests* (Trenton, 1900), 13–174; F. Shreve, M. A. Chrysler, F. Blodgett, and E. W. Berley, *The Plant Life of Maryland,* Maryland Weather Service Special Publication VIII (Johns Hopkins University Press, Baltimore, 1910).

47. Vermeule, The forests of New Jersey, 7–8.

48. Ibid., 10, 40–41.

49. Westveld, *Applied Silviculture,* 84.

50. J. B. Smith, The role of insects in the forest. In Geological Survey of New Jersey, *Report on Forests,* 229–32.

51. Russell et al., Recent centuries.

52. Lorimer, The oak regeneration problem.

53. Fralish et al., Comparison of presettlement, second-growth and old-growth forest, abstract.

54. Ibid., 307.

55. M. D. Abrams and M. L. Scott, Disturbance-mediated accelerated succession in two Michigan forest types, *Forest Science* 35:42–49, 1989.

56. Lorimer, The oak regeneration problem. See also chapter 5.

57. Abrams and Scott, Disturbance-mediated succession.

58. R. H. Westveld, *Applied Silviculture in the United States,* 2d ed. (John Wiley and Sons, New York, 1949).

59. P. J. Kramer and T. T. Kozlowski, *Physiology of Woody Plants* (Academic Press, New York, 1979), 354–58; H. L. Mitchell and R. E. Chandler, The nitrogen nutrition and growth of certain deciduous trees of northeastern United States, *Black Rock Forest Bulletin* 11, 1939.

60. C. P. Dunn, R. Guntenspergen, and J. R. Dorney, Catastrophic wind disturbance in an old-growth hemlock-hardwood forest, Wisconsin, *Canadian Journal of Botany* 61:211–17, 1983.

61. W. C. Johnson and C. S. Atkisson, Dispersal of beech (*Fagus grandifolia*) nuts by blue jays (*Cyanocitta cristata*) in fragmented landscapes, *American Midland Naturalist* 113:319–24, 1985.

62. W. C. Johnson and T. Webb III, The role of blue jays (*Cyanocitta cristata* L.) in the postglacial dispersal of fagaceous trees in eastern North America, *Journal of Biogeography* 16:561–71, 1989.

63. M. W. Shaw, The reproductive characteristics of oak. In *The British Oak,* M. G. Morris and F. H. Perring, eds. (Classey, Farringdon, 1974), 162–81.

64. Millers, *History of Hardwood Decline,* 3.

65. D. Botkin and R. A. Nisbet, Projecting the effects of climate change on biological diversity in forests. In *Global Warming and Biological Diversity,* R. L. Peters and T. E. Lovejoy, eds. (Yale University Press, New Haven, 1992), 277–93.

66. D. T. Streeter, Ecological aspects of oak woodland conservation. In Morris and Perring, *The British Oak,* 341–53.

67. H. H. Shugart, Jr., and D. C. West, Forest succession models, *BioScience* 30(5):308–13, 1980.

68. N. Oreskes, K. Shrader-Freshette, and K. Belitz, Verification, validation, and confirmation of numerical models in the earth sciences, *Science* 263:641–48, 1994.

69. I. G. Simmons, Green biogeography? Guest editorial, *Journal of Biogeography* 16:501–02, 1989. Simmons's points also included the use of historical analogues.

## Chapter 13. Toward the Future

1. H. P. Santmire, Historical dimensions of the American crisis. In I. Barbour, *Western Man and Environmental Ethics* (Addison, Wesley, Reading, Mass., 1973), 66–92.

2. H. R. Delcourt and P. A. Delcourt, *Quaternary Ecology. A Paleoecological Perspective* (Chapman and Hall, London, 1991).

3. R. K. Peet, D. C. Glenn-Lewin, and J. W. Wolf, Prediction of man's impact on plant species diversity. In *Man's Impact on Vegetation*, W. Holzner, M. J. A. Werger, and I. Ikusima, eds. (Dr W. Junk, The Hague, 1983), 41–53.

4. M. B. Davis, Climatic instability, time lags, and community disequilibrium. In *Community Ecology*, J. Diamond and T. J. Case, eds. (Harper and Row, New York, 1984), 269–84; T. Webb III, Is vegetation in equilibrium with climate: How to interpret late-Quaternary pollen data, *Vegetatio* 67:75–91, 1986.

5. Delcourt and Delcourt, *Quaternary Ecology*, 106–11.

6. P. L. Chesson and T. J. Case, Overview: nonequilibrium community theories: chance, variability, history and coexistence. In Diamond and Case, *Community Ecology*, 229–39.

7. L. White, Jr., The historical roots of our ecologic crisis, *Science* 155:1203–07, 1967.

8. C. J. Glacken, *Traces on the Rhodian Shore* (University of California Press, Berkeley, 1967); B. Piasecki, Environmental ambivalence: an analysis of implicit dangers. In *Environmental History: Critical Issues in Comparative Perspective*, K. E. Bailes, ed. (University Press of America, Lanham, Md., 1985), 83–98; S. P. Bratton, Oaks, wolves and love: Celtic monks and northern forests, *J. Forest History* 33:4–20, 1989; F. H. Russell, The bifurcation of creation: Augustine's attitudes toward nature. In *Man and Nature in the Middle Ages*, S. J. Ridyard and R. G. Benson, eds. (University of the South Press, Sewanee, Tenn., 1995), 83–96.

9. Glacken, *Traces*; M. Williams, *The Making of the South Australian Landscape* (Academic Press, New York, 1974); G. Wynn, Changing the face of the earth: Old themes, current concerns, and new perspectives, *J. Forestry and Conservation History* 36:29–32, 1992.

10. M. Oelschlager, *The Idea of Wilderness: From Prehistory to the Age of Ecology* (Yale University Press, New Haven, 1991); R. Nash, *Wilderness and the American Mind*, rev. ed. (Yale University Press, New Haven, 1982).

11. M. Hunziker, Wenn wiesen zu Wald werden . . . ein Verlust für das Landschaftserlebnis? *Informationsblatt des Forschungsbereiches Landschaftsökologie* 18:1–2, 1993.

12. M. Henberg, Wilderness, myth, and American character, *Key Reporter*, Spring, 1994, 7–11.

13. Y. Tuan, Discrepancies between environmental attitudes and behavior: examples from Europe and China, *The Canadian Geographer* 12:176–91, 1968.

14. T. Palmer, The case for human beings, *Atlantic Monthly* 269(1): 83–88, 1992.

15. J. T. Overpeck, P. J. Bartlein, T. Webb III, Potential magnitude of future vegetation change in eastern North America: Comparisons with the past, *Science* 254:692–95, 1991; T. Webb III, Past changes in vegetation and climate: lessons for the future. In *Global Warming and Biological Diversity*, R. L. Peters and T. E. Lovejoy, eds. (Yale University Press, New Haven, 1992), 59–75; H. R. Delcourt and P. A. Delcourt, *Quaternary Ecology*, 3–7.

16. C. O. Sauer, Forward to Historical Geography, *Annals of the Association of American Geographers* 31:1–24, 1941 (reprinted in J. Leighly, ed., *Land and Life: A Selection from the Writings of Carl Ortwin Sauer* [University of California Press, Berkeley, 1965], 351–79); Glacken, *Traces*.

17. Nash, *Wilderness and the American Mind,* chap. 1.
18. Williams, *The Making,* 14–15
19. L. W. Milbraith, Culture and environment in the United States, *Environmental Management* 9:161–72, 1985.
20. H. P. Santmire, Historical dimensions of the American crisis. In *Western Man and Environmental Ethics,* I. Barbour, ed. (Addison Wesley, Reading, Mass., 1973), 66–92.

# Index